**Employee Well-being Support: A**

# Employee Well-being Support
## A Workplace Resource

**Andrew Kinder, Rick Hughes and Cary L. Cooper**

John Wiley & Sons, Ltd

Copyright © 2008      John Wiley & Sons Ltd, The Atrium, Southern Gate, Chichester,
West Sussex PO19 8SQ, England
Telephone (+44) 1243 779777

Email (for orders and customer service enquiries): cs-books@wiley.co.uk
Visit our Home Page on www.wiley.com

**Other Wiley Editorial Offices**

John Wiley & Sons Inc., 111 River Street, Hoboken, NJ 07030, USA

Jossey-Bass, 989 Market Street, San Francisco, CA 94103-1741, USA

Wiley-VCH Verlag GmbH, Boschstr. 12, D-69469 Weinheim, Germany

John Wiley & Sons Australia Ltd, 42 McDougall Street, Milton, Queensland 4064, Australia

John Wiley & Sons (Asia) Pte Ltd, 2 Clementi Loop #02-01, Jin Xing Distripark, Singapore 129809

John Wiley & Sons Ltd, 6045 Freemont Blvd, Mississauga, Ontario L5R 4J3, Canada

Wiley also publishes its books in a variety of electronic formats. Some content that appears in print
may not be available in electronic books.

*Library of Congress Cataloging-in-Publication Data*

Kinder, Andrew.
   Employee well-being support : a workplace resource / Andrew Kinder, Rick Hughes and Cary
L. Cooper.
      p. cm.
   Includes bibliographical references and index.
   ISBN 978-0-470-05899-2 (cloth) − ISBN 978-0-470-05900-5
1. Employee assistance programs. 2. Job stress. 3. Employees–Mental health. 4. Industrial
hygiene. I. Hughes, Rick, 1967- II. Cooper, Cary L. III. Title.
   HF5549.5.E42K56 2008
   658.3'8–dc22                                                                    2007050336

*British Library Cataloguing in Publication Data*

A catalogue record for this book is available from the British Library

ISBN 978-0-470-058992 (H/B) 978-0-470-05900-5 (P/B)

Typeset in 10/12 Palatino by Thomson Press (India) Limited, New Delhi
Printed and bound in Great Britain by Antony Rowe Limited, Chippenham, Wiltshire

# Contents

# About the Editors

**Andrew Kinder** is a Chartered Counselling and Chartered Occupational Psychologist, is the Chair of the Association for Counselling at Work (www. counsellingatwork.org.uk a Division of the British Association for Counselling and Psychotherapy) and is an Associate Fellow of the British Psychological Society. He is also a Chartered Scientist. He is currently principal psychologist with Atos Healthcare with responsibility for a large counselling and employee assistance programme service. He has worked in the area of stress, trauma and employee assistance within organisations for over 13 years and has run numerous courses for all levels on managing stress, maximising performance under pressure, coping with change and trauma support while, as a counsellor and coach, having his own case-load of clients, many of whom have stress-related issues. He was a member of the steering group which produced the Mind Out for mental health line managers' resource: *A Practical Guide to Managing and Supporting Mental Health in the Workplace*. He has been active as a researcher – his latest being a collaboration with the Institute of Employment Studies, Royal Mail Group, University of Sheffield and the British Occupational Health Research Foundation into the evidence for organisational interventions used following a work-related trauma. He has published articles on stress, substance misuse and trauma. His most recent publication is co-authoring with Rick Hughes best practice guidelines in relation to counselling in the workplace (BACP, Rugby). He also has an interest in media psychology and has carried out numerous assessments on contributors for reality TV programmes plus providing after-care.

**Rick Hughes** has widespread experience within the world of workplace counselling, employee assistance programmes (EAP) and employee development fields having worked for several international EAP providers and consultancies. He is head Adviser for Counselling in the Workplace of the British Association for Counselling and Psychotherapy. He was Deputy Chair of the Association for Counselling at Work (ACW) and a founding member of the Association for Coaching (AC). He has been a guest lecturer on the MBA course at Edinburgh University Management School. Rick's publications include co-author of *Experiences of Person-Centred Counselling Training* (2000,

PCCS Books), editor of *An Anthology of Counselling at Work II* (2004, BACP) and current editor of *Counselling at Work* journal. With fellow editor, Andrew Kinder, he co-wrote *Guidelines for Counselling in the Workplace* on behalf of ACW and the British Association for Counselling and Psychotherapy (BACP). Rick has an MPhil, 'An emotions perspective – extending the role of employee assistance programmes', under Professor Dave Mearns at University of Strathclyde, where he retains an Honorary Research Fellowship.

**Professor Cary L. Cooper** is Professor of Organisational Psychology and Health, Lancaster University Management School and Pro Vice Chancellor (External Relations) at Lancaster University. He is the author of over 100 books (on occupational stress, women at work, and industrial and organisational psychology), has written over 400 scholarly articles for academic journals, and is a frequent contributor to national newspapers, TV and radio. He is currently founding editor of the *Journal of Organizational Behavior* and co-editor of the medical journal *Stress and Health* (formerly *Stress Medicine*). He is a Fellow of the British Psychological Society, the Royal Society of Arts, the Royal Society of Medicine, the Royal Society of Health, the British Academy of Management and an academician of the Academy for the Social Sciences. Professor Cooper is the immediate past president of the British Academy of Management, is a Companion of the Chartered Management Institute and one of the first UK-based Fellows of the (American) Academy of Management (having also won the 1998 Distinguished Service Award for his contribution to management science from the Academy of Management). In 2001, Cary was awarded a CBE in the Queen's Birthday Honours List for his contribution to organisational health. He holds honorary doctorates from Aston University (DSc), Heriot-Watt University (DLitt), Middlesex University (Doc. Univ) and Wolverhampton University (DBA); an Honorary Fellowship of the Faculty of Occupational Medicine of the Royal College of Physicians; and in 2006 was awarded an Honorary Fellowship of the Royal College of Physicians (Hon FRCP).

Professor Cooper is the editor-in-chief of the international scholarly *Blackwell Encyclopedia of Management* (13-volume set); and the editor of *Who's Who in the Management Sciences*. He has been an adviser to two UN agencies; the World Health Organisation and ILO; published a major report for the EU's European Foundation for the Improvement of Living and Work Conditions on 'Stress Prevention in the Workplace'; and was a special adviser to the Defense Committee of the House of Commons on their Duty of Care enquiry (2004–2005). Professor Cooper is Chair of the Sunningdale Institute, a think tank on management and organisational issues, in the National School of Government in the Cabinet Office. Professor Cooper is also the President of the Institute of Welfare Officers, President of ISMA, President of the British Association of Counselling and Psychotherapy (from October 2006), an ambassador of the Samaritans and patron of the National Phobic Society

# List of Contributors

**Stephanie Beer** is an independent EAP consultant based in the UK. She has eight years' direct experience with Accor Services as Head of Operations responsible for the delivery of both Psychological and work/life services. Before this she had seven years' experience in the delivery of telephone helplines following social broadcasting with BBC and ITV. She was also a specialist debt advisor with Citizen Advice Bureaux for 10 years. She is a Board Director of EAPA Inc, responsible for all non-American members. She has served as Chairman of EAPA UK and as Chair of the subcommittee responsible for revising and updating the current UK EAPA standards.

**Dr Steve Boorman** is an experienced specialist in occupational medicine, after beginning his career as a general practitioner. He holds honorary appointments as Senior Clinical Lecturer to the Institute of Occupational Medicine, Birmingham University; Chief Examiner to the Faculty of Occupational Medicine's Diploma in Occupational Health and as an appeal board referee under Merchant Shipping Regulations. He is a previous president of the Royal Society of Medicine's Section of Occupational Medicine and a regular lecturer/presenter on occupational health topics.

As Chief Medical Adviser to Royal Mail Group, he has had responsibility for commissioning occupational health and welfare services for one of the UK's largest employers.

**Mark Brayne** is a psychotherapist and trainer specializing in trauma and journalism, having served for 30 years as foreign correspondent and senior editor for Reuters and the BBC World Service. Mark is Director Europe of the US-based Dart Centre for Journalism and Trauma, working with journalists, mental health professionals and educators towards improving media coverage of violence and trauma, and mitigating the emotional consequences of such coverage on those who report the stories. He developed and implemented for the BBC a programme of trauma awareness and support training in which he has also trained journalists, editors and managers at news organisations around the world including the *Washington Post* and *Newsweek*, WDR Television in Germany, the Arabic news channel al Jazeera and the *Financial Times* in

London. Mark is a Visiting Fellow at Bournemouth University Media School in the UK, and lectures regularly on journalism and trauma at other universities such as Cardiff and City in the UK. He is a member of the Board of the European Society for Traumatic Stress Studies.

**Andrew Buckley** is founder of mental well-being organisation Kipepeo and has been helping individuals and organisations understand mental health since the mid-1990s. He is a psychotherapist, coach and co-author of *A Guide to Coaching and Mental Health: The Recognition and Management of Psychological Issues* (Routledge, 2006). He is regularly invited to speak at conferences and events on the topic of managing mental health issues at work and advocates a simple approach that looks for practical and effective means that will help all concerned.

**Tony Buon** is a well-known psychologist, educator and consultant. Tony was born in Scotland but it took 25 years in Australia for him to lose his Glaswegian accent! He is now based in the north of Scotland and works throughout the UK, Europe and the Middle East. A part-time lecturer in HRM at Robert Gordon University, he is also the Managing Partner of ScotCoach, an Edinburgh-based consultancy. He speaks internationally on conflict resolution, mediation, leadership and employee assistance.

**Dr Sharon Clarke** is a Senior Lecturer in Organisational Psychology at Manchester Business School, the University of Manchester. She has published widely in the area of health and safety management, including articles published in some of the top international journals for organisational psychology (e.g., *Journal of Occupational and Organizational Psychology* and *Journal of Organizational Behavior*) as well as internationally recognised specialist safety and risk publications (such as *Safety Science* and *Risk Analysis*). She has co-authored the books *Managing the Risk of Workplace Stress* with Professor Cary L. Cooper (Routledge, 2004) and *Human Safety and Risk Management* (2nd edn) with Professors Ian Glendon and Eugene McKenna (CRC Press, 2006). She is currently the Principal Investigator on an IOSH-funded project (2007–2009) examining the long-term effectiveness of safety training interventions. Her research features regularly at leading conferences.

**Professor David Clutterbuck** is one of the international pioneers of structured mentoring, having introduced the concept to Europe in the early 1980s and, with colleagues at the Mentoring and Coaching Research Unit at Sheffield Hallam University, facilitated the emergence of developmental mentoring as a non-directive alternative to the US model of sponsorship mentoring. He co-founded in 1992 the European Mentoring Centre, which evolved in 2000 to become the European Mentoring and Coaching Council (EMCC), for which he is current chair of research.

Visiting professor of coaching and mentoring at both Sheffield Hallam and Oxford Brookes Universities, he is the author or co-author of 10 books in this field (out of almost 50 books overall):

- *Everyone Needs a Mentor*, (1985, rev. 1992, 1998, 2002)
- *Mentoring in Action* (volumes 1 and 2)
- *Mentoring Executives and Directors*
- *Learning Alliances*
- *Situational Mentoring*
- *Mentoring and Diversity: An International Perspective*
- *Implementing Mentoring Schemes*
- *Coaching at Work: Creating a Coaching Culture*
- *Coaching the Team at Work*

David leads an international consultancy, Clutterbuck Associates, which specialises in helping organisations establish and sustain coaching and mentoring capability. www.clutterbuckassociates.co.uk

**Professor Philip Dewe** is Vice-Master of Birkbeck and Professor of Organisational Behaviour in the Department of Organisational Psychology, Birkbeck, University of London. He graduated with a Master's degree in management and administration from Victoria University in Wellington, New Zealand, and with an MSc and PhD (in organisational psychology) from the London School of Economics. After a period of work in commerce in New Zealand he became a Senior Research Officer in the Work Research Unit, Department of Employment (UK). In 1980 he joined Massey University in New Zealand and headed the Department of Human Resource Management until joining the Department of Organisational Psychology, Birkbeck, University of London, in 2000. Research interests include work stress and coping, emotions and human resource accounting. He is a member of the editorial board of *Work and Stress*. He has written widely in the area of work stress and coping.

**Alison Dunn** is Head of Treatment Services, in the Occupational Health Department at Transport for London, which provides a range of services for London Underground and the Transport for London group. In this role she oversees the management of the Counselling and Trauma Service, the Physiotherapy Service, and the Drug and Alcohol Assessment and Treatment Service. Alison's background is in social work and then counselling - she was awarded a Master's degree in psychological counselling and psychotherapy in 2000. Alison has thorough experience of providing counselling in an organisational setting, managing a proactive workplace counselling service and responding to critical incidents. She has co-ordinated the counselling teams' response to several incidents that have taken place during past years as well as the response to the events on 7 July. Alison has previously written about a four-stage model for trauma aftercare in Thom Spiers' book – *Trauma: A Practitioner's Guide to Counselling*.

**Emily Duval** earned her Master's in psychology with a concentration on marriage and family therapy from Golden Gate University, San Francisco, CA. In 1994 she earned certification in suicide intervention and first began counselling in 1998 when she became certified as a grief counsellor in Marin County where she specialised in sudden death and grief after suicide, working with individuals, couples and as co-facilitator of 'SOS' groups for those who had lost someone to suicide. Emily has ample experience in university counselling centre settings, both in the USA and the UK. She currently works part-time for a workplace employee assistance programme and has a private practice in Bristol, England, offering organisational consulting services and presentations on grief after suicide.

**Professor Ståle Einarsen** was one of the early pioneers in research on bullying and harassment in the workplace, a field in which he has published extensively. He has also published in the fields such as creativity and innovation, psychosocial work environment, and leadership, and has been a licensed clinical psychologist since 1991 with a PhD in organisational psychology from 1996. Einarsen is Professor of Work and Organisational Psychology and Managing Director of the Bergen Bullying Research Group at the University of Bergen, Norway. His work has appeared in journals such as *Aggressive Behaviour, Leadership Quarterly, Violence and Victims, Journal of Applied Social Psychology* and *European Journal of Work and Organizational Psychology*. He has co-edited the book *Bullying and Emotional Abuse in the Workplace*, which gives an extensive overview of both research and best practice in the field.

**David Fairhurst** has enjoyed a rich and varied career in human resources. Since joining Lucas Industries as a graduate trainee, he has built an HR department from scratch for Transport Development Group; was the youngest group manager at H J Heinz; and was European Director of Recruitment and Leadership Planning for SmithKline Beecham where he ran a large shared services department and took the company to 'European Employer of Choice' in its sector. David moved to Tesco Stores in November 2000 as Group Resourcing Director and was quickly given the additional accountability of Corporate HR Director. In May 2005 David joined McDonald's Restaurants Ltd as Vice President of People, and in January 2007 was promoted to Senior Vice President, Chief People Officer – Northern Europe with responsibility for HR, training, education, and customer services. David is a Fellow of the Chartered Institute of Personnel and Development, a Fellow of the RSA, a member of the Council of People 1st, an associate member of Investors in People's Human Capital Management Standards board, and Chair of the Advisory Board to the Centre for Professional Personnel and Development (CPPD). In July 2006 David was voted HR Director of the Year by readers of *HR Magazine* and in June 2007 he secured No. 1 position in *Personnel Today's* Top-40 HR Power Players list. In July 2007 he was given an honorary doctorate in business administration by Manchester Metropolitan University Business School.

**M. Lance Frazier** is a PhD candidate at Oklahoma State University with an emphasis on organisational behaviour. He received his MBA from Oklahoma City University and is a student member of the Academy of Management, Society of Industrial Organisational Psychology and Southern Management Association. His current research interests include organisational justice, trust, occupational stress and personality at work. He recently was honoured as one of the Spears School of Business Outstanding Graduate Teaching Associates. Before returning to pursue his doctorate, Mr Frazier had nearly 10 years of corporate experience in the telecommunications industry.

**Neil Greenberg is** the Head of Department at the Department of Community Mental Health for Portsmouth Naval Base and a Senior Lecturer in Military Psychiatry at King's College London. Dr Greenberg studied medicine at Southampton University, graduating in 1993. He has served with the Royal Marines. Neil has specialised in psychiatry, completing a Masters degree in clinical psychiatry and become a Member of the Royal College of Psychiatrists. He is a specialist in general adult, forensic and liaison psychiatry. Since 1997 Neil has been part of the team at the forefront of developing a novel peer-led traumatic stress support package. He has provided psychological input for Foreign Office personnel after the events of 11 September 2001 and in Bali after 12 October 2002. More recently he has been a key advisor to the London Ambulance Service helping them manage their staff support in the wake of the London bombings in 2006.

**Kristina Gyllensten** is a chartered counselling psychologist and a coach. She currently works as a therapist, lecturer and researcher at a centre for cognitive therapy in Gothenburg, Sweden and is also involved in the development of a new coaching organisation, providing courses in cognitive coaching. Her particular interests are coaching, workplace stress, stress management, gender and stress, and cognitive therapy, on which she has co-authored a number of articles. She is the co-author of various publications on coaching and workplace stress including *Can Coaching Reduce Workplace Stress? The Coaching Psychologist.*

**Dr Helge Hoel** is a lecturer at Manchester Business School, the University of Manchester, England. Together with Professor Cary L. Cooper he carried out the first nationwide study of bullying in Britain and has recently completed the first evaluation study examining the effectiveness of organisational anti-bullying interventions. He has written and contributed to a number of books, journal articles and reports in the area of bullying, violence and harassment. He is co-editor of the book *Bullying and Emotional Abuse in the Workplace.*

**Peter Jenkins** is Co-Director of Counselling and Psychotherapy at Salford University, and a BACP accredited counsellor trainer. He is a former member of the Professional Conduct Committee of the British Association for Counselling and Psychotherapy, and is currently a member of the Ethics Committee of the United Kingdom Council for Psychotherapy. He has extensive experience of training counselling practitioners and organisations on legal aspects of therapy, and has published widely on this topic. His most recent publication is *Counselling, Psychotherapy and the Law* (2nd edn, Sage, 2007).

**Professor E. Kevin Kelloway** is Professor of Management and Psychology at Saint Mary's University and Senior Research Fellow at the CN Centre for Occupational Health and Safety. He is a prolific researcher having published over 100 articles and book chapters and has edited or authored eight books. His research interests include occupational health psychology, leadership, workplace violence and workplace safety. Dr Kelloway also maintains an active consultancy advising both public and private sector firms on issues related to leadership development, performance management and occupational health and safety.

**Dr Laura M. Little** is a Visiting Professor of Management at Oklahoma State University. She received her BA from Vanderbilt University, her MBA from the University of Texas at Austin and her PhD from Oklahoma State University in May 2007 where she was the recipient of the Robert W. and Jean M. Schuetz Distinguished Graduate Fellowship Award. Dr Little's research has been published in several books as well as the *Journal of Organizational Behavior, Journal of Management Studies* and *Journal of Occupational Health Psychology*.

**Gladeana McMahon** is considered one of the leading personal development and transformational coaches in the UK. She was instrumental in founding the Association for Coaching for which she now holds the positions of Fellow and Vice-President. She is also a Fellow of the BACP, the Institute of Management Studies and the Royal Society of Arts. Gladeana is widely published with some 16 popular and academic books on coaching and counselling including *Essential Business Coaching* and *Achieving Excellence in Your Coaching Practice* (Brunner-Routledge), *How to Make Life Happen* and *Confidence Works* (Sheldon Press) and *No More Anxiety* and *No More Anger* (Karnac Publications). An innovator, Gladeana is one of the UK founders of cognitive behavioural coaching and currently works as the Head of Executive Coaching for Fairplace plc and Co-Director of the Centre for Coaching. She is passionate about her work in coaching business and public sector leaders to master the psychological complexities of 21st-century corporate life.

**Dr Derek Mowbray** has over 25 years of top management experience in the public, private and education sectors including that of Director of the Management Advisory Service to the NHS – the first NHS internal advisory service that focused on service delivery and organisation development. He is credited with facilitating the most significant recent development of clinical psychology in the UK with his review of clinical psychology in 1989. More recently he completed the feasibility study into the role of associate psychologist in 2003, now being implemented, and his work is underpinning the direction of new ways of working for applied psychologists in 2007. He is currently encouraging a new focus for psychologists on organisational health. Dr Mowbray is Director of the Centre for Organisation Health, an organisation that concentrates on the primary prevention of stress and mental distress at work by facilitating changes in organisational culture. He is an organisation health psychologist, a Visiting Professor at Northumbria University, an Independent Technical Expert for the European Commission and an Expert Witness in stress (www. orghealth.co.uk)

**Professor Deborah L. Nelson** is the Spears School of Business Associates' Distinguished Professor of Business Administration and Professor of Management at Oklahoma State University. She received her PhD from the University of Texas at Arlington, where she was the recipient of the R.D. Irwin Dissertation Fellowship Award. Dr Nelson is the author of over 70 journal articles and book chapters focusing on work stress, gender issues in the workplace and positive organisational behaviour. Dr Nelson's research has been published in the *Academy of Management Executive, Academy of Management Journal, Academy of Management Review, MIS Quarterly, Journal of Organizational Behavior* and other journals. Among Dr Nelson's books are *Stress and Challenge at the Top: The Paradox of the Successful Executive, Organizational Leadership, Preventive Stress Management in Organizations, Gender, Work Stress and Health*, and *Organizational Behavior: Foundations, Realities, Challenges*. Dr Nelson has been honoured with a host of teaching and research awards, including the Burlington Northern Faculty Achievement Award, the Regents Distinguished Research Award, the Greiner Graduate Teaching Award, and the Chandler-Frates and Reitz Graduate Teaching Award. She has served on the editorial review boards of *Academy of Management Journal, Journal of Occupational Health Psychology, Academy of Management Executive, Leadership, Journal of Leadership and Organizational Studies* and the *Journal of Organizational Behavior*. Dr Nelson has also served as a consultant/executive coach for several organisations including AT&T, Sonic Corporation, ONEOK, State Farm Insurance Companies and Southwestern Bell. She has presented leadership, emotional intelligence and preventive stress management seminars in a variety of organisations, including American Fidelity Assurance, Blue Cross/ Blue Shield, Conoco/Phillips, FAA, Enogex, Kerr-McGee Corporation, Oklahoma Gas and Electric, and Oklahoma Natural Gas.

**Professor Vanja Orlans**, PhD, Dip. GPTI, AFBPsS, is a Chartered Occupational Psychologist, a Chartered Counselling Psychologist, a UKCP Registered Psychotherapist, Foundation Member with Senior Practitioner Status, BPS Register of Psychologists Specialising in Psychotherapy, and Visiting Professor at Middlesex University. She has extensive training and experience in a range of approaches to therapeutic work, as well as in the understanding of group and organisational dynamics, and has been working with individuals and groups in many different settings for over 20 years.

Vanja is currently Joint Head (with Maria Gilbert) of the Integrative Department at the Metanoia Institute in London, which offers both psychotherapeutic and coaching trainings. She also runs a private practice in psychotherapy, counselling, coaching and supervision. She has published a wide range of articles and book chapters on both clinical and organisational topics. Recent writing includes: Counselling psychology in the workplace, in R. Woolfe, W. Dryden and S. Strawbridge (Eds.), *Handbook of Counselling Psychology* (2nd edn), 2003; From structure to process: ethical demands of the postmodern era, *British Journal of Psychotherapy Integration*, 4:54–61, 2007. She is also currently co-authoring a book on counselling psychology which will appear in early 2008.

**Professor Stephen Palmer** PhD is an international stress expert and helped to launch the coaching psychology movement in the UK. He is Honorary Professor of Psychology and Founder Director of the Coaching Psychology Unit at City University, London. He is a Visiting Professor of Work Based Learning and Stress Management at the National Centre for Work Based Learning Partnerships, Middlesex University, and Director of the Centre for Stress Management. His honorary posts include being President of the Association for Coaching. He is a Chartered Psychologist, APECS Accredited Executive Coach and Supervisor, and a UKCP Registered Psychotherapist. He has written or edited over 35 books and numerous articles and book chapters on stress, coaching, counselling and health. His forthcoming book is the *Handbook of Coaching Psychology* (with Whybrow). He is editor of the *International Journal of Health Promotion and Education*, and the UK co-ordinating editor of the *International Coaching Psychology Review*. He has received awards for his contribution to counselling psychology and the development of REBT.

**Matthew A. Prosser** MSc is a PhD student in industrial/organisational psychology at Saint Mary's University, Halifax, Nova Scotia, Canada. He is a graduate of Atlantic Baptist University (music and philosophy), the Southern Baptist Theological Seminary (Master of Divinity in church history), and Saint Mary's University (BA, MSc in psychology). His research interests include: leadership, eyewitness identification, retirement well-being, and workplace sabotage. Mr Prosser is the recipient of both the Nova Scotia Health Sciences Research Foundation Doctoral Grant and the Social Science and Humanities Research Council of Canada Doctoral Graduate Scholarship. Mr Prosser plans to complete his doctoral studies in 2009.

**Dr Jo Rick** is a Chartered Occupational Psychologist based at the University of Sheffield's Institute of Work Psychology. Here Jo runs a programme of research into the workplace factors that affect psychological health with particular emphasis on well-being, trauma, human resource management (HRM) and performance, organisational culture and change management.

Prior to this, Jo led the Work, Health and Well-being programme at the Institute for Employment Studies, where she published and consulted on many aspects of work-related health and well-being including psychological trauma and rehabilitation and led the review of evidence to underpin the HSE's Management Standards for Work-related Stress.

Jo provides research and consultancy support to both organisations and policy makers on workplace mental health issues and is regularly invited to speak at conferences and in the media on work, health and well-being.

**Professor Ivan Robertson** is currently Managing Director of Robertson Cooper Ltd (a University of Manchester spin-off business founded in 1999) specialising in well-being and motivation. The company has offices in Manchester, London and Sydney – (www.robertsoncooper.com) and has developed some of the leading tools for developing well-being as a platform for organisational success. Ivan's experience covers over 30 years working at senior levels with industry/national government, education and business. He has advised many organisations, on a worldwide basis, on a wide range of issues including: well-being management, work–life balance, leadership development and training, the psychological assessment of employees, and the selection and development of top teams.

He has been responsible for over 35 books on work and organisational psychology and over 150 scholarly articles/conference papers. His publications cover management and leadership development, stress assessment and management, managerial assessment, personnel selection and personnel psychology, personality, performance management and assessment. He has held visiting academic posts in the USA (Michigan State University), Singapore (National University of Singapore) and Australia (Queensland University of Technology).

**Michael Teed** MSc is a PhD candidate (industrial/organisational psychology) at Saint Mary's University. Mike received his Master's degree in industrial and organisational psychology from Saint Mary's University. He has consulted in both private and public organisations, working on organisational stress intervention techniques, conducting needs analysis, and personnel selection/evaluations. He has also completed a two-year teaching contract for the Williams School of Business at Bishop's University. His current research interests include leadership, occupational health and safety, violence and aggression, and stress.

**Gordon Tinline** is a Chartered Occupational Psychologist and has been a Director of Robertson Cooper Ltd since the company was founded in 1999. During this time, he has become a recognised expert in the field of well-being, work-related stress, leadership and people performance. Gordon has worked extensively across the public sector, including local authorities, central government, the Prison Service and with 18 UK police forces, as well as in the private sector. Much of this work attempts to go beyond compliance with Health and Safety stress guidelines to focus on positive well-being and, ultimately, the productivity of employees and organisations.

**Dr Louise Tomson** is an independent consultant and researcher specializing in work-related stress and employee absence. She has previously held posts as a Research Fellow at the Institute for Employment Studies, and as a Lecturer in Occupational Health Psychology at the Institute of Work, Health and Organisations at the University of Nottingham. Louise has conducted research into the role of psychological, social and organisational factors in occupational health conditions, particularly work-related stress. She has designed and evaluated organisational interventions for work-related stress in a wide variety of organisations in both the private and public sectors. She has also worked with organisations to identify the causes of employee absence and develop absence management strategies. She has conducted research to identify examples of best practice following absence due to stress-related illness, and the various factors that influence the effectiveness of organisational practices in rehabilitating employees.

**David Weaver** is Chairman and Senior Partner of Freeman Oliver, a talent management consulting firm. He has over 15 years experience as an independent change management and organisational development consultant. A former social worker, university lecturer and local government senior manager, he has worked with numerous organisations in the public, private and not-for-profit sectors - primarily on issues relating to organisational change, leadership and diversity.

David holds the distinction of having led the development of one of the UK's first major entrants into the public sector recruitment and executive search market in the mid 1990s. He has personally 'head-hunted', recruited and 'coached' an impressive number of board members, chief executives and senior managers in the public and private sectors and is a frequent commentator on themes relating to leadership and public services.

He is noted as a leading consultant in the area of change management, and has used these skills to great effect within training, diversity, public speaking, mediation, conflict management and facilitation interventions. David's client base has spanned the UK, USA, France and the Eastern Caribbean and he continues to act as a mentor for young black males in inner city London.

He is a former political advisor to two senior government ministers, has represented the UK government on a Council of Europe body, European Monitoring Centre on Racism and Xenophobia and is a Vice President of the British Association for Counselling and Psychotherapy (BACP). David also acts as advisor to a number of charitable bodies, is a Vice President of the British Association for Counselling and Psychotherapy (BACP) and Chairman of Human Rights campaigning body - The 1990 Trust.

**Dr Michael Walton** is a Chartered Psychologist and a Fellow in the Centre for Leadership Studies at the University of Exeter. For many years his interests and work have focused on executive behaviour-in-context and on the unhelpful dynamics of organisation life. In addition to his academic links Dr Walton runs his own business psychology consultancy 'People in Organisations Ltd' (established in 1990) working primarily with directors and senior executives on organisational and personal change. He is seeking to establish a Centre for the Study of Executive Success and Failure; a new venture that will examine the bases for executive derailment, dysfunction and toxicity through research-based field-work studies with partner organisations. Michael has published three management titles in the area of self-management in organisations – one has been translated into German – as well as several articles on management development and change; he has co-edited a book on counselling in organisations and is the lead editor for a special issue on 'leadership toxicity' for *Organizations and People* to be published in August 2008.

**Dr Patrick Williams** One of the early pioneers of coaching, Patrick Williams MCC began executive coaching in 1990. In 1998 he founded the Institute for Life Coach Training, an ICF Accredited Coach Training Program. He speaks internationally on purposeful living, vital aging and new eldering, and the power of the coach approach in empowering and sustaining change. He is the co-author of *Therapist as Life Coach: Transforming Your Practice; Total Life Coaching: 50+ Life Lessons, Skills, and Techniques to Enhance your Practice and Your Life; Law and Ethics of Coaching: How to Solve and Avoid Difficult Problems in Your Practice* and *Becoming a Professional Life Coach: Lessons From the Institute for Life Coach Training.* Dr Williams was awarded (June 2006) the honour of being named the first Global Visionary Fellow by the Foundation of Coaching for his project, Coaching the Global Village ... bringing the coaching approach to the underserved through NGOs, leaders in developing countries, and non-profit boards.

**Dr Mark Winwood** has been a Chartered Counselling Psychologist since 1995 and is an Associate Fellow of the British Psychological Society. He has spent the last 10 years managing and developing AXA PPP healthcare's EAP product 'Employee Support', which plays a significant role in the UK market. He is interested in the development of products that integrate EAP and other employee well-being and health systems. Mark has researched extensively into telephone psychological intervention and was a member of the working party establishing the BACP *Guidelines for Telephone Counselling and Psychotherapy.* He manages a telephone counselling service that provides support for over two million private healthcare customers. He is also a Chartered Scientist. He plays an active part in EAPA both nationally and internationally. He has trained as a systemic family therapist and prior to his role in EAPs spent 10 years with the NHS. As an NHS psychologist he was involved in neuropsychological research and clinical work with a range of patients experiencing terminal illness.

**Dr David Wright** has an extensive background in occupational medicine. He served in the Army for 20 years in a wide variety of posts at regimental, formation and Ministry of Defence level. This included appointment as Chief

Medical Officer to the United Nations Protection Force in Yugoslavia for which he was awarded the CBE. Since leaving the Army he has worked as a senior occupational physician in the railways and subsequently the Post Office before transferring to Atos Origin as Chief Occupational Physician. He lectures regularly and was a joint author of the Society of Occupational Medicine handbook on the Disability Discrimination Act and of the British Society of Rehabilitation Medicine publication *Vocational Rehabilitation – the Way Forward*. He has lectured on a programme under the auspices of the Royal Society of Medicine on the biopsychosocial aspects of disability and rehabilitation back into the workplace and has been involved in the launch of the Work and Health booklet jointly produced by the Faculty of Occupational Medicine, the Society of Occupational Medicine and the Royal College of General Practitioners. He is a regular reviewer for the *Journal of Occupational Medicine* and has recently completed a term as President of the Society of Occupational Medicine.

# Foreword – The Fourth Wave

**David Fairhurst**
*Senior Vice President, Chief People Officer – Northern Europe McDonald's Restaurants*

It's very easy to forget that 'going to work' is a relatively new phenomenon.

In 1703, when the British farmer and inventor Jethro Tull first advertised a mechanical seed drill in his book *Horse-Hoeing Husbandry*, over three-quarters of the English population worked in agriculture, with most of the remaining quarter engaged in small-scale manufacturing and service occupations. For most where they lived was where they worked, and the nature of the work they were engaged in reflected the pattern of the seasons.

Tull's seed drill, however, was a catalyst. A catalyst for a revolution which lead to just one-third of people being employed in agriculture by the early 19th century, and a mere 4% by the mid-20th century – the Industrial Revolution.

But the transition from an agrarian to an industrialised economy was a tough one for employees. After thousands of years of following the natural rhythms of nature, the demands of the newly mechanised industries meant that wholly unnatural shifts and working patterns were introduced which people found difficult to adjust to. In response, employers imposed fines for lateness and absence. They also kept the wages low in the hope that an empty belly would heighten the appetite for hard work.

In this light, it is clear that the past century has seen the workplace become a significantly more humane place. But has it yet become a truly employee-centred place?

Workplaces are about getting things done as efficiently and effectively as possible – a truth that applies as much to a public service organisation or a charity as it does to a commercial firm. And over the past 300 years the transformation in organisational efficiency and effectiveness has been dramatic.

The First Wave of transformation came from machines. Tull's seed drill created a step-change in performance with a single operator doing the work of 10 people. But as machines became ever more sophisticated step-change improvements became harder to find, so the Second Wave of performance enhancement emerged – 'scientific management'.

In 1895 F.W. Taylor first put forward his ideas on the division of labour and time-and-motion studies, and these were taken to their natural conclusion by Henry Ford with his moving assembly line. The step-change was dramatic – Ford increased the productivity of his Highland Park plant from one car every 13 hours in 1913 to one car every 93 minutes in 1914. And so, for a short time the process was king.

But before too long processes were in pretty good shape and once again organisations were looking for the source of the next step-change. And the Third Wave of transformation, the Information Revolution, was heralded by the bulky form of the Electronic Numerical Integrator and Calculator (ENIAC) – the world's first general-purpose electronic digital computer. Forty feet long and 20 feet high, ENIAC consumed enough power to cause the lights of Philadelphia to dim when it was first switched on in 1946. However, when ENIAC was turned off for the last time in 1954 it was estimated to have done more mathematics in its eight-year life than the entire human race had done prior to 1945.

Today, the computer I am using to write this foreword does more computations per second than ENIAC did in eight years. And this observation alone prompts me to suggest that maybe the Third Wave is nearing its end too. But where will the Fourth Wave be found? What underutilised resource is there left in the workplace that might deliver a step-change improvement in organisational performance?

Well, in a 2001 survey Gallup found that 26% of US employees were 'engaged' with their work, 55% 'not engaged' and 19% 'actively disengaged' – a group who psychologically, Gallup said, had already left their jobs. And a similar survey in the UK revealed 19% 'engaged', 61% 'not engaged' and 20% 'actively disengaged'.

It isn't hard to imagine the performance improvements organisations would enjoy if they could get this resource working at optimum levels. And this is why I firmly believe that improving the way organisations manage their people will deliver the Fourth Wave of transformation. But the Fourth Wave will not be an easy ride.

Machines, processes and information technology all share one thing in common – they are soulless, mindless entities designed to fulfil a role in the workplace. People on the other hand have been hard-wired over millennia to be effective in the role of hunter-gatherers and farmers. As a result they are a poor fit in most workplace roles and I think this may go some way towards explaining why people – often an organisation's single most expensive resource – have always come second. After all, if organisations were able to gain performance improvements from their custom-built, compliant resources, why expend unnecessary effort wrestling performance improvements out of something as wilful, spirited and unfit for purpose as the workforce?

Well, that's exactly the challenge we face with the Fourth Wave – and it's a challenge that at this moment many organisations are ill-equipped to tackle.

Just as the Second Wave forced organisations to adopt Taylor's ideas of 'scientific management', so the Fourth Wave will force a reappraisal of what we currently consider to be standard practice.

From the perspective of the early 21st century we can look back and identify the three waves of transformation which have shaped today's organisations. At the same time, we can also identify and condemn the inhuman way organisations have treated people in the past.

But I wonder how history will judge today's organisations when the Fourth Wave of workplace transformation has become fully embedded? Will organisations which fail to support employees who are suffering from high levels of stress, who are being bullied and mistreated, or who are simply failing to cope with the demands of the workplace be considered as deviant as those of an earlier age which fined or starved their employees to ensure compliance?

I suspect that they will. Which is why I consider this to be an important book. A book which will be seen in the years ahead as containing many of the ideas which defined the Fourth Wave of transformation. The wave which will finally put people where they belong – at the heart of the organisation.

# Acknowledgements

Writing this book has been a fantastic experience for us as it has opened up our world to the thoughts and practices of many leading experts in the field of well-being. We would like to convey our thanks and appreciation to each contributor. We are particularly grateful to our publishers, to Claire Ruston and Sarah Tilley at Wiley-Blackwell, and to our families for their respective support during the development of this book.

# INTRODUCTION

# Adapting to Change

Andrew Kinder, Rick Hughes and Cary L. Cooper

Change is about the only constant within today's organisational life and as economies yo-yo and organisations adapt their cultures, processes and systems to fit, people still remain the organisation's most prized resource. Employment legislation continues to evolve to offer protection and rights and whilst this might be seen to be weighted in the employee's favour, the longer-term outcome is part of the duty of care rightly afforded to all staff.

Organisations understand that to operate successfully in a competitive marketplace with the best possible human resources, they need to support and nurture their people. The working life has changed immeasurably over the last decade – the working hours of many people have significantly increased, jobs are no longer for life and most families now have two earners. Whilst job flexibility and adaptive employment practices undoubtedly help some, pressures within the workplace remain. Work can never be stress-free.

## THE COST OF STRESS

The collective cost of stress to US organisations has been estimated at approximately US$ 150 billion a year. In European countries, stress costs the economy an estimated 5–10% of GNP per annum. Studies show that workplace stress was responsible for more long-term sickness absence than any other core factor. With absence come increased workloads, longer working hours, lower morale, increased mistakes and accidents, culminating in reduced productivity.

We are seeing the 'Americanisation' of Europe spreading throughout the continent. This trend towards what is euphemistically called the 'flexible' workforce originated in the UK. Britain led the way in Europe towards privatising the public sector in the 1980s. Its workforce was substantially downsized during the recession of the late 1980s and early 1990s. Outsourcing

*Employee Well-being Support: A Workplace Resource.* Edited by A. Kinder, R. Hughes and C.L. Cooper.
© 2008 John Wiley & Sons, Ltd.

many of its corporate functions, it left the recession behind in the early 1990s, faster than its European counterparts. However this scenario of 'leaner' organisations, intrinsic job insecurity and a culture of longer working hours is beginning to have an adverse effect on employee attitudes and behaviour. The short-termist approach or corporate 'X-Factor' syndrome might save companies money in the interim, but will undoubtedly cost more in the longer term.

## THE STRESS FACTORS

What is so disturbing about the trend towards a long-hours culture is the employees' perception of the damage it is inflicting on them and their families. Although there has been some improvement over the last five years, the recent CMI Quality of Working Life survey of a new cohort of 10,000 managers found that 56% of them (from shop floor to top floor management) reported that these long hours seriously damaged their health; 54% that they adversely affected their relationship with their children; 60% that they damaged their relationship with their partners' spouse; and 46% that their long hours substantially undermined their productivity at work. In addition, when the managers felt 'less productive', it was found that they averaged nearly 10 days off a year with a sickness absence in contrast to 2.5 days a year for those who felt productive and worked less hours.

Another manifestation is the increasing level of job insecurity. Historically in Europe, very few white-collar, managerial and professional workers have experienced high levels of job insecurity. Even blue-collar workers who were laid off were frequently re-employed when times got better. The question that we have to ask is 'Can human beings cope with permanent job insecurity?'

The constant 'change for change sake' mentality amongst many companies is also beginning to take its toll on employee mental well-being at work. The recent CMI survey found that 63% of managers at all levels indicated that their organisation was engaged in a substantial cost reduction program, 57% in the use of short-term contract staff, 36% in a major redundancy program and 25% in substantial outsourcing. It was found that this constant change, and the underlying breaking of the psychological contract between employer and employee by these activities, led to declining motivation (57%), reduced sense of job security (66%), poorer morale (61%), poorer employee well-being (48%) and decreased loyalty to the organisation (47%).

## A STRATEGY FOR MANAGING STRESS IN A CHANGING WORKFORCE

For the prevention and management of stress at work, the following three approaches can provide a comprehensive strategic framework: primary (e.g. stress reduction), secondary (e.g. stress management) and tertiary pre-vention (e.g. employee assistance programs/workplace counselling).

- *Primary prevention* is concerned with taking action to modify or eliminate sources of stress inherent in the work environment, so reducing their negative impact on the individual. The focus of primary interventions is in adapting the environment to 'fit' the individual.
- *Secondary prevention* is concerned with the prompt detection and manage-ment of experienced stress. This can be done by increasing awareness and improving the stress management skills of the individual through training and educative activities.
- *Tertiary prevention* is concerned with the treatment, rehabilitation and recovering process of individuals who have suffered, or are suffering, from serious ill-health as a result of stress. In most cases this is done by workplace counselling.

This book caters for each of these intervention stages within an amalgam of articles, each building on the other to offer a template for employee support options.

## THIS BOOK

This book was developed with John Wiley & Sons, Ltd to provide the reader with a comprehensive insight into contemporary employee support theory and practice, and to offer guidance on best practice. This provides organisations a chance to maintain their competitive advantage in a commercial world prone to change and stress within the workplace.

We have brought together respected experts from around the globe to share their specialities within the world of employee support. Written by leading practitioners, prominent academics and business leaders, the book seeks to educate and inform the reader about opportunities for a positive emotionally and psychologically healthy workplace.

This book is an authoritative resource designed to give practical guidance to the reader along with summary checklists and case-studies to illustrate key points. We believe the book has relevance for the business community, such as senior executives and directors as well as human resources personnel, people development, welfare, occupational health, and health and safety functions. 'Externals' such as union representatives, employee assistance professionals, counsellors, occupational therapists, coaches, mentors, trainers and consul-tants will also find this a useful employee support compendium.

## STRUCTURE OF THE BOOK

The book is split into three sections:

## 1. Organisational Behaviour Issues and Well-Being

How people behave at work and how they are treated by others will have a considerable influence on productivity. Organisational structures and the cultures within will shape the mould in which employees function. More open cultures that favour consultative approaches to employee communication will allow staff more opportunity to express their views and offer creative options for business improvement. More autocratic styles will instil a greater rigidity and reduce the communication flow potential.

Chapter 1 assesses what might make a working environment 'toxic' – does it inspire and motivate, or drain and suppress? Chapter 2 goes on to reflect on what makes up a supportive organisation, which is reinforced by Chapter 3 where we hear about employee psychological well-being. In fact, the lead for effective support comes from their orgnisational behaviour or style (Chapter 4) but can be mapped out depending on the scale of operations (Chapter 5). Proactive intervention strategies help to keep an organisation on the right track – whether this is management coaching (Chapter 6), behaviour risk management (Chapter 7) or developing positive coping strategies (Chapter 8), though more reactive approaches help realign the organisation if it is on the wrong track, including developing an effective duty of care approach (Chapter 9), learning about diversity (Chapter 10) and having a sufficient knowledge of mental health issues (Chapter 11).

## 2. Responding to Specific Organisational Challenges

Part 2 examines specific organisational challenges that occur within an organisation and which can impact significantly on employee well-being if not addressed properly. These include traumatic incidents (Chapter 12), suicide and sudden death (Chapter 13) and bullying and mistreatment at work (Chapter 14). Setting up effective support systems for employees such as employee assistance programmes is important to minimise the distress of such difficult challenges. Using psychological approaches from counselling and coaching traditions to understand how an organisation can be helped can be useful when looking to understand how the organisation is behaving (Chapter 15). Research highlights that counselling in the workplace does have a net positive cost benefit, meaning that the benefit of providing the service to staff is greater than the cost (McLeod, 2001, 2007). Indeed, counselling is now well regarded as a crucial component of employee welfare. Organisations bringing in a counselling/employee assistance programme need to understand how to get the most out of the service (Chapter 16). Tackling a macho culture (Chapter 17) illustrates how a combination of employee support and organisational change initiatives can make big changes to the improved output of an organisation.

## 3. Mental Health, Emotions and Work

When employees need support, it is important to identify the source of the problems and then which options are most appropriate for remedial action. Section 3 looks at mental health issues in supporting people returning to work following absence (Chapters 18 and 19) as well as how stress can be tackled (Chapter 20).

Conflict can be a source of positive organisational energy but if not harnessed correctly can be destructive, requiring conflict resolution approaches such as workplace mediation (Chapter 21). Mediation is one of many active interventions – others include counselling (Chapter 22), coaching (Chapter 23) and mentoring (Chapter 24). A further chapter explores whether building emotional resilience into the culture is an effective strategy for increasing well-being (Chapter 25).

Whether employee support initiatives fall into the reactive or proactive camps is to some extent immaterial. The value for an organisation (and their staff) is choosing a package that fits; they generate a synergy of positive emotional health and positive cost benefits.

At the end of the day, life at work is not inherently 'bad' – and employee support interventions do not automatically imply organisation guilt or complicity in 'stress' (quite the opposite). Mental health studies all agree that work and employment is the greatest predictor of good mental health. Absence and unemployment impacts negatively on mental health. Work gives us structure, routine and boundaries.

Employee support is simply a set of practices and initiatives that help to guide and nurture employees to make the best contribution to their jobs and work. It's bottom-line productivity-enhancing strategy at its best.

## REFERENCES

McLeod, J. (2001). *Counselling in the Workplace: The Facts. A Systematic Study of the Research Evidence*. Rugby: British Association for Counselling and Psychotherapy.

McLeod, J. (2007). *Counselling in the Workplace: A Comprehensive Review of the Research Evidence*, 2nd edn. Lutterworth: British Association for Counselling and Psychotherapy.

# PART 1

# Organisational Behaviour Issues and Well-being

# CHAPTER 1

# In Consideration of a Toxic Workplace: a Suitable Place for Treatment

**Michael Walton**
*Fellow in the Centre for Leadership Studies at the University of Exeter*
*Director, People in Organisations Ltd, UK*

This chapter suggests that all workplaces will be, to some degree, toxic and that such conditions are to be expected and thus to be viewed as a regular feature of organisational life. It advocates that those in positions of organisational leadership should anticipate, prepare for and handle more openly and frankly the dynamics, features and characteristics of a toxic workplace as described rather more than currently appears to be the case.

Whilst much is rightly made of the critical impact of leadership behaviour on an organisation's well-being this may not be the primary determinant of an organisation's health and condition. In considering organisational toxicity this chapter asserts that more attention should be given to considering the internal culture of an organisation and the organisation's external environment in *combination* with an examination of leadership behaviour-in-context.

## INTRODUCTION

For the purposes of this chapter a toxic organisation is defined as one within which behaviours which poison, are disruptive, destructive, exploitive, dysfunctional and abusive are pervasive and tolerated. Instances of this would include workplace bullying and harassment in its various forms, deception and fraudulent dealings, the forced imposition of unrealistic workloads and the fostering of disruptive internal competition resulting in bitter and destructive 'turf' battles. In such environments feuding between different departments and functions is likely to lead to a 'blame' culture, embedded patterns of

*Employee Well-being Support: A Workplace Resource.* Edited by A. Kinder, R. Hughes and C.L. Cooper.
© 2008 John Wiley & Sons, Ltd.

misinformation and misrepresentation, together with the condoning of overly competitive and aggressive interpersonal behaviour.

Such destructive and self-servicing misuse of power is likely to create organisations that become increasingly internally divided and composed of competing 'power blocs' of winners and losers. The losers are likely to be discredited, captured, demolished, suppressed, seduced or driven under-ground. These could be described as 'war-zone' organisations in which the weapons employed whilst not of a military form can be just as deadly. The type of organisation I am depicting, and have experienced, is likely to become progressively unhealthy and protective of its 'ruling elite' resulting in ways of working that will ultimately undermine the effective functioning – and perhaps continuation – of the organisation itself.

'Corruption, hypocrisy, sabotage, and manipulation, as well as other assorted unethical, illegal, and criminal acts, are part of the poisonous repertoire of toxic leaders' is how Lipman-Blumen (2005:18) describes such leaders 'who, by virtue of their destructive behaviours and their dysfunctional personal qualities or characteristics, inflict serious and enduring harm on the individuals, groups, organisations, communities and even the nations that they lead'.

In spite of much of the 'positive' hype promoted by the 'leadership industry' leaders are not, by definition, always good, ethical or correct in their behaviour as has been evidenced in recent times by the deluge of material describing toxic leadership behaviour. High profile toxic leadership within companies such as Enron and WorldCom reinforces the importance of addressing, examining, understanding better – and anticipating – the toxic presence of such facets of leadership (Anand et al., 2004; Frost, 2003; Hogan & Smither, 2001; Kellerman, 2004; Sankowsky, 1995; Smith & Quirk, 2005; Thomas & Herson, 2002; Wright & Smye, 1996).

Such examples have been described as evidence of 'the dark side of leader-ship', a side which whilst always present has often remained in the shadows so far as much of the conventional training for leadership is concerned, yet a side which exerts a profound influence on the well-being of those at work (Babiak, 1995; Cavaiola & Lavender, 2000; Conger, 1990; Frost, 2003; Furnham & Taylor, 2004; Babiak & Hare, 2006; Gabriel, 1999; Hogan & Hogan, 2001; Kellerman, 2004; Kets de Vries, 1985; Lipman-Blumen, 2005; Zaleznik & Kets de Vries, 1985). It may well be that these high profile examples are but the tip of the iceberg of such behaviour in many of our organisations and institutions. It is salutary to speculate that – to some degree – all organisations could be experienced as toxic and thus to think otherwise would be naïve, illusory and fanciful in the light of the day-to-day perversity and pain that is experienced by many.

Whilst examining the behaviour of those in positions of leadership and influence is important in any consideration of a toxic workplace so is the need to look at the internal culture (the 'how we do things around here' dimension) and the 'climate' (what it is like to experience being and working there) (Osrin, private conversation, 2006).

## THE PECULARITY OF ORGANISATIONS

Working in an organisation can be quite a strange experience and generate intense feelings and tensions ranging from unsuppressed delight to the deep depths of depression. But why is this so? What is it that working in an organisation does to many of us when we report for work each day? What is it about conformity, anonymity, collectivity, power and authority, and the exercise of leadership and followership that generates the blocking and negativity, stupidity and closed-thinking, selfishness and arrogance we often see around us at work? After all as Bolden and Gosling (2006) observe, leaders do not exist in splendid isolation; they do have a need for meaningful relationships with others yet such needs may be persistently and continuingly damaged by counterproductive and destructive workplace practices. Why should such behaviour be so prevalent and undermine the constructive and productive work generally accomplished?

It makes you wonder why there seem to be so many people problems at work and why this is such a common and continuing experience for so many? Why don't people work harmoniously all the time? Just what is it that seems to trigger the competition, animosity, rivalry, jealousy and one-upmanship that seem to be all too common at work? What is it about the work of Scott Adams and 'Dilbert' and 'Dogbert' that is so pertinent, accurate, appealing and captivating to the legions of us who are, or have felt, captive at work? What is it that Adams (1996a, b) brings to life so vividly that is ever present yet rarely openly discussed and considered about the dysfunctional and toxic nature – because that is what Adams is so aptly highlighting in much of his work – many experience on a regular basis within their working environments?

Irrespective of the formal and logical bases underpinning their inception, business organisations remain, in terms of how they function, socially constructed entities. They combine – for a variety of specified purposes – disparate groups of people many of whom would otherwise have very little interest in freely meeting or socializing with those they find around themselves. It is highly likely that a more transactional than transformational orientation would describe why most are at work and consequently each person will want to protect and secure the best they can for themselves (Avolio, 1999).

Whilst leaders may wish to believe otherwise, relatively few employees are likely to be profoundly committed to the organisation even though they will want to protect their status and position within it. Furthermore there is unlikely to be any universal experience about what it means to work in any particular organisation even though its internal rules, communications and entreaties will have been scripted for a common audience. Indeed the presented veneer of universality within organisations could be more accurately described as a thin and fragile one punctuated and punctured by vested interests, hidden agendas, competing alliances and personal objectives. With such a mix of personal and sectional interests at play, corporate communications are unlikely to be interpreted at face value but will be interpreted through personal, professional and functional filters. Given such a matrix of dynamics the frequent emergence of misunderstandings, conflicts, misperceptions, internal intrigue, the interplay of power and politics and resistance to change in organisations should come as no surprise but be anticipated more acutely and addressed more openly.

With such an unpinning, a challenge – real or imagined – to a person's emotional attachment, status and standing at work is likely to trigger defensive and self-protective responses to counter emergent feelings of vulnerability, confusion, shock and anxiety (Roberts & Hogan, 2002). Such reactions are likely to be more keenly felt and more intensely experienced the more senior the person involved is as they will probably consider that they have more to lose and thus may be prompted to try to maintain the *status quo* in a robust – not to say, potentially toxic – manner irrespective of what they may say to the contrary! If so such a working hypothesis could help explain 'seemingly' overly defensive and aggressive over-reactions from senior executives when they feel under threat or under criticism. Reactions which may significantly increase toxicity in the workplace.

There is a further important dimension to organisational life that helps to explain why change in organisations all too often generates stern resistance, dysfunctional reactions and why people may behave with such emotion when they feel under threat. If viewed as a 'containing institution' an organisation comes to be seen as offering a welcomed measure of security, continuity and protection in an otherwise ambiguous and changing world. Consequently challenges and threats to the *status quo,* as well as periods of internal uncertainty, are likely to increase internal tension and trigger self-protective reactions. Such defensive reactions could result and begin to explain the origins of some of the toxic behaviours outlined earlier.

When combined within such a complex and multi-layered context, toxic behaviour and dysfunctional practices may be present when individuals and groups feel the need to protect their own interests and advantages. Whilst not desirable such defensive individual and collective responses within an organization can be expected, should be acknowledged and could be valued as evidence of an organization being 'alive and well'. The challenge can then be redefined to become that of maintaining such 'festerings' but within productive limits and to avoid apathy, internal anarchy and extreme internal workplace toxicity overwhelming the productive working through of the tensions of change. This however may be more difficult to achieve than one would wish. Whilst Case & Gosling (2006) note that 'Logic as a practice depends on non-attachment towards subjective feelings (such as those generated by interactions within organisations)' much of what actually goes on interpersonally in organisations is high in subjectivity.

Whilst interactions within organisations will be presented 'logically', just how deep that veneer goes and how well that can be sustained is variable when those involved feel vulnerable, marginalized, threatened, and under duress or strain.

Instances of illogical and even absurd behaviour at work – over 'seemingly' trivial events – which can be out of all proportion to the events themselves – may however be surfacing just how seriously interactions within organisations are taken when the actors involved feel under threat. It may be that we are all prone to developing high levels of attachment to things at work, which, when we consider them to be under threat, will trigger defensive behaviour, causing 'logic' to fly out of the window! Within the hot-house of an organisation we will scrutinise and interpret peoples' interactions, watch for status plays, power ploys and the like particularly when we feel our position to be vulnerable. In turn, unconsciously perhaps, we may then position and prepare ourselves to repel potential 'attacks'. Organisations, and the dynamics contained within them really are peculiar – albeit interesting – things to consider!

One way of getting more of a grip on toxicity and dysfunctionality is to examine the organisation through different contextual filters – such as the internal culture and climate, the stakeholder network, the predominant disciplines and functions represented, and the main markets and products/ services provided – focussing on different aspects of the organisation. The results can then be combined into a more detailed assessment to provide a more integrated 'view' of what may be going on.

## 'CONTEXT' IS KING

The tone, the feel and the culture of the workplace conditions, how those 'inside' feel enabled, or conversely, disabled to undertake their work. It shapes how an employee experiences and makes sense of what they see going on around them; it legitimizes their actions, commissions and omissions. It guides them towards what is expected and what is unwelcome in what they say, observe and do. The *context* defines and describes what is wanted, what is 'healthy' and acceptable and what is not deemed to be so; it defines the behaviour of executives as 'good' and 'bad', constructive and destructive, caring and selfish, exploitative or paternalistic, threatening and welcoming, functioning and dysfunctional, harmless and toxic.

Yet in spite of this it seems to me that the assessment of an organization's internal context receives relatively little attention when set against the deluge of material emphasizing individual task achievement, personal advancement, the acquisition of charismatic & transformational leadership behaviours, technical skills development and on the successful deployment of one-upmanship behaviour at work. This poses the question 'Why might such neglect, of such an important aspect of organisational functioning, persist?'

In addition the skills of 'spin', impression management and the promotion of self combined with the avoidance of blame seem to attract far more attention, as significant mediating forces for executive success and employee well-being, than examining the internal organisational context and its impact on executive performance.

It may be that examining the internal context, in contrast with a more headline-grabbing numbers driven assessment of the organization, and grappling with the 'challenge of change' takes too long, is low on media interest, isn't sexy enough and could worry investors if it got out that the organisation had an internal culture problem! If so this may help to account for less attention being placed on culture and context than is merited even though such factors exercise a crucial influence on organizational success and failure. But it may also be that it is more convenient and appealing to hold the leader(s) responsible for success and failure as they can relatively easily be replaced – like sports coaches – when the going gets tough, when their personal allure fades or when an alternative 'Mr Fix-It Saviour' becomes available on the market.

The internal context and culture will also influence how, and in what manner, an executive's vulnerabilities are triggered. Vulnerabilities, to which all are susceptible, such as anxiety, fear of failure and ridicule, rivalry, jealousy and dysfunctional competition and the threat of humiliation and perhaps annihilation (which in this context may mean being pushed out of the organisation)! So what then do we need to watch out for? How and in what ways should we be on our guard? To what extent does the behaviour of senior executives and other key influential figures set the tone and demand certain types of behaviour – some of which may indeed be toxic – against which a person's success, compliance and acceptability may well be measured? The extent to which those in positions of influence tolerate behaviour different from their own and the degree to which behavioural compliance is demanded as a mark of loyalty to the flag may well hold some of the clues to the level of toxicity in the workplace (Harvey, 1988; Janis, 1982 amongst others).

So what then do we need to watch out for? Kellerman for example posits seven categories of bad leadership practices which she describes as being incompetent, rigid, intemperate, callous, corrupt, insular and evil (2004) whereas Lipman-Blumen's (2005) primary focus concerns the *allure* of toxic leaders and on toxic *follower* behaviour (see also Janis, 1982; Finkelstein, 2003; Kets de Vries, 1989; Lowman, 1993; McCalley, 2002; Offermann, 2004; Sperry, 2002, Stein, 2005; Sulkowicz, 2004; Zaleznik, 1970). In addition to leaders and followers we should also be concerned about those whom Frost & Robinson (1999) terms 'toxic handlers' as the pervasiveness of toxic leader/follower behaviour also exerts a pressure and a cost on those who seek to keep the place going, in spite of the internal trauma and angst generated, such as a client of mine who described themselves as the 'Director of Disease, Divorces, Dysfunctions and Deaths'.

## INDICATORS OF A TOXIC WORKING ENVIRONMENT

The most obvious and overt indicators will be those relating to the behaviour of 'the people in charge'. The literature suggests that the most frequently reported disruptive executive behaviours are characterised by dramatic, histrionic, emotionally demanding, narcissistic, aggressive and somewhat grandiose leadership behaviours (Babiak, 1995; Conger, 1990; Hogan & Hogan, 2001; Kets de Vries, 1979, 1985, 1989; Khurana, 2002; Levinson, 1978; Lubit, 2002; Maccoby, 2000, 2004; Price, 2000; Sankowsky, 1995).

The work of the above reinforces the key contributions from the Center for Creative Leadership (CCL) whose research on executive derailment highlighted patterns of abrasive and abusive behaviour, insensitivity to the needs of others, distant, aloof and arrogant ways of behaving, unnecessary and intrusive micro-management, the manipulation of situations and continuing self-serving behaviour as significant contributors to an executive's derailment and demise (Kofodimos, 1989, 1990; Lombardo & Eichinger, 1989; McCall & Lombardo, 1983) – and thus, to my mind, a culture of toxic leadership.

Recent years have seen the lure of charisma in leadership generate enthusiasm for such styles of heroic leadership and a relative decline in the appeal of less overt styles of leader behaviour. McCall (1998) quotes Harry Levinson on the grandiose self-image which can develop as executives become more senior: 'They think they have the right to be condescending and contemptuous to people who serve them. They (executives) think they are entitled to privilege and the royal treatment.' McCall concludes: 'In summary, the development of arrogance is one of the most insidious of the derailment dynamics. It is a negative that grows from a positive, deriving as it does from actual talent and success.' (1998:46)

Unsurprisingly then the dangers of excessive charisma attract particular attention when thinking about the potential for toxic leadership as the heightened level of self-aggrandizement that can accompany the enactment of overly 'heroic' and 'transformational' approaches to leadership can so readily drift into excess (see Khurana, 2002; Lubit, 2002; Maccoby, 2000, 2004; Tourish, 2005, amongst others).

A toxic working environment will show itself primarily:

(i) through the behaviour of an organisation's key personnel,
(ii) by the rules and regulations formally established governing people's behaviour and ways of working and
(iii) how these rules are implemented in practice.

Whilst this chapter resists the temptation to place all of the responsibility for toxic working onto the behaviour of an organisation's key executives, how they behave – and what they sponsor – will be indicative of what is deemed constructive and 'acceptably disruptive' about their organisation.

Yet this is not the whole story as one of the difficulties in addressing toxicity in the workplace is the way in which 'toxic' demands can be cast in such a manner as to be difficult to fault, counter, challenge or deny. Demands such as to the need to 'build for the future', the need 'to strip out dead wood and embrace 20th-century thinking', to 'beat the competition', to 'endure the pain for the longer gain', and to 'work harder & smarter' may all sound reasonable yet may prompt and encourage – and legitimise – uncaring, abusive and toxic behaviour. Whilst demands such as these need not be punitive nor abrasive how they are enacted may be. So the issue is not that such exhortations are inappropriate so much as *how* they are then pursued. *The means* do not always justify *the ends* yet in an organisation which displays toxic characteristics this is far more likely to be the case.

The workplace situation can be further complicated as behaviours, now increasingly recognised as toxic and abusive, may have previously been excused, denied, or even encouraged, because of the results they delivered and may over time have:

(i) reinforced and intensified leadership behaviour now viewed as toxic,
(ii) discouraged others from addressing the unacceptable behaviours experienced, and
(iii) generated a groupthink and/or acceptant mentality within that setting that may have become deeply embedded and is now resistant to change (Harvey, 1988; Janis, 1982; Milgram, 1974; Zimbardo, 1969, 2007).

Toxic organisational behaviour could be said to exist within the 'white space' of an organisation – between the lines of what is going on and what is seen as acceptable to discuss – and where a culture of 'Omerta' may have taken hold. This makes it difficult to initiate discussions about such matters as they expose the instigator – as in the fable of *The Emperor's New Clothes* (Anderson, 1991) – as a more neutral and distanced observer of what is actually going on as opposed to what many, collusively, pretend is happening within the workplace. In adopting such a position the naïve observer makes themselves vulnerable:

 (i) to possible accusations of being unable to cope,
 (ii) of being unsuitable and untrustworthy for the job in the first place,
(iii) of being a naysayer,
(iv) of betraying colleagues,
 (v) of being a troublemaker, and
(vi) of being labelled as someone to watch for the future. A person perhaps whose card may be then be marked as unreliable, as someone not likely to be 'one of the boys', a snitch and a person who could at some point in the future be brave (or foolish!!) enough to be a whistleblower (Alford, 2001; Wright and Smye, 1996).

Influential though they are the behaviour of those in positions of power and influence will give a clue about the toxicity of an organisation but that is not the whole story . . .

## REVIEWING THE SITUATION

Whilst this was not, to my knowledge, their primary purpose frameworks such as the 7-S model (Peters & Waterman, 1982) and Galbraith's (1977) 'Fit' model can be used to examine how different facets of an organisation are working in support of each other or if they may be skewing the way an organisation is

(i) orientated and (ii) functioning. In effect highlighting whether the organisation is in-tune internally or if its ways of working are mutually competing and antagonistic. For example when the reward structure fails to encourage the very outcomes the organisation needs to accomplish to survive or if it rewards behaviour that is destructive and self-serving (but perhaps financially beneficial to the few).

This section introduces another method – based on field work – that can be used to re-view the behaviour of executives and consider the organisation's susceptibility for excess toxicity by focusing on:

  (i) the key influencers,
 (ii) the internal state of the organization, and
(iii) on the conditions in the external environment within which the organisation is operating and trading.

Although it remains very appealing to attribute to the leader the successes and the misfortunes of an organisation's performance, to do so fails to give sufficient weight to the wider range of factors at play which influence and determine the success and the failure of an executive's performance and that of their organisation. Whilst the personal characteristics, behaviour and pedigree of key executives will influence an organisation's performance – and set the tone and feel of the working environment – my research suggests other facilitating factors will influence organisational toxicity (Walton, 2005). Based on a review of consulting cases, three dimensions emerged as significant in reviewing the behaviour of senior executives and their impact on the internal workplace climate and sense of well-being. These were:

1. The behaviour of the *executive*(s) themselves.
2. The internal *context* of the organization (its internal culture and climate).
3. The *external* environment (the 'external' world) in which the organization finds itself.


## The First Dimension: The Executive-in-action: Personality Characteristics

Although, as has been noted earlier, the psychological composition of the key executives exerts a significant effect on an organization, no one set of personality characteristics emerged that led to the range of dysfunctions I had witnessed and studied. For example 'toxic' behaviours were recorded which led to problems in some organisations, but also where the same behaviours did not in others! I had examples of those who could be described as 'heroic' and as 'villains' who were creating positive and less than helpful outcomes. I had examples of charismatic extroverts and introverted thinkers, some providing helpful and some providing unhelpful leadership, and I had examples of executives offering directive and more transformational approaches again with varying effects (Avolio, 1999; Burns, 1978; Kellerman, 2004; Lipman-Blumen, 2005; Lowman, 1993).

The personality characteristics of those in charge seemed, on their own, insufficient to account for a toxic workplace. Considering the internal contexts and cultures of the case material I was studying seemed the logical next focus to take.

## A Second Dimension: Working within the Culture and Climate of the Organisation

Executive behaviour does not occur in a vacuum but within contexts and settings which shape the ways in which leadership is defined and accomplished. Just as form without function could be said to have little – other than an aesthetic – meaning on its own so examining an executive's personality and make-up without reference to how these are presented at work offers a similarly incomplete picture.

In sharp contrast to a view that it is what the executive does 'that gets results' it may be more accurate to explore how (i) the internal context(s) mediate what the executive is able to do and (ii) how those contexts define executive success and failure (Ackroyd & Thompson, 1999; Cavaiola & Lavender, 2000; Giacalone & Greenberg, 1997). A more extensive exploration of the contextual determinants of effective leadership behaviour, whilst currently somewhat neglected in the literature, is needed and may help to avoid excessive and penalistic toxic leadership practices taking hold.

Contextual conditions that appeared to facilitate the likelihood of a toxic workplace revolved around:

(i) disruptions to previously long-standing internal processes and procedures,
(ii) loss of well established colleagues (who held the internal 'wisdom and history' of the place),
(iii) a too rapid level of internal staff movement across and within departments,
(iv) too rapid promotion to levels of responsibility,
(v) a climate of expediency, of structural 'transition', and
(vi) a loss of belief in the internal integrity of the organisation and its future.

Such internal 'fragmentation', if combined with executives who may have psychological predispositions for the misuse and manipulation of influence and power, dramatically increases the possible degree of toxicity that could be induced. The research however suggested the presence of a third dimension, which, if present, would place an organisation at severe risk of toxic danger. The third dimension influencing leader and workplace toxicity was the stability of the organisation's external environment. If it was deemed to be unstable this was likely to facilitate toxic behaviour, if not a tolerance for extreme internal toxicity will be much reduced.

## The Third Dimension – Conditions in the External Environment

Disruptive and intrusive conditions in the external environment became the third dimension as a determinant of internal disruption and toxic leader behaviour. Examples of which would include a market collapse, a local disaster, an emergency alert, threat of a public humiliation or Federal Inspection, a hostile bid, bankruptcy protection under a Chapter 7 or Chapter 11 filing, the threat of an external Inquiry, media pressure, 'Wall Street' and 'City' intrusion and high profile stakeholder pressure.

My hypothesis is that a significant increase in toxic behaviour and internal instability is more likely to occur and be sustained when all three of these dimensions, like three tumble locks on a combination safe, are sufficiently aligned for the 'spring' into dysfunction and toxicity to be released.

The likelihood for executive dysfunction is increased where the following conditions are present:

1. A personal predisposition for errant working.
2. An internal context which permits or encourages errant behaviour to occur.
3. Significant external circumstances which provide the wider context, cover and excuse for toxic behaviour.

Thus, when in alignment, these three conditions may trigger – or perhaps invite – latent negative and potentially destructive and disruptive executive behaviour resulting in an increasingly toxic working environment.

The resultant 'ACE-R' framework as illustrated in Figure 1.1 can be used to prompt a more rounded look at organisational situations and specifically to identify combinations of conditions in which executive dysfunction and extreme toxic working environments may be more likely to be present.

Factor 4 proposes that even though the other three dimensions may make dysfunction likely the executive may still hold off exhibiting such behaviour if they considered it to be too risky. The combinations of these dimensions are summarised in Table 1.1 and indicate how these can work to either block or prompt toxic behaviour to be more or less likely to occur.

The ACE-R framework can be used to prompt sufficient attention being given to each of the three dimensions it highlights to reduce the conditions that may intensify toxic working conditions.. The tendency to ascribe toxic and dysfunctional behaviour to the organisation's leadership – triggered when executives feel under psychological threat – can be too easily adopted and result in the internal and external contextual features noted above being neglected.

This framework invites a broader consideration of the underpinnings of executive success and failure and of the contextual conditions that may

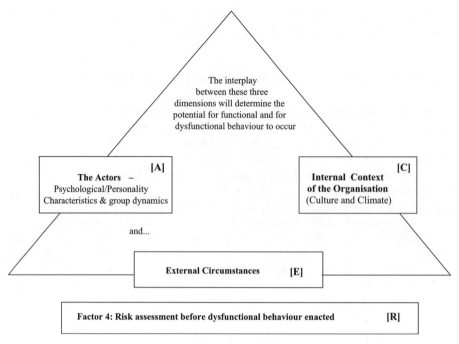

**Figure 1.1**   The ACE-R framework

**Table 1.1**   Assessing the likelihood of a toxic surge

| The ACE-R framework | The Actors–the personal dispositions of those key people (A) | Internal context: the climate and culture of the organisation(C) | External circumstances (E) |
|---|---|---|---|
| Condition 1: Latent potential for dysfunction, but awaiting the opportunity | Yes, person(s) predisposed | Yes, allowing | No, not suitable |
| Condition 2: Executive quite prepared to take advantage but culture won't condone this | Yes, person(s) predisposed | No, not allowing | Yes, suitable |
| Condition 3: Executive not prepared to take advantage of the situation | No, person(s) not predisposed | Yes, allowing | Yes, suitable |
| Condition 4: Potential for executive dysfunctional behaviour is high | Yes, person(s) predisposed | Yes, allowing | Yes, suitable |

encourage or discourage toxic working patterns to take hold. It can be used to prompt timely, defensive and protective action should 'Condition 4' appear likely.

## CONCLUSIONS AND REFLECTIONS

Perhaps as Thomas & Hersen suggest (2002), 'within many organizations there is a heightened and continuing level of strain, expectation, stress and vigour beyond that which is "healthy" for most of us for too long' (see also Kahn & Langlieb, 2003; Tobias, 1990). If this were so it raises questions:

(i) as to how might executives be better prepared for such unhealthy conditions, and

(ii) as to what may be the resultant impact of such pressures on their overt behaviours and on the organisations and departments they lead.

It may be timely to remember that whilst business organisations are constitutionally and legally formulated they remain – through their dynamics – socially constructed environments in which those within them will seek to meet their own individual goals some of which will be mutually congruent and some of which will be mutually antagonistic to the expressed needs of their organisation.

In conclusion the studies on which this chapter is based suggest that an executive's success is not determined primarily by their own behaviour (or psychological characteristics) but is significantly conditioned and constrained by both the internal organizational contexts within which they are working, *and* the wider external circumstances affecting that organization.

Toxic behaviours by leaders – and from followers – could be described as silent killers as they operate below the surface and sabotage, block, and penalise those who raise issues for discussion (Beer & Eisenstat, 2000). A combination of toxic leaders, vulnerable and demeaned followers, and conducive contexts results in an unhealthy 'toxic triangle' (Padilla *et al.*, 2005; Paulhus & Williams, 2002). With such forces threatening an organisation's success it remains surprising that a fuller exposition and exploration of the darker side of leadership, and the misuse of institutional power, is not at the top of the curricula for organisational studies (Dotlich & Cairo, 2003; Schell, 1999).

What is apparent is that appointment to a position of formal leadership does not guarantee positive, constructive leadership behaviour. The leader as a person will remain susceptible to the full range of human strengths and vulnerabilities irrespective of their title, professional background and experience (Zimbardo, 2007). All working environments are likely to be toxic to some degree; if so a key question revolves around how we prepare ourselves for such conditions and how we engage with them insightfully, constructively, purposefully, ethically and maturely (Walton, 2007).

## REFERENCES

Ackroyd, S. & Thompson, P. (1999). *Organizational Misbehaviour*. London: Sage.

Adams, S. (1996a). *The Dilbert Principle*. New York: Boxtree.

Adams, S. (1996b). *Dogbert's Management Handbook*. New York: Boxtree.

Alford, C. (2001). *Whistleblowers: Broken Lives and Organizational Power*. Ithaca, New York State: Cornell University Press.

Anand, V., Ashforth, B. & Joshi, M. (2004). Business as usual: The acceptance and perpetuation of corruption in organizations. *Academy of Management Executive, 19*.

Anderson, H. (1991). *The Emperor's New Clothes*. Neugebauer Press.

Avolio, B. (1999). *Full Leadership Development*. Thousand Oaks, CA: Sage.

Babiak, P. (1995). When psychopaths go to work: A case study of an industrial psychopath. *Applied Psychology: An International Review*, 44:171–188.

Babiak, P. & Hare, R. (2006). *Snakes in Suits*. New York: HarperCollins.

Beer, M. & Eisenstat, R. (2000). The silent killers of strategy implementation and learning. *Sloan Management Review*.

Bolden, R. & Gosling, J. (2006). Leadership competencies. *Leadership*, 2:147–163.

Bramson, R. (1996). *What Your Boss Doesn't Tell You Until It's Too Late*. New York: Fireside.

Burns, J. (1978). *Leadership*. New York: Harper & Row.

Case, P. & Gosling, J. (2006). Wisdom of the moment. *Social Epistemology, 20*. Special issue on Wisdom and Stupidity in Management.

Cavaiola, A. & Lavender, N. (2000). *Toxic Coworkers*. Oakland, CA: Harbinger.

Charan, R. & Colvin, G. (1999). Why CEOs fail. *Fortune Magazine*.

Conger, J. (1990). The Dark side of leadership. *Organizational Dynamics*, 19:44–55.

Dotlich, D. & Cairo, P. (2003). *Why CEOs Fail*. San Francisco: Jossey-Bass.

Finkelstein, S. (2003). *Why Smart Executives Fail*. New York: Portfolio, Penguin.

Frost, P. (2003). *Toxic Emotions at Work*. Boston: HBS.

Frost, P. & Robinson, S. (1999). The toxic handler. *Harvard Business Review*, 97.

Furnham, A. & Taylor, J. (2004). *The Dark Side of Behaviour at Work*. Basingstoke: Palgrave Macmillan.

Gabriel, Y. (1999). *Organizations in Depth*. London: Sage.

Galbraith, J. (1977). *The Age of Uncertainty*. London: Andre Deutsch.

Giacalone, R. & Greenberg, J. (1997). *Antisocial Behaviour in Organization*. Thousand Oaks, CA: Sage.

Harvey, J. (1988). *The Abilene Paradox*. Lexington, MA: Lexington Books.

Hogan, R. & Hogan, J. (2001). Assessing leadership: A view from the dark side. *International Journal of Selection and Assessment*, 9:40–51.

Hogan, R. & Smither, R. (2001). *Personality: Theories and Applications*. Boulder, CO: Westview Press.

Janis, I. (1982). *Groupthink*. Boston: Houghton Mifflin.

Kahn, J. & Langlieb, A (2003). *Mental Health and Productivity in the Workplace*. San Francisco: Jossey-Bass.

Kellerman, B. (2004). *Bad Leadership*. Boston: HBS.

Kets de Vries, M. (1979). Managers can drive their subordinates mad. *Harvard Business Review*, 125–134.

Kets de Vries, M. (1985) The dark side of entrepreneurship. *Harvard Business Review*, 160–167.

Kets de Vries, M. (1989) Leaders who self-destruct: the causes and cures. *Organizational Dynamics*, 17:5–17.

Khurana, R. (2002). The curse of the superstar CEO. *Harvard Business Review*, 60–66.

Kilburg, R. (2000). *Executive Coaching*. Washington DC: American Psychological Association.

Kofodimos, J. (1989). *Why Executives Lose Their Balance*. Greensboro, North Carolina: Centre for Creative Leadership.

Kofodimos, J. (1990). Why executives lose their balance. *Organizational Dynamics*, 19: 58–73.

Levinson, H. (1978). The abrasive personality. *Harvard Business Review*, 86–94.

Lipman-Blumen, J. (2005). *The Allure of Toxic Leaders*. New York: Oxford University Press.

Lombardo, M. & Eichinger, R. (1989). *Preventing Derailment: What to Do Before It's Too Late*. Greensboro, North Carolina: Centre for Creative Leadership.

Lowman, R. (1993). *Counselling and Psychotherapy of Work Dysfunctions*. Washington, DC: American Psychological Association.

Lubit, R. (2002) The long-term organizational impact of destructively narcissistic managers. *Academy of Management Executive*, 16:127–138.

Maccoby, M. (2000). Narcissistic leaders: The incredible pros, the inevitable cons. *Harvard Business Review*, 69–77.

Maccoby, M. (2004). Why people follow the leader: The power of transference. *Harvard Business Review*, 76–85.

McCall, M. (1998). *High Flyers*. Boston: HBS.

McCall, M. & Lombardo, M. (1983). Off The Track: *Why and How Successful Executives Get Derailed*. Greensboro, North Carolina: Centre for Creative Leadership.

McCalley, R. (2002). *Patterns of Management Power*. Westport, CT: Quorum Books.

Milgram, S. (1974). *Obedience to Authority*. New York: HarperCollins.

Offermann, L. (2004). When followers become toxic. *Harvard Business Review*.

Padilla, A., Hogan, R. & Kaiser, R. (2005). *The Toxic Triangle: Destructive Leaders, Vulnerable Followers, and Conducive Environments*. Department of Business Management, NC State University.

Paulhus, D. & Williams, K. (2002). The dark triad of personality: Narcissism, Machiavellianism, and psychopathy. *Journal of Research in Psychology*, 36:556–563.

Peters, T. & Waterman, R. (1982). *In Search of Excellence*. New York: Harper & Row.

Price, T. (2000). Explaining ethical failures of leadership. *The Leadership and Organization Development Journal*, 21:177–184.

Roberts, B. & Hogan, R. (2002). *Personality Psychology in the Workplace*. Washington DC: American Psychological Association.

Sankowsky, D. (1995). The charismatic leader as narcissist: Understanding the abuse of power. *Organizational Dynamics*, 23:57–71.

Schell, B. (1999). *Management in the Mirror*. Westport, CT: Quorum Books.

Smith, N. & Quirk, M. (2005). From grace to disgrace: The rise and fall of Arthur Anderson. *Journal of Business Ethics Education*, 1:93–132.

Sperry, L. (2002). *Effective Leadership*. New York: Brunner-Routledge.

Stein, M. (2005). The Othello conundrum: The inner contagion of leadership. *Organization Studies*, 26:1405–1419.

Sulkowwicz, K. (2004). Worse than enemies: The CEO's destructive confident. *Harvard Business Review*.

Thomas, J. & Hersen, M. (Eds.) (2002). *Handbook of Mental Health in the Workplace*. Thousand Oaks, CA: Sage.

Tobias, L. (1990). *Psychological Consulting to Management*. New York: Brunner Mazel.

Tourish, D. (2005). Charismatic leadership and corporate cultism at Enron: The elimination of dissent, the promotion of conformity and organizational collapse. *Leadership*, 1.

Walton, M. (2005). Executive Behaviour-in-Context. Unpublished MPhil thesis, University of Bradford.

Walton, M. (2007). Leadership toxicity – an inevitable affliction of organisations? *Organisations and People*, February, 14.

Wright, L. & Smye, M. (1996). *Corporate Abuse*. New York: Macmillan.

Zaleznik, A. (1970). Power and politics in organizational life. *Harvard Business Review*.

Zaleznik, A. & Kets de Vries, M. (1985). *Power and the Corporate Mind*. Chicago: Bonus Books.

Zimbardo, P. (1969). *The Cognitive Control of Motivation*. Glenview: Scott Foresman.

Zimbardo, P. (2007). *The Lucifer Effect: How Good People Turn Evil*. London: Rider Books.

# CHAPTER 2

# Leading to a Healthy Workplace

**E. Kevin Kelloway, Mike Teed and Matt Prosser**
*Saint Mary's University, Halifax, Nova Scotia, Canada*

The suggestion that leaders have an impact on employees' well-being is neither novel nor particularly startling. Research documenting the effects of leadership on employee well-being has been available for over 30 years (Day & Hamblin, 1964) and the conclusions of this research would not surprise any adult who has held a job for any length of time (Gilbreath, 2004). Poor leadership is associated with increased levels of employee stress (Offerman & Hellman, 1996; Richman *et al.*, 1992), alienation (Ashforth, 1994, 1997) and may provoke counter-productive behaviors such as retaliation (Townsend, Phillips & Elkins, 2000). What may be surprising is just how extensive are the effects of leadership on individuals' well-being. In this chapter, we argue for the position that leaders, and their leadership styles and behaviors, are major determinants of whether or not a workplace is healthy. In doing so, we first describe three types of leadership (transformational, passive and abusive), we then review the literature linking these styles of leadership to safety, stress and health practices.

## LEADERSHIP AND THE HEALTHY WORKPLACE

A useful definition of a healthy workplace is one that encompasses the physical environment (i.e. the traditional domains of occupational health and safety), the psychosocial environment (i.e. job stress) and the practice of healthy behaviors (e.g. lifestyle factors, see http://www.nqi.ca/nqistore/product_details. aspx?ID=63). This is a comprehensive definition that encompasses a diverse array of healthy behaviors and conditions. Leadership in organisations has been associated with every aspect of the healthy workplace. The following review examines many of the ways in which a particular leadership style can affect the health of the workplace and, ultimately, the health of the employees who work there.

*Employee Well-being Support: A Workplace Resource.* Edited by A. Kinder, R. Hughes and C.L. Cooper.
© 2008 John Wiley & Sons, Ltd.

## Leadership and Stress

Several studies have found that leaders' behavior affects employees' well-being. The available evidence supports the notion of two opposite effects of leadership on well-being. First, positive leadership behaviors have a positive impact on well-being. Conversely, negative leadership behaviors have adverse consequences for individual well-being.

For example, Gilbreath and Benson (2004) found that positive supervisory behavior (e.g. increasing employee control, improved communication and organisation, considering employees and their well-being, just treatment of employees) predicted employee well-being over and above the effects of age, lifestyle, social support from co-workers and at home, and stressful work and life events. Similarly, Van Dierendonck et al. (2004) found that that high quality leadership behavior was associated with increased employee well-being.

Other studies have focused on the notion of transformational leadership – shown to be an effective leadership style. In two studies, Arnold et al. (in press) provided evidence for the link between transformational leadership and well-being. Moreover, they began to consider the mechanisms through which these linkages occur. Specifically, Arnold et al. (in press) found that transformational leaders helped employees to experience more meaning in their work environment, and that these perceptions of meaningfulness predicted individual well-being. Other potential mechanisms also seem promising. For example, a recent experimental study showed that 'charismatic leaders enable their followers to experience positive emotions' (Bono & Ilies, 2006:331). Another study found that transformational leadership behavior was positively related to mentoring and negatively related to job-related stress (Sosik & Godshalk, 2000).

The positive effects of effective leadership extend to the physical consequences associated with stress. For example, Karlin, Brondolo and Schwartz (2003) examined the stressful occupation of New York City traffic enforcement agents and found that social support from immediate supervisors tended to be negatively correlated with systolic blood pressure. In addition to directly enhancing well-being, these results suggest that effective supervision may also help individuals cope with the stressful aspects of their jobs.

The stress of poor supervision also manifests in physical outcomes. Wager, Fieldman and Hussey (2003) reported that on days when a sample of nurses worked for a supervisor that was seen as being punitive and unfair, they experienced a 15 mm increase in systolic blood pressure and a 7 mm increase in diastolic blood pressure compared to days when they worked for a supervisor who was seen as being fair. These results provide direct evidence that working for an unfair supervisor results in a greater likelihood of a cardio-vascular incident. Similarly, in a recent extension to the Whitehall studies, Kivimaki et al. (2005) showed that how an individual was treated by their supervisor predicted incident coronary heart disease (CHD) over a nine-year span. The risk of CHD attributable to supervisory treatment was independent of risks attributable to traditional job stress or lifestyle risk factors.

## Leadership and Safety

There is now considerable research evidence suggesting that organisational leaders play a central role in influencing workplace safety. For example, Cree and Kelloway (1997) noted that perceptions of managers' and supervisors' commitment to health and safety were strongly related to perceived risk and willingness to participate in safety programs. Similarly, Mullen (2005) found that perceptions of managerial receptiveness to health and safety predicted individuals' willingness to raise safety issues in the workplace. Hofmann and Morgeson (1999) found that high quality leader–member exchange contributed to improved safety communication and safety commitment, which in turn contributed to reduced incidence of accidents. Specifically pertaining to the importance of leadership as a predictor of occupational health and safety related outcomes, Barling, Loughlin and Kelloway (2002) reported that perceptions of supervisors' safety-specific transformational leadership were related to individual safety consciousness and perceptions of safety climate and, through these intervening variables, safety events and actual injuries.

Overall, the data suggest that when leaders actively promote health and safety, organisations experience better safety records and greater positive safety outcomes (Hofmann, Jacobs & Landy, 1995; Shannon, Mayr & Haines, 1997; Zohar, 1980; 2002b). Of particular interest is the finding that training leaders in safety had an impact on employees' number of accidents (Zohar, 2002b).

## Leadership and Healthy Lifestyle Practices

While the suggestion that organisational leadership is linked to job stress or job safety is not at all surprising, many would have more difficulty accepting the suggestion that leadership may be linked to healthy lifestyle practices. Nonetheless, the available data, albeit scarce, does in fact seem to support such a link.

Substance use in the workplace is prevalent and the role of supervisors in managing substance use and its consequences are well documented. For example, based on his national (US) prevalence data, Frone (2006) reported that just over 14% of the workforce engaged in illicit drug use with 3.9% of respondents engaging in illicit drug use at work. As he notes, these are global estimates and in certain sectors of the workforce illicit drug use may be substantially higher. Supervisors are expected to intervene when they detect problems related to substance use (Ames, Grube & Moore, 2000) and to enforce policies (e.g. Bamberger & Donahue, 1999). More recently, there is evidence that supervisory behavior may be a causal factor in substance use. Bamberger and Bacharach (2006) found that when supervisors engage in abusive supervision employees are more likely to engage in problem drinking. Similarly, supervisors who treat employees unfairly may precipitate health-related behaviors such as lack of sleep. Greenberg (2006) reported that employees treated unjustly were more likely to display insomnia and that training supervisors in interactional justice substantially reduced these adverse consequences.

While this suggests that poor leadership can predict unhealthy behaviors in subordinates, it may also be the case that positive leadership behaviors can encourage healthy lifestyle behaviors. For example, leadership has also been associated with the success of health promotion programs. In their evaluation of a health promotion program in the US Navy, Whiteman, Snyder and Ragland (2001) found that tobacco usage declined as a result of the program and that program success was attributable to leadership and command involvement.

Leaders can influence health behaviors via several routes. First, leaders can create the conditions that inhibit or encourage employees to engage in health behaviors (or not). Certainly the need for managerial support for programs such as employee assistance programs (Mio & Goishi, 1988) and workplace health promotion programs (Fielding, 1984) is well documented. Second, leaders are role models who perform a communicative role in organisations. Just as managers may communicate the importance (or not) of working safely (Kelloway et al., 2005), they may, through their actions, communicate the importance of health-enhancing activities. In doing so, there may be some additional benefits. There are data suggesting that leaders who engage in regular programs of exercise are rated higher on standardised measures of leadership style (McDowell-Larson, Kearney & Campbell, 2002). By engaging in health promoting activities, leaders may enhance both their own health and their reputation as a leader.

## HOW DO ORGANISATIONAL LEADERS CONTRIBUTE TO A HEALTHY WORKPLACE?

Organisational leaders influence the health of the workplace in two primary ways. First, because of their organisational position and power, leaders create the organisational conditions that lead to a host of health-related outcomes. Second, the behavior of leaders toward individuals or 'leadership style' exerts an influence on health related outcomes.

### Leaders as a Root Cause

Kelloway et al. (2005) drew the parallel with traditional occupational health and safety analysis in suggesting that leaders are a root cause of employee health outcomes. That is, leaders create the conditions that may lead to safety-related or health-related outcomes. Leaders are suggested to have a direct impact on the most common job stressors (i.e. workload and pace, roles stress, career concerns, work schedules, interpersonal relations, job content and control; Sauter, Murphy & Hurrell, 1990). This suggestion has received at least initial empirical support (Skogstad *et al.*, 2007).

Similarly, Gilbreath (2004) suggested that supervisors (as the most immediate manifestation of leadership in the organisation) influence a diverse array of psychosocial job conditions including task autonomy, demands, control, balance, and self-efficacy. In doing so, supervisors make a direct contribution to individual well-being by creating the conditions that either promote, enhance or detract from employee positive health-related employee behavior in the workplace.

## LEADERSHIP STYLE: THE GOOD, THE BAD AND THE UGLY

In commenting on their experiences with leadership development programs, Kelloway and Barling (2000) note that all participants, regardless of group composition, unanimously identify exactly the same two distinct sets of behaviors, one constituting good leadership and the other poor leadership; suggesting that these behavioral sets are intuitive and generalisable. The set of good leadership behaviors are those comprising the style called 'transformational leadership' (Avolio, 1999; Bass & Avolio, 1990; 1994). In contrast, Kelloway *et al.* (2005) suggested that the set of poor leadership behaviors may be classified as one of two types: passive and abusive. Passive leaders may lack appropriate leadership and/or social skills and thus avoid engaging in any leadership behaviors at all. Abusive leaders may be abusive, aggressive, violent or punitive. Of particular importance is the fact that this tripartite characterisation of leadership behaviors (i.e. transformational, passive and abusive leadership) parallels styles of personal interaction in other contexts (e.g. positive, withdrawal and angry behaviors in marital interaction; MacEwen, Barling & Kelloway, 1992).

### The Good: Transformational Leadership

In the past 10 years, more research has been conducted on transformational leadership than on all other leadership theories combined (Judge & Bono, 2000). The resulting literature clearly illustrates that transformational leadership positively affects critical organisational attitudes and outcomes (Avolio, 1999; Bass, 1998). Transformational leadership has been defined as superior leadership performance that occurs when leaders 'broaden and elevate the interests of their employees, when they generate awareness and acceptance of the purposes and mission of the group, and when they stir their employees to look beyond their own self-interest for the good of the group' (Bass, 1985:21). Empirical data largely support the effectiveness of such behaviors.

For example, leaders' use of transformational leadership behaviors is associated with subordinates' satisfaction (Hater & Bass, 1988; Koh, Steers & Terborg, 1995), commitment to the organisation (Barling, Weber & Kelloway,

1996; Bycio, Hacket & Allen, 1995; Koh *et al.*, 1995), trust in management (Barling *et al.*, 1996), and organisational citizenship behaviors (Koh *et al.*, 1995). Laboratory-based experimental investigations show that transformational leadership styles result in higher task performance (e.g. Howell & Frost, 1989; Kirkpatrick & Locke, 1996). Field studies also support the performance impact of transformational leadership. In longitudinal studies, for example, Howell and Avolio (1993) linked transformational leadership to unit financial performance. Similarly, Barling *et al.* (1996) showed that subordinates' perceptions of supervisors' transformational leadership led to enhanced affective commitment to the organisation and, through this effect on affective commitment, to enhanced group performance. Barling *et al.* (1996) reported on a field experiment in which training leaders in transformational leadership resulted in improved branch-level financial performance.

Transformational leaders go beyond exchange relationships and motivate others to achieve more that they thought was possible (Bass, 1998). Bass and Avolio (1990) suggested that the transformational leadership style comprises four dimensions, namely idealised influence, inspirational motivation, intellectual stimulation and individualised consideration. Idealised influence occurs when leaders engender the trust and respect of their followers by doing the right thing, thereby serving as a role model. Leaders who engage in inspirational motivation 'raise the bar' for their employees, encouraging them to achieve levels of performance beyond their own expectations. Intellectual stimulation involves engaging the rationality of subordinates, getting them to challenge their assumptions and to think about old problems in new ways. Lastly, individualised consideration deals with treating employees as individuals and helping them to meet their needs.

In demonstrating these behaviors, transformational leaders may have a dramatic effect on followers. First, of particular importance for this discussion, Shamir, House and Arthur (1993:578) note that transformational leadership 'gives meaningfulness to work by infusing work ... with moral purpose and commitment'. Moreover, transformational leaders implicitly and explicitly tell followers what is important in the workplace, about their work, and about themselves (Salancik & Pfeffer, 1978; White & Mitchell, 1979). In doing so, transformational leaders create a sense of meaning which, in turn, may translate into enhanced well-being among followers (Arnold *et al.*, in press).

## The Bad: Passive Leadership

Although the foregoing discussion focused on the notion of transformational leadership, we also recognise that failing to enact positive leadership, or refusing to engage in the most basic of leadership behaviors, may also be a source of stress for individuals. We term this lack of enacted positive leadership, passive leadership (Kelloway, Mullen & Francis, 2006). We define passive leadership as comprising elements from both the laissez-faire and management-by-exception (passive) styles articulated in the theory of transformational leadership (Bass & Avolio, 1994). Leaders who use the laissez-faire style avoid decision -making and the responsibilities associated with their position (Bass, 1985; Hater & Bass, 1988). Leaders engaging in the management by exception (passive) style do not intervene until problems are either brought to their attention or become serious enough to demand action (Bass, 1985).

The leader who fails to provide feedback or who fails to stand up for employees (Neuman & Baron, 2005; Skogstad et al., 2007) is displaying passive leadership. To some extent such behaviors may be characteristic of passive aggression (Buss, 1961).

Not surprisingly, passive leadership is generally considered to be ineffective. For instance, Howell and Avolio (1993) reported that passive management by exception is negatively related to business unit performance and laissez-faire leadership is generally accounted to be the least effective style (Bass & Avolio, 1994). Frischer and Laarson (2000) found that leaders' lack of initiative is negatively related to subordinates' satisfaction and efficiency. Kelloway et al. (2006) suggested that there were both conceptual and empirical grounds on which to suggest that passive leadership is (a) distinct from and (b) has negative effects beyond those attributable to a lack of transformational leadership skills.

Bass (1985) distinguished 'active' and 'passive' leadership as separate higher-order factors underlying his leadership measure. Researchers have since investigated this distinction, often combining Bass and Avolio's (1990) management by exception-passive and laissez-faire dimensions into a single higher-order 'passive' leadership dimension (e.g. Bycio et al., 1995; Den Hartog et al., 1997). Garman, Davis-Lenane and Corrigan (2003) found that management by exception (passive), is negatively correlated with transformational, but positively correlated with laissez-faire, leadership. In the same study, active and passive management by exception emerged as independent constructs, thereby furthering the empirical support for the distinction between active and passive leadership.

It is generally accepted that passive leadership correlates negatively, and transformational leadership positively, with numerous organisational outcomes (Den Hartog et al., 1997, Howell & Avolio, 1993). However, until recently it was unclear whether the deleterious effects of passive leadership were attributable to a lack of more positive leadership behaviors or whether passive leadership in and of itself constituted a destructive form of leadership. Indeed, few studies specifically examined the impact of passive leadership on organisational outcomes. (for an exception see Zohar, 2002a). Rather, the existing research has focused on the positive organisational impact of more active forms of leadership.

Recent research has begun to change this emphasis, documenting the destructive impact that passive leadership has on individual and organisational outcomes (e.g. Kelloway et al., 2006; Skogstad et al., 2007). First, in a recent study, Kelloway, Mullen and Francis (2006) examined the impact of transformational and passive safety leadership on safety outcomes. Following Barling, Loughlin and Kelloway's (2002) earlier analysis, they examined the

ns between leadership and safety-related outcomes. The results of
showed that passive safety leadership was both empirically distinct
ɛformational leadership and negatively related to safety outcomes.
passive leadership offered an incremental prediction of outcome
ᵼe. over and above that attributable to transformational leadership).
Kelloway *et al.* (2006) suggested that passive leadership may explain variance
beyond that attributable to transformational leadership for other leadership-
related outcomes.

Similarly, Skogstad *et al.* (2007) empirically tested the suggestion made by
Kelloway *et al.* (2005) that passive leadership may be a root cause of workplace
stress. Consistent with this suggestion, Skogstad *et al.* (2007) found that laissez-
faire leadership by one's supervisor led to the experience of conflicts with co-
workers and role stress (i.e. conflict and ambiguity). In turn, role stress and
conflict predicted the experience of bullying and psychological distrust. As the
authors note, their data are consistent with the view that laissez-faire or passive
leadership is not a 'neutral' form of leadership but, rather, is a destructive
leadership style that impairs individual well-being. Furthermore, passive
leadership can be identified by particular leadership behaviors, such as
avoidance or withdrawal. That is, passive leadership is not merely the absence
of leadership behavior (be it transformational or otherwise), rather the behaviors expressed by passive leadership are observable and quantifiable.

## The Ugly: Abusive Leadership

A great deal of research attention has focused on issues related to aggressive
and violent behaviors in the workplace (Kelloway, Barling & Hurrell, 2006).
Variously termed 'workplace harassment' (e.g. Rospenda, 2002), 'emotional
abuse' (e.g. Keashly, 1998, 2001; Keashly & Harvey, 2006), 'bullying' (e.g.
Einarsen, 1999; Hoel, Rayner & Cooper, 1999; Rayner & Cooper, 2006), or
simply workplace aggression (for a review see Schat & Kelloway, 2005), such
behaviors have deleterious consequences for both individuals and organisations (Schat & Kelloway, 2005). Abusive leadership occurs when individuals in
a formal leadership role engage in aggressive or punitive behaviors toward
their employees (Tepper, 2000). These behaviors can vary widely, from leaders
degrading their employees by yelling, ridiculing and name-calling to terroris-
ing employees by withholding information or threatening employees with job
loss and pay cuts or by isolating the employee in the workplace. Ashforth
(1994, 1997) has suggested that such behaviors constitute 'petty tyranny' in
organisations.

While the incidence of physical violence from supervisors is extremely low
(LeBlanc & Kelloway, 2002; Schat, Frone & Kelloway, 2006) acts of non-physical
aggression from supervisors are more common. For example, Pizzino (2002)
reported that supervisors accounted for 20% of aggressive behaviors reported
by unionised respondents compared to members of the public who accounted
for 38% of aggressive behavior. It is worth noting that such acts by supervisors

might have more detrimental effects on employee outcomes than do similar acts committed by members of the public or other sources. The available data suggest that those exposed to abusive supervision are more likely to be distressed, dissatisfied and to leave their jobs (Zellars, Tepper & Duffy, 2002).

There are several reasons to highlight the adverse effects of abusive supervision. First, organisational context, such as the leadership role of the perpetrator, plays a crucial role in understanding the effects of aversive behaviors in the workplace (Barling *et al.*, 2002; Fitzgerald *et al.*, 1997). Leaders may, for example, be more likely than others to engage in abusive behaviors (see for example Keashly, Trott & MacLean, 1994) perhaps because of a sense of invulnerability (Dekker & Barling, 1998). Moreover, these actions may be more salient to the target because of the aggressor's ability to control organisational sanctions and rewards. Moreover, abusive supervision is associated with a leaders' reliance of an authoritarian leadership style (Aryee *et al.*, 2007) suggesting that such behaviors may be a frequent occurrence in the lives of employees.

LeBlanc and Kelloway (2002) provided evidence that the effects of aggression varied with the source of the aggression. In particular, the effects of public aggression/violence on outcomes were indirect, being mediated by fear of future violence (see also Barling, Rogers & Kelloway, 2001; Rogers & Kelloway, 1997; Schat & Kelloway, 2000, 2003). However, the effects of co-worker aggression (including that from leaders) on personal and organisational outcomes were direct, suggesting that the actions of leaders may have a stronger impact on personal well-being than the actions of members of the public.

## CONCLUSION

There is little doubt that organisational leaders have a pervasive influence on the well-being of employees. In terms of the tripartite definition of a healthy workplace as comprising physical safety, the psychosocial environment and healthy lifestyle practices, the available data consistently suggest that organisational leaders affect employees' experience of job stress, job safety and engagement in healthy lifestyle behaviors. These effects are pervasive enough that the quality of supervisory behavior has been recognised as a risk factor by the legal systems in several jurisdictions. For example, courts have recognised that supervisory behavior is a stressor in the workplace (e.g. Hollis & Goodson, 1989). With regard to workplace safety, several jurisdictions have operationalised the concept of corporate homicide by holding managers/supervisors criminally liable for workplace deaths caused by a lack of appropriate safety procedures (see for example, Kelloway, Francis & Montgomery, 2002).

As Gilbreath (2004) notes, these observations come as no surprise to anyone who has ever held a job. However, research is now accumulating documenting the extent and nature of these effects. Perhaps more importantly, research is beginning to demonstrate the effectiveness of leadership interventions in enhancing organisational well-being and truly creating a healthy workplace.

## ACKNOWLEDGEMENTS

Preparation of this manuscript was supported by grants from the Social Sciences and Humanities Research Council of Canada, the Nova Scotia Health Research Foundation and Saint Mary's University. Correspondence regarding the manuscript may be addressed to the first author at the Department of Management, Saint Mary's University, Halifax, Nova Scotia, B3H 3C3 Canada or kevin.kelloway@smu.ca.

## REFERENCES

Ames, G. M., Grube, J. W. & Moore, R. S. (2000). Social control and workplace drinking norms: A comparison of two organizational cultures. *Journal of Studies on Alcohol*, **61**:203–219.

Arnold, K., Turner, N., Barling, J. *et al.* (in press). Transformational leadership and psychological well-being: The mediating role of meaningful work. *Journal of Occupational Health Psychology*.

Aryee, S., Chen, Z. X., Sun, L. & Debrah, Y. A. (2007). Antecedents and outcomes of abusive supervision: Test of a trickle-down model. *Journal of Applied Psychology*, **92**:191–201.

Ashforth, B. (1994). Petty tyranny in organizations. *Human Relations*, **47**:755–778.

Ashforth, B. (1997). Petty tyranny in organizations: A preliminary examination of antecedents and consequences. *Canadian Journal of Administrative Sciences*, **14**:1173–1182.

Avolio, B. J. (1999). *Full Leadership Development: Building the Vital Forces in Organizations.* Newbury Park, CA: Sage Publications.

Bamberger, P. A. & Bacharach, S. B. (2006). Abusive supervision and subordinate problem drinking: Taking resistance, stress and subordinate personality into account. *Human Relations*, **59**:723–752.

Bamberger, P. A. & Donahue, L. (1999). Employee discharge and reinstatement: Moral hazards and the mixed consequences of last chance agreements. *Industrial and Labor Relations Review*, **53**:3–20.

Barling, J., Loughlin, C. & Kelloway, E. K. (2002). Development and test of a model linking safety-specific transformational leadership and occupational safety. *Journal of Applied Psychology*, **87**:488–496.

Barling, J., Rogers, G. & Kelloway, E. K. (2001). Behind closed doors: In-home workers' experience of sexual harassment and workplace violence. *Journal of Occupational Health Psychology*, **6**:255–269.

Barling, J., Weber, T. & Kelloway, E. K. (1996). Effects of transformational leadership training on attitudinal and financial outcomes: A field experiment. *Journal of Applied Psychology*, **81**:827–832.

Bass, B. M. (1985). *Leadership and Performance beyond Expectations.* New York: Free Press.

Bass, B. M. (1998). *Transformational Leadership: Industrial, Military, and Educational Impact.* Lahwah, NJ: Lawrence Erlbaum Associates.

Bass, B. M. & Avolio, B. J. (1990). *Transformational Leadership Development: Manual for the Multifactor Leadership Questionnaire.* Palo Alto, CA: Consulting Psychologists Press.

Bass, B. M. & Avolio, B. J. (1994). *Improving organizational Effectiveness through Transformational Leadership.* Thousand Oaks, CA: SAGE Publications.

Bono, J. E. & Ilies, R. (2006). Charisma, positive emotions and mood contagion. *Leadership Quarterly*, **17**:317–334.

Buss, A. H. (1961). *The Psychology of Aggression.* New York: John Wiley & Sons, Inc.

Bycio, P., Hackett, R. D. & Allen, J. S. (1995). Further assessments of Bass's (1985) conceptualization of transactional and transformational leadership. *Journal of Applied Psychology*, **80**:468–478.

Cree, T. & Kelloway, E. K. (1997). Responses to occupational hazards: Exit and participation. *Journal of Occupational Health Psychology*, **2**:304–311.

Day, R. C. & Hamblin, R. L. (1964). Some effects of close and punitive styles of supervision. *American Journal of Sociology*, **69**:499–510.

Dekker, I. & Barling, J. (1998). Personal and organizational predictors of workplace sexual harassment of women by men. *Journal of Occupational Health Psychology*, **3**:7–18.

Den Hartog, D. N., Van Muijen, J. J. & Koopman, P. (1997). Transactional versus transformational leadership: An analysis of the MLQ. *Journal of Occupational and Organizational Psychology*, **70**:19–34.

Einarsen, S. (1999). The nature and causes of bullying at work. *International Journal of Manpower*, **20**:16–27.

Fielding, J. E. (1984). Health promotion and disease prevention at the worksite. *Annual Review of Public Health*, **5**:237–265.

Fitzgerald, L. F., Drasgow, F., Hulin, C. L. *et al.* (1997). Antecedents and consequences of sexual harassment in organizations: a test of an integrated model. *Journal of Applied Psychology*, **82**:578–589.

Frischer, J. & Larsson, K. (2000). Laissez-faire in research education: An inquiry into a Swedish doctoral program. *Higher Education Policy*, **13**:131–155.

Frone, M. (2006). Prevalence and distribution of illicit drug use in the workforce and in the workplace: findings and implications from a US national survey. *Journal of Applied Psychology*, **91**:856–869.

Garman, A. N., Davis-Lenane, D. & Corrigan, P. W. (2003). Factor structure of the transformational leadership model in human service teams. *Journal of Organizational Behavior*, **24**:803–812.

Gilbreath, B. (2004). Creating healthy workplaces: the supervisor's role. In C. Cooper & I. Robertson (Eds.), *International Review of Industrial and Organizational Psychology, Volume 19*. Chichester, UK: John Wiley & Sons, Ltd.

Gilbreath, B. & Benson, P. G. (2004). The contribution of supervisor behaviour to employee psychological well-being. *Work and Stress*, **18**:255–266.

Greenberg, J. (2006). Losing sleep over organizational injustice: Attenuating insomniac reactions to underpayment inequity with supervisory training in interactional justice. *Journal of Applied Psychology*, **91**:58–69.

Hater, J. J. & Bass, B. M. (1988). Superiors' evaluations and subordinates' perceptions of transformational and transactional leadership. *Journal of Applied Psychology*, **73**:695–702.

Hoel, H., Rayner, C. & Cooper, C. L. (1999). Workplace bullying. In C. L. Cooper and I. T. Robertson (Eds.), *International Review of Industrial and Organizational Psychology (Vol. 14)*. Chichester, UK: John Wiley & Sons, Ltd.

Hofmann, D. A. & Morgeson, F. P. (1999). Safety-related behaviour as a social exchange: The role of perceived organizational support and leader-member exchange. *Journal of Applied Psychology*, **84**:286–296.

Hofmann, D. A., Jacobs, R. & Landy, F. (1995). High reliability process industries: Individual, micro, and macro organizational influences on safety performance. *Journal of Safety Research*, **26**:131–149.

Hollis, D. & Goodson, J. (1989). Stress: The legal and organizational implications. *Employee Rights and Responsibilities Journal*, **2**:255–262.

Howell, J. M. & Avolio, B. J. (1993). Transformational leadership, transactional leadership, locus of control and support for innovation: Key predictors of consolidated-business-unit performance. *Journal of Applied Psychology*, **78**:891–902.

Howell, J. M. & Frost, P. J. (1989). A laboratory study of charismatic leadership. *Organizational Behavior and Human Decision Processes*, **43**:243–269.

Judge, T. A. & Bono, J. E. (2000). Five-factor model of personality and transformational leadership. *Journal of Applied Psychology*, **85**:751–765.

Karlin, W. A., Brondolo, E. & Schwartz, J. (2003). Workplace social support and ambulatory cardiovascular activity in New York city traffic agents. *Psychosomatic Medicine*, **65**:167–176.

Keashly, L. (1998). Emotional abuse in the workplace: Conceptual and empirical issues. *Journal of Emotional Abuse*, **1**:85–115.

Keashly, L. (2001). Interpersonal and systemic aspects of emotional abuse at work: The target's perspective. *Violence and Victims*, **16**:233–268.

Keashly, L. & Harvey, S. (2006). Workplace emotional abuse. In E. K. Kelloway, J. Barling & J. J. Hurrell (Eds.), *Handbook of Workplace Violence*. Thousand Oaks, CA: Sage Publications.

Keashly, L., Trott, V. & MacLean, L. M. (1994). Abusive behavior in the workplace: A preliminary investigation. *Violence and Victims*, **9**:125–141.

Kelloway, E. K. & Barling, J. (2000). What we've learned about developing transformational leaders. *Leadership and Organization Development Journal*, **21**:157–161.

Kelloway, E. K., Barling, J. & Hurrell, J. J. (Eds.) (2006). *Handbook of Workplace Violence*. Thousand Oaks, CA: Sage Publications.

Kelloway, E. K., Francis, L. & Montgomery, J. (2002). *Management of Occupational Health and Safety in Canada*, 3rd edn. Toronto, ON: Thomson-Nelson.

Kelloway, E. K., Mullen, J. & Francis, L. (2006). Divergent effects of passive and transformational leadership on safety outcomes. *Journal of Occupational Health Psychology*, **11**:76–86.

Kelloway, E. K., Sivanthan, N., Francis, L. & Barling, J. (2005). Poor leadership. In J. Barling, E. K. Kelloway & M. Frone, *Handbook of Workplace Stress*. Thousand Oaks: Sage Publications.

Kirkpatrick, S. A. & Locke, E. A. (1996). Direct and indirect effects of three core charismatic leadership components on performance and attitudes. *Journal of Applied Psychology*, **81**:36–51.

Kivimaki, M., Ferrie, J. E., Brunner. E. *et al.* (2005). Justice at work and reduced risk of coronary heart disease among employees: The Whitehall II Study. *Archives of Internal Medicine*, **165**:2245–2251.

Koh, W. L., Steers, R. M. & Terborg, J. R. (1995). The effects of transformational leadership on teacher attitudes and student performance in Singapore. *Journal of Organizational Behavior*, **16**:319–333.

LeBlanc, M. & Kelloway, E. K. (2002). Predictors and outcomes of workplace violence and aggression. *Journal of Applied Psychology*, **87**:444–453.

MacEwen, K. E., Barling, J. & Kelloway, E. K. (1992). Effects of acute role overload on individual well-being and marital interaction. *Work and Stress*, **6**:117–126.

McDowell-Larsen, S. L., Kearney, L. & Campbell, D. (2002). Fitness and leadership: is there a relationship?: Regular exercise correlates with higher leadership ratings in senior-level executives. *Journal of Managerial Psychology*, **17**:316–324.

Mio, J. S. & Goishi, C. K. (1988). The employee assistance program: Raising productivity by lifting constraints. In P. Whitney & R. B. Ochsman (Eds.), *Psychology and Productivity*, pp. 105–125. New York: Plenum Press.

Mullen, J. (2005). Testing a model of employee willingness to raise safety issues. *Canadian Journal of Behavioural Science*, **37**:273–282.

Neuman, J. H. & Baron, R. M. (2005). Aggression in the workplace: A social-psychological perspective. In S. Fox and P. E. Spector (Eds.), *Counterproductive Behavior: Investigation of Actors and Targets*. Washington, DC: APA Books.

Offermann, L. R. & Hellmann, P. S. (1996). Leadership behavior and subordinate stress: A 360° view. *Journal of Occupational Health Psychology*, **1**:382–390.

Pizzino, A. (2002). Dealing with violence in the workplace: the experience of Canadian unions. In M. Gill, B. Fisher & V. Bowie (Eds.), *Violence at Work: Causes, Patterns, And Prevention*, pp. 165–179. Cullompton, England: Willan.

Rayner, C. & Cooper, C. L. (2006) Workplace bullying. In E. K. Kelloway, J. Barling & J. J. Hurrell (Eds), *Handbook of Workplace Violence.* Thousand Oaks, CA; Sage Publications.

Richman, J. A., Flaherty, J. A., Rospenda, K. M. & Christensen, M. (1992). Mental health consequences and correlates of medical student abuse. *Journal of the American Medical Association,* **267**:692–694.

Rogers, K. & Kelloway, E. K. (1997). Violence at work: Personal and organizational outcomes. *Journal of Occupational Health Psychology,* **2**:63–71.

Rospenda, K. M. (2002). Workplace harassment, services utilization, and drinking outcomes. *Journal of Occupational Health Psychology,* **7**:141–155.

Salancik, G. R. & Pfeffer, J. (1978). A social information processing approach to job attitudes and task design. *Administrative Science Quarterly,* **23**:224–253.

Sauter, S. L., Murphy, L. R. & Hurrell, Jr., J. J. (1990). Prevention of work-related psychological disorders: A national strategy proposed by the National Institute for Occupational Safety and Health (NIOSH). *American Psychologist,* **45**:1146–1158.

Schat, A. & Kelloway, E. K. (2005). Workplace violence. In J. Barling, E. K. Kelloway & M. Frone (Eds.), *Handbook of Workplace Stress.* Thousand Oaks: Sage Publications.

Schat, A., Frone, M. R. & Kelloway, E. K. (2006). Prevalence of workplace aggression in the US workforce: Findings from a national study. In E. K. Kelloway, J. Barling & J. J. Hurrell (Eds.), *Handbook of Workplace Violence,* Thousand Oaks, CA: Sage Publications.

Schat, A. C. H. & Kelloway, E. K. (2000). The effects of perceived control on the outcomes of workplace aggression and violence. *Journal of Occupational Health Psychology,* **4**:386–402.

Schat, A. C. H. & Kelloway, E. K. (2003). Reducing the adverse consequences of workplace aggression and violence: the buffering effects of organizational support. *Journal of Occupational Health Psychology,* **8**:110–122.

Shamir, B., House, R. J. & Arthur, M. B. (1993). The motivational effects of charismatic leadership: A self-concept based theory. *Organization Science,* **4**:577–594.

Shannon, H. S., Mayr, J. & Haines, T. (1997). Overview of the relationship between organizational and workplace factors and injury rates. *Safety Science,* **26**:201–217.

Skogstad, A., Einarsen, S., Torsheim. T. *et al.* (2007). The destructiveness of laissez-faire leadership behavior. *Journal of Occupational Health Psychology,* **12**:80–92.

Sosik, J. J. & Godshalk, V. M. (2000). Leadership styles, mentoring functions received, and job-related stress: A conceptual model and preliminary study. *Journal of Organizational Behavior,* **21**:365–390.

Tepper, B. J. (2000). Consequences of abusive supervision. *Academy of Management Journal,* **43**:178–190.

Townsend, J., Phillips, J. S. & Elkins, T. J. (2000). Employee retaliation: The neglected consequence of poor leader-member exchange relations. *Journal of Occupational Health Psychology,* **5**:457–463.

van Dierendonck, D., Haynes, C., Borrill, C. & Stride, C. (2004). Leadership behaviour and subordinate well-being. *Journal of Occupational Health Psychology,* **9**:165–175.

Wager, N., Feldman, G. & Hussey, T. 2003. The effect on ambulatory blood pressure of working under favourably and unfavourably perceived supervisors. *Occupational and Environmental Medicine,* **60**:468–474.

White, S. E. & Mitchell, T. R. (1979). Job enrichment versus social cues: A comparison and competitive test. *Journal of Applied Psychology,* **64**:1–9.

Whiteman, J. A., Snyder, D. A. & Ragland, J. J. (2001). The value of leadership in implementing and maintaining a successful health promotion program in the Naval Surface Force, US Pacific Fleet. *American Journal of Health Promotion,* **15**:437–440.

Zellars, K. L., Tepper, B. J. & Duffy, K. M. (2002). Abusive supervision and subordinates' organizational citizenship behavior. *Journal of Applied Psychology,* **87**:1068–1076.

Zohar, D. (1980). Safety climate in industrial organizations: Theoretical and applied implications. *Journal of Applied Psychology*, **65**:96–102.

Zohar, D. (2002a). The effects of leadership dimensions, safety climate, and assigned priorities on minor injuries in work groups. *Journal of Organizational Behavior*, **23**: 75–92.

Zohar, D. (2002b). Modifying supervisory practices to improve subunit safety: A leadership-based intervention model. *Journal of Applied Psychology*, **87**:156–163.

# CHAPTER 3

# Understanding and Improving Psychological Well-being for Individual and Organisational Effectiveness

**Ivan Robertson and Gordon Tinline**
*Robertson Cooper Ltd and Leeds University Business School*

It always seems somewhat counter-intuitive to have to justify the case for the 'healthy, happy, productive worker' (e.g. Cropanzano & Wright, 2001). On an individual basis how many of us enjoy being unhealthy, unhappy and unproductive, or believe we at our best when we feel like this? How many organisations, however hard headed and commercially oriented their leadership ethos, can demonstrate positive performance outcomes they can attribute to keeping their staff unhappy? Nevertheless there remains a need to demonstrate that psychological well-being is not a 'touchy feely' issue or something that organisations need concern themselves with, and that its benefits are tangible and important.

The main goal of commercial and public service organisations is to achieve the best possible results. The key to getting the best possible results lies with the organisation's workforce, in a group of individuals. Successful organisations are good at directing and sustaining the energy of people who work within them – to produce results.

Although it is results that count and provide the final test of success, organisations generally look for a wider range of key outcomes. In particular, they look for the following:

- High productivity.
- Low levels of sickness/absence.
- High numbers and quality of applicants for jobs.

*Employee Well-being Support: A Workplace Resource.* Edited by A. Kinder, R. Hughes and C.L. Cooper.
© 2008 John Wiley & Sons, Ltd.

- Retention of good people.
- Excellent behaviour towards customers.
- Good levels of organisational citizenship.
- Effective learning and problem-solving.

It is more or less self-evident that if an organisation can achieve all of the above it will be successful – as long as its strategic goals and mission are well-targeted. Conversely, any organisation that fails to achieve these, over any sustained period of time, will be under threat. The really successful organisations do well on all of the above requirements. For example, low levels of sickness/absence and good organisational citizenship, high productivity together with effective learning and problem-solving make it possible to deliver an impressive and consistent level of response to customers. The recruitment and retention of good people enables an organisation to build an experienced and effective workforce that compares well with the competition and provides competitive advantage.

At the heart of these needs is a requirement for the organisation to build a workforce that is highly engaged and working positively in ways that are aligned with the goals and mission of the organisation. It is clear that organisations increasingly recognise the importance of building a positive, engaged workforce and many are working hard to address a range of important factors.

## CURRENT FRAMES OF REFERENCE AND INTERVENTIONS

In practice, there is a limited range of activities that organisations can undertake to achieve these outcomes. Broadly, all initiatives can be classified as:

- *composition* (the procedures used to recruit, select and place people into specific roles in the organisation);
- *training and development* (processes for learning and development); and
- *situational engineering* (e.g. the design of the work that people do, the structure and processes that operate in the organisation, the work environment – including less tangible factors such as culture and climate).

Many organisations work hard on all of these categories – designing recruitment and selection processes to recruit the best talent, taking a strategic approach to identifying training and development needs and aligning these with the strategic goals of the organisation and bringing expertise to bear on issues of work design, organisational structure, change management, etc.

All of the approaches used by organisations are designed to build a workforce that is highly engaged and working positively towards their respective goals and missions. Several common approaches are currently used by organisations to build success. For example, performance management practices are often developed and managers in the organisation are trained and encouraged to put these into practice. Of course, performance management can work very effectively. There is a great deal of support to show that employees who are clear about their goals and receive plentiful feedback on progress are more effective. But care is needed in applying performance management processes to achieve high levels of performance. Heavier and more forceful levels of performance management can cause negative reactions from employees. Recent high profile legal cases have also established, quite clearly, that employers are liable for the bad behaviour of employees towards each other – and will not be excused even if they have tried to train people to behave differently.

Another interesting example of an intervention designed to improve organisational outcomes (in this case levels of sickness/absence) is attendance management. The processes used to manage attendance (return-to-work interviews, etc.) can bring about reductions in rates of sickness/absence. But without further follow-up work the causes of sickness/absence will not be tackled. When implemented properly, attendance management processes should also provide some information about the underlying causes of sickness absence. To sustain reduced levels of sickness absence without resorting to firmer and firmer attendance management practices (likely to eventually produce adverse reactions) the underlying reasons have to be identified and tackled.

These examples highlight two key points.

- The role of the line manager is clearly central in building and sustaining an engaged and enthusiastic workforce.
- Management processes, intended to ensure that employees' behaviour is aligned with the goals of the organisation, are limited by the reactions that they produce from the workforce.

This second point reinforces the central issue in this chapter – that organisations need an engaged and positive approach from their people, otherwise changes and other interventions, whatever they are intended to achieve, will not produce a positive reaction from the workforce – and will therefore be less effective.

## ORGANISATIONS WANT AN ENGAGED WORKFORCE – WHAT IS IT THAT INDIVIDUALS WANT?

There is a very simple answer to this question. What individuals want is to feel good. All theories of motivation at their heart have the individual being motivated to feel better. Of course circumstances, background factors, personal history and many other factors mean that exactly what will make one person feel good at any particular moment is quite individual and specific. For one person, at any given time, acquiring a minimal amount of money could give a big psychological high – for another, giving away a large sum of money could have the same effect, but essentially, the key motivator is the same for all of us – to feel good. When people feel good it is fundamentally because they have a sense of psychological well-being (PWB) and therefore this goal of feeling good will be referred to as PWB in the remainder of this chapter.

In an organisation where people are committed, engaged and enthusiastic, the behaviour required by the organisation and the activity that makes people feel good (i.e. enhances PWB) coincide. Building a committed and engaged workforce involves using management behaviours, organisational processes and work practices that enhance and sustain PWB and, most important of all, are not damaging to PWB.

PWB is the central motivational goal for people. This means that organisations need to find ways of enabling employees to enhance psychological well-being – directly through the work that they do. It is important to emphasise that humans do not derive high levels of PWB when there is an absence of goals, achievement and striving. In other words people do not experience PWB when they are not challenged. Obviously, it's nice from time to time to put one's feet up and completely relax. But this is not how most people want to spend their lives – it does not deliver enough 'feel good'. Actually, people feel at their best after the achievement of a significant challenge – for example, consider the high that comes after reaching a difficult goal. People benefit from measured degrees of challenge and from achieving goals that they think are important. Workplaces are potentially very good places for providing the challenge and the feelings of achievement that go with them.

The most successful psychological theory of motivation, goal-setting theory (e.g. Locke and Latham, 1990) gives convincing support to this view. If goals are set under conditions where people are committed to them (e.g. through a participative goal-setting process) the most effective goals are hard and challenging, rather than easy. There is a great deal of evidence that the achievement of goals alone (without extrinsic monetary reward) is extremely psychologically rewarding for people. The harder the goal (as long as it is not impossible) the better the feeling. Of course, if goals are impossible, muddled or not valued, people react in a very different way. This is where management and organisational processes should be working positively to enhance PWB, or can end up being actively pitted against people's efforts to achieve PWB.

## WHY PSYCHOLOGICAL WELL-BEING MATTERS

So PWB is important for individuals. But it is, in fact, even more important for employers and organisations. There are four main reasons for this:

1. The first reason has been explained above. If PWB is the main motivational force for individuals, the processes and systems of an organisation need to work in ways that enable employees' PWB to be sustained. The processes of goal-setting and the provision of clear and rewarding feedback are good

examples of important areas where organisations can leverage the benefits of PWB.

2. The second reason is that PWB in itself is associated with a number of highly desirable characteristics. For example, people with lower levels of psychological well-being are more likely to see ambiguous events as threatening (Seidlitz & Diener,1993; Seidlitz *et al.*, 1997). This can mean that when change is taking place, it will immediately be seen as negative and threatening by people with lower levels of PWB. Evidence also shows that unfavourable feedback is seen by those lower on PWB as more hurtful, and that favourable feedback produces fewer benefits. People lower on PWB also use more contentious interpersonal tactics (Larsen & Ketelar, 1991; Derryberry & Read, 1994). In short, people with higher levels of PWB learn and problem-solve more effectively, are more enthusiastic about change, relate to others more positively and accept change more readily. It is difficult to think of another set of characteristics, apart from job-specific skills, that are more important to an organisation's success.

3. The third reason is that PWB is dynamic. It ebbs and flows. Most researchers who study PWB acknowledge that PWB is not fixed and stable. It can be enhanced or it can be damaged as time passes. Individuals have a reservoir of PWB. Events and relationships that damage PWB, or call on people to use up their reserves of PWB, are damaging. Of course some people are more resilient than others, and people's PWB is damaged or enhanced by different things. But no one can go on for too long without replenishing their reservoir.

4. A final reason, perhaps the most compelling, is that the research evidence shows that when people are higher on PWB their organisations do better (e.g. Harter, Schmidt & Hayes, 2002; Wright & Cropanzano, 2004; Donald *et al.*, 2005), PWB delivers direct benefits.

## THE BENEFITS OF PSYCHOLOGICAL WELL-BEING

PWB plays a central role in delivering most of the important outcomes that are associated with successful, high performing organisations. Individuals who are high on psychological well-being have a number of advantages as leaders, managers and employees. Research has shown that almost 25% of the variance in reported levels of productivity is predicted by PWB (along with the perceived commitment of the organisation to the employee and resources and communication, which are also important factors in sustaining PWB) (Donald *et al.*, 2005). In one study, data from nearly 8,000 separate business units in 36 companies were analysed and revealed that engagement/well-being was linked to business unit performance, predicting customer satisfaction, productivity, profitability, employee turnover, sickness/absence levels and other key business unit outcomes (Harter, Schmidt & Hayes, 2002).

• PWB is the platform for low rates of sickness/absence, optimal levels of employee turnover and high productivity. Furthermore, from a talent management perspective, an organisation with a reputation for PWB amongst its workforce is also more likely to be able to attract the best from the talent pool of potential employees, as people are increasingly seeing PWB and work–life balance as being equally as important factors as economic reward.

It is also clear, from even a cursory review of current political and business leaders, that there is strong and growing recognition that, above all else, people want to be happy! Although economic and material factors will always be attractive to people, especially when people are making comparative judgements PWB is increasingly a factor to be evaluated, in its own right, alongside material and economic ones, in ways that previous generations have never done. Organisations and leaders that ignore this growing trend will increasingly be out of step with their workforces.

As emphasised earlier, it is important to stress that PWB comes from achievement not sloth. The view of PWB in an organisational setting that we advocate involves providing people with a level of challenge that enables them to experience achievement, not simply inventing one pointless 'happy-clappy' event after another to try to make people more committed. PWB is much deeper than this and will not be influenced by schemes to make people bond and relate to each other in a setting that fits with the organiser's idea of having a good time.

Figure 3.1 provides a summary diagram showing the role of PWB in supporting levels of engagement and an indication of the key sources of pressure that can damage the PWB reservoir. The diagram also indicates some of the core organisational processes that need to be working to support and enhance PWB, rather than conflicting with it.

Figure 3.1 introduces a new factor into the argument – the leadership and management actions required to achieve the organisation's strategic goals. These actions cover a range of approaches and relate to the priorities for the organisation, whether this is to bring about major changes, increase performance and productivity, improve the attachment of employees to the organisation, or some combination of these. The strategic focus and the actions required in any specific organisation will depend on strategic goals, history, culture and a number of other factors. The important point is that the leadership and management actions are critical to the success of the organisation. These actions are important because improved engagement underpinned by high levels of PWB will not automatically bring about desired outcomes. These factors do provide an essential platform for the managers and leaders of the organisation to improve organisational performance and they will make employees at all levels much more responsive to improvement opportunities, but they cannot magically bring about improvements themselves. The management and leadership of any organisation are critical to its success and it is important to recognise that effective leadership and management involves building and supporting key actions, focused on the organisation's strategic goals. These are the ingredients that will actually bring about improved organisational performance.

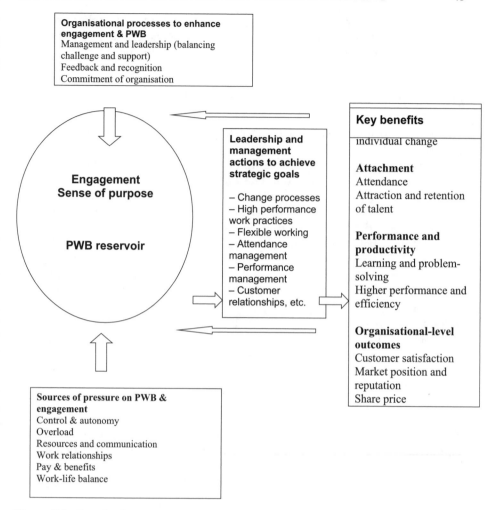

**Figure 3.1**    Benefits from PWB

When researchers and practitioners comment on shortcomings in organisational performance, leadership and management are identified more often than anything else as the key factors. To be effective in their own roles, leaders and managers must understand how they can build PWB and engagement in their workforces. This goes beyond understanding the factors that need to be addressed to maintain or improve PWB and engagement; it also involves raising self-awareness and providing leaders with a clear view of their own impact on the members of their workgroup(s).

Key findings from the field of positive psychology have informed our approach to this area (e.g. Fredrickson, 1998; Fredrickson & Joiner, 2002; Seligman *et al.*, 2005). The development of PWB is dependent on having an overall 'sense of purpose' that gives direction and meaning to people's actions.

This is why it is important to focus on the area of leadership when trying to instil a sense of PWB, as organisational leaders have the primary responsibility for providing this sense of purpose and direction for the workforce.

## ORGANISATIONAL PROCESSES AND PWB

There are two major ways of maximising PWB through key organisational processes.

The first of these involves focusing on the behaviour of the line managers and leaders in the organisation. The line manager relationship is the most important for anyone in an organisation. When people leave an organisation over one third cite their line manager as a key reason for wanting to leave. The line manager is the link between the goals and mission of the organisation and the day-to-day behaviour of the employee. As far as PWB is concerned, the core issue in this relationship is the success of the manager in managing the extent to which the employee is challenged and supported. Feeling suitably challenged and being able to reach goals is a critical factor in building PWB and self confidence, both within the workplace and elsewhere. However, when challenge is too great, or the goals are really unachievable people need support. Balancing challenge and support is a key, and perhaps the most important, managerial skill.

The second major way in which organisational processes can build PWB is to ensure, as far as possible, that when employees have to make decisions or commit high degrees of effort the choice that will maximise PWB is also the choice that is in the best interests of the organisation. If the consequences of a decision damage or deplete the employee's reservoir of PWB in some way employees will find it more difficult to take that decision. Similarly, people will choose to commit effort to a PWB-rewarding task in preference to one that damages PWB. Congruence between the behaviours that the organisation requires and the behaviours that enhance PWB creates a virtuous cycle that enhances PWB as it improves the success of the organisation.

## QUANTIFYING THE BENEFITS OF PWB

Low levels of psychological well-being are damaging for individuals and organisations. As already shown, psychological well-being is important for people's overall happiness and is the basis for a range of positive behaviours, including how people behave towards others, levels of confidence, problem-solving ability, mental strength and resilience. Damage to psychological well-being occurs when people are living or working (or both) in a situation that does not allow the PWB reservoir to be maintained and topped up. When PWB is high it will produce individual and organisational benefits (Cropanzano & Wright, 1999). These benefits are closely connected. People who feel good have a positive approach to things, see change and challenge positively and are

**Table 3.1** Benefits from assessment centres and PWB compared (based on correlations with performance of 0.3 for both AC scores and PWB scores)

|  | Proportion of high performers | Proportion of average and low performers |
|---|---|---|
| Low PWB | 35 | 65 |
| High PWB | 65 | 35 |
| Low score on AC | 35 | 65 |
| High score on AC | 65 | 35 |

happier and better-adjusted individuals. They also make stronger contributions to their workplaces, leading to better organisational outcomes such as: low levels of sickness-absence; lower employee turnover; higher customer satisfaction; better performance and productivity.

Because the statistical relationships between PWB and the key organisational outcomes are becoming clear it is possible to estimate the impact that PWB has on the outcomes. For example, the correlation between PWB and work performance is between 0.3 and 0.4 (e.g. Wright & Cropanzano, 2004). To provide a benchmark for the size of effect involved here, consider the impact of leadership development on leader performance, or the strength of the correlation between assessment of performance in a selection process and actual levels of work performance. Both of these are a similar order of magnitude (i.e. correlations of between 0.3 and 0.4). Consider how much organisations currently spend on leadership development and assessment processes. It is likely that investment in improving PWB would provide just as much pay off, but for much less cost. Table 3.1 shows how the benefits from an assessment centre (AC) are broadly comparable with the benefits of improving PWB.

Of course, the benefits of assessment centres apply only to people who have been selected using this approach; whereas the benefits of improved PWB could be obtained for the whole workforce.

Researchers have developed various utility analysis procedures for estimating the benefits of interventions and it is relatively easy to apply these established methods to PWB. In simple terms, with a correlation of 0.33, an increase in PWB of 1 standard deviation would produce an improvement in performance of about one third of a standard deviation. This improvement would move someone from being an average performer to being in the top 40% of performers.

Improvements in PWB can bring competitive advantage. As an illustration of the benefits: an organisation with 200 people has 50% of its people classified as high performers and 50% classified as low performers. PWB is also evenly split, with half of the workforce high on PWB and half low on PWB. With a correlation of PWB with performance of 0.3 (a value that would be expected based on the research evidence), the initial organisational situation could be described by the figures in Table 3.2.

The workforce of 200 has 65 people who are high on both performance and PWB – there are also 35 people who are high performers but low on PWB – this

**Table 3.2**  Initial organisational situation

|            | Low performance | High performance | Totals |
|------------|-----------------|------------------|--------|
| High PWB   | 35              | 65               | 100    |
| Low PWB    | 65              | 35               | 100    |
| Totals     | 100             | 100              | 200    |

**Table 3.3**  Organisation after intervention to raise PWB

|            | Low performance | High performance | Totals |
|------------|-----------------|------------------|--------|
| High PWB   | 45              | 95               | 140    |
| Low PWB    | 39              | 21               | 60     |
| Totals     | 84              | 116              | 200    |

reflects the fact that, although there is a link between PWB and performance the relationship is not perfect, just like the link between assessment centre performance and subsequent work performance. An intervention that improved the average level of PWB for the whole workforce would move some people from the low to the high PWB group. For example, the intervention could improve PWB so that another 20% of the workforce had high levels of PWB. In turn, because of the link between PWB and performance, this would create higher levels of performance for the workforce as a whole. In fact, with 20% more people in the high PWB group there would be an extra 16 high performers. The changes are shown in Table 3.3.

As this case illustrates, the changes in PWB would pay off for the organisation in terms of better performance. The example above has focused on performance; in practice, of course, the changes in PWB also would be likely to have an impact on other key outcomes, such as sickness-absence, employee recruitment, employee turnover and customer satisfaction.


## PSYCHOLOGICAL WELL-BEING: THE POSITIVE APPROACH TO BETTER INDIVIDUAL AND ORGANISATIONAL EFFECTIVENESS

Psychological well-being is the platform for low rates of sickness absence, optimal levels of employee turnover and high productivity. It is worth emphasising that the general reaction of employees to a PWB initiative is likely to be positive – because the aim is to make them feel good at work. This is very different from some other types of initiatives that are designed to improve organisational performance and which often elicit more guarded, or even actively negative, reactions. This is another facet of the benefits associated with pursuing a PWB approach.

# REFERENCES

Cropanzano, R. & Wright, T. A. (1999). A 5-year study of change in the relationship between well-being and performance. *Consulting Psychology Journal: Practice and Research*, **51**, 252–265.

Cropanzano, R. & Wright, T. A. (2001). When a 'happy' worker is really a 'productive' worker: A review and refinement of the happy-productive worker thesis. *Consulting Psychology Journal: Practice and Research*, **53**:182–199.

Derryberry, D. & Read, M. A. (1994). Temperament and attention: orienting toward and away from positive and negative signals. *Journal of Personality and Social Psychology*, **68**:1128–1139.

Donald, I., Taylor, P., Johnson, S. *et al.* (2005). Work environments, stress and productivity: An examination using ASSET. *International Journal of Stress Management*, **12**:409–423.

Fredrickson, B. L. (1998). What good are positive emotions? *Review of General Psychology*, **2**:300–319.

Fredrickson, B. L. & Joiner, T. (2002) Positive emotions trigger upward spirals toward emotional well-being. *Psychological Science*, **13**:172–175.

Harter, J. K., Schmidt, F. L. & Hayes, T. L. (2002). Business unit level outcomes between employee satisfaction, employee engagement and business outcomes: A meta-analysis. *Journal of Applied Psychology*, **87**:268–279.

Larsen, R. J. & Ketelar, T. (1991). Personality and susceptibility to positive and negative emotional states. *Journal of Personality and Social Psychology*, **61**:132–140.

Locke, E. A. & Latham, G. P. (1990). *A Theory of Goal-setting and Task Performance*. Englewood Cliffs, New Jersey: Prentice Hall.

Seidlitz, L. & Diener, E. (1993). Memory for positive versus negative events: Theories for the differences between happy and unhappy persons. *Journal of Personality and Social Psychology*, **64**:654–664.

Seidlitz, L., Wyer, R. S. and Diener, E. (1997). Cognitive correlates of subjective well-being: The processing of valenced life events by happy and unhappy persons. *Journal of Research in Personality*, **31**:240–256.

Seligman, M. E. P., Steen, T. A., Park, N. & Petersen, C. (2005). Positive psychology progress: empirical validation of interventions. *American Psychologist*, **60**:410–421.

Wright, T. A. and Cropanzano, R. (2004). Psychological well-being and job satisfaction as predictors of job performance. *Journal of Occupational Health Psychology*, **5**:84–94.

# CHAPTER 4

# Employee Well-being: the Heart of Positive Organizational Behavior

**Debra L. Nelson, Laura M. Little and M. Lance Frazier**
*Oklahoma State University*

A movement is growing in organisational behavior and management that calls for emphasising the positive in organisations. Often referred to as positive organisational behavior (POB), it has roots in positive psychology and focuses on positive states, traits and processes that lead to positive outcomes in organisations (Nelson & Cooper, 2007). Fred Luthans (2002a, 2002b) pioneered the positive approach in organisational behavior and recommended the elevation of human strengths at work rather than only managing weaknesses. Kim Cameron and his colleagues (Cameron, Dutton & Quinn, 2003) called for the study of what goes right in organisations, identifying human strengths, producing resilience and restoration, fostering vitality and cultivating extraordinary individuals. These and many other researchers have led the charge to study what is positive and provide balance in a field that in some cases emphasises the management of the negative.

In this chapter, we examine the growing POB movement specifically in terms of its implications for employee support and well-being. We view well-being in its broadest and most comprehensive sense, recalling Aristotle's eudaemonia, the realisation of one's true potential, as an overarching indicator of well-being (Rothman, 1993). Another part of well-being includes happiness and its causes, described by Russell (1958), defined as zest, work and affection. Ryff & Singer (1998, 2002) advocated a more comprehensive view of health, one that would include both mind–body interactions and wellness. Thus, we view well-being not as simply the absence of the negative; instead, we see it as the presence of the positive.

POB encompasses positive states, traits and processes, and there are multiple candidates for discussion in each category that are linked with well-being. Due

*Employee Well-being Support: A Workplace Resource.* Edited by A. Kinder, R. Hughes and C.L. Cooper.
© 2008 John Wiley & Sons, Ltd.

to space considerations, we found it impossible to present them all, so we will include a reasonable subset. For purposes of illustration, we have selected one to represent each category: positive emotions and mood (states), core self-evaluations (traits), and eustress (processes). Each has implications for well-being as an important positive outcome in organisations, and can give a hint of POB's promise for assisting those individuals who are working to support employee well-being.

## POSITIVE EMOTIONS AND MOOD: HEALTHY STATES

The study of mood and distinct emotions is gaining momentum in organisational research and has grown out of the 'affective revolution' that began in the 1980s and 1990s (Brief, 2001). Around this time, researchers acknowledged that mood and emotions are an integral part of the working environment and their effects on workplace outcomes in general, and well-being specifically should be studied. Mood or state affect is comprised of feeling states that are relatively enduring and without a salient antecedent cause (Watson & Clark, 1992) whereas distinct emotions are more intense, shorter-lived and have a definite cause (Russell, 2003). Whereas mood is typically thought of as positive and/or negative and is hierarchical to emotion such that emotions are subsumed under mood, emotions are distinct constructs such as anger, pride, joy and contentment directed at specific entities. Thus, shorter-lived emotions are experienced in reaction to some specific entity and the variety of different emotions one feels over a short period of time will influence one's more enduring mood.

Mood, as it relates to well-being, has been studied a great deal and results have generally indicated that positive mood is positively related to well-being while negative mood is negatively related to well-being. For example, mood is positively related to subjective health (Benyamini et al. , 2000) and negatively related to reported pain (Gil et al., 2003). Positive mood has also been linked to more objective health measures. Studies have found correlations between positive mood and immune system functioning (Stone, Cox, Valdimarsdottir & Jandorf, 1987; Stone, Neale, Cox & Napoli, 1994) and positive mood and less frequent health-care use (Gil et al., 2003). Positive mood has been shown to positively influence success-related variables as well, such as marital happiness, satisfaction with friendships, self-esteem and job performance (Glenn & Weaver, 1981; Lucas et al., 1996; Erez & Isen, 2002). Negative mood, on the other hand, has been linked to increased same-day pain (Gil et al., 2003) and decreases in self-reported health (Benyamini et al., 2000) and Evans and Egerton (1992) found that negative mood led to a higher incident of colds.

Distinct emotions have been studied less often than mood; however, ample theoretical rationale exists explaining a positive relationship between positive emotions and well-being. Frederickson's (1998) Broaden and Build Model of Positive Emotions, for example, argues that negative emotions are related to many negative outcomes because they narrow one's thought-action repertoire and cause individuals to be overly focused on problems. She contends that positive emotions are positively related to well-being because positive emotions broaden the scope of attention, action and cognition and build social, physical and intellectual resources. Specifically, Frederickson argues that positive emotions such as joy, interest and contentment increase one's thought–action repertoire and can help individuals undo the negative affects of negative emotions. Thus, the experience of positive emotions has both an immediate impact on well-being in that feeling joy, interest, etc. will make an individual feel good at that moment, and broadening one's scope and desire to build resources can have more long-term effects.

For example, joy or happiness is said to relate to well-being because it creates an urge to play. Play involves examination, discovery and fooling around. Play increases one's thought–action repertoire and has been shown to promote skill acquisition. Thus, joy not only broadens one's momentary thought–action tendencies but also allows one to acquire skills that can be drawn upon later. Interest or curiosity/intrigue creates feelings of becoming involved with the person or object that has stimulated it. Interest causes individuals to explore and seek out new information that, again, can be drawn upon later. Contentment arises in situations appraised as safe and as having a high degree of certainty. Research on contentment suggests that this emotion 'prompts individuals to savor their current life circumstances and recent successes' (Frederickson, 1998:306). Thus, contentment allows an individual to take pleasure in and assimilate recent events and experiences creating a new sense of self. As these examples illustrate, positive emotions can have both immediate and lasting impacts on well-being and thus should be encouraged in the workplace.

If positive mood and emotions are linked to well-being, then how can managers help their employees feel positive? One of the most promising aspects of mood and emotion and their effects on well-being is that both mood and emotion are malleable. Thus, managers can have a great deal of influence on the experience of these feelings in their employees. By creating a work environment that encourages positive experiences and allows employees to relish previous successes, managers can promote positive mood and emotions such as joy at work. Additionally, promoting an environment that allows an employee to feel safe and able to explore can encourage individuals to feel both content and interested. Because positive emotions are subsumed under mood, creating situations in which employees feel many positive emotions will also encourage an overall positive mood which again, should influence well-being.

## CORE SELF-EVALUATIONS: HEALTHY TRAITS

We next discuss the broad personality trait of core self-evaluations (CSE) and its relationship with both job satisfaction and job performance. In the opening of this chapter, we stated that well-being has been characterised as the presence of the positive. Positive outcomes at work such as job performance and job satisfaction are included in this view and have been identified as influences on the well-being of an employee. For example, Hart and Cooper (2002) developed a model of employee well-being and at the core of this model is job satisfaction. If an employee is satisfied with his or her job, the thought is that the employee will be happy and more productive in the workplace. Other well-being research has shown that well-being is associated with job performance. Warr (1999) reviewed research that suggested that employee well-being is significantly associated with job performance. Based on our definition of well-being and previous well-being research, we feel that as employees are more satisfied with their jobs and are performing at a high level, their well-being will also be enhanced.

Research on job satisfaction and job performance has shown a significant association between these outcomes and personality traits. Therefore, although positive mood and emotions clearly have influence on these outcomes, dispositional factors explain additional variance in job satisfaction and job performance. In fact, Dormann and Zapf (2001) recently estimated that a substantial percentage of the variance in job satisfaction could be attributed to stable personality traits.

Core self-evaluations are defined as the fundamental assessments people make about their worthiness, competence and abilities (Judge, Locke & Durham, 1997). Introduced by Judge et al. (1997), core self-evaluations consist of four self evaluative traits: self-esteem, generalised self-efficacy, neuroticism and locus of control. Self-esteem is the value one places on oneself as a person (Harter, 1990) and is identified as the broadest and most fundamental self-evaluation (Judge et al., 1997). Drawing on the work of Bandura (1982), Judge et al. defined generalised self-efficacy as the estimate a person makes about his or her ability to cope, perform and be successful in various situations. People high on neuroticism, which is one of the 'Big Five' personality traits (Barrick & Mount, 1991), are characterised as worriers, plagued by self-doubt and tending to be nervous. This trait has also been called emotional stability, which is essentially a person who is low on neuroticism. Finally, locus of control is the degree to which people feel they can control their environment and the outcomes associated with it.

Empirical studies examining the relationship between the individual traits that comprise CSE and job satisfaction have shown strong support for the relationship. For example, Judge and Bono (2001) examined the relationship between the four individual traits of CSE and found that each had a positive relationship with job satisfaction. For example, generalised self-efficacy is a person's view of his or her ability to perform in a variety of situations. The positive relationship between self-efficacy and job satisfaction suggests that as an employee has a higher belief in his or her ability, the more likely the employee will be satisfied with the job he or she is performing. However, more recently, researchers have examined the relationship between the overarching, broad trait of CSE and job satisfaction, and concluded that the real promise of CSE is as a broad personality construct in that the relationship with job satisfaction becomes stronger when the four traits are considered in aggregate. In other words, an employee high in CSE will likely be more satisfied with his or her job than an employee high on any one of the individual traits that comprise CSE. This positive relationship between CSE and job satisfaction extends across cultures, as well. Judge, Van Vianen and De Pater (2004) reported a strong positive relationship between job satisfaction and CSE among a sample of Dutch employees. Research with a sample of Japanese employees showed a similar relationship (Piccolo *et al.*, 2005).

Though the majority of CSE research has examined the relationship with job satisfaction, CSE has also shown a significant positive relationship with job performance (Erez & Judge, 2001). Individuals high on core self-evaluations see themselves as worthy and capable of performing in a variety of situations, feel they have control over what happens to them and are likely to remain calm in the face of challenges. In other words, employees high on core self-evaluations have been shown to be better performers (Erez & Judge, 2001). As employees have a positive view of themselves, they will believe in their abilities to persevere in the face of adversity and succeed when presented with new challenges and opportunities.

Why should managers care about core self-evaluations? The evidence presented thus far suggests that employees with positive self-evaluations are more likely to find satisfaction in their jobs and more likely to be better performers. Additionally, CSE has been shown to be negatively related to job burnout (Best, Stapleton & Downey, 2005), thus potentially reducing turnover.

Core self-evaluations have also shown stability over a period of time. A recent study by Dormann, Fay, Zapf and Frese (2006) found that CSE was highly stable over a two-year time frame. This stability indicates that core self-evaluations may predict performance and job satisfaction consistently over time. This stability also indicates that, although managers can and should promote environments that allow individuals to thrive, identifying CSE may be very important during the selection and hiring.

The tasks and responsibilities of today's employee are constantly changing and employees must be able to adapt to these changes. An employee who can take constant change in stride and be calm in the face of change, that sees oneself as able to perform well in a variety of situations, and also be satisfied with the job would certainly be viewed as an asset to managers. In an ever changing work environment, the consistency of CSE should promote the well-being of both employee and manager.

## EUSTRESS: A HEALTHY PROCESS

Stress is an inevitable feature of working life. Although there is a considerable knowledge base about distress, the negative form of stress, and its negative medical, psychological and behavioral consequences, less is known about *eustress*, the positive form of stress, and its positive consequences. Eustress is defined as a positive response to a stressor, as indicated by the presence of positive psychological states (Nelson & Simmons, 2004). The experience of eustress can leave employees invigorated, motivated and productive.

Viewing stress as only negative is missing half of the picture; it is similar to a bathtub with only one faucet (distress). We know a lot about the sources of cold water, and we can tell individuals how to either decrease the flow of cold water into or increase the flow of cold water out of their bathtub. In other words, we know how to limit individuals' exposure to distress, and how to reduce or eliminate it. We also know quite a bit about the negative consequences of exposure to a bathtub full of cold water for a prolonged period of time. This view, however, does not give us a comprehensive understanding of the water (stress) in the bathtub. A more holistic model of stress must acknowledge that the bathtub does indeed have two faucets – hot (eustress) and cold (distress) – and both are necessary for a comfortable bath.

A cornerstone of research on eustress is the cognitive appraisal approach in which it is not the stressor itself but the individual's appraisal of the stressor that determines how the individual will respond. When an individual appraises a stressor, he/she examines the stressor in terms of its potential implications for well-being. Positive appraisals happen when the outcome of the encounter is expected to preserve or promote health (Lazarus, 1966; Lazarus & Folkman, 1984). Feelings of exhilaration often accompany such positive appraisals. The positive assessment of a stressor also produces different psychological and physiological responses than does a negative assessment. Eustress can thus result in improvement in, rather than a deterioration of, well-being (Nelson & Simmons, 2006). Several research studies have indicated support for a direct link between eustress and health (cf. Edwards & Cooper, 1988; Simmons & Nelson, 2007).

Individuals who experience eustress describe it as being totally 'in the moment', in the zone, or in a state of flow (Csikszentmihalyi, 1990). Time suspends, concentration is focused in a state of mindful challenge, and the individual is engaged in a healthy state of arousal. Among nurses, who have extremely demanding jobs, eustress was experienced at work, as indicated by their active engagement in their work and their hope, both of which contributed to their feelings of well-being (Simmons, Nelson & Neal, 2001). Despite their exposure to stressors such as work overload and death of patients, nurses who found meaning in their work and remained emotionally attached to their work experienced positive stress and its health benefits. Eustress is therefore related to health and well-being, and in turn to work performance.

The research on distress focuses on coping or managing negative stress in order to prevent dysfunctional consequences such as psychological or physiological illness. The companion process to coping as applied to eustress is *savoring*, which means enjoying something with appreciation or dwelling on it with great delight. Employees not only prefer eustress, they actually *savor*, or enjoy with appreciation, this positive response to aspects of demands they encounter at work. When athletes speak of being in the zone or at the top of their game, or opera singers describe complete immersion in the performance and attunement with the audience, they are referring to eustress. Descriptions such as these are often accompanied by a desire to savor that positive, productive state more frequently, or for longer periods of time.

Given the preference for eustress and its positive consequences, and employees' desire to savor the experience, leaders can design ways to encourage eustress at work. In the parlance of distress, the task for leaders is distress prevention; in the case of eustress, the leader's task becomes one of eustress generation. How can leaders generate eustress? One way is by creating cultures and work settings that give individuals the opportunity to experience the eustress response. The ability to generate hope among an organisation's members may be particularly important during radical change efforts and it may be key to experiencing eustress in difficult times. Hope is an important indicator of eustress, which is the employee's belief that he/she has both the will (self-efficacy) and the way (resources) to successfully accomplish a goal. When people believe that their actions will lead to positive results, they may be more willing to accept difficult challenges. Managers can generate hope by establishing goals that are challenging to all members, providing ample resources to enable individuals to excel at their jobs, and engaging in inspirational dialogues with their employees.

Managers must strive to find out which aspects of work are most meaningful, engaging and invigorating, and design jobs around these activities. These actions demonstrate that employees' well-being is worthy of investment and commitment from managers, and that the challenges of improving the employees' work experience are important.

Another thing managers can do is to provide an environment in which employees can completely immerse themselves in their work without unnecessary interference or interruptions. Impediments to eustress may include policies, procedures and physical working conditions that may need to be altered. Removing obstacles to flow can allow employees to savor, or prolong, the experience of eustress. Although it may not be possible to remove all negative stress from a job, it is certainly realistic to add more eustress.

## POB AND WELL-BEING

The POB movement has much to offer in terms of guidance for researchers, and for managers who want to encourage well-being in organisations. There are many other states (vigor, engagement, hope), traits (interdependence, resilience, humility) and processes (flourishing, positive deviance, forgiveness) to be explored by managers and researchers in joint endeavors. Well-being, in its broadest sense, is at the heart of the individual outcomes that are positive, which in turn lead to positive outcomes at the work, team and organisational levels.

It is important to note that POB does not advocate blind optimism. It does, however, call for a shift in emphasis for those supporting employee well-being. Part of the task is managing symptoms and preventing the negative from occurring to preserve health. The other part of the task, emphasised in POB, is building strengths and creating positive workplaces that promote well-being, commitment, job satisfaction and performance. Recognising and rewarding exceptional performance should go hand-in-hand with correcting poor performance. We believe that encouraging positive emotions, lifting up and emphasising positive core self-evaluations, and generating eustress are high payoff pursuits for those who want to support employee well-being.

# REFERENCES

Bandura, A. (1982). Self-efficacy mechanism in human agency. *American Psychologist*, **37**:122–147.

Barrick, M. R. & Mount, M. K. (1991). The Big Five personality dimensions and job performance: A meta-analysis. *Personnel Psychology*, **44**:1–26.

Best, R. G., Stapleton, L. M. & Downey, R. G. (2005). Core self-evaluations and job burnout: The test of alternative models. *Journal of Occupational Health Psychology*, **10**:441–451.

Benyamini, Y., Idler, E. L., Leventhal, H. & Leventhal, E. A. (2000). Positive affect and function as influences on self-assessment of health: Expanding our view beyond illness and disability. *Journals of Gerontology*, **55B**:107–116.

Brief, A. P. (2001). Organizational behavior and the study of affect: Keep your eyes on the organization. *Organizational Behavior and Human Decision Processes*, **86**:131–139.

Cameron, K., Dutton, J. E. and Quinn, R. E. (Eds.) (2003). *Positive Organizational Scholarship: Foundations of a New Discipline*. San Francisco: Berrett-Koehler Publishers.

Csikszentmihalyi, M. (1990). *Flow: The Psychology of Optimal Experience*. New York: Harper & Row.

Dormann, C. & Zapf, D. (2001). Job satisfaction: A meta-analysis of stabilities. *Journal of Organizational Behavior*, **22**:483–504.

Dormann, C., Fay, D., Zapf, D. & Frese, M. (2006). A state-trait analysis of job satisfaction: On the effect of core self-evaluations. *Applied Psychology – an International Review*, **55**:27–51.

Edwards, J. R. & Cooper, C. L. (1988). The impacts of positive psychological states on physical health: A review and theoretical framework. *Social Science Medicine*, **27**: 1147–1459.

Erez, A. & Isen, A. (2002). The influence of positive affect on the components of expectancy motivation. *Journal of Applied Psychology*, **87**:1055–1067.

Erez, A. & Judge, T. A. (2001). Relationship of core self-evaluations to goal setting, motivation, and performance. *Journal of Applied Psychology*, **86**:1270–1279.

Evans, P. D. & Egerton, N. (1992). Mood states and minor illness. *British Journal of Medical Psychology*, **65**:177–186.

Frederickson, B. L. (1998). What good are positive emotions? *Review of General Psychology*, **2**:300–319.

Gil, K. M., Carson, J. W., Porter, L. S. *et al.* (2003). Daily stress and mood and their association with pain, health-care use, and school activity in adolescents with sickle cell disease. *Journal of Pediatric Psychology*, **28**:363–373.

Glenn, N. D. & Weaver, C. N. (1981). The contributions of marital happiness to global happiness. *Journal of Marriage and the Family*, **43**:161–168.

Hart, P. M. & Cooper, C. L. (2002). Occupational stress: Toward a more integrated framework. In N. Anderson, D. S. Ones, H. K. Sinangil & C. Viswesvaran (Eds.), *Handbook of Industrial, Work and Organizational Psychology*, Vol. 2, pp. 93–114. Thousand Oaks, CA: Sage Publications.

Harter, S. (1990). Causes, correlates, and the functional role of global self-worth: A life-span perspective. In R. J. Sternberg & J. Kolligan (Eds.), *Competence Considered*, pp. 67–97. New Haven: Yale University Press.

Judge, T. A. & Bono, J. E. (2001). Relationship of core self-evaluations traits – self-esteem, generalized self-efficacy, locus of control, and emotional stability – with job satisfaction and job performance: A meta-analysis. *Journal of Applied Psychology*, **86**:80–92.

Judge, T. A., Locke, E. A. & Durham, C. C. (1997). The dispositional causes of job satisfaction: A core evaluations approach. *Research in Organizational Behavior*, **19**:151–188.

Judge, T. A., Van Vianen, A. E. M. & De Pater, I. E. (2004). Emotional stability, core self-evaluations, and job outcomes: A review of the evidence and an agenda for future research. *Human Performance*, **17**:325–346.

Lazarus, R. S. (1966). *Psychological Stress and the Coping Process*. New York: McGraw-Hill.

Lazarus, R. S. & Folkman, S. (1984). *Stress, Appraisal, and Coping*. New York: Springer Publishing Company.

Lucas, R. E., Diener, E. & Suh, E. M. (1996). Discriminant validity of well-being measures. *Journal of Personality and Social Psychology*, **71**:616–628.

Luthans, F. (2002a). The need for and meaning of positive organizational behavior. *Journal of Organizational Behavior*, **23**:695–706.

Luthans, F. (2002b). Positive organizational behavior: Developing and managing psychological strengths. *Academy of Management Executive*, **16**:57–72.

Nelson, D. L. & Cooper, C. L. (2007). *Positive Organizational Behavior*. London: Sage Publications, forthcoming.

Nelson, D. L. & Simmons, B. L. (2004). Eustress: An elusive construct, an engaging pursuit (monograph). In P. Perrewe & D. Ganster (Eds.), *Research in Occupational Stress and Well-Being*, **3**:265–322.

Nelson, D. L. & Simmons, B. L. (2006). Eustress and hope at work: Accentuating the positive. In A. M. Rossi, S. Sauter & P. Perrewe (Eds.), *Stress and Quality of Working Life: New Perspectives in Occupational Health*, pp. 121–134. Greenwich, CT: Information Age Publishing.

Piccolo, R. F., Judge, T. A., Takahashi, K. *et al.* (2005). Core self-evaluations in Japan: Relative effects on job satisfaction, life satisfaction, and happiness. *Journal of Organizational Behavior*, **26**:965–984.

Rothman, J. C. (1993). *Aristotle's Eudaemonia, Terminal Illness, and the Question of Life Support*. New York: P. Lang.

Russell, B. (1958). *The Conquest of Happiness*. New York: Liveright. (Original work published 1930).

Russell, J. A. (2003). Core affect and the psychological construction of emotion. *Psychological Review*, **110**:145–172.

Ryff, C. D. & Singer, B. (1998). The contours of positive human health. *Psychological Inquiry*, **9**:1–28.

Ryff, C. D. & Singer, B. (2002). From social structures to biology: Integrative science in pursuit of human health and well-being. In C. R. Snyder and S. J. Lopez (Eds.), *Handbook of pPositive Ppsychology*, (pp. 541–555). New York: Oxford University Press.

Simmons, B. L. & Nelson, D. L. (2007). Eustress at work: Extending the Holistic Stress Model. In D. L. Nelson & C. L. Cooper (Eds.), *Positive Organizational Behavior*. London: Sage Publications, forthcoming.

Simmons, B. L., Nelson, D. L. & Neal, L. J. (2001). A comparison of positive and negative work attitudes of home healthcare and hospital nurses. *Health Care Management Review*, **26**:64–75.

Stone, A. A., Cox, D. S., Vladimarsdottier, H. & Jandorf, L. (1987). Evidence that secretory IgA antibody is associated with daily mood. *Journal of Personality and Social Psychology*, **52**:988–993.

Stone, A. A., Neale, J. M., Cox, D. S., & Napoli, A. (1994). Daily events are associated with a secretory immune response to an oral antigen in men. *Health Psychology*, **13**:400–418.

Warr, P. (1999). Well-being and the workplace. In D. Kahneman, E. Diener & N. Schwarz (Eds.), *Well-being: The Foundations of Hedonic Psychology*, pp. 392–412. New York: Russell Sage Foundation.

Watson, D. & Clark, L. A. (1992). Affects separable and inseparable: On the hierarchical arrangement of negative affects. *Journal of Personality and Social Psychology*, **62**: 489–505.

# CHAPTER 5

# Employee Support Strategies in Large Organisations

**Steve Boorman**
*Institute of Occupational Medicine, Birmingham University*

'Good health = good business' was the underpinning principle of a campaign by the Health and Safety Executive in the UK. Businesses frequently refer to their staff as their greatest assets and even the most automated of factories rely on people to ensure their products are successfully produced, distributed and sold. Delivering employee support in larger businesses is often thought to be easier–however, it is erroneous to think that larger organisations have bigger pockets and many more resources to enable supporting people more easily. The reality is that larger businesses are often more complex and in today's commercial marketplace it is rare to have large sums of money simply waiting around to be spent on employee support (e.g. counselling, well-being initiatives and occupational health).

## THE BUSINESS CASE

In the commercial environment of a large organisation, there needs to be a compelling reason to provide employee support. Without such then quite simply the money is best spent elsewhere and almost certainly will be! The business case for employee support has many facets:

- Duty of care (legal)
- Duty of care (ethical/moral)
- Avoidance of cost
- Improved efficiency or effectiveness.

All employers have duties of care under Health and Safety legislation; as a basic principle an employer is required to assess risks that may harm employees

*Employee Well-being Support: A Workplace Resource.* Edited by A. Kinder, R. Hughes and C.L. Cooper.
© 2008 John Wiley & Sons, Ltd.

and take steps, as far as reasonably practicable, to reduce the likelihood of harm arising. The 'as far as reasonably practicable' test is important – as larger organisations effectively have a higher hurdle to satisfy, which can be important in considering the allocation of resources to enable employee support.

Organisations must therefore as a first step consider whether there are any hazards – physical, biological or psychosocial – that may give rise to harm. Where hazards exist the legislation places a duty to consider a hierarchy of control – firstly to consider whether the risk can be avoided completely; if this is impracticable steps should be taken to consider substitution (alternative ways of doing the work tasks to again avoid or reduce the risk of harm). Failing this, risk reduction is required – the use of strategies to minimise the harm likely to arise – and finally if the risk cannot be practicably taken away consideration is needed of measures to protect the individual from harm.

Until recently this has been well understood in relation to physical hazards, but less well so for psychosocial hazards. Greater emphasis from the Health and Safety Executive, with the development of guidance on the assessment and control of workplace stress and the wider availability of simple assessment tools has increased awareness (as has the prosecution of large organisations with much publicity for failure to control psychosocial risks).

Most large organisations are also concerned about their brand image – this is important to continued sales of their products or services (customer brand), and also to the recruitment and retention of good quality staff (employer brand). The ethical and moral aspects of the duty of care are an important feature strengthening brand value – a caring employer is perceived as a responsible one and research reinforces the commercial value of such and the benefits in terms of staff loyalty.

Businesses exist to generate profit for their shareholders; even in service industries funds need to be realised to maintain investment for the future. In relation to this most large organisations are concerned at the financial impacts of employee ill health or distress. For a large organisation a sickness absence rate of 5% or more can easily equate to many millions of pounds a year and, since pension funds have begun to recognise potentially disastrous deficits, the costs of ill health retirement are beginning to be taken more seriously. Replacing an ill employee requires spend on advertising, recruitment, induction and further training, aside from additional costs arising from lost experience, expertise and destroyed contact networks. In generating a business case to underpin investment in employee support these costs are sometimes underestimated or overlooked.

In addition to the costs associated with absent employees it can also be difficult to quantify the costs associated with employees who attend work, but who underperform due to illness, distraction or distress. The 'sick present' costs businesses through mistakes, inefficiencies, poor employee relations, time spent on performance management, grievances and dealing with discontent (and linked litigation).

For the reasons outlined in previous paragraphs there is a clear business case to be made to provide financial and legal arguments supporting investment in employee support. For a large organisation particularly the question 'whether or not to provide' is therefore relatively simple to answer – much more difficult is the 'what to provide'.

## EMPLOYEE SUPPORT CHOICES

A simple review of what is or isn't provided in a random trawl of large businesses suggests scope for variation exists. There is no standard model and clear information on comparative cost/benefit between alternative strategies is not always available. An additional factor that deserves consideration is organisational styles and culture – approaches that work in one organisation do not always transfer successfully to others.

Physical access may influence the choice of approach used, for example different communication and dissemination methods are required in organisations that operate on multiple sites compared with a large single site. Workers with different backgrounds may favour alternative means of delivering approaches – for example 'blue collar' male workers are less receptive to written health information than female 'white collar' workers who often prioritise health and well-being messages more easily.

The demographics of a workforce will also influence behaviours and uptake of support services. This is particularly true of support delivered via intranet or internet – younger age groups are generally more computer-literate and experience has shown that some ethnic groups find the 'anonymity' of remote support easier to accept than 'face to face' services.

Management attitudes also impact on service provision choices – telephone-based support (at least for initial contact) may clearly have cost benefits in comparison with onsite counsellor provision, but cost-saving needs careful balancing against perceived quality of support. Studies of trauma care provision have shown that perceived levels of organisational support are significantly associated with attendance post trauma (Rick, O' Regan & Kinder, 2006).

Availability in the wider community of support services will also influence the organisational need to provide, as there is significant geographical variability in the provision of charitable, voluntary or state-provided care services. Where good services exist locally – often free or at low cost, with ready access and low waiting times – then clearly organisational provision risks duplication. However, some organisations may still choose to provide workplace-based support services from a perspective of enhancing their 'employer brand', seeking to strengthen employee engagement through branded care provision.

Volume is an important factor in determining the resource needed. High demand, particularly if associated with urgency and requirements for delivery across wide geographical areas, will clearly tend towards favouring remote service delivery models (telephone- or computer-based support). Lower volumes, particularly if relatively predictable in nature (without large fluctuation) make it easier to deliver face-to-face onsite services. Marketing and promotion of service availability can have high impact on demand, and trust in the service (and its practitioners) is also key to uptake levels.

## OPTIONS

A range of options exist and the previous section suggests some of the factors that help to drive choices for provision:

- Simple self-help information – leaflets (which may include self-help advice and contact points for resources such as advisory sources, charitable providers, NHS resources, etc.).
- Telephone-based services – these may be self-help contact points or may be services that managers or colleagues can source advice/support from. Such services may be solely telephone support-based or may be linked to other options to provide more comprehensive assistance programmes.
- IT-based services – these vary from local 'free-standing' assessment and support programmes, including for example simple cognitive behavioural therapy-based approaches, through to complex internet or intranet support packages that may enable interactivity or provision of additional support via other modalities. Whilst all services have similar trust and confidentiality issues, web-based data collection is often viewed with suspicion and deserves attention regarding data confidentiality and use. Increasing availability of web-based teleconferencing/remote care software is enabling interactive IT-based services to deliver flexible distant support with less loss of personal interaction.
- Face-to-face services – support and care often benefits from direct contact, with empathy and rapport being easier to establish. However such provision is often more expensive (especially when travel costs and suitable accommodation is also included) and the health and safety of practitioners needs consideration (especially if visiting remote sites or highly distressed individuals without benefit of chaperone). Care needs to be given to ensure appropriate standards of ethical delivery and simple protocols (such as timed telephone check-in with a colleague) can help to reduce risk of incident.
- Specialist provision – you would not expect to visit a gynaecologist to have neurosurgery, and in a similar fashion some areas of employee support require particular specialist skills or knowledge (e.g. after rape or major trauma). Such incidents are usually rare, but in certain industries may be more commonplace (e.g. an industry handling large amounts of money may be more prone to hostage-taking incidents). The predicted frequency of such events will determine whether service provision should contain such specialists permanently available (for early intervention and response) or whether access via third party or sub-contract arrangements is sufficient to meet need.
- Beyond employee support – particularly for large organisations, attendance management and rehabilitation to work services often need to be linked to the employee support offering to provide more comprehensive care. Large organisations often have access to occupational health provision and this may or may not be integrated directly with the employee support services. Where such services are not provided by a common provider (and even

sometimes when they are) there is a need to consider carefully ethical issues such as those of client confidentiality in managing referrals between one professional and another. Multi-disciplinary case management can provide individuals with high quality support, but only if well managed with careful attention to avoid unnecessary repetition whilst avoiding sharing inappropriate information.

Whatever service model is chosen, it is important for the organisation to understand that it remains responsible for the standards of care provided (whether the service is an 'in-house' provided by directly employed staff or is a contracted-in service). The business has a responsibility to ensure that the service is provided by adequately trained, competent staff complying with professional body recommendations (and registered where appropriate) and operating to ethical standards complying with published guidance.

## PRACTICALITIES

Much attention is often focused on counselling models and the professional aspects of service provision, discussed elsewhere (see Chapter 22). However simple practical arrangements are also important in ensuring an effective support service.

Whatever chosen model of provision, accessibility is a key first step. For those with long-term disability, legislation may help to support the case for careful consideration of access needs (not just physical, but also for those with sensory, mental impairments or other needs), but it is worth remembering that simple adjustment, to enable flexible service access, can make services easier to use by all and improve satisfaction levels.

Support services stand or fall on the trust and confidence of those using them. In busy workplaces it can be difficult to guarantee that confidential or sensitive information cannot be overheard, and discrete, quiet and welcoming environments are sometimes hard to find. However professional high quality support provision does require good quality accommodation, accompanied by high standards of discretion in managing contacts between client, practitioner and management.

Recipients of support services are often vulnerable, and deserve reassurance of their own safety. Simple environmental issues such as lighting, heating and ventilation can have significant contribution to the success of support provision – distractions, discomfort and noise rapidly break the rapport needed to provide empathetic support.

Employee support is often provided by lone practitioners, and their clients' needs are sometimes considered in isolation from the practitioner's needs. Practitioners' personal safety is of paramount importance; distressed, angry or mentally unwell clients may react unpredictably or violently, and support practices should take steps to minimise risk. Simple measures such as avoiding situations where help is unavailable, security 'panic' buttons linked to receptionist (care needs to be taken that reliance is not placed on an alarm ringing in an empty room!) and visits may be planned with a contact schedule agreed to ensure that the practitioner reports in when a call is complete.

## MANAGEMENT INFORMATION

In smaller organisations client confidentiality may limit the information that can be fed back to the business without breach of confidentiality. For larger organisations such information is an important resource to promote employee support and improvement. The identification of 'hotspots' – areas with unexpectedly high rates of a particular issue arising – or trends suggesting an issue is becoming more widespread enables a business to recognise issues affecting more than one individual and to take steps to reduce the risk of further problems arising.

Recognition and use of such data may be important for risk control under health and safety legislation and can help an organisation reduce its risk of liability for future claims. The information is also useful in planning for future resource needs and to ensure that practitioner resource is allocated where most needed.

In addition to simple volume information (number and types of consultation or problem), information on waiting times and cancelled or non-attended appointments can be useful in planning service provision and targeting improvement.

Prevention is better than cure – and the costs of intervention are an important factor in understanding the need for workplace improvement. Average cost per case can be estimated in relation to the cost of intervention, but additional costs such as sickness absence, costs of substitution if required, lost opportunity costs and costs of reduced quality also deserve inclusion and consideration.

## OUTCOME MEASURES

For the providers of many health-related services, clinical or client progress is seen as the most important benchmark of successful support. This is certainly of value (particularly to the client!), but practitioners should be wary that in organisational terms a successful intervention is one that promotes work function. Early return or retention in work (where possible) are desirable outcome measures for those commissioning or buying support services – a good functional outcome may be considered in terms of return to work, retention at work without recurrent problems or improved productivity.

## CONCLUSION

Good employee support doesn't happen by accident – it needs careful planning and a clear understanding of why it is being provided. Many different models of provision exist, and an understanding of organisational needs will inform the best delivery method. – often driven by simple practical considerations, such as available accommodation. Organisations are responsible for support services delivered – information on service performance and effectiveness is an important tool to ensure investment is well made.

## CASE STUDY – ROYAL MAIL

*Royal Mail has provided workplace-based employee support via its welfare service for over 50 years. Welfare advisers have been providing support to distressed colleagues with a wide range of personal issues, and since the 1980s this has extended to include a range of counselling services (see Kinder & Park, 2004). In the 1990s telephone-based employee assistance began to complement locally based services, with the service being further developed in 2006 and branded HELP (Health and emotional well-being, Employment advice, Legal and Practical assistance). This provides stressed employees on request with a broad range of advice and practical help to enable problems to be rapidly resolved. Careful evaluation (with independent research) has assessed the efficacy and value of specialised support services – such as those used to support victims of traumatic events.*

## REFERENCES

Kinder, A & Park, R. (2004). From welfare to workplace counselling. *Counselling at work, Spring*, 14–17.
Rick, J., O' Regan, S & Kinder, A. (2006). Early intervention following trauma: A controlled longitudinal study at Royal Mail Group Institute of Employment Studies. Report 435.

## CHAPTER 6

# Coaching Skills for Managers

**Gladeana McMahon**
*Association for Coaching*

## BACKGROUND

The 'coaching culture' continues to expand such that coaching is now a mainstream component part of human resource development for many organisations (Palmer & Neenan, 2001; Sommers, 2001). There are a number of definitions of coaching, but one that relates directly to managers is that coaching is:

> A process that enables learning and development to occur and thus performance to improve. To be a successful Coach requires a knowledge and understanding of process as well as the variety of styles, skills and techniques that are appropriate to the context in which the coaching takes place. (Parsloe, 1999)

Coaching is growing in popularity because of the value it adds to staff relationships and team working, as well as individual and organisational productivity. No one has yet been able to provide a globally agreed model for evaluating the return on investment (ROI) that coaching makes. However, what studies do exist demonstrate a variety of return figures. Examples include the Metrix Global Study (Anderson, 2001) and the return figures stated range from 5% to 529%. The lack of consensus and continuity in these studies leads one to question the figure but not the fact that there is a return on investment.

The Chartered Institute of Personnel and Development (CIPD) stated in their report *Coaching and Buying Coaching Services* (CIPD, 2004) that the benefits of coaching for the line manager are:

- Improved staff performance, productivity, quality and business results.
- Improved morale and employee commitment (retention).
- A support to other learning and development activities, reinforcing new ways of embedding them quickly.
- Supporting individuals through personal change (promotion).

*Employee Well-being Support: A Workplace Resource.* Edited by A. Kinder, R. Hughes and C.L. Cooper.
© 2008 John Wiley & Sons, Ltd.

- Supporting organisational change.
- Helping staff members to sort out personal issues that might affect performance at work.
- Support employees who have been promoted to cope with new responsibilities.

In addition, the Association for Coaching, one of the fastest-growing professional coaching bodies in the UK, also found a number of organisational benefits for the use of coaching skills within an organisation such as increased staff motivation and alignment to organisational values (AC, 2004).

It is now commonplace for managers to be required to take on more of a coaching role with their direct reports (Parsloe, 1999). A 'coaching culture' means moving away from the traditional control and command model, into one that encourages independent working and personal responsibility amongst employees. A coaching approach fosters a more self-directed way of working. As Redshaw states in his 2001 article, 'Do we really understand coaching? How can we make it work better?' for the *Industrial and Commercial Training Journal*:

> Coaching has enormous benefits for both organisations and for the individuals they employ. When good coaching is widespread, the whole organisation can learn new things more quickly and therefore can adapt to change more effectively. Individuals not only learn the new skills they are coached in, they also become better and proactive learners. For coaching to be effective in an organisation, a supportive climate is required; one where coaching is regarded as a normal part of managing and where greater importance is placed on learning from mistakes than on blaming people for them. This is too often overlooked by many organisations that wish to introduce coaching. Effective coaching requires that both organisations and the learning establishments that support them, adopt a more informed strategy to develop coaches and to build and maintain a climate where coaching can happen.

## WHAT ARE COACHING SKILLS?

A number of different approaches to coaching exist. Currently, these include: reflective coaching, transpersonal coaching, solution-focused coaching, cognitive-behavioural and co-active coaching. Although many individuals train as professional coaches on courses that have been university-accredited starting from basic certificated training through to that of PhD, the basic skills of coaching are now often taught to managers in the form of two- to four-day training programmes (Leimon, Moscovici & McMahon, 2005).

In the late 1980s and early 1990s, managers were often offered the opportunity of undertaking 'counselling skills' training as a way of improving communication skills within existing teams, thereby enabling the manager to deal more effectively with the people side of management.

However, the term 'counselling' was often felt to be an inappropriate one as it tended to suggest that those who would benefit were linked to the needs of a clinical population. The term 'coaching' has none of these negative connotations and is regarded as a way of helping individuals to maximise their performance. Indeed the term 'performance coaching' is now commonly used. However, it is interesting to note that the basic communication skills used in coaching, such as paraphrasing, summarising and use of body language, are taken directly from counselling skills but are usually renamed either 'coaching' or 'basic communication skills'.

One very common coaching model for helping managers develop coaching skills is that devised by Sir John Whitmore (2002) entitled the '**GROW** Model'. It provides a simple framework that can be applied by the manager:

- **Goals** – The setting of goals is intrinsic to coaching – if you do not know where you are going how will you know if you have achieved that which you set out to do? The coach asks specific questions of the individual in order to ensure that the goal is in the best interests of the individual and those with whom he/she interacts.
- **Reality** – the client needs to have a realistic grasp of where they are now, where they are starting from, and whether his or her goal is a realistic goal and can be achieved.
- **Options** – the coaching manager guides the individual in thinking of a number of ways of achieving the goal(s) and the individual decides how he or she will pursue this. Although the manager needs to manage, and no one wishes to deny the fact that there will be times when he or she has to direct an individual when using the coaching process, the manager does not aim to lead the individual but rather assist the person explore possibilities so they can decide which option is best for them. The philosophical position is that, by doing this, the individual is more likely to develop creative ways of approaching problems that can be used successfully in the future without the need to resume the coaching process. In effect, this part of the process is more akin to self-directed learning.
- **Will/Wrap-up** – the client will only achieve a goal if he or she is motivated to do so. Therefore, the manager assists the individual to look at the possible obstacles he/she may encounter and how these can be overcome. In addition, the manager helps the person consider whether there is a secondary gain to be had in the client not achieving the goal. For instance, it may be more comfortable to remain in the current position than make the effort it takes to achieve the goal he/she has in mind.

The GROW Model works because it ensures that there is nothing which might prevent the client from going for the goal. It checks whether the goal itself fits with the individual's capabilities, ambitions, personal and professional values and establishes whether the client needs to change current behaviours or requires new skills in order to successfully obtain their desired goal(s).

Although the GROW Model may seem a rather simplistic model to some, it has a number of advantages when used as a coaching skills model for managers. Whilst managers gain a number of advantages from adopting a coaching skills approach, as mentioned earlier, with their staff, they also have to do so alongside the day-to-day task of keeping the business going.

The GROW Model provides a clear structure the manager can follow. The manager is not a substitute for a professional coach and therefore there will be times when he or she will call upon such individuals to work with an employee, having recognized the needs of the individual concerned. Some individuals are unable to gain the benefit that the GROW Model offers as issues such as 'perfectionism' or 'negative thinking' may be the root cause of the presenting problem. If this is the case, then the manager may need to either employ a psychological coaching model such as cognitive behavioural coaching if he or she has the skills to do so or call upon such external coaching resources (Palmer & Neenan, 2001).

The GROW Model encourages the manager to use questions instead of commands to raise awareness and individual responsibility and can be taught in a relatively short space of time. By keeping the format simple, yet fostering this type of thinking, the model aims to synthesise ease of use with effective outcomes.

Like all models, the GROW Model has its limitations. For example, given the growth of coaching skills within the workplace it is important to evaluate the success of coaching interventions from a corporate perspective; something that the existing model fails to do.

Another model that can be used to hold the coaching process together is the Seven-Stage Problem Solving Model (Wasik, 1984).

Palmer and Neenan (2001) assert that presenting individuals with a problem-solving model to follow may seem at first glance to stifle their creativity, but thinking things through in a structured and systematic way actually encourages it. McMahon (2002) also used this model as a way of providing individuals with a structure for both professional and personal goal setting.

The seven-step problem-solving sequence and accompanying questions that people can ask themselves at each step are shown in Table 6.1. Once the person becomes adept at using the seven-step model, he/she may want to use a shorter model to quicken the problem-solving process (Palmer & Neenan, 2001). For example, **STIR** and **PIE**, as shown in Table 6.2.

**Table 6.1**  Seven-step problem-solving model

| Steps | Questions/actions |
|---|---|
| 1. Problem identification | *What is the problem/challenge?* |
| 2. Goal selection | *What do I want to achieve?* |
| 3. Generation of alternatives | *What can I do to achieve my goal?* |
| 4. Consideration of the consequences | *What are the pros and cons?* |
| 5. Decision-making | *What am I going to do?* |
| 6. Implementation | *Time to do it!* |
| 7. Evaluation | *What worked and why and do I need to amend my action plan?* |

**Table 6.2**  STIR and PIE models

| | |
|---|---|
| Select a problem | Problem definition |
| Target a solution | Implement a solution |
| Implement a solution | Evaluate outcome |
| Review outcome | |

These shorter models of problem-solving are usually used for rapid processing of a problem in order to deal with a crisis or make a quick decision. With these shorter models, deliberation is exchanged for speed, so it is possible that the person will experience a less personally or emotionally satisfactory outcome. Although these models focus on problem-solving, the manager uses his or her coaching skills to enable the individual to find his or her own solutions. These models provide the structure within which coaching can take place; however, the process is still very much one of assisting the individual to find his or her own solutions with the manager acting as a guide rather than an instructor.

The models above provide the structure for coaching to take place, and once the process is understood, the manager is then provided with the basic coaching skills that he or she requires to assist the coaching process to be effective.

The micro-skills of coaching include helping the manager develop the skills and attitudes to help an individual manage situations from within their own resources (Egan, 2004). During this stage of the training, the manager learns about the concepts of empathy, respect and genuineness.

Empathy is the ability to put oneself in the shoes of the other person, which requires the manager to be able to tentatively explore the individual's thoughts and feelings while putting aside personal thoughts and/or prejudices. In addition, by showing an understanding for the individual, this aids the person concerned to explore his or her own ideas and feelings in a safe way.

Respect is the ability to refrain from judgement of the person as an individual, regardless of the manager's personal responses to an individual's actions. If a person fears being unfairly or less favourably judged, then he or she may provide the information the manager wants to hear and not that which is actually attached to the situation in question. As a manager is involved in the appraisal of staff, this can prove a challenge for both the manager and his or her direct report. After all, the manager is making judgements about the individual's ability and there is an expectation that he/she will do so by the organization. Indeed, he or she may be responsible for providing information that could directly affect an individual's promotion prospects and/or any bonuses that may be due. For the manager to use effective coaching skills he or she needs to be clear with the individual as to the boundaries that exist between those occasions when he or she is engaging in what could be termed good management practice using coaching skills, and those occasions when a more formal direct line management approach is being used. However, if a manager is using coaching skills to assist an individual improve performance, this process is unlikely to be successful if the individual perceives the manager as being antagonistic.

Genuineness relates to the ability to remain sincere and genuine. If a manager has a reputation for breaking confidences, or speaking to others in an indiscriminate manner about individuals, it is unlikely that any protestations of assistance will be seen as genuine.

Carl Rogers was the first person to recognise that the personal attitudes of empathy, respect and genuineness (Thorne, 2003) were central to developing effective rapport.

Skills training then goes on to include the techniques of what has been termed 'active listening'. Active listening is a process whereby through using a set of micro-skills, the listener is intent on listening for meaning. The goal of active listening is to improve mutual understanding.

The micro-skills of active listening include:

- Attending (i.e. mirroring and matching the body language of the other person).
- Listening to the end of the sentence.
- Paraphrasing content (i.e. encapsulating the factual essence of what is being said and feeding this back).
- Reflecting feeling – emotion (i.e. catching the explicitly expressed or inferred emotion, for example: 'It sounds as if you were disappointed').
- Summarizing information.
- Asking for examples of what an individual has tried in order to deal with the situation or about the ways that the challenges being faced are impacting on performance.
- Using open questions (i.e. those starting with what, where, when, how and why as a way of getting an individual to expand on his/her situation and/ or thoughts or emotions).
- Minimal encouragers (i.e. the use of simple terms such as 'ah ha', 'mmm', etc. to acknowledge that information has been understood without interrupting).

In Egan's Problem Management Model (Egan 2004), there are three stages to the helping process. Stage One is termed 'Exploration' and here the manager is encouraged to allow the other person to fully expand upon his or her situation, thoughts and feelings. During this stage, the manager, using coaching skills, attempts to illicit information about the situation rather than attempting to assist the individual resolve it. Egan believes that the success of this stage lies in the ability of the individual to explore the situation while the manager facilitates this process.

Stage Two is entitled 'Understanding', during which the manager as coach uses the skills of probing and challenging to assist the individual think more deeply about what is happening. Part of the aim is to help the person look for his or her own contribution to the situation, those aspects that he or she has not explored, or those aspects that could be termed 'blind spots'.

**Table 6.3** The SMART model

| | |
|---|---|
| Specific | Ensuring that a goal is stated in specific terms (e.g. 'to make a presentation to the board at the next quarterly meeting regarding the advantages of a global strategic response') |
| Measurable | Choosing goals that can be measured (e.g. either the individual will make the presentation concerned or not) |
| Achievable | Checking to see that the goal can be achieved (i.e. can this goal be achieved in the time available or is the goal itself even achievable?) |
| Realistic | Designing goals that are within the person's ability (e.g. is this subject something the person knows about, can talk about and is within their professional scope or does the person need additional training?) |
| Time-bound | Deciding on what timeframe the goal needs to be achieved in (e.g. the date of the next quarterly board meeting) |

Stage Three is called the 'Action' stage and it is during this stage that the individual is encouraged to consider what he or she needs to do in order to change the situation and how to go about enacting such changes.

One aspect of successful coaching is ensuring that the goals set by the individual are clear and realistic and, as such, managers are often introduced to the SMART model for goal-setting (Neenan & Dryden, 2001) in order to achieve this (Table 6.3). The concept of SMART goal-setting is one taught on a variety of training courses within business and industry to assist individuals in their problem-solving efforts, and many managers are already conversant with this model when they undertake their coaching skills training.

'Behavioural contracting' is another way of achieving a clear set of outcomes that can then be measured (McMahon, 2005). A behavioural contract sees the manager asking the client what general objectives he or she may be seeking and then sets about breaking these down into a set of measurable outcomes. For example, an individual may be taking on too much work, some of which is of a non-essential nature due to his or her inability to say 'no', and may state that he or she wants to be able to be more 'assertive with others', which would be seen as an overall objective. However, this would then translate into a series of outcomes such as 'identifying mechanisms to identify non-essential pieces of work' and 'demonstrating the ability to say "no" to non-essential items'. Both of these outcomes are measurable as the mechanism for identifying non-essential pieces of work as well as identifying those situations where the individual said 'no' are observable by the individual as well as objectively by others.

## THE DIFFERENCES BETWEEN COACHING, COUNSELLING AND MENTORING

Although coaching, counselling and mentoring may share some of the same skills, such as the micro-skills of active listening, they are different in what they aim to achieve and the ways in which they do this.

## Coaching

Coaching is about improving the performance of an individual or group, not by telling but by questioning to facilitate awareness and self-directed learning. Coaching is not necessarily about fixing problems but about helping successful individuals and teams to become more so. Coaching is positive, non-judgemental, solution-focused and challenging. It aims to empower and motivate the individual. Although the structure of the process lies with the coach, the content always lies with the individual (Wilson & McMahon, 2006).

## Counselling

Counselling is aimed at helping people with emotional distress that is stopping them from being able to function as well as they would like. The types of problems that are suitable for counselling are bereavement, relationship difficulties, parenting problems, work-related issues such as bullying, stress or a general unhappiness with life and family challenges.

## Mentoring

Mentoring is a halfway point between consulting and coaching; mentors may empower and motivate, but it is not their primary role to do so. Like coaches, they provide support, but it is through imparting their own experience, knowledge and case histories to those they are mentoring (Megginson *et al.*, 2005).

## CASE STUDY

John was the branch manager of a group of 10 branches of a major high street retail organisation. He had recently taken up this appointment having spent the previous six years successfully managing a group of five branches in the north-west of England. His previous success had resulted in his recent promotion.

John was enthusiastic and his high-energy style had always served him well in the past. He came across as self-confident. However, he confided in his manager, the regional director, that he was starting to lack confidence in his ability to tackle these new challenges and his director offered to support him in his new role.

His regional manager could have chosen to mentor John by drawing on his own experiences as a manager and helping John come up with a plan of action based on these. However, he had recently completed a coaching skills training course and decided that he would use his newly acquired coaching skills to enable John to work out his own solutions. The organisation had recently made the decision to encourage a 'coaching culture' and, as such, provide an environment that was based more on encouraging individuals to find personal solutions and develop skills, awareness and individual ways of dealing with the challenges faced.

At the initial meeting, his manager helped John establish the two areas that required attention – his leadership style and his lack of change management skills. One of his stated goals was 'to identify my leadership style together with the associated strengths and weaknesses'.

Using the GROW Model his manager assisted John to recognise that whilst he perceived his style to be fairly inclusive and democratic, his new team saw him as highly directive and having little tolerance of under-performance. Although this style had worked for him in the past, it was apparent that he needed to try a more collaborative approach with his new and more experienced management team.

From discussions, it became apparent that John had received minimal training in the skills required for effective change leadership. His manager suggested that he should contact the training department who, in turn, recommended a reading list that included a number of books, articles and case studies for him to study in his own time as well as arranging for him to attend a series of management and managing change seminars.

In combining his desire to develop a more inclusive leadership style with his increasing knowledge of effective change management, he worked on a strategy for his new role. This included identifying a core team from within his group who would guide and inform the process; including both managers and clerical staff. The core team were responsible for identifying a vision for the newly structured group, communicating this within their teams, and feeding back both best practice and obstacles to the programme. In addition, in line with the organisation's desire to develop a 'coaching culture', John was also offered a place on a two-day 'introduction to coaching skills' training course as a way of providing him with the practical skills required to communicate with and encourage his team in their endeavours rather than reverting to his usual directive style of communication.

His manager met with John at first on a regular basis but on a less frequent basis as it became apparent that he was now managing his team more effectively. In addition, John sought feedback from his staff team regarding the changes he had instigated and in his personal style and received positive feedback about the enhancing effects of both. The coaching skills approach used by his regional director also strengthened their relationship which, in turn, led to a more productive way of working between them and also helped John develop a new set of skills that benefited the organisation, his staff team and the profitability of the organisation.

## SUMMARY

Coaching skills are now part of everyday corporate life, and managers from all sectors are increasingly taking on the style of a 'coaching manager' for which appropriate training is given. A number of different training models to teach coaching skills exist, some of which are philosophically at odds with each other. However, at the most basic level they are all based on 'basic coaching skills' and the techniques of active listening used within a structured framework. Managers trained in such skills have found them useful in dealing with the day-to-day issues of person management and in creating a more self-directed learning environment for staff.

## REFERENCES

AC, Association for Coaching (2004). *Guidelines for Coaching in Organisations*. London, UK: Association for Coaching.

Anderson, M. C. (2001). *Metrix Global ROI Study*. USA: Metrix Global, LLC.

CIPD (2004). *Coaching and Buying Coaching Services: A Guide*. London, UK: CIPD.

Egan, G. (2004). *The Skilled Helper: A Problem Management and Opportunity Development Approach to Helping/Skilled Helping Around the World*, 7th edn. California, USA: Wadsworth Publishing Company, USA.

Leimon, A., Moscovici, F. & McMahon, G. (2005). *Business Coaching*. Essential Coaching Skills and Knowledge Series, Eds. G. McMahon, S. Palmer & A. Leimon. London, UK: Brunner Routledge.

McMahon, G. (2002). *Confidence Works: – Learn to be Your Own Life Coach*. London, UK: Sheldon Press.

McMahon, G. (2005). *Behavioural Contracting in Organisations:, Coach the Coach*. Kent, UK: Fenman Publications.

Megginson, D., Clutterbuck, D., Garvey, B. *et al.* (2005). *Mentoring in Action: A Practical Guide for Managers*. London, UK: Kogan Page.

Neenan, M. & Dryden, W. (2001) *Life Coaching – The Cognitive-Behavioural Way*. London, UK: Brunner Routledge.

Palmer, S. & Neenan, M. (2001). Cognitive behavioural coaching. *Stress News*, **13**, July.

Parsloe, E. (1999). *The Manager as Coach and Mentor*. London, UK: CIPD.

Redshaw, B. (2001). Do we really understand coaching? How can we make it work better? *Industrial and Commercial Training Journal*, **32**, June.

Sommers, M. (2001). *Coaching in Call Centres: Summary Report*. Articles, Coaching and Mentoring Network, www.coachingnetwork.org.uk

Thorne, B. (2003). *Carl Rogers*, 2nd edn. Key Figures in Counselling and Psychotherapy, Ed. Windy Dryden. London, UK: Sage Publications.

Wasik, B. (1984). *Teaching Parents Effective Problem-Solving: A Handbook for Professionals*. Unpublished manuscript. University of North Carolina.

Whitmore, J. (2002). *Coaching for Performance: Growing People, Performance and Purpose*, 3rd edn. Boston, USA: Nicholas Beasley Publishing.

Wilson, C. & McMahon, G. (2006). What's the difference? *Training Journal*, pp. 54–57, September.

# CHAPTER 7

# Behaviour Risk Management

**Sharon Clarke**
*Manchester Business School, the University of Manchester*

The use of a risk management approach to control physical risks to the health, safety and well-being of employees is well-established. In the United Kingdom, the requirement for employers to conduct a systematic examination of hazards and identify the potential for the risks arising to cause harm is enshrined in Regulation 3 of the Management of Health and Safety at Work Regulations 1992. Similar legislation operates in other countries, for example, Australia and New Zealand have a national risk management standard (AS/NZ 4360) as well as legislation referring to specific risk assessment issues. The concept of risk assessment has become ubiquitous, at least in the British media, where reports of excessive and banal uses of risk assessment for health and safety purposes frequently appear (e.g., a local council that collected conkers from trees around schools and distributed them to the children, to avoid the slight risk of harm to the children by climbing trees to retrieve them – *Daily Express*, 10 October 2006). Although more recent, there is a growing recognition of the need to manage psychosocial hazards, that is, those aspects of the design, organisation and management of work, and their social and organisational contexts, which have the potential for causing psychological or physical harm (NIOSH, 1996; Cox & Griffiths, 1996; Cox *et al.*, 2000). However, the establishment of legislative requirements in relation to the risk assessment of psychosocial hazards is less evident. For example, whilst the European Framework Directive on Health and Safety at Work (1989) states that the employer has a duty to ensure the safety and health of workers in every aspect of their work, few European countries have developed specific legislation relating to psychosocial hazards.

The process of risk management involves the collection of information about hazards followed by an evaluation of the risks that they pose; where risks cannot be eliminated, they must be reduced to an acceptable level through risk control measures or interventions. The final step in the risk management cycle involves monitoring interventions and reviewing their effectiveness (see Figure 7.1).

*Employee Well-being Support: A Workplace Resource.* Edited by A. Kinder, R. Hughes and C.L. Cooper.
© 2008 John Wiley & Sons, Ltd.

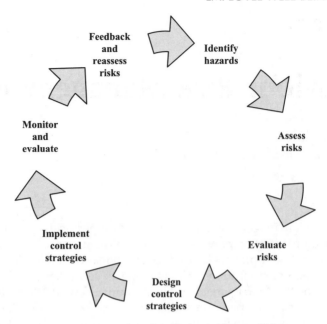

**Figure 7.1**   The risk management cycle (after Clarke & Cooper, 2004)

Occupational safety and health interventions may react to existing conditions (e.g., targeted at reducing stress symptoms, or responding to high injury
rates) or be preventive in nature (e.g., decreasing the likelihood of stress
symptoms or accidents occurring in future). Interventions may focus at an
individual level, with the objective of changing the individual employee's
behaviour, or at an organisational level, by targeting the work environment,
work design, or organisational policies and structures (see Table 7.1).
Individual-level interventions are the most commonly used measures.

This chapter will discuss the effectiveness of interventions designed to
manage the risks associated with employee behaviour, and to develop
recommendations for best practice.

## MANAGING PHYSICAL RISKS

Safety interventions designed to manage employee behaviour employ a variety
of techniques, including direct behavioural change programmes (which use
applied behavioural analysis or behaviour modification techniques), training
and education, or the enforcement of behavioural restrictions, such as procedures, rules and regulations.

Behaviour-based safety interventions use behaviour modification techniques
which aim to remove a targeted unsafe behaviour and introduce a safe one,
through the systematic use of observation, feedback and reinforcement
(e.g., observing and rewarding critical behaviours). These interventions are
most effective when the desired behaviour can be defined with some degree of

**Table 7.1** Examples of interventions

| Safety interventions | Individual-level | Organisational-level |
| --- | --- | --- |
| Reactive | Behaviour-based safety, training, rule enforcement | Rules and procedures, control and monitoring systems, ergonomics (changes to equipment, work environment or design), inspections and safety audits |
| Preventive | Health and safety training (problem-solving, hazard awareness) | Team-working, cultural change, leadership development, employee participation |
| *Stress interventions* | | |
| Reactive | Employee assistance programmes, counselling, training in coping skills | Company-wide policies on managing stress |
| Preventive | Selection procedures, health promotion, stress management training | Job redesign, employee participation, flexible working |

precision – for example, wearing personal protective equipment (PPE), such as hard hats or reflective clothing. Reviews have concluded that behavioural safety interventions which target specific behaviours, such as rule compliance, are effective if rewards are suitable and given in an appropriate manner (e.g., Sulzer-Azaroff & Austin, 2000; Fleming & Lardner, 2002; Lund & Aaro, 2004). Whilst empirical work has illustrated the success of behavioural safety programmes within manufacturing (e.g., Zohar & Fussfeld, 1981) and construction (e.g., Cooper *et al.*, 1994), recent studies have demonstrated their utility in high hazard industries, such as offshore oil production (Zhu, Wallin & Reber, 2000) and nuclear power plants (Cox, Jones & Rycraft, 2004). However, whilst the short-term effects can be spectacular, the long-term effectiveness of behavioural safety programmes is less certain, and depends on the cultural context within which the programme is being implemented (Glendon, Clarke & McKenna, 2006). DePasquale and Geller (1999) highlighted the important role played by the visible commitment of managers and supervisors and, in particular, managerial support for the provision of the necessary time for observations and analysis of results, in addition to a commitment to implementing changes recommended by the programme, such as environmental conditions or procedures. The study also found that programmes were more successful when workers trusted that managers were capable of supporting the process (with beliefs in managers being well-intentioned having no effect). Hopkins (2006) identifies the focus on 'mono-causality' as one of the main reasons why behavioural safety programmes may prove ineffective; that is, observers are restricted to the focus on managing worker behaviours, and are not supported in reporting unsafe conditions or hazards. DeJoy (2005) describes the behavioural change approach to workplace safety as a 'bubble up' effect, where changing the behaviour of workers on the 'front line' can lead to cultural change within the organisation. The success of such approaches depends on managers sending appropriate messages to workers (i.e., that they are interested in their welfare and genuinely committed to improving safety) and also the effective communication of information from workforce to management. Given these factors, DeJoy (2005) proposed that behavioural change programmes should not be used in isolation, but in combination with wider safety management systems. Thus, managing behavioural risk through the direct manipulation of employee behaviour is most effective in combination with managerial support and commitment, and changes to work design or environment.

Training is used to reduce behavioural risks through the improvement of employees' safety knowledge, skills and values, recognition and awareness of hazards, problem-solving and decision-making skills (Burke & Sarpy, 2003). There is evidence that the effective use of safety training (i.e., adequate training on a regular basis) is successful in lowering injury rates (Shannon, Mayr & Haines, 1997). However, Wright and Geary (2001) noted that safety training may be too narrowly focused on current jobs, rather than developing people's broader capabilities, such as identifying and evaluating hazards on a day-to-day basis. Colligan and Cohen (2004) emphasised that when used as an isolated intervention to control risk, training success will depend on management commitment to providing a safe work environment. If training is received in procedures that are impossible to implement due to inadequate equipment, resources or supervisory commitment, then employees may view training as an unsatisfactory substitute for investing in newer and safer equipment or machinery, or as a measure that focuses on the worker's contribution to accidents, rather than situational factors. Thus, it is important to be concerned not only with training individuals, but also to ensure that the organisational environment within which those individuals operate is consistent with training provision.

At an individual level, safety interventions may also focus on the strict enforcement of existing rules and procedures or the implementation of new ones, i.e., attempting to manage behaviour through administrative controls (Reason, Parker & Lawton, 1998). However, safety rule infringements are not usually acts of deliberate risk-taking, but shortcuts designed to make work more efficient, quicker, or easier (Reason, Parker & Free, 1994). As employees are not usually able to assess the impact of breaking rules on the system as a whole, and because there may be no obvious or immediate negative consequences, their actions are often reinforced. In addition, rules and procedures designed to ensure safe behaviour are not always appropriate. For example, workers on the North Sea oil-rig, *Piper Alpha*, had been instructed never to jump from the side of the platform in the event of an emergency, but to await rescue by helicopter. However, during an emergency on the rig (which led to its destruction), those who ignored these instructions survived, while those who followed the rules perished in the fire, as the clouds of smoke prevented the rescue helicopter from landing (Cullen, 1990). Correct rule violations, that is, breaking a rule because an immediate hazard assessment indicates that the rule is inappropriate, demand that individuals are given latitude to make decisions. To do so, they must be appropriately trained and empowered to assess and evaluate hazards accurately. However, the purpose of training is often to enhance worker knowledge in order to comply with safety rules and regulations, rather than equipping workers with sufficient knowledge and skills regarding the system so that they can develop an understanding that is accurate enough to enable a competent level of hazard evaluation.

A limitation of individual-level safety interventions is that behavioural risks are considered in isolation from the organisational and social context. Research has demonstrated that the level of employee support from the organisation, managers, supervisors and co-workers has a significant impact on the success of safety interventions. Social support (from supervisors and co-workers) is associated with lower injury rates in manufacturing workers (Iverson & Erwin, 1997) and hospital nurses (Hemingway & Smith, 1999). In a longitudinal study of manufacturing employees, Parker, Axtell and Turner (2001) found that supportive supervision had a lagged positive effect on safe working 18 months later. Therefore, there is consistent evidence of a significant relationship between social support and occupational safety, suggesting that social support encourages safer working and reduces the number of occupational injuries experienced by workers. Further research has found that high perceived organisational support was predictive of reduced injury and accident rates (Hofmann & Morgeson, 1999; Wallace, Popp & Mondore, 2006). Oliver *et al.* (2002) demonstrated that supervisory and co-worker support not only had significant direct effects on injuries, but also significant indirect effects, mediated by general health and safe behaviour. These findings suggest that social support may reduce injuries by two means – directly by facilitating safe behaviour, and indirectly by buffering workers from psychological strain, thereby protecting their mental well-being. Thus, the degree of support from co-workers, supervisors and managers has a significant effect on occupational safety, demonstrating the importance of considering the social context of risk management activities.

Many interventions within the tradition of behavioural risk management take a control orientation, where emphasis is placed on identifying behaviours which pose a risk of physical or psychological harm, and instituting control measures. An enhanced risk management cycle, which incorporates a commitment orientation, would involve not only risk assessment and monitoring of performance, but also developing strategies that enhance worker commitment. High-commitment management creates conditions that encourage workers to identify with organisational goals (such as prioritising safety) and to expend extra effort to achieve them (for example, engaging in safety-related citizenship behaviours). This approach avoids the over-reliance on compliance by means of rules, regulations, and monitoring to minimise injuries (Whitener, 2001). The findings of Vredenburgh (2002) provide support for combining control and commitment-oriented practices in relation to safety; the study found that the emphasis on control-oriented activities alone was associated with increased injuries, whilst a combination of control-oriented and more preventive measures (selection and training) was associated with reduced injuries. Thus, an integrated approach, combining traditional risk management techniques with high commitment strategies, will lead to more effective safety interventions.

## Recommendations for Best Practice

- Avoid using behaviour-based safety interventions in isolation, but use within a broader safety management system;
- Provide adequate information and consult with personnel before the introduction of any intervention programme to ensure that participants feel involved and to demonstrate the commitment of all parties, particularly senior management;
- Ensure that there are adequate resources allocated to the programme, not only in terms of financial support, but also time and commitment;
- Enhance communication systems to ensure a good flow of information regarding the purpose of the intervention and to gather feedback on its implementation;
- Monitor the ongoing effectiveness of the intervention and take measures to ensure its continued impact;
- Capitalise on the increased awareness of safety issues in the workforce by introducing measures that allow further participation and involvement and so increase employee commitment.

## MANAGING PSYCHOSOCIAL RISKS

The majority of stress interventions are targeted at an individual level, with the aim of changing employee behaviour through enhancing stress management and coping skills (e.g., programmes that encourage more healthy lifestyles or provide education on coping strategies) or mitigating stress symptoms (e.g., programmes that help individuals to cope with their anxiety through counselling). This is particularly evident within the United States, although in Europe and Scandinavia organisational level interventions are more widely found (Geurts & Grundemann, 1999). In a comprehensive review, Giga, Faragher and Cooper (2003) found that the most widely used individual-level techniques were cognitive behaviour therapy (CBT) and relaxation (each featuring in 30% of interventions), whilst training and education were used in 15–20% of interventions and selection featured in only 1% of intervention programmes. Thus, whilst interventions that involve preventive action may be targeted at individuals (e.g., health promotion programmes, selection and placement), these tend to be underutilised.

There is consistent evidence that changing employee behaviour in relation to stress can have positive effects, e.g., an improved lifestyle can feed back into the stress process by boosting individuals' resistance to stress, and counselling can improve workers' psychological well-being by increasing their confidence and self-esteem (Berridge, Cooper & Highley-Marchington, 1997). However, whilst stress management activities have a moderate effect in temporarily reducing the stress symptoms experienced, these positive effects tend to diminish over time (Cooper, Liukkonen & Cartwright, 1996; Murphy, 1988). Research has suggested that individual-level techniques may be more successful in combination with measures that take the social and organisational context into account. For example, support groups have been successfully combined with CBT and relaxation, evaluation studies indicating that in addition to reducing stress symptoms, participants' support-seeking skills and adequacy of coping also improved (Elliot & Maples, 1991; Lees & Ellis, 1990; McCue & Sachs, 1991). In combination with preventive interventions, such as work redesign, training and communication, long-term maintenance of low levels of stress has been reported (Griffin, Hart & Wilson-Evered, 2000; Kalimo & Toppinen, 1999). For example, Kalimo and Toppinen (1999) examined work- and health-related factors over a 10-year period for 11,000 forestry industry workers who participated in a stress intervention programme involving work redesign, training and co-worker support groups. The study found that a majority of staff rated their psychological working capacity as good and that stress remained low.

The traditional approach to behavioural risk management is to identify and manage those factors which increase the risk of physical or psychological harm (risk factors). An alternative perspective, in keeping with the movement towards a more 'positive psychology', is to focus on the identification of protective factors, which develop resilience to stress and promote safe working. The underlying philosophy is that 'strength-based' developmental models should increasingly supplant 'deficit-based' models of human functioning. In relation to stress interventions, protective factors are those individual characteristics and environmental conditions that can moderate an individual's vulnerability to stress, e.g., positive self-evaluations, optimism, feeling of being in control, and social support from co-workers. Risk management interventions would consider each individual's balance sheet, in terms of risk factors versus protective factors, and design a programme which targets those individuals with a negative stress balance by aiming to reduce the number of risk factors and to promote protective factors for them. Whilst such an approach takes a more positive view of the individual, there is a danger that the focus may remain at the individual level, rather than assessing the social and organisational context. However, on the other hand, the emphasis on protective factors encourages a preventive approach to managing risks, rather than a reactive one. For example, training can be used as a reactive measure to refresh knowledge of rules and encourage compliance, but it can be more effective as a preventive measure, by focusing on developing 'protective' skills, such as the ability to recognise, assess and evaluate workplace hazards.

## Recommendations for Best Practice

- Avoid a 'fire-fighting' approach to managing occupational stress, that is, implementing measures that only deal with stress symptoms that have already occurred;
- Reactive measures are best used in conjunction with preventive measures that aim to build resilience to stress, e.g., health promotion, stress management skills, etc.;
- Consider how risk factors may be managed at source – organisational-level interventions may provide more cost-effective benefits in the long-term.

## CONCLUSIONS

The risk management approach has led to the predominance of control-oriented measures that aim to reduce risks through a focus on changing individual behaviour. However, this chapter has demonstrated that such measures, particularly when used in isolation, are not always the most effective means of managing physical or psychosocial risks. Table 7.2 illustrates an

**Table 7.2**   Example of a safety intervention programme

|         | Intervention |
| --- | --- |
| Level 1 | |
| 1.1 | Statement of intent from senior manager/director |
| 1.2 | Ongoing feedback from management to employees |
| 1.3 | Accurate communication systems |
| 1.4 | Near-miss reporting system |
| 1.5 | Analysis of training needs |
| 1.6 | Sanction and reward scheme |
| 1.7 | Communication and safety committees |
| Level 2 | |
| 2.1 | Action planning for leaders |
| 2.2 | Developing employee team-work |
| 2.3 | Employee involvement |
| 2.4 | Integrating safety into appraisals |
| 2.5 | Feedback communication |
| 2.4 | Training |
| 2.5 | Job design and hazard analysis |
| Level 3 | |
| 3.1 | Leadership workshops |
| 3.2 | Management education sessions |
| 3.3 | Management safety review tool |
| 3.4 | Well-being programme |
| 3.5 | Health and safety appraisal system |
| 3.6 | Behaviour modification programme |

*Source*: Specialist Training and Consultancy Services, Ltd, in conjunction with the University of Manchester (see www.specialisttraining.co.uk)

example of a safety intervention programme designed across a number of different levels, where each level reflects the degree of provision already provided within the company. The intervention programme combines individual and organisational measures, and is intended to be preventive rather than reactive. Interventions at Level 1 are designed to enhance safety through the implementation of systems to increase the flow of safety information, e.g., feedback systems from managers to employees (such as safety bulletins) or a near-miss reporting system. At Level 2, interventions are designed to integrate preventive measures into the organisation, e.g., inclusion of safety criteria within staff appraisals or facilitating the use of safety action planning. At Level 3, amongst other measures, a behavioural change programme is included. However, this intervention would be implemented within the context of improved communication, information flow and commitment from managers and employees achieved at Levels 1 and 2. Thus, the success of managing behavioural risk using an individual-based intervention is maximised by first considering the social and organisational context. In addition, behavioural risk is considered not only at the level of the workforce, but also at a managerial level, with the inclusion of leadership workshops and management education sessions. A company participating in the intervention programme would undergo a safety audit to identify existing areas in need of improvement. A tailored package of interventions would then be implemented and the effects on safety outcomes monitored.

There has tended to be a division between interventions aimed at different types of risk, that is, initiatives designed to manage occupational stress and to enhance workplace safety are considered separately. Yet, research has demonstrated the links between these two areas. For example, Goldenhar, Williams and Swanson (2003) found that occupational stressors (job demands, job control and responsibility for others' safety) had significant direct effects on near-accidents and, in addition, responsibility for others' safety also had a direct effect on injuries; these effects were partially mediated by psychological (tension, depression and anger) and physical (nausea, headaches, insomnia and back pain) symptoms. In addition, Oliver et al. (2002) found that the effect of 'organisational involvement' (including aspects of supervisory and co-worker support, as well as safety management) on work injuries was partially mediated by general health (measures of anxiety and depression). Thus, interventions should be designed with due regard to their potential impact on both safety and health-related outcomes, rather than in isolation. Specific interventions such as bonus pay, sensitivity training for supervisors, or provision of on-site exercise facilities tend to affect single outcomes, such as satisfaction with pay, supervision or stress, respectively (Morrow & Crum, 1998). However, safety interventions tend to have wider implications, affecting a broad range of outcomes, such as improved job satisfaction (Goldenhar et al., 2003) and stress interventions, such as health promotion programmes, have led to reductions in injury rates (Mearns, Whitaker & Flin, 2003; Shannon et al. 1997). However, there is little recognition of the wider impacts that intervention programmes can achieve if effectively managed to encompass the health, safety and well-being of employees (Clarke & Cooper, 2004).

## REFERENCES

Berridge, J., Cooper, C. L. & Highley-Marchington, C. (1997). *Employee Assistance Programmes and Workplace Counselling*. Chichester: John Wiley & Sons, Ltd.

Burke, M. J. & Sarpy, S. A. (2003). Improving worker safety and health through interventions. In D. A. Hofmann & L. E. Tetrick (Eds.), *Health and Safety in Organizations: A Multilevel Perspective*, pp. 56–90). San Francisco: Jossey-Bass.

Clarke, S. & Cooper, C. L. (2004). *Managing the Risk of Workplace Stress: Health and Safety Hazards*. London: Routledge.

Colligan, M. J. & Cohen, A. (2004). The role of training in promoting workplace safety and health. In J. Barling & M. R. Frone (Eds.), *The Psychology of Workplace Safety*, pp. 223–248. Washington, DC: American Psychological Association.

Cooper, C. L., Liukkonen, P. & Cartwright, S. (1996). Stress Prevention in the Workplace: Assessing the costs and benefits to organizations. European Foundation for the Improvement of Living and Working Conditions. Luxembourg: Office for Official Publications of the European Communities.

Cooper, M. D., Phillips, R. A., Sutherland, V. J. & Makin, P. J. (1994). Reducing accidents using goal setting and feedback: A field study. *Journal of Occupational and Organisational Psychology*, **67**:219–240.

Cox, S., Jones, B. & Rycraft, H. (2004). Behavioural approaches to safety management within UK reactor plants. *Safety Science*, **42**:825–839.

Cox, T. & Griffiths, A. (1996). Assessment of psychosocial hazards at work. In M. J. Schabracq, J. A. M. Winnubst & C. L. Cooper (Eds.), *Handbook of Work and Health Psychology*, pp. 127–143. New York: John Wiley& Sons, Inc.

Cox, T., Griffiths, A., Barlowe, C. *et al.* (2000). *Organizational Interventions for Work Stress: A Risk Management Approach*. Sudbury: HSE Books.

Cullen, W. D. (1990). *Report of the Official Inquiry into the Piper Alpha Disaster*. London: HMSO.

DeJoy, D. (2005). Behavior change versus culture change: Divergent approaches to managing workplace safety. *Safety Science*, **43**:105–129.

DePasquale, J. P. & Geller, E. S. (1999). Critical success factors for behaviour-based safety: A study of twenty industry-wide applications. *Journal of Safety Research*, **30**:237–249.

Elliot, T. R. & Maples, S. (1991) Stress management training for employees experiencing corporate acquisition. *Journal of Employment Counselling*, **28**:107–114.

European Framework Directive on Health and Safety at Work (1989). Council Directive 89/391/EEC of 12 June 1989 on the introduction of measures to encourage improvements in the safety and health of workers at work. Official Journal No. L183, pp. 1–8.

Fleming, M. & Lardner, R. (2002). Strategies to promote safe behaviour as part of a health and safety management system. Contract Research Report 430/2002 for the Health & Safety Executive. Sudbury: HSE Books.

Geurts, S. & Grundemann, R. (1999). Workplace stress and stress prevention in Europe. In M. Kompier & C. Cooper (Eds.), *Preventing Stress, Improving Productivity: European Case Studies in the Workplace*. London: Routledge.

Giga, S., Faragher, B. & Cooper, C. L. (2003). Part 1: Identification of good practice in stress prevention/management. In J. Jordan, E. Gurr, G. Tinline *et al.* (Eds.), *Beacons of Excellence in Stress Prevention.*, pp. 1–45. HSE research report no. 133. Sudbury: HSE Books.

Glendon, A. I., Clarke, S. G. & McKenna, E. (2006). *Human Safety and Risk Management*, 2nd edn. Boca Raton, Florida: CRC Press.

Goldenhar, L. M., Williams, L. J. & Swanson, N. G. (2003). Modelling relationships between job stressors and injury and near-miss outcomes for construction laborers. *Work and Stress*, **17**:218–240.

Griffin, M. A., Hart, P. M. & Wilson-Evered, E. (2000). Using employee opinion surveys to improve organizational health. In L. R. Murphy & C. L. Cooper (Eds.), *Healthy and Productive Work: An International Perspective*, pp. 15–36. London: Taylor & Francis.

Hemingway, M. & Smith, C. S. (1999). Organizational climate and occupational stressors as predictors of withdrawal behaviors and injuries in nurses. *Journal of Occupational and Organizational Psychology*, **72**:285–299.

Hofmann, D. A. & Morgeson, F. P. (1999). Safety-related behavior as a social exchange: The role of perceived organizational support and leader-member exchange. *Journal of Applied Psychology*, **84**:286–296.

Hopkins, A. (2006). What are we to make of safe behaviour programs? *Safety Science*, **44**:583–597.

Iverson, R. D. & Erwin, P. J. (1997). Predicting occupational injury: The role of affectivity. *Journal of Occupational and Organizational Psychology*, **70**:113–128.

Kalimo, R. & Toppinen, S. (1999). Finland: Organizational well-being. Ten years of research and development in a forest industry corporation. In M. Kompier & C. L. Cooper (Eds.), *Preventing Stress, Improving Productivity: European Case Studies in the Workplace*, pp. 52–85. London: Routledge.

Lees, S. and Ellis, N. (1990) The design of a stress-management programme for nursing personnel. *Journal of Advanced Nursing*, **15**:946–961.

Lund, J. & Aaro, L. E. (2004). Accident prevention: Presentation of a model placing emphasis on human, structural and cultural factors. *Safety Science*, **42**:271–324.

McCue, J. D. and Sachs, C. L. (1991) A stress management workshop improves residents' coping skills. *Archives of International Medicine*, **151**:2273–2277.

Mearns, K., Whitaker, S. M. & Flin, R. (2003). Safety climate, safety management practice and safety performance in offshore environments. *Safety Science*, **41**:641–680.

Morrow, P. C. & Crum, M. R. (1998). The effects of perceived and objective safety risk on employee outcomes. *Journal of Vocational Behaviour*, **53**:300–313.

Murphy, L. R. (1988). Workplace interventions for stress reduction and prevention. In C. L. Cooper & R. Payne (Eds.), *Causes, Coping and Consequences of Stress At Work*, pp. 301–339. New York: John Wiley & Sons, Inc.

NIOSH, National Institute of Occupational Safety and Health (1996). *National Occupational Research Agenda (NORA)*. Cincinnati, OH: National Institute of Occupational Safety and Health. Available at: www.cdc.gov/niosh/nora.html.

Oliver, A., Cheyne, A., Tomás, J. M. & Cox, S. (2002). The effects of organizational and individual factors on occupational accidents. *Journal of Occupational and Organizational Psychology*, **75**:473–488.

Parker, S. K., Axtell, C. M. & Turner, N. (2001). Designing a safer workplace: Importance of job autonomy, communication quality and supportive supervisors. *Journal of Occupational Health Psychology*, **6**:211–218.

Reason, J. T., Parker, D. & Free, R. (1994). *Bending the Rules: The Varieties, Origins and Management of Safety Violations*. Leiden, The Netherlands: Rijks Universiteit Leiden.

Reason, J. T., Parker, D. & Lawton, R. (1998). Organizational controls and safety: The varieties of rule-related behaviour. *Journal of Occupational and Organizational Psychology*, **71**:289–304.

Shannon, H. S., Mayr, J. & Haines, T. (1997). Overview of the relationship between organizational and workplace factors and injury rates. *Safety Science*, **26**:201–217.

Sulzer-Azaroff, B. & Austin, J. (2000). Does BBS work? *Professional Safety*, **45**:19–24.

Vredenburgh, A. G. (2002). Organizational safety: Which management practices are most effective in reducing employee injury rates? *Journal of Safety Research*, **33**: 259–276.

Wallace, J. C., Popp, E. & Mondore, S. (2006). Safety climate as a mediator between foundation climates and occupational accidents: A group-level investigation. *Journal of Applied Psychology*, **91**:681–688.

Whitener, E. M. (2001). Do 'high commitment' human resource practices affect employee commitment? A cross-level analysis using hierarchical linear modeling. *Journal of Management*, **27**:515–535.

Wright, P. M. & Geary, G. (2001). Changing the mindset: The training myth and the need for world class performance. *International Journal of Human Resource Management*, **12**:586–600.

Zhu, Z., Wallin, J. A. & Reber, R. (2000). Safety improvements: An application of behavior modification techniques. *Journal of Applied Management Studies*, **9**:135–140.

Zohar, D. & Fussfeld, N. (1981) A systems approach to organisational behavior modification: Theoretical considerations and empirical evidence. *International Review of Applied Psychology*, **30**:491–505.

# CHAPTER 8

# Positive Coping Strategies at Work

**Philip Dewe**
*Department of Organisational Psychology, Birkbeck, University of London*

Research on coping with work stress has, over the last 40 years, been the subject of numerous books and articles. While this sustained interest could be explained in terms of the topic developing a popular momentum all of its own simply because exploring how people cope is in itself appealing, it is more likely to reflect the view that the better we understand coping the better we can understand work stress and how to deal with it. Coping is the fundamental part of the stress equation. It must, as Zeidner and Saklofske (1996) suggest, be thought of as something more than simple adjustment because it lies at the very heart of individual growth and development. Coping has an immediate personal relevance for us all and this chapter explores the role of positive coping in dealing with work stress. However, coping research has not been without its controversies and in order to understand the role of positive coping at work we need to first explore what we mean by coping, the different ways in which coping strategies have been classified, the emergence of positive coping, how coping effectiveness is judged and what all this means for organisations and organisational interventions.

## WHAT DO WE MEAN WHEN WE USE THE TERM COPING?

The first step towards understanding positive coping is to consider what it is we mean when we talk about coping. Defining what we mean by coping is not without its difficulties. To describe something as coping assumes that we have some knowledge of what a person is thinking or doing. It is therefore important to think of coping as a process as part of the way the individual transacts with the environment and so coping is generally defined as 'the cognitive and behavioural effort a person makes to manage demands that tax or exceed

*Employee Well-being Support: A Workplace Resource.* Edited by A. Kinder, R. Hughes and C.L. Cooper.
© 2008 John Wiley & Sons, Ltd.

personal resources' (Lazarus, 1991:5). Put simply coping is the effort required to manage stress (Lazarus, 2001). It is a dynamic and unfolding process. A brief account of Lazarus's view follows. Two aspects of his theory are crucial when thinking about coping: how it should be defined and the processes that take place in a stressful encounter. The first is that in any stressful transaction the individual makes an appraisal that the situation is demanding and represents, in terms of well-being, some sort of threat, harm/loss or challenge. It is the appraisal that something of significance is at stake. Threat refers to some anticipated demand, harm/loss to some demand that has already occurred and challenge to the opportunity for achievement and personal development.

The second appraisal is the recognition that something has to be done about it and so individual coping options and resources are considered for dealing with those demands (see Lazarus, 1991). Resources and options generally refer to those social, economic, organisational and personal characteristics that can be drawn on to aid coping, and so, stressful encounters are all about the balance between the demands of the situation and the individual's resources for dealing with them. Coping then involves purpose, effort and planning; is present- and future-focused and is consciously set within the context of a demanding event. Perhaps what we are beginning to see emerge from the stress literature are attempts to broaden what we understand by coping to now include both negative and positive appraisals (Lazarus, 1991), the depletion and the accumulation of coping resources (Hobfoll, 2001), and a 'time perspective' that gives as much emphasis to positive (proactive) coping as has traditionally been given to reactive coping (Schwarzer, 2001). Many of these issues are, of course, intensely debated and while agreement has yet to be reached as to how exactly coping should best be defined (Aldwin, 2000) when coping is considered in relation to many of these issues then attention, inevitably, is drawn to the nature of coping and the functions it is supposed to perform.

A second step in developing our understanding of positive coping is to consider just what it is that coping strategies actually do. Many attempts have been made to classify the different functions that coping strategies play. By far the most well known is the distinction first made by Lazarus and Folkman (1984) between *problem-focused* and *emotion-focused* coping. Problem-focused coping best describes direct action involving rational task-oriented behaviors (e.g. consider a range of plans for handling the situation; set priorities; stand back and try and rationalise the situation; find out more about the situation; seek out additional information) aimed at the source of stress. Emotion-focused strategies on the other hand are aimed at the emotional discomfort accompanying a stressful encounter. Emotion-focused strategies include, for example, emotional relief (e.g. express your irritation to other work colleagues just to be able to let off steam), distracting activities (e.g. leave your desk and go to another part of the office for a while), getting support from work colleagues (e.g. draw on support from your boss and discuss the problem), family and friends (leave the problem and try and resolve it later by talking it through at home), and passive attempts to tolerate, and preparing to deal with the situation (e.g. do nothing and carry on as usual). Building on this problem-focused–emotion-focused distinction, Latack and Havlovic (1992) have suggested that any attempt to distinguish between the function coping strategies play must take into account not just the *focus* of different strategies (i.e. problem/emotion) but also their *form* (i.e. cognitive-thoughts/behaviors). These two examples aside it is clear from the literature (Dewe & Cooper, 2007) that researchers have used a variety of terms to describe coping functions including control, escape, management, instrumental, active, preventative, passive, palliative, approach, avoidance and existential.

Despite this array of terms and the fact that many of them have a problem/emotion-focused quality about them, there is still little agreement as to what is the best template to use when describing the functions coping strategies play. What is even more significant in the context of this chapter is to note that describing the functions coping strategies play is qualitatively different from describing how effective they are or whether they represent a positive or some other form of coping. To evaluate coping, effectiveness or the positive impact of coping must be considered in relation to other factors including the context within which the coping occurs, how and when coping strategies are used, what is trying to be achieved and who is making the evaluation. It is important to establish at this stage that describing coping functions should not be confused with whether they are effective or positive. This is a more complex distinction as noted above. Yet with this caution in mind it is possible to explore forms of coping that have the potential to improve the quality of life, develop a sense of self worth, mobilise self-confidence and promote better health (Greenglass, 2002; Schwarzer, 2004).

## FROM REACTIVE TO PROACTIVE COPING

It is important, when thinking about what may constitute positive coping and its qualities, to have a context within which to judge such ideas. There is every reason to believe that the emphasis on positive coping, best illustrated perhaps, by proactive coping, grew out of two recent developments. The first is the rise in what is described as the positive psychology movement (Seligman & Csikszentmihalyi, 2000) where the emphasis is on the positive experience, the search for positive human functioning and those factors that allow individuals to flourish and which enrich the quality of individual lives (Fredrickson, 2001). This movement has also drawn attention to what has been described as the underrepresented 'other side of coping' (Folkman & Moskowitz, 2000:647), that is its positive affect, and the role of positive emotions such as pride, joy, happiness and contentment (Fredrickson, 1998) and the adaptational importance of coping in helping to produce these kinds of emotions. While the idea of a positive psychological movement is robustly debated (Lazarus, 2003) such a discussion has motivated researchers to think more broadly about the nature of coping and the positive ways in which it can sustain individuals during stressful encounters.

The second development that has contributed to the growing interest in positive coping has grown out of the work of Hobfoll (2001) and his resource-based theory of coping. The basic tenet of Hobfoll's (2001) conservation of resource theory is, in brief, that stress occurs when there is, for the individual, a threat that resources will be lost, are lost or there is a failure to regain resources after they have been invested. The importance of Hobfoll's theory is that it points to both resource depletion as well as resource accumulation. It is this latter idea of resource accumulation that is a 'highly attractive concept' (Schwarzer, 2001:403) that enriches and broadens our understanding of coping because resources empower individuals to more effectively cope (Greenglass, 2002). This idea that resources energise individuals and build up their capacity to cope provides the opportunity for researchers to consider the positive benefits of how resources are developed and nurtured and how they can be put to best use. From these two developments – a positive psychology and the conservation of resources – it is possible to identify what may well reflect the basic qualities of positive coping.

These qualities would include:

(a) the appraising of events that produce positive meanings that develop and sustain positive emotions,
(b) strategies that are forward-looking and which contribute to the accumulation of resources and personal growth, and
(c) positive emotions themselves that 'broaden an individual's thought and action repertoire and thereby build the individual's enduring personal resources' (Fredrickson, 2001:219).

There is no mutual exclusivity about these qualities; each depends on the other and all should be viewed as part of the transaction between the individual and the environment. It is also important to recognise that the growing emphasis on positive coping is not an argument for ignoring the more traditional approach where coping is viewed more in terms of dealing with or reacting to events that have already occurred. As we shall see, determining how a coping strategy is used and its affect is no easy matter. Both approaches aid our understanding of the impact of coping and the current emphasis on positive coping may, as Folkman and Moskowitz suggest, 'be indicative of a catch-up phase for an area that has been under-emphasised in recent years' (2003:121).

If the qualities outlined above reflect positive coping and if the 'prototype' of positive coping is proactive coping (Schwarzer & Knoll, 2003) then it is time to explore proactive coping in more detail. By drawing attention to the time element in the stress process, Schwarzer (2001, 2004) distinguishes proactive coping from other forms of coping on the basis that it is forward-looking and oriented more towards the future. In this way proactive coping can be defined as 'an effort to build up general resources that facilitate promotion toward challenging goals and personal growth' (Schwarzer, 2001:406). Two other qualities distinguish proactive coping from other forms of coping. The first is that proactive coping is regarded as 'goal management' rather than 'risk management', while the second is that proactive coping is motivated by the desire to meet the challenges of goal attainment (Greenglass, 2001, 2002). In this way proactive coping is all about developing an action plan that facilitates the promotion of challenging goals and creates opportunities for personal development. In contrast (see Schwarzer, 2001, 2004) other forms of coping are more oriented towards 'risk management' in that they are aimed at dealing with a situation that has happened (*reactive coping*), dealing with an impending demand (*anticipatory coping*) and preparing to deal with possible demands (*preventative coping*).

Schwarzer describes the proactive coper as one who 'strives for improvement of work or life and builds up resources that assure progress and quality of functioning' (2001:406). The positive nature of proactive coping is reinforced by the fact that demanding situations are appraised in terms of personal challenges (Schwarzer & Knoll, 2003) where coping, as mentioned, becomes more about goal management than risk management. But what does proactive coping involve? Building on Schwarzer's (1999) proactive coping theory, Greenglass (2002) describes the development of the Proactive Coping Inventory (PCI) to assess different dimensions of a proactive approach to coping. The seven subscales of the PCI can be viewed via the on-line publication available at http://userpage.fu-berlin.de/~health/greenpci.htm (Greenglass, 2001; Greenglass, Schwarzer & Taubert, 1996). In order to illustrate what proactive coping entails the emphasis here is on the 14-item Proactive Coping Scale that 'combines autonomous goal setting with self-regulatory goal attainment cognitions and behaviours' (Greenglass, Fiksenbaum & Eaton, 2006:16). Such coping involves, for example, 'When I experience a problem, I take the initiative in resolving it', 'After attaining a goal, I look for another, more challenging one', 'I turn obstacles into positive experiences', 'I try to pinpoint what I need to succeed' and 'I visualise my dreams and try to achieve them.'

It is also worth, at this stage, returning to one of the other coping strategies mentioned above – *preventive coping* – as it too seems to reflect coping activities (e.g. skill development, resource accumulation, capacity-building) that have a proactive element, although as Schwarzer and Taubert (2002) point out, the motivation to use this type of coping will be different, depending on whether it results from demands that are appraised as challenging, versus those that are appraised as threatening. It is interesting to speculate if preventive coping is all about building up general resistance; whether techniques such as exercise, relaxation, meditation and a balanced approach to life would qualify as proactive coping. If such strategies are used to develop an inner sense of energy, self-awareness and well-being and in doing so develop a greater capacity for managing stress and meeting challenges, then a strong case can be made for including them under the general rubric of proactive coping.

It is important to return to two other aspects of the stress process – appraisal and emotions – and to consider how they too contribute to positive coping. The significance of any demanding encounter is determined by the way in which an individual appraises those demands and gives meaning to what is at stake. The meaning an individual gives to any encounter is the most powerful influence on the sort of coping that occurs and the positive outcomes that may follow. In terms of the meanings individuals give to any encounter, Lazarus (2001), for example, talks about the positive aspects of appraisals not just when the encounter is appraised as challenging but also when it is appraised in terms of the potential benefit(s) that may flow from it. So, positive appraisals include both identifying challenges and finding benefit. Because positive coping leads to positive emotions it is also important to consider the 'broad and build' (Fredrickson, 1998:315) qualities that flow from experiencing positive emotions. Positive emotions such as joy and pride have qualities that prompt individuals to pursue a wider range of thoughts and actions that help to build personal resources that 'serve as reserves to be drawn on later, to improve coping' (Fredrickson & Branigan, 2005:315). Positive emotions also, in terms of their 'broad and build' qualities, have the potential to undo or correct the lingering effects of negative emotions, build resiliency and enhance subsequent well-being (Fredrickson, 2001). The experience of positive emotions seems to be one where they act as 'vehicles for individual growth and social connection' (Fredrickson, 2001:224).

By now a picture of positive coping is beginning to emerge. It involves a number of not mutually exclusive elements. These would include positive appraisals of events that involve meeting challenges and searching for the benefits that may emerge in terms of personal growth and development. Coupled with this are coping strategies that, more often than not, are forward-looking and involve taking the initiative, accepting the challenge, turning events into a positive experience, developing and accumulating resources and taking time to build an inner sense of awareness and well-being. Such strategies are associated with positive emotions that have a dual quality where, in contrast to negative emotions (e. g. tension; anxiety), they not only broaden the range of thoughts and actions that individuals take, helping to expand possible alternatives and motivating the drive for creative solutions, but also they help to build a variety of 'enduring personal resources' that 'fuel resilience' (Fredrickson, 2001:219).

If all these elements reflect proactive coping can other forms of coping such as problem-focused and emotion-focused coping also produce positive results? The answer is that of course they can. However, determining whether any coping strategy is positive is not as straightforward as perhaps one would imagine even though proactive coping is forward-looking with qualities that involve meeting challenges and taking the initiative. The question that needs to be answered is how you go determining the positive nature of any form of coping. One way to do this is to begin to better understand *why* a coping strategy is being used; what motivates the choice of a coping strategy, *how*, in what way is that strategy being used, *what* it is that is hoped to be achieved from using that strategy and *how* are those achievements to be evaluated in relation to outcomes. As these questions illustrate, to understand the positive nature of coping requires something more than just asking or knowing whether or not a particular coping strategy is being used. So, while attention may be shifting to seeking out the positive through proactive coping this does not mean that other types of coping should be ignored or that they cannot produce positive results. Developing our understanding of positive coping is important because it does allow us to explicitly explore what has been described as the 'underrepresented' side of coping (Folkman & Moskowitz, 2000). The point that needs reinforcing though, and which should not be lost sight of as this 'other side of coping' is explored, is that understanding what constitutes effective coping and what can be achieved by understanding more about positive coping is an emphasis that needs to be applied across all types of coping so that individuals can develop and achieve utilising many forms of coping strategies.

So, what does this mean for organisations and organisational intervention strategies? Organisational interventions must, as Lazarus (1991) suggests, be developed from the premise that stress does not reside solely in the individual or solely in the work environment but from the transaction between the two. So, when it comes to intervening, organisations have a responsibility to ensure that strategies need to treat the individual and the environment as a *single analytic unit*, rather than as separate sets of variables to be manipulated independently' (Lazarus, 1991:10). In this way the needs of the individual and the resources of the environment can be brought together to provide the context for developing interventions that facilitate positive coping and enhance well-being. Researchers too have a responsibility. Theirs is to ensure that, as our understanding of coping develops, we are better placed to answer the question, of how coping helps to unlock the positive, releasing opportunities for personal growth and fulfilment.

# REFERENCES

Aldwin, C. M. (2000). *Stress, Coping and Development: An Integrative Perspective*. London: The Guilford Press.

Dewe, P. & Cooper, C. (2007). Coping research and measurement in the context of work related stress. In G. Hodgkinson & K. Ford (Eds.). *International Review of Industrial and Organizational Psychology*, **22** (in press). Chicester: John Wiley & Sons, Ltd.

Folkman, S. & Moskowitz, J. T. (2000). Positive affect and the other side of coping. *American Psychologist*, **55**:647–654.

Folkman, S. & Moskowitz, J. T. (2003). Positive coping from a coping perspective. *Psychological Inquiry*, **14**:121–124.

Fredrickson, B. L. (1998). What good are positive emotions? *Review of General Psychology*, **25**:364–372.

Fredrickson, B. L. (2001). The role of positive emotions in positive psychology. *American Psychologist*, **56**:218–226.

Fredrickson, B.L., & Branigan, C. (2005). Positive emotions broaden the scope of attention and thought-action repertoires. *Cognition & Emotion* 19, 313–332.

Greenglass, E. R. (2001). Proactive coping, work stress and burnout. *Stress News*, **13**: 1–5.

Greenglass, E. R. (2002). Proactive coping and quality of life management. In E. Frydenberg (Ed.), *Beyond Coping: Meeting Goals, Visions, and Challenges*, pp. 37–62. Oxford: Oxford University Press.

Greenglass, E., Fiksenbaum, L. & Eaton, J. (2006). The relationship between coping, social support, functional disability and depression in the elderly. *Anxiety, Stress, and Coping*, **19**:15–31.

Greenglass, E. R., Schwarzer, R. & Taubert, S. (1996). *The Proactive Coping Inventory (PCI): A Multidimensional Research Instrument.* [Online publication]. Available at: http://www.psych.yorku.ca/greenglass/

Hobfoll, S. E. (2001). The influence of culture, community, and the nested-self in the stress process: Advancing conservation of resources theory. *Applied Psychology: An International Review*, **50**:337–421.

Latack, J. C. & Havlovic, S. J. (1992). Coping with job stress: A conceptual evaluation framework for coping measures. *Journal of Organizational Behavior*, **13**:479–508.

Lazarus, R.S. (1991). Psychological stress in the workplace. In P. L. Perrewé (Ed.) Handbook on job stress [special issue], *Journal of Social Behavior and Personality*, **6**:1–13.

Lazarus, R. S. (2001). Conservation of Resources Theory (COR): Little more than words masquerading as a new theory. *Applied Psychology: An International Journal*, **50**:381–391.

Lazarus, R. S. (2003). Does the positive psychology movement have legs? *Psychological Inquiry*, **14**:93–109.

Lazarus, R. S. & Folkman, S. (1984). *Stress, Appraisal and Coping.* New York: Springer.

Schwarzer, R. (1999). *Proactive Coping Theory.* Paper presented at the 20th International Conference of the Stress and Anxiety Research Society (STAR), Cracow, Poland, 12–14 July.

Schwarzer, R. (2001). Stress, resources, and proactive coping. *Applied Psychology: An International Review*, 50:400–407.

Schwarzer, R. (2004). Manage stress at work through preventive and proactive coping. In E. A. Locke (Ed.), *The Blackwell Handbook of Principles of Organizational Behavior*, pp. 342–355. Oxford: Blackwell Publishing.

Schwarzer, R. & Knoll, N. (2003). Positive coping: Mastering demands and searching for meaning. In S. Lopez & C. R. Snyder (Eds.), *Positive Psychological Assessment: A Handbook of Models and Measures*, pp. 393–409. Washington DC: APA.

Schwarzer, R. & Taubert, S. (2002). Tenacious goal pursuits and strivings: Toward personal growth. In E. Frydenberg (Ed.), *Beyond Coping: Meeting Goals, Visions, and Challenges*, pp. 19–35. Oxford: Oxford University Press.

Seligman, M. E. P. & Csikszentmihalyi, M. (2000). Positive psychology: An introduction. *American Psychologist*, **55**:5–14.

Zeidner, M. & Saklofske, D. (1996) Adaptive and maladaptive coping. In M. Zeidner & N. S. Endler (Eds.), *Handbook of Coping: Theory, Research, Applications*, pp. 505–531. New York: John Wiley & Sons, Inc.

# CHAPTER 9

# Organisational Duty of Care: Workplace Counselling as a Shield against Litigation?

**Peter Jenkins**
*Salford University*

The term 'duty of care' is very much in vogue at present, holding a degree of popularity amongst therapists which is at least equivalent to that enjoyed by the term 'workplace stress' in the previous decade. The term duty of care is used, variously, to include an organisational responsibility for reporting child abuse (Sher, 2003), for providing supervision to therapists (Copeland, 2005), and for assessing suicide risk to clients (Reeves, 2005). Major institutions have been directly criticised by coroners' courts for being in breach of their duty of care. In one instance, this related to Styal Women's Prison, for failing to prevent the suicide of a young inmate (*Guardian*, 25 January 2005, 27 September 2006). In another case, the BBC was held to account for the quality of the risk assessment, which was made prior to sending a journalist to Mogadishu, Somalia, where she was killed on a reporting assignment (*Guardian*, 30 September 2006). Elsewhere, concerns have been raised by the Financial Services Authority about the lack of effective disaster management measures for affected staff, following terrorist incidents occurring in the heart of London (*Guardian*, 10 April 2006).

However, using the term duty of care, particularly when applied broadly to organisations in the context of workplace health, safety and well-being, is quite likely to lose its essential sharpness of focus. It runs the risk of simply becoming yet another 'persuasive definition' (McDermott, 1975) in the much wider debate about the respective responsibilities of employers, staff and workplace counsellors. The term duty of care is capable of very precise definition in terms of English law, and this will set the parameters for discussion in this chapter. The term duty of care can also carry a strong ethical and professional loading in the hands of practitioners. The latter may be seeking to use it both as a means of

*Employee Well-being Support: A Workplace Resource.* Edited by A. Kinder, R. Hughes and C.L. Cooper.
© 2008 John Wiley & Sons, Ltd.

setting ever higher standards, in terms of practice and resource provision for workplace counselling, and also to buttress the professional standing of therapists relative to that of other professional groups. This chapter will, therefore, explore the developing role of work-based counselling provision as a potential 'shield' against litigation by employees for 'workplace stress'.

## LEGAL ASPECTS OF DUTY OF CARE

The organisation's duty of care to its employees has a number of sources in English law. These duties derive, firstly, from statute, and, secondly, from common law. Under common law, organisations have duties to employees under the law of contract, and also under negligence law. It is primarily the latter area, namely litigation for personal injury, which has seen a major recasting of organisational responsibilities for workplace well-being in the past decade. While this chapter specifically addresses UK law, many features of organisational duty of care will also be found in other common law jurisdictions, such as the USA, Canada and Australia.

Organisations have clearly defined statutory responsibilities to staff under key pieces of legislation, such as the Health and Safety at Work Act 1974. Under this Act, employers must ensure the health, safety and welfare at work of employees, and to provide a safe working environment. This duty has been widened by the Management of Health and Safety at Work Regulations 1999 (SI 1999/3242) to make health and safety risk assessments, and to provide appropriate health surveillance of employees. Employers also have a duty to prevent bullying and harassment towards members of staff by colleagues, following a successful case brought under anti-stalking legislation, the Protection from Harassment Act 1997. Employers, particularly in the public sector, have wide responsibilities towards staff under a growing range of legislation on equal opportunities, regarding sex, race, disability and age. It is likely that statutory employer responsibilities towards staff with mental health problems under the Disability Discrimination Acts of 1995 and 2005 will become increasingly complex over time, as further case law develops (see Wright, Chapter 18 in this volume).

Furthermore, employer statutory duties are actively monitored by agencies such as the Health and Safety Executive. This has adopted a proactive, interventionist stance in key cases regarding unacceptably high levels of reported staff stress, for example at a West Dorset hospital and at De Montfort University. It has also taken action in the courts against a mental health trust for systematic failures, which lead to the death of a nurse at the hands of a psychiatric patient.

However, the concept of duty of care relates more accurately to liability under *common law*, rather than to duties under statute. Under the law of negligence, individuals and agencies can be deemed to hold a duty towards other parties, who may suffer foreseeable damage through acts of omission or commission, on the 'neighbour' principle, established by the landmark

*Donoghue* case in 1932. Under negligence law, a plaintiff needs to establish that the defendant owed him or her a duty of care, was in breach of that duty, and that he or she suffered foreseeable harm as a direct result. Apart from any physical injury, the plaintiff needs to establish that the damage amounted to a psychological injury, such as clinical depression. Such injury needs to be consistent with diagnostic criteria employed by psychiatric manuals, such as the DCM-4 or ICD-10. In the well-known *Walker* case in 1995, a senior social worker brought the first successful case for damages against his employer for 'workplace stress' (*Walker v Northumberland CC* [1995]). John Walker had experienced, crucially, a *second* onset of severe anxiety and depression. This was held to be due to the employer's failure to take adequate steps to provide effective management, support and workload monitoring, after the *first* reported onset of severe distress.

This was followed by a number of similar cases, with employers admitting liability for personal injury. In the *Hatton* case in 2002, the Court of Appeal heard four conjoined cases, where the principles underlying the original *Walker* case were comprehensively restated. Employers were seen to be under a duty to take reasonable care with regard to the psychological health of their employees, but with a number of important qualifying statements. Firstly, the court held that no job was inherently stressful, given that stress itself is a subjective concept, and therefore, in the wider scheme of things, 'some things are no one's fault'. The simplistic notion that 'work causes stress, which causes harm', was decisively rejected. The crucial factor in personal injury cases remains that of establishing, on the civil test of the 'balance of probabilities', that the employer was in breach of their duty of care to avoid foreseeable harm (see Figure 9.1).

Employers are required to act on the basis of information that is brought to their attention. They can normally assume that the employee is up to the demands of the job, unless the latter has a known vulnerability to stress. Employers can discharge their duty of care to staff by providing retraining where appropriate, or by negotiating a redistribution of duties. This would apply where an individual is subject to an undue pressure of work, which is unreasonable and likely to cause foreseeable harm. Of critical importance, the Court of Appeal held that where an employer provided a confidential counselling service, then it was unlikely to be held in breach of its obligations. However, no detail was provided by the court as to the precise form that such a confidential counselling service should take.

## FORESEEABLE DAMAGE

The *Hatton* case sets out the terrain for future cases of personal injury which allege psychological damage (see Table 9.1). This harm must be attributable, not simply to 'workplace stress' but, rather, must take the form of foreseeable psychological injury, directly or materially caused by breach of the employer's duty of care. However, in this context, there is also another

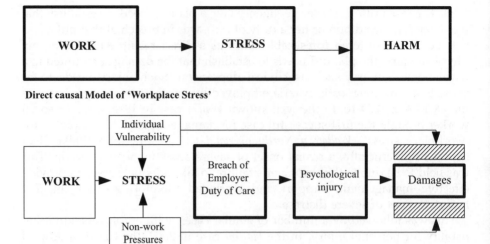

**Figure 9.1** Comparison of direct causal model and duty of care model of 'workplace stress'

dimension to the concept of duty of care, relating to the competence of the *individual* therapist. An aggrieved employee could seek to bring a case not only against the employer on the grounds outlined above, but also against a workplace counsellor, for breach of their own individual duty of care to the client. Action against an individual counsellor, or a staff counselling service,

**Table 9.1** Checklist for employer liability

---

- Is the individual subject to undue pressure of work which is:
  - unreasonable by any standard?
  - unreasonable judged in comparison with the workload of others in a similar job? or
  - due to individual vulnerability, which is known to the employer?
- Has the individual received an injury to health, either physical or psychological, which is directly attributable to stress at work?
- Was this injury reasonably foreseeable by the employer?
- Is this injury directly and mainly attributable to the employer's breach of duty of care, in failing to reduce workplace stress (by providing confidential counselling, redistribution of duties, training, etc.)?

---

*Source:* Adapted from: *Hatton v Sutherland* [2002]

would be covered by the employer's vicarious liability for its employed counsellors. The test applied to the standard of counselling provided by the counsellor would be the *Bolam* test, namely that of the ordinarily competent practitioner.

UK case law in the field of therapist negligence is still limited, with the case of *Werner v Landau* (1961) as the main reported case at Appeal Court level (Jenkins, 2007). The *Bolam* test of practitioner competence derives from medical case law, and is based on a form of peer defence, or justification of therapeutic standards and technique. The *Bolam* test, which tends to militate heavily against successful claims by clients and patients, has been further modified by the *Bolitho* judgement. This requires the justification of a chosen medical (or therapeutic) approach, not just via the support of a body of responsible and competent professional opinion, but also on the basis of a more objective rationale, such as reference to a sound evidence or research base.

This brief summary points to an underlying reason why practitioners should perhaps be cautious about seeking to develop an ever more expansive and inclusive duty of care. In legal terms, duty of care crucially denotes *liability*. For counsellors and organisations, it might therefore be prudent to work to a restricted, rather than all-encompassing definition of duty of care, simply in order to establish limits to future employer and counsellor liability. In any event, the parameters of duty of care are set and decided by the courts, and not by professionals. In the absence of legislation on workplace counselling or statutory regulation of therapists, the relevant standard is set by the courts, relying, in part, on the evidence of expert witnesses, as well as on previous case law.

This points to a key structural weakness in the debate about organisational duty of care regarding workplace counselling. The actual, and rather limited, baseline, of providing a confidential counselling service for employees, is set by the *Hatton* case. Practitioners might attempt to raise the bar on this, by arguing in favour of a duty of care to provide supervision, suicide assessment, or reporting child abuse, as outlined earlier in the introduction to this chapter. However, these constitute elements of a wider, more highly developed *ethical or professional interpretation* of a duty of care, rather than one which is likely to carry much influence with the courts. The process of trying to develop an enhanced sense of the organisation's duty of care is perhaps most evident in the case of higher education (HE). Here, universities have consciously attempted to widen access to enrolment, by recruiting students with significant, and often enduring, mental health problems (CVCP, 2000; AMOSSHE, 2001). The actual nature of the university's obligations to students with mental health support needs is, in fact, largely untested, given that its statutory duties are based on disability law, rather than on pre-existing mental health legislation.

Practitioners in HE and elsewhere may be attempting to flesh out the notion of organisational duty of care, admittedly in this context towards students rather than to staff, with concepts drawn from best professional practice.

However, from a sociological point of view, writers, such as Blomberg (1978), have accurately described this process as one of 'net-widening'. Agencies and professionals tend to move well beyond the original boundaries of their role, by identifying yet more areas requiring their unique expertise and the application of their specialist professional knowledge and skill. This expanded notion of organisational duty of care thus becomes a powerful lever for promoting the professional status of counsellors within the highly competitive market for providing psychological services to employers. This is most strongly evident in the debate over the value of post-trauma care, such as psychological debriefing, which is discussed below.

## PSYCHOLOGICAL DEBRIEFING

The debate over psychological debriefing and other forms of post-trauma support provides the sharpest expression of the debate over a *restricted*, versus an *expanded*, definition of organisational duty of care. At one level, there is a continuing debate between proponents and critics of psychological debriefing, over its status as an effective form of post-trauma care for employees and members of the public. The influential National Institute for Clinical Excellence guidelines on Post-Traumatic Stress Disorder state explicitly that 'brief, single session interventions (often referred to as debriefing) should not be routine practice when delivering services' (NICE, 2005:4). Critics of psychological debriefing have marshalled comprehensive evidence in the form of a *Cochrane Review*, which is highly critical of the use of debriefing as an intervention (Rose *et al.*, 2002). However, the position is made more complex by the counter-argument that debriefing can take many forms, and is not, strictly speaking, a *counselling* intervention as such (Hughes, 2002:26).

On the other hand, defenders of debriefing, such as Tehrani, claim that the research evidence indicates that it remains an effective and valuable part of post-trauma care (2004:161). Decisive case law would be necessary to clearly establish whether the provision of debriefing could be seen to constitute sub-standard care, in the event of litigation against an employer, by aggrieved staff alleging damage following trauma at work. In part, the courts would rely on the *Bolitho* principle, in the case of litigation against individual counsellors, namely whether there was a robust evidence and research base in favour of debriefing, as opposed to other measures. The Ministry of Defence (MOD) case (discussed below) suggests that the courts may well be very reluctant to prescribe specific interventions for trauma care, when applying the test of the 'reasonable employer' in cases of alleged negligence.

The second aspect of the debriefing debate relates to the push to refine and expand the definition of the organisation's duty of care, beyond established case law, and to include debriefing as demonstrable evidence of an organisation actually *discharging* its duty of care (Beale, 2002:34). This stance is highly problematic, since the *content* and *form* of the organisation's duty of care is defined by the courts, with reference to statutory legislation and guidelines, together with previous case law. Tehrani, for example, argues that:

> The law attempts to protect employees by placing a duty of care on the employer. In order to meet this duty the organisation has to put in place a number of policies and procedures including ensuring that there are adequate risk assessments, safe practices and post-trauma support for employees that become involved in traumatic events. (Tehrani, 2004:62)

The inclusion of 'post-trauma support' in the already established statutory duties, of risk assessment and safe practices, rests on future and as yet undecided case law, however desirable it may appear from a wider ethical and professional point of view. Certainly, recent discussion of the limited case law available on debriefing (Wheat, 2002:56), tends to suggest that it is ambiguous and inconclusive to date (*Howell v State Rail Authority NSW* [1996]).

## COUNSELLING AS A SHIELD AGAINST LITIGATION?

The courts, so far, have been notably reluctant to prescribe the actual *form* of the 'confidential counselling service', identified in *Hatton* as a shield against litigation by employees for breach of duty of care. This is perhaps not surprising, given the traditional reluctance of the courts to stray into issues of policy and resource allocation, which is acknowledged to be the preserve of parliamentary legislation. However, employers should be cautious about assuming that the simple provision of a confidential counselling service for employees provides automatic protection against future litigation. In the recent *Intel* case, an employee with a history of depression won her negligence case against the firm, despite the existence of a staff counselling service provided by the company (*Intel v Daw* [2007]). Provision of confidential staff counselling can substantially reduce, but clearly not *eliminate*, the risk of employee litigation for psychological injury.

A striking illustration of the rapidly changing contours of the debate about organisational duty of care comes from a military source. In response to adverse publicity surrounding the deaths of young recruits at the Princess Royal Barracks at Deepcut, Surrey, between 1995 and 2002, the House of Commons Defence Committee issued a report on its duty of care to recruits and trainees across the three armed services. The report makes challenging reading, with the frank admission that '(f)or too long in the past the Armed Forces, and the Army in particular, failed to grasp the nettle of duty of care' (HoCDC, 2005:19). The report concludes that bullying exists in the Armed Forces and that it is under-reported. In order to respond effectively to this problem, it is acknowledged that the system of reliance on 'Empowered Officers', as the first point of contact for recruits experiencing bullying, is ineffective. Instead, it is proposed that the services introduce professionally trained counsellors.

Such counsellors should be able to initiate monitoring and support for individuals at risk without hindrance from the chain of command. We expect the MOD will consider best practice in this area from other disciplined organisations including the police force. (HoCDC, 2005:11).

The provision of employee counselling has clearly emerged both as cost-effective human resource management (McLeod, 2007) and also as a viable defence against litigation. For instance, in the Hutton Inquiry into the death of weapons expert Dr David Kelly, the issue of emotional support was clearly a persistent sub-text in the dogged cross-examination of senior MOD staff ('Was there any counselling offered?' www.the-hutton-enquiry.org.uk). Elsewhere, major employers such as the National Health Service have rapidly moved towards the provision of access to counselling services for all staff (NHSE, 1998). While such services flesh out the employer's duty of care, it is widely recognised that counselling provision can present complex issues for managing the disclosure of sensitive personal information, and fine-tuning these processes with professional counsellors' expectations of confidentiality. For instance, the Bullock Inquiry referred to the problems caused by the existence of 'two parallel universes of knowledge', where occupational health holds employee information, which is not directly available to line managers (Bullock, 1997:16). Legal commentators have also identified the difficulties facing staff counsellors in managing confidential client disclosures of disability, and the complexity involved in reporting malpractice within organisations, despite the apparent protection offered by the Public Interest Disclosure Act 1998 (Pattenden, 2003:719, 731).

## MOD CASE

If *Walker* and *Hatton* set out the key principles for judging an employer's duty of care for psychological injury, then the class action against the Ministry of Defence provides the template for its future application to cases involving organisational duty of care. This was an action brought by a number of former soldiers, alleging MOD negligence in failing to take adequate steps to prevent the development of psychiatric illness, and secondly, failing to detect, diagnose or treat such illness. While the case may be seen to be somewhat atypical of the usual type of employer and employee relationship, it represents, albeit in extreme form, the issues of liability at the heart of this debate. The courts established in *Hatton* that *no* job can be considered to be inherently stressful, even within the military, with its constant exposure to war, conflict and trauma. Furthermore, the military enjoy an unprecedented level of protection against litigation. Legal action for negligence committed prior to 1987 is excluded by virtue of Crown immunity. Other action is largely, but not completely, limited by means of combat immunity, which will apply in a theatre of war.

The judgement in the *MOD* case, which found against the claimants, repays careful reading for anyone interested in the future of organisational 'duty of care' cases. It provides an extremely detailed examination of the history of military psychiatry, and of the changing medical and military perspectives on psychiatric illness amongst soldiers exposed to trauma. The test applied is that of the 'reasonable and prudent employer', rather than that of ideal, or even optimal, care. In the *MOD* case, the guidelines from the earlier *Hatton* case are quoted approvingly:

> There may be a temptation, having concluded that some harm was foreseeable and that harm of that kind has taken place, to go on to conclude that the employer was in breach of his duty of care in failing to prevent that harm (and that the breach of duty caused the harm). (Owen, J. at para 2.E.4, *Multiple Claimants v MOD* [2003])

In fact, the judge accepted that there *were* definite breaches of duty of care by the MOD. These included the failure to provide mandatory training on battleshock for officers and non-commissioned officers after 1985, and the failure to liaise with the NHS between 1976 and 1992, over the medical history of military patients. However, the crucial element in negligence cases is to establish that any breach *caused, or materially contributed towards*, the damage experienced – the so-called 'causation test'. Simply establishing the fact of employer breach of duty of care is not sufficient on its own to prove the case. Hence future arguments in court over whether or not an employer should have used psychological debriefing, or cognitive behaviour therapy, for its employees following workplace trauma are completely secondary to the task of establishing the close, causal relationship of such provision, or its absence, to any psychological damage incurred by employees as a result.

## A TEST FOR DUTY OF CARE?

In terms of duty of care, the close reasoning evident in the MOD case points to a number of different dimensions of the test of the prudent and reasonable employer. These might be described in organisational terms as *vertical*, i.e. relating to the *internal* policies operating within the organisation, and *horizontal*, i.e. in relation to *comparable organisations* in the UK and abroad (see Table 9.2).

These questions seem to underpin the systematic, and even painstaking, judicial analysis of MOD policy and provision for discharging its duty of care to serving soldiers. If this proves to be an accurate translation from the legal argument, then cases challenging organisational 'duty of care' will face an equally high bar to overcome in the future.

**Table 9.2**   Test for organisational duty of care:

What should a prudent and reasonable employer have been doing with regard to employee welfare at this time?

**Vertical dimension** (i.e. relating to the *internal* policies operating within the organisation):

- What provision was in place?
- What policies or approach underpinned this provision?
- What was the stated rationale for this approach?
- What was the evidence base for this approach?
- What factors would reasonably have delayed, or prevented, the adoption of certain policies or provision designed to respond to this issue?

**Horizontal dimension** (i.e. in relation to *comparable organisations* in the UK and abroad):

- What were other comparable employers doing about this issue at this time?
- What was the state of research and received professional and academic opinion at this time, both 'cutting edge' and mainstream?
- How robust was this research, in terms of its use of randomised controlled trials, sample size and methodology?
- What were the relevant statutory guidelines (such as Health and Safety Executive, General Medical Council) applying at this time?

*Source*: Adapted from: *Multiple Claimants v MOD* [2003]

## REFERENCES

AMOSSHE, Association of Managers of Student Services in Higher Eduction (2001). *Responding To Student Mental Health Issues: 'Duty of Care' Responsibilities in Student Services in Higher Education: Good Practice Guide*. Winchester: AMOSSHE.

Beale, D. (2002) Organisational issues related to psychological debriefing. In British Psychological Society, *Psychological Debriefing*, pp. 31–41. Leicester: BPS.

Blomberg, T. (1978). *Social Control and the Proliferation of Juvenile Court Sessions*. San Francisco: R & E Research Associates Inc.

Bullock, R. (1997). *Report of the Independent Inquiry into the Major Employment and Ethical Issues Arising from the Events Leading to the Trial of Amanda Jenkinson*. Nottingham: North Nottinghamshire Health Authority.

CVCP, Committee of Vice Chancellors and Principals (2000). *Guidelines on Student Mental Health and Procedures for Higher Education*. London: CVCP.

Copeland, S. (2005). *Counselling Supervision in Organisations: Professional and Ethical Dilemmas Explored*. London: Routledge.

HoCDC, House of Commons Defence Committee (2005). *Duty of Care: Third Report of Session 2004–5*. Volume 1. NC 63-1. London: Stationery Office.

Hughes, O. (2002). Training, supervision and the assessment of competence. In British Psychological Society, *Psychological Debriefing*, pp. 25–30. Leicester: BPS.

Jenkins, P. (2007). *Counselling, Psychotherapy and the Law*, 2nd Edn. London: Sage.

McDermott, F. (1975). *Self-determination in Social Work*. London: Routledge & Kegan Paul.

McLeod, J. (2007) *Counselling in the Workplace: A Comprehensive Review of the Research Evidence*. 2nd Edn. Rugby: BACP.

NHSE, National Health Service Executive (1998). *Working Together: Securing a Quality Workforce for the NHS*. London: HMSO.

NICE, National Institute for Clinical Excellence (2006). *Post-traumatic Stress Disorder: The Management of PTSD in Adults and Children in Primary and Secondary Care*. Clinical Guideline 26. London: NHS.

Pattenden R. (2003). *The Law of Professional-Client Confidentiality: Regulating the Disclosure of Personal Information*. Oxford: Oxford University Press.

Reeves, A. (2005). Supporting staff dealing with suicide. *Association of University and College Counsellors Journal*, Autumn, pp. 8–12.

Rose, S., Bisson, J. and Wessely, S. (2002). Psychological debriefing for preventing post traumatic stress disorder (PTSD). *Cochrane Database of Systematic Reviews*, Issue 2. Art. No.: CD000560. DOI: 10.102/14651858.CD000560.

Sher, M. (2003). Ethical issues for therapists working in organisations. In H. F. Solomon & M. Twyman (Eds.), *The Ethical Attitude in Analytic Practice*. London: Free Association.

Tehrani, N. (2004). *Workplace Trauma: Concepts, Assessment and Intervention*. Hove: Brunner-Routledge.

Wheat, K. (2002). Psychological debriefing and legal issues. In British Psychological Society, *Psychological Debriefing*, pp. 51–58. Leicester: BPS.

## Internet Reference

www.the-hutton-enquiry.org.uk/content/transcripts/hearing-trans36.htm

## Legal References

*Bolam v Friern HMC* [1957] 2 All ER 118.

*Bolitho v City and Hackney Health Authority* [1997] 3 WLR, 1151, [1997] 4 All ER 771 (HL).

*Donoghue v Stevenson* [1932] AC 562 (HL).

*Hatton v Sutherland* [2002] 2 All ER 1.

*Howell v State Rail Authority of New South Wales* Sup. Ct. NSW 7/6/96; Ct. of App. NSW 19/12/96; Sup. Ct. NSW 7/5/98 (Unreported).

*Intel Incorporation Ltd v Tracy Ann Daw* [2007] EWCA Civ 70.

*Multiple Claimants v MOD* [2003] EWHC 1134 (QB).

*Walker v Northumberland County Council* [1995] 1 All ER 737.

*Werner v Landau* TLR 8/3/1961, 23/11/1961, Sol Jo (1961) 105, 1008.

# CHAPTER 10

# Managing Diversity

**David Weaver**
*Freeman Oliver*

*Diversity is a fact not an ideology...*

High level strategic discussions about 'managing diversity' are no longer an unusual feature of business life. Indeed it is increasingly rare for any organisation proclaiming 'serious status' to openly shun or argue against the principles of 'addressing diversity'. Even in the commercial world where such virtues as 'meeting the bottom line' or 'protecting the margins' predominate, the language of 'diversity' is, at least on the surface, given some airtime. Why is this now the case? Why are a growing number of organisations, not only in the UK but throughout the western world, concerned about diversity?

These questions were posed to managers from a mixture of private and public sector organisations in a symposium I addressed. The responses were interesting. One view, supported by many, was that international terrorism, and particularly the events of 11 September 2001 in New York, had brought to the doorstep of every person in the United Kingdom the importance of understanding diversity and difference. Other responses identified ethical/legal reasons and even that vexed, well-known but difficult to define concept called 'political correctness'. However the most consistent contribution was a supposition that 'managing diversity potentially brings business benefit'.

If this is correct – and I start from the premise that it is, why is it so difficult to list examples of organisations that are exemplars and regarded as successful in this area? And what can you as managers and leaders do to make a difference for your organisations, the customers they serve – and even to enhance your own leadership career? This chapter explores some of these questions and presents a framework for mainstreaming diversity and making it part of the 'DNA of your organisation'.

*Employee Well-being Support: A Workplace Resource.* Edited by A. Kinder, R. Hughes and C.L. Cooper.
© 2008 John Wiley & Sons, Ltd.

## BUT FIRST – WHAT IS MANAGING DIVERSITY?

As implied earlier, 'diversity speak' is now part of the everyday parlance for many organisations – but what does diversity management mean?

As part of a research study I conducted in 2003, 10 so-called 'diversity experts' were placed in a room and asked to individually define 'diversity'. The outcome was at least seven radically different responses. An astonishing level of rhetoric and jargon pervaded those definitions and to be candid whilst responses such as 'it's about good practice', 'equal chances for all' or 'recognising and respecting difference' are all worthy and sound, their responses did not pass the 'so what' test of the business-focused private sector boss, local government politician, board member or company shareholder.

So how do we commonly describe or perceive diversity management? Thomas and Ely (1996), in an article written for the *Harvard Business Review*, claim that most definitions are based on an assumption that workplace diversity is about increasing racial, national, gender or class representation – in essence, recruiting and retaining more people from traditionally underrepresented 'identity groups'. They argue that even though the intention behind this is understandable, the downside is that it leads to organisations' encouraging and expecting women, people of colour, disabled people, etc., to blend in or predominate in jobs that relate specifically to their backgrounds. In effect, they are simply required to interface with clients or customers of their same identity group.

Thomas and Ely's view is that companies lose out because they operate on the limited and limiting assumption that the main virtue identity groups offer is knowledge of their own people. My own emerging research into 'diversity and leadership behaviour' shows that this view is gaining widespread currency amongst business leaders. In short, definitions of diversity should go above reaching numerical targets by giving emphasis on the actual benefit their knowledge, experience, skills, perspectives and background will bring to the business. I call this the 'non-benevolent approach' (Weaver, 2001) – an acknowledgement that a diverse customer base demands organisations have diverse skills and perspectives to gain a competitive edge. Benevolence is not warranted or necessary!

This should not undermine the importance of numbers and targets. Discuss with any successful leader what makes for organisational effectiveness and the virtues of targets and goals will feature near the top. What is fundamental is the need to be clear about 'why the organisation is addressing diversity and for what *business benefit*'.

So is there a case for an all embracing definition? Yes – but not as a substitute for taking action. Joe Montgomery, one of the most senior black leaders in UK central government, in speaking about career development in a symposium with black managers said, 'The trick is for you and your organisations to deal with definitions at the same time as taking action. It never ceases to amaze me how often the action informs the definition; and the outcomes are much more meaningful and relevant to you and your organisation'.

## 'DIVERSITY IS A FACT, NOT AN IDEOLOGY'

The population of the United Kingdom and its workforce is changing. These changes are shaped by irrevocable demographic, global economic and social trends. Knowledge of this is critical to organisational planning and effectiveness. The need for organisations to come up to speed with this is well exemplified by an analysis of London.

Londoners speak over 300 languages and belong to at least 14 different faiths. Nearly a third of the population is from black, Asian or other ethnic minority groups and over the next decade will account for 80% of the increase in London's working-age population. One fifth of the working-age population has a disability, yet only 11% are in employment. At least 5% of London's residents are gay or lesbian – the economic value of the 'pink economy' in the UK is estimated to be around £ 95 billion. London's economic output would be £ 1.5 billion higher if part-time employment rates for women with children in London were raised to equal those in the rest of the country (London Development Agency, 2005).

It is notable that London's mayor, Ken Livingstone, often speaks about the benefits of London's diversity. His body, the Greater London Authority (GLA), set up a high profile initiative called 'Diversity Works' that partners with businesses in the City. The active interest and involvement from many of the City's large multinationals demonstrates the importance of managing diversity to their success. A major aspect of the mayoral plan is focused on acknowledging the role that the diversity of London can play in meeting the City's aim of 'increasing the economic impact and making London the economic capital of the world'.

Similar statistics are mirrored across the United Kingdom, Western Europe and the USA. The challenge is for leaders to tap into the potential that this diversity brings.

## FROM RHETORIC TO REALITY

'All organisations (should) have a concern for their customers. The successful organisation of the new millennium will move from good to great only if they connect with customer markets which they have traditionally ignored.' When I recently said this at a conference, I was met with a heavy rebuff by a public sector chief executive who said: 'I agree – but what do we do next and what can I do to get the ball rolling?'

In 2001, I formed a task force called 'Organisations Fit for a Diverse Society – from Rhetoric to Reality'. The remit of this body was to determine what could be done by organisations to make them more 'fit for purpose' in meeting the needs of a diverse customer base. A series of focus groups and one-to-one sessions discussed with public service managers, business leaders and ethnic minority customers (including potential customers) their views on the issue. The result of this led to a charter called 'Diversity Change Management – The

Seven-point Plan'. The outcomes outlined below go some way towards addressing the chief executive's rebuff:

## DIVERSITY CHANGE MANAGEMENT – THE SEVEN-POINT PLAN

### Leadership from the Top

Leadership of the message has to be visible and should (and be seen to be) driven from the top. The messages need to be explicit, unambiguous and be linked directly with the core purpose of the business. The benefits of diversity should be evident in the business plan and made integral to other business objectives in a meaningful way. If the concept is not understood by the leadership, then they should do what leaders generally do – seek external expertise. If leaders have executive coaches, ensure they can give effective support on these issues. If they can't – don't appoint them. This is a 'business critical' issue. Treat it as such!

The 'behaviour of leaders' must also reflect the 'diversity values' of the organisation. The way in which they relate to their employees, customers and other stakeholders must convey respect and fairness and demonstrate a willingness to listen and learn.

Seek involvement at board level and aim to garner diverse representation at this level too. If as a business you are looking for investment, note: people of colour, lesbians and gay men, disabled people and women invest too – and have significant economic capability.

### Recruit in View of the Future – Not the Past or Present

'If you do what you have always done, you will get what you have always got'. This statement represents the case for change in recruitment practices. The customer base is becoming increasingly diverse. Managing and understanding diversity and difference is going to be one of the foremost competencies of tomorrow's organisations and will either help or hinder the organisation's aspiration to gain competitive advantage. To use job profiles and competencies that are the hallmark of yesterday's and today's organisations is a recipe for disaster. On the other hand, to invest time in 'futures thinking' – involving existing (and potential) customers – will not only help build outstanding and sustainable relationships, but will also help develop a prophetic insight into the business and give a vision of what is possible.

Review all of the job profiles within your organisation. Yes – all of them – and with some urgency. This is good practice anyway! Ensure that they are fit for purpose going forward, and recognise the diversity of your customer base as well as the important attribute of being able to 'manage and work with difference'. Give training and development to employees to help their performance. Most important, incorporate the key elements of the profiles into the recruitment process and treat them seriously. Don't change your mind and give someone a chance because 'they were OK aside from the diversity question ... so I think we could let them through'. This may sound funny, but I can tell you as someone who leads a headhunting firm that I have seen this happen on numerous occasions. And the ironic thing is that those who 'fail the diversity test' are usually those that are poor people managers, can't work in teams and in general are not good for the business!

## Performance Manage – Incentivise and (Yes) Impose Sanctions where Necessary

Like all good performance management models, it is important that there is a clear alignment to the business objectives. To enable effective management of this process, it is important that 'working with diversity' is integral to the work of individuals and directly linked to the organisation's overall objectives.

'People are the organisation's greatest asset' is probably one of the best-known truisms. But it is true! Give proper support and challenge to them, and ensure that they are aware of the business critical nature of this aspect of their role. It is also vital to incorporate the issues into generic learning and development programmes in a meaningful way. If you outsource management development training, ensure providers are able to deal with the issues in an effective manner. If they can't – don't use them. Management development is too important to be left to unaccountable consultants! The success of these programmes can have a direct impact on the organisation's future success, and diversity issues are an integral component part of the business proposition going forward. Notwithstanding the need for intensive learning and development and acknowledgement that this to be the first consideration, equal to this is the need to enact appropriate sanctions if standards are not being met. This will send a powerful signal throughout the organisation that diversity is being taken seriously.

## Involve Everyone in the Organisation

Everyone needs to know what diversity means for the organisation and should be able to contribute their views and opinions in an open, respectful manner. This could happen at a formal level, e.g. through training and development programmes, or by inviting external speakers, using drama, showing videos or even managers skilfully initiating conversations in informal settings.

The middle management level of organisation is viewed by many as critical to organisational success. In a lot of organisations, they have the power to move the organisation almost overnight to the next level up, block progress or, at worst, cause business failure. The buy-in of this cadre of management is critical. This is well captured by 'The Good Boss Company' who in their prominent research in 2005 stated: 'People don't leave organisations, they leave their bosses.'

The people in your organisation know more than is often realised. Full and open debate, with people knowing that the leadership of the organisation takes the issues seriously, will give the organisation a competitive edge.

## Involve Under-represented People in Your Organisation

Ask them their views on all aspects of the business. They are more than their identity group! Women, people of colour, disabled people and other under-represented professionals often hold leadership and other influential roles in their communities, be that through their faith organisations, children's schools, as mentors or as individuals consulted by a range of bodies interested in the 'minority opinion'. For many of them, it is an opportunity to 'give back' (Hewlett, Luce & West, 2005). For others, it is to compensate for the non-utilisation of their talent by their employers.

A significant amount of research indicates that under-represented groups lose out at work due to limited access to the people who make key decisions. Managers and leaders should look at formal and informal ways of creating channels for communication. Consideration should be given to the creation of interest groups. If the organisation decides not to have these, do so with the assurance that you have addressed the reasons behind the request (if there was one). If there is not a request – still consider whether the creation of such a group would be beneficial. Ask. If the organisation creates interest groups, make sure there is a direct link to the business and that senior managers listen and take on board legitimate concerns. Always challenge yourself to ensure that you are not being the barrier to change because of your own prejudices and views informed by your own background.

## HR Play a Key Role – But It's Not Their Job

Far too many organisations 'dump' responsibility for diversity into human resources departments. HR clearly plays an important role but they can only tackle certain parts of the equation. It is important to centralise the strategy and to ensure that it is driven by the corporate leadership agenda. If you are in HR and you're given it – give it back to the leadership team! I have witnessed many an isolated HR victim who has been deemed to have failed when in reality the organisation did not take on its corporate leadership responsibilities in this area.

## Have a Robust Stakeholder Engagement Drive that Captures the Diversity of the Organisation's Environment

This is an important increasingly utilised approach. It can range from simply getting to know the area, e.g. developing relationships with the local women's centre or sponsoring raffle tickets for the local community centre through to giving grant aid to the local Bangladeshi advice centre or having a work experience placement from a local mentoring initiative for black boys of school age.

Engaging with your community is not only a key element of a corporate responsibility strategy (CRS) but can also have a direct positive impact on the bottom-line. It can also make your organisation into an employer of choice for the diverse talent in your area who, as a result of your stakeholder engagement initiatives, feel positive about working with your organisation.

## AND WHAT ABOUT THE WELL-BEING OF THE PEOPLE YOU EMPLOY?

The past 10 years have witnessed a significant amount of research about health and well-being and, in particular, on the potential for psychological well-being as a vehicle for improving the experiences of employees and the success of their organisations. Many organisations, within both private and public sectors, have begun to take this seriously and have invested time in consulting with their employees and devising policies as a means of enshrining some of the positive principles in practice.

Boniwell and Henry (2007), Robertson (2007) and others have argued that a key component of well-being is purpose.

> Most people will accept that living a life that involves moving from one positive experience to another will not be particularly enjoyable, unless the experiences have a purpose beyond pure enjoyment, or they lead towards achieving a worthwhile goal of some kind. (Robertson, 2007)

So what does this have to do with diversity?

There has been a plethora of research that shows that black and minority people are more likely to be at the wrong end of disciplinaries and grievances in comparison to their white counterparts. Sexual harassment and discrimination are still unacceptable phenomena within organisations in the West, and disabled professionals often complain about being ignored by colleagues and being defined simply by their disability. In essence, discrimination is unfortunately a significant facet of organisational life and all too stark a reality for under-represented groups.

Much of the research in the field of psychological well-being shows a high correlation between high psychological well-being and personal and organisational productivity. The challenge for managers is to harness this to get the best from their people for the benefit of their organisations. Discrimination can cause low self-esteem to the victim and low psychological well-being. Effective management of diversity and difference can help make a positive difference in this regard. Conversely the lack of this competence can have devastating impacts on 'minority employees' and on the performance of the organisation.

As interest in the subject of health and well-being increases, it will be crucial for organisations to ensure that diversity forms a central component part of their approach. It will also be important for academics to give some attention to the connections between diverse workforce and well-being. There is a sparcity of literature in this area and failure to do so will surely be a significant flaw in this important exploration.

## AND SO WHAT?

Managing diversity is not simple – but it's not that complex either. Much of it is down to plain and simple good practice and most of all – strong and effective leadership. Many of today's organisations may feel that the issue (whilst important) is not centre stage. Tomorrow's organisations are hostage to the realities of a changing world.

Let's put it like this: 'The future is not orange', contrary to the message of a well-known telecommunications company. Actually, it's multi-coloured and very diverse. The management of diversity and difference will therefore be the key core managerial and leadership competence of this millennium – not for moral reasons or even because of the shift towards 'principle-centred leadership'. Simply put it's about demographics and the demands of more empowered customers who are insisting that organisations meet their needs.

Those organisations and leaders that respond will succeed. Those organisations and leaders that don't will fail. It's as straightforward as that!

## REFERENCES

Boniwell, I. & Henry, J. (2007). Developing conceptions of well-being: Advancing subjective, hedonic and hedonic series. *Social Psychological Review*, 9:3–8.

Good Boss Questionnaire (2006). Version 0.7, p. 3. Good Boss Company, Surrey.

Hewlett, S.A., Luce, C.B. & West, C. (2005). Leadership in your midst. *Harvard Business Review*. November, **83**(11):74–82.

London Development Agency (2005). Diversity Works for London, London.

Robertson, I. (2007) Using business psychology to close the well-being gap. *Selection and Development Review*, **23**(4): p. 13.

Thomas, D. & Ely, R. (1996). Making differences matter: A new paradigm for managing diversity. *Harvard Business Review*, September to October, **74**(5):79–90.

Weaver, D. (2002). Diversity change management – the 7 point plan. Making Difference Pay Conference, Trust, London, 1990.

# CHAPTER 11

# Understanding Mental Health – a Guide for All Employees

**Andrew Buckley**
*Kipepeo*

## INTRODUCTION

Every human being has a view of mental illness, not just the 'experts' working in the field. Pejorative terms start to be used in the playground and continue in films, TV, and the media. These all impact on our view of the meaning of both mental health and mental illness. The rare but horrific instances of murder being committed by a so-called 'paranoid schizophrenic' and reported instances of successful suicide by a worker 'who had everything to live for' further impact on the views that many hold of mental illness.

The attitude of all employees to mental ill health is important in any organisation. Managing the effects of mental ill health within an organisation is the responsibility of everyone, not just specialist and expert services such as the human resource manager and occupational health specialist. 'An open, non-stigmatising culture in which staff feel free to talk about mental health issues is crucial' (St John, 2005:44) in allowing individuals with mental health problems to feel free to discuss their feelings and problems at work. Attitudes of colleagues, managers and the culture of the organisation are fundamentally important in easing the path to support, care and recovery.

Thomas and Secker suggest a three-pronged approach to managing the impact of mental health issues in the workplace (Grove, Secker & Seebohn, 2005:123).

1. Primary prevention; focuses on creating a healthy workplace. A culture that supports employees and takes an active role in managing stress and other factors.
2. Secondary prevention; includes early recognition of possible problems and prompt and appropriate action.

*Employee Well-being Support: A Workplace Resource.* Edited by A. Kinder, R. Hughes and C.L. Cooper.
© 2008 John Wiley & Sons, Ltd.

3. Tertiary prevention; focuses on those employees who have become ill and usually need the services of the health professional. Return to work and rehabilitation strategies sit here.

This chapter looks at issues and solutions in the category of secondary prevention.

The organisation that promotes mental wellbeing as an integral part of culture and actively manages the workplace to limit adverse effects can, nonetheless, never be immune from the effects of distress and mental illness. Employers who follow the best practice advice as outlined in other chapters of this book will still see employees who suffer and need support. The effects of non-work-related issues have an impact on an employee's behaviour, ability to work and mental well-being. No employer can manage their workplace in a way that removes these factors.

Relying on medical care once an employee has become ill, tertiary prevention, as outlined above, is arguably the traditional approach. But mental illness is not a clear 'have or have not' as is often the case with a physical illness. Consultant Psychiatrist, Dr Mike Nowers says:

> Most mental illnesses lie on a spectrum between health and illness and an individual may slide from health into illness over a period of time and in a way that may be hard to identify. You do not catch mental illness and in general it is not amenable to tests or measurements but diagnostically is based on a careful assessment of symptoms and signs. (Buckley & Buckley, 2006:X).

The Department of Health in the United Kingdom has acknowledged the importance of attitudes to mental illness in organisations in their initiative, *Action on Stigma: Promoting Mental Health, Ending Discrimination At Work* (Department of Health, 2006) and includes the provision of mental health awareness training and promoting an understanding of mental health issues for all employees as two of the five key actions that employers can take to give benefit to the individual and the organisation.

Widening the responsibility and ability to offer support has been shown to be a successful part of the strategy in many organisations that have reaped the benefits of addressing mental health issues. One such company is British Telecommunications plc (BT). Dr Paul Litchfield, Chief Medical Officer, says:

> We haven't rejected any job applications on grounds of mental illness since our strategy has been in place. Mental health sickness absence are down 30%, stress claims have been reduced dramatically, 75% of long term absentees return to their own job and the medical retirement rate for mental illness is down by 80%. (Department of Health, 2006:5)

The BT approach is wide-ranging, covering primary, secondary and tertiary prevention.

Secondary prevention, for BT, means identifying early signs of distress and supporting individuals. Stigma is addressed through multi-channel communication, training is provided for management, and mental health issues are kept mainstream with the issues de-medicalised.

Pharmaceutical company Glaxo Smith Kline takes a broadly similar approach with a wide-ranging programme of workplace strategies to promote mental well-being, a comprehensive care programme for those employees who become ill and an innovative approach to secondary prevention that includes 'team resilience', a team-based training programme that encourages all employees to take responsibility for their colleagues, support them through times of difficulty, and eliminate inappropriate work pressures.

Widening the responsibility for mental ill health beyond the expert services of human resources, occupational health and medical professionals, is showing real benefit to many organizations. The goal is to help with early recognition and prompt action once an employee shows signs that may indicate a mental health issue. The rewards can be substantial and varied as summarised in Table 11.1.

Recognising and managing mental health issues at work will be a small part of any manager's workload. It is, nonetheless, an important skill, and training and resources need to reflect this fact. What the manager needs is the ability to decide what to do; whether to make adjustments, offer personal support at the team level, or to refer to occupational health or the employee's family doctor as appropriate. 'What to do?' as a question is not the same as 'What is wrong? or

**Table 11.1**  The rewards of managing mental health issues

Benefits at the organisational level:

- Reductions in sickness absence
- Reductions in retirement/redundancy on medical grounds
- Improving and maintaining productivity
- Overall increase in staff well being resulting in a more healthy and effective workforce.

Benefits at the team level:

- Accepting and compensating for the normal emotional ups and downs of individuals
- Knowing how to approach an employee appropriately to offer early help and accommodate with minor adjustments
- Understanding how to facilitate a referral to specialist support (in house or external)
- Supporting the rest of the team and creating a sense of caring for the well being of all staff.

Benefits to the individual:

- Early intervention, which increases the likelihood of a speedy return to normal
- Early intervention, which facilitates the involvement of the professional at an early date if appropriate
- A sense of being cared for and understood
- A reduction in feelings associated with possible stigma and the fear of talking about issues.

'How to help?' Diagnosing a problem and deciding on treatment, the 'what is wrong' and 'how to help' questions, are the province of the expert, the nurse, doctor or other clinician.

What follows is an outline of the information that any manager will find useful in helping them recognise and manage those employees who start to struggle; whether this is a temporary reaction to a normal life event, the result of increasing pressures at work or the early signs of mental illness.

There are four parts to this:

1. An understanding of mental health and mental ill health.
2. How to identify the changes in behaviour of an employee who may be starting to struggle.
3. The questions to ask to gather more information.
4. Deciding 'What to do?', how best to manage this individual in a work-based setting.

## UNDERSTANDING MENTAL HEALTH AND MENTAL ILLNESS

How mental health and mental illness are conceptualised, the language used to describe behaviours and symptoms or effects, and the basis for the possible problem (is it an organic illness or a reaction to events?) impact on how the issues are perceived and dealt with. For the purposes of this piece and as an aid to the management of issues in the workplace there are two models of mental health/ill health that the manager will find useful.

### The Medical Model

The medical model, or bio-medical model, of mental illness promotes the view that problems are an illness similar to any physical problem.

> Applying the concept of medical disease to psychiatric disorders with states of health and illness representing two distinct categories. The bio-medical model tends to promote the view that 'mental illness is an illness like any other'; 'mental illness is a brain disease'. Science provides the foundation for understanding the causes of mental health problems. (Rethink, 2004:6)

At the core of the medical model are definitions and categories of disorders that can be used to link an individual with a named disorder. These are exemplified by the *Diagnostic and Statistical Manual of Mental Disorders IV* (APA, 1994) and the *International Classification of Diseases*, 10th revision (WHO, 1994) that have lengthy and complex lists of diagnostic criteria.

The medical model fits most closely those patients whose symptoms are clear and unequivocal. Normally this is the more seriously affected individual; hence the medical model fits best in those people seen by a psychiatrist, or other clinician.

The medical model of mental illness is dominant throughout most of the world and is at the centre of the language and treatments available to doctors. For the layperson or the manager at work understanding what is wrong, in the terms used by the medical model, may have attractions. There can be a sense of knowledge by using technical terms and a veneer of understanding and common purpose when sharing the terms used by experts. When used inappropriately the language of the medical model – including such common words as depression, anxiety and stress, and labels used for mental illness, autism, anorexia and bipolar affective disorder for example – can lead to problems. My suggestion is that these terms should be avoided by managers in all cases, with the one exception of a colleague who has been diagnosed by an appropriate clinician and then chooses to use the term of him- or herself.

Training managers in the medical model has many difficulties. It is a complex area, and would require a high level of expertise before the manager could use the training to help support colleagues. The medical model may lead to an over-emphasis on 'illness' for many employees who are temporarily struggling and make the return to normal harder to achieve unless 'cure' has been effected. Inappropriate diagnosis, so-called 'spot-labelling' based on a limited understanding, stigmatising and discriminatory language and prejudice based on personal views make the medical model inappropriate for the non-specialist who is seeking to decide what to do when a colleague is behaving unusually.

There is some research evidence pointing to the potential difficulties of training managers using the medical model. One study found that teachers were less effective in recognising depression in their students after training (Moor et al., 2007) and another found that whilst the ability of managers to recognise the severe problem of schizophrenia was improved, their ability to recognise the common problem of depression was not improved with training, and yet the latter is far more likely to be encountered on a day-to-day basis in a work-based setting (Kitchener & Jorm, 2004).

Furthermore, 'the media hyperbole and the pseudo-science that tends to surround stress at work' sums up the need for managers to leave medicine, and the medical model of mental health, to the qualified clinician (Miller et al., 2002:xi).

## The Social Model

The social model of mental illness, sometimes called the bio-psycho-social model, emphasises a continuum of behaviours from 'normal' through to 'abnormal' (cf. the mentally ill of the medical model) and links the individual's place in society with their physiology and individual psychology. The interplay of behaviours, feelings and changes in physiology leads to distress for the individual and, potentially, difficulties for those around him or her.

The strategy of those who adopt a social model approach is often to present mental health and mental illness as a continuum connecting 'ordinary' living (thinking, feeling, behaving) to mental disorder. It locates social stigma and discrimination within social institutions and not exclusively 'in' the individual. The labelling of psychiatric disorders is avoided and people's experiences of mental health 'problems', 'distress' or 'crisis' are the focus of awareness training. (Rethink, 2004:6).

The social model emphasises the normality of psychology for all of us, and how every day of our lives we have 'psychology' in the same way as we have 'physiology'. Sometimes something is not quite as expected, as it is with physical well-being.

Focussing on the actual experience of the employee has many advantages at work:

- The individual is talked to, not the illness
- Support can be explored, not treatment
- The support may be in the system, not just the individual (e.g. adjusting working hours)
- Support can be offered without first finding a 'cure'
- This supportive approach benefits everyone.

> Most people who suffer from a mental illness will make a full recovery with appropriate diagnosis, management and treatment. Doing what is right and, more importantly, not doing what is wrong, is the cornerstone of good quality care. (Buckley & Buckley, 2006:x11).

Good quality care in an organisation revolves around the answer to the question, 'What to do?' rather than deciding what is wrong and identifying the best treatment. This must remain the focus of good quality care for the clinician. The social model provides a route to this for the manager when coupled with the knowledge that the medical model lives with the expert.

This may be seen as a quite radical approach to the norm, where mental illness is the province of occupational health, and health and safety. It is a different way of looking at mental health and mental illness that looks for support for individual employees, their colleagues and the organisation.

Bob Grove, Jenny Secker and Patience Seebohm provide some very powerful arguments for a 'new paradigm' in thinking (and actions) to address the challenges presented by mental health issues at work (Grove et al., 2005). Their book *New Thinking about Mental Health and Employment* changes the 'illness' definition to a focus on individual needs and individual contributions to the workplace, irrespective of any label and even life-long treatment for clear mental illnesses.

For organisations to benefit financially and strategically, widening the responsibility to find solutions further than the treatment focus of expert services, is vital. To achieve this the manager needs to be able to recognise and explore unusual behaviour as early as possible by having an awareness of the signs, the knowledge to explore issues sensitively and an understanding of the support systems in place within the organisation and the wider society.

# RECOGNISING PSYCHOLOGICAL AND MENTAL HEALTH PROBLEMS

Table 11.2 lists a variety of ways that someone may behave that could indicate a mental health problem. None of these signs when viewed in isolation will demonstrate categorically that the person has a mental illness. These would often be quite normal behaviours shown by many of us at times.

**Table 11.2**  Signs to look for which may indicate some action is needed

Appearance

- Unusual dress?
- Lack of personal care?
- Body language or movement?

Behaviour

- Agitated and nervous?
- Lethargic and uninterested?
- Repetitive behaviours?
- Is there a mismatch between what is being said and how they appear?

Mood

- Incongruent with what would be expected?
- Overly pessimistic?
- Optimistic in a way that seems inappropriate?
- Sad, hopeless or apathetic?

Thoughts

- Fixations or preoccupations?
- Irrational or delusional thoughts?

Perception

- Experiencing as real something that is not?
- Hallucinations of sight, hearing, smell, taste or touch?
- Not experiencing the world as would be normally expected?

Intellect

- Changes in intellect or intellect not as expected?
- Lack of thought processes that would be expected?
- 'In a different world'?

Insight

- Is there a rational and believable explanation?
- Does the person seem aware that they may be behaving unusually?

**Table 11.3**   Watch out for:

- Changes in work patterns
- Unexplained absences and sick leave
- Use of alcohol or other products
- Isolating or withdrawing from usual social contact
- Tiredness, apathy, lack of energy
- Changes in capacity to make good judgements
- Changes in ability to make appropriate decisions
- Unusual emotional displays
- Changes in usual behaviour
- Difficulties in relationships at work.

It is an accumulation of signs and behaviours that provide the clarity around any future diagnosis arrived at by a mental health specialist.

The important point is not to ignore these signs but to find out more information to discount them, or as additional information that indicates a possible problem. The first priority is to look for a rational reason for the changes in behaviour. Strange and unusual behaviour does not necessarily mean a psychological problem. Avoid ignoring unusual behaviour, but do not assume it is a mental health issue.

Table 11.3 shows a slightly different approach to help raise awareness when there may be a developing issue that needs exploration. It is more about seeing evidence that needs looking at than the specific signs from Table 11.2.

The key point, in both these tables of signs and other evidence, is change. Change is the most important indicator that there may be a problem.

Has timekeeping changed? For some this may be spending much longer at work than normal and is not limited to poor time-keeping. Outwardly positive change could well be a sign that someone is starting to struggle.

Has sociability changed? A common desire with anyone suffering from psychological 'distress' is to isolate. If someone stops joining the group for a coffee, or seems to be in their office with the door shut more than usual, it may be worth talking to the individual. Conversely if someone were to start spending more time with others or seem to want company all the time there could be a need to check this out. Another sign that could, outwardly, suggest an increase in sociability would be the person who starts to join the group that goes to the bar after work, or at lunchtime. It may not be a desire for friendship but an increasing use of alcohol that is driving this behaviour.

## HOW TO APPROACH PEOPLE

Once some unusual or worrying behaviour has been noticed it seems sensible to try to find out more information. To do this means having a conversation with the employee, and addressing those behaviours that have given rise to the concerns. A straightforward, matter-of-fact approach that neither ignores nor dramatises any unusual behaviour is most likely to have positive results. It can

**Table 11.4**   How to approach people

1. Avoid telling the person what to do.
   - Let the employee remain in control.
   - Avoid intrusive questions.
   - Allow time for them to decide what, if anything, to tell you.

An important part of this basic principle is that the employee remains in control. If you ask anything that takes away their control then you may lose the chance to positively affect the outcome. Taking control may lead to them closing down or telling you what they think you want to hear and will almost certainly lead them away from working with you to find a resolution.

2. Ask non-controlling or open questions only.

   - 'I wonder if anything has happened recently?
   - 'I've noticed you've been quieter than usual.'
   - 'I am wondering how are you doing at the moment?'

All of these allow the person plenty of freedom to choose what to say. Often maintaining a silence after asking the question allows the employee both the time and a sense of safety to be able to answer you instead of feeling pressured.

3. Never push for an answer.

Even if an employee is starting to behave in ways that are giving real concern, be patient. It is not necessary to know what is really going on for the employee. You don't need to know the detail, only information that will help towards a plan.

4. Don't attempt to diagnose

Avoid medical language unless the employee has seen a mental health specialist and received a diagnosis, and then, only if the employee chooses to use the words about themselves. 'You seem depressed' may label someone unhelpfully. 'You seem very low today' however, acknowledges their mood without any link to an illness.

---

be difficult for anyone, even the professionals, to pick the right words, the right way and the right time to broach a difficult subject (Table 11.4.)
Remember:

- Let the employee remain in control
- Be patient; allow time for them to choose what to tell you
- Ask open and non-controlling questions
- Let the employee decide what and how much to say
- Never push for information
- You don't need to know everything to be really helpful
- Don't make suggestions about any illness.
  - Use non-medical language
  - Discourage others from using medical terms
- Let the employee decide what terms to use.

# WHAT TO ASK

The section above, giving some pointers as to how to approach the employee who is struggling, includes some 'do not's. This section covers the three areas where questioning will give information that helps work towards a plan of what to do. Following the basic principles of sensitivity and respect, as outlined above, ask about the history of the problem, its prevalence or pervasiveness and if there is any plan of action to help resolve the issues.

Table 11.5 lists the three key areas that are helpful to explore once an employee has shown signs that could indicate a mental health issue. Unless a crisis has occurred it is likely that some exploration of what is actually happening for the individual will be necessary and helpful before making any decision as to what to do.

## The Past

Asking about the past gives two important pieces of information. Firstly, just because something unusual has been noticed does not mean that it is necessarily a new feeling or behaviour; the person may have kept their suffering well hidden. So, knowing how long the employee has felt like this is very important. Someone who is really low, but was fine until last week, would normally be a lower level of concern to someone who has been low for some months, but been

**Table 11.5**   PPP questioning

Past

- What is the history of this behaviour or feeling?
- How long has the client had similar feelings?
- Has this happened before?

Pervasive

- How much of the client's life is involved?
- Is this a home issue that has crossed over to work today?
- Is it a work issue that is impacting on home life?
- Or are all parts of the client's life affected?

Plan

- Is there a plan?
- Is the plan positive?
- Is the plan realistic, will it work?
- Will the plan be carried out, is there commitment?

*Note*: PPP questioning is © Andrew Buckley

able to hide their feelings from colleagues at work. Secondly, asking if this has ever happened before gives information that is helpful in deciding how to help and what to do. A repeating pattern of difficulties could emerge, and the employee may be able to use strategies and tactics that helped in the past during this present period of difficulty.

## How Pervasive?

Knowing how much of the employee's life is impacted by the signs that have been observed gives clues as to how to proceed. Someone whose low mood, emotional outbursts or other changes in behaviour are primarily a problem at work points to an organisational issue. If the focus of the issues lies in the employee's personal life there may be less that the organisation can do except support the employee.

If the issues impact all parts of the employee's life then the level of concern will be higher as the employee will not have the respite of either going home, or coming to work, to provide a period of rest from their problems.

## A Plan?

A substantial barrier to helping and treating anyone with a psychological problem, or mental illness, is the individual accepting that there is something wrong and that they need to have a plan of what to do. The best predictor for recovery from a psychological problem is recognition that something is wrong and a plan to do something about it. But the plan does need to be realistic and positive.

## WHAT TO DO?

The action that is taken once a colleague has shown signs of a possible mental health problem is the most important step. It is also the step most difficult to give advice about. Every individual, every team, every organisation and every locality or country is different. For the manager, knowing what is available in the way of support within the organisation is vital.

- If there is an employee assistance programme, how is it accessed?
- If there is medical cover, what is the route to this support for the employee?
- Is an occupational health service available on site?
- Is there a designated contact in human resources for advice?
- What access does the employee have to his or her own family doctor or other mental health professional?

The larger organisation is more likely to have policies and procedures in place. For the smaller business an ad hoc system of offering support may be more likely. However an organisation structures the support for an employee who is having difficulty, the key is to make access to this as straightforward as possible and for all managers, at least, to be fully aware.

But access to formal support is only one part of the picture. Much can be achieved without the need for the employee to be seen by any clinician or expert. As indicated in the introduction, mental health/mental illness is often a sliding scale and an employee may need little more than some relatively minor adjustments to allow them to manage their own issues and return to normal functioning. The social model of mental health emphasises the importance of social factors in mental ill health. Most people will accept that bereavement, for example, can be a very painful experience and that a caring approach possibly with some temporary adjustment to working hours and responsibilities will help the employee. Similarly an employee experiencing a relationship problem, possibly divorce, or illness of a family member, may be helped by common-sense adjustments.

Similar adjustments will help many employees who show signs of distress, whatever the cause or even when there is no apparent focus to the problems.

The goal in all these cases, from bereavement, divorce, family problems or no obvious reason, is to help the employee to cope with the situation so that they are able to return to normal. Many people who are, eventually, diagnosed with a mental illness could have been helped to avoid sliding from relative health, or at least temporary ill health, into mental illness by the timely and sensible accommodation of their situation by family, friends and their employers.

Widening the responsibility for the recognition and management of mental health and psychological issues from the expert service of human resources and occupational health to all managers is one key part in the story that is well-being at work.

## REFERENCES

APA, American Psychiatric Association (1994). *Diagnostic and Statistical Manual of Mental Disorders*, 4th edn. Washington, DC: APA.

Buckley, A. & Buckley, C. (2006). *A Guide to Coaching and Mental Health: The Recognition and Management of Psychological Issues*. London: Routledge.

Department of Health (2006). *Action on Stigma: Promoting Mental Health, Ending Discrimination at Work*. London: Shift. Available online at www.shift.org.uk (accessed 5 May 2007).

Grove, B., Secker, J. & Seebohm, P. (2005). *New Thinking about Mental Health and Employment*. Oxford: Radcliffe Publishing.

Kitchener, B. A. & Jorm, A. F. (2004). Mental health first aid in a workplace setting: A randomized controlled trial. *BMC Psychiatry*, **4**:23.

Miller, D. M., Lipsedge, M. & Litchfield, P. (2002). *Work and Mental Health, an Employers Guide*. London: Gaskell.

Moor, S., Maguire, A., McQueen, H. *et al.* B. (2007). Improving the recognition of depression in adolescence: Can we teach the teachers? *Journal of Adolescence*, **30**:81–95.

St John, T. (2005). Mental health at work: The hard facts. *Training Journal*, May, pp. 44–47.

Rethink (2004). How can we make mental health education work? Rethink. Available online at www.rethink.org.uk (accessed 5 May 2007).

WHO, World Health Organisation (1994). *International Statistical Classification of Diseases and Related Health Problems*, 10th Revision (ICD-10), 2nd edn. Geneva: WHO.

# PART 2

# Responding to Specific Organisational Challenges

CHAPTER 12

# Organisational Responses to Traumatic Incidents

**Alison Dunn**
*Occupational Health Department at Transport for London*

## INTRODUCTION

Very little has been written on the specific subject of organisational response to disaster. This chapter aims to provide a practical guide to the issues and challenges of planning and implementing an organisational response to a critical incident from a counselling/psychological perspective. It is hoped that readers will find this to be a useful and informative contribution – opening up areas for debate that practitioners will recognise.

This chapter will look at organisational responses to disaster from the perspective of the emotional, psychological and humanitarian needs of employees involved.

### Individual and Organisational Responses to Trauma

It is widely understood that immediate responses during traumatic incidents are directed by the reptilian part of the brain – the primitive part designed to maximise our chances of survival in the most dangerous situations. The first split second response may be to fight, flee or freeze – depending on the nature of the danger and our own individual psychological makeup. Tehrani suggests that there is a fourth possible response – which is to "'deal" with the demands of the traumatic situation' (2004:26).

One of the issues that is clear when working within an organisation is that just as traumatised individuals can have insufficient internal and external resources in the face of an overwhelming experience, so can the organisation – and of course one impacts on the other. However, good support structures,

*Employee Well-being Support: A Workplace Resource.* Edited by A. Kinder, R. Hughes and C.L. Cooper.
© 2008 John Wiley & Sons, Ltd.

clearly defined roles and responsibilities, adequate resources, effective training, planning and communications will aid recovery post incident.

Those responsible for organizing the supportive response may experience
the collective response in different ways, for example:

- Demands or requests – spoken or unspoken – to 'make it better now'.
- Anxiety that some people are forgotten.
- Anger that not enough is being done.
- Miscommunications, confusion.
- Conversely – that everything is back to normal – when it clearly isn't.
- An assertion that help isn't needed.

The role of the counsellors working in this context is to root their understanding of these responses in their knowledge of trauma, to hear and contain
them on an emotional level, and to hold the belief that things can and will move
on. Counsellors themselves may experience these feelings and need to be
aware and support each other when inevitable feelings of overwhelm occur. It
is not helpful when counsellors get stuck in the hopelessness and overwhelm
experienced by others.

## CASE STUDY: PROVIDING SUPPORT TO TRANSPORT FOR LONDON EMPLOYEES FOLLOWING THE BOMBINGS ON 7 JULY 2005

London Underground staff were not only caught up in the immediate aftermath of the bombings, but they also provided the initial rescue response
following the bombings on 7 July 2005. They continued to provide a service to
Londoners despite the further attacks on 21 July and the ongoing threat of
further incidents. Employees were significantly affected by this, and it was the
role of the Counselling and Trauma Service to respond to their needs for
trauma support. The team worked closely with Emerald-Jane Turner of EJT
Associates, in developing and delivering the interventions that formed this
response.

When it first became known that some very major incidents had occurred on
London's transport system on 7 July, it was immediately clear that the
counselling team were facing their biggest ever challenge in terms of providing
employee support. As the rescue operation unfolded at the four explosion sites,
the process of planning got underway. It was unnaturally quiet as clients were
unable to come in for sessions; however the phones were busy with calls from
senior managers, checking out that support was available. Communications
were a priority – to reassure everyone that support was indeed available. This
was done through discussions with managers, through email and the company
intranet.

The most difficult part of these very early hours was when a manager requested counsellors to go to the site immediately. This was difficult to organise at the time; however volunteers from the Trauma Support Group were able to provide support to colleagues on site. Volunteers are trained to offer 'emotional first aid' and they did an excellent job on that day.

Counsellors were available by phone to listen, normalise responses and offer advice on how to manage stress symptoms. It was important to ensure that this was available constantly so another task on that first day was to set up a 24-hour helpline for employees, which we did through liaison with ICAS. This service was kept in place for many months after 7 July.

The following day counsellors went to the site of each incident to talk to managers and staff. They discussed with managers what help might be needed and spoke to some employees. It became clear that teams of employees were working together well and supporting each other. Managers were concerned about some individuals; however, many employees were still very much involved in the ongoing response and not ready to think about their own needs. In the meantime, employees from all over the organisation with differing needs were being referred and were being offered telephone support by a counsellor.

Face-to-face counselling sessions were offered to all employees who wanted this. Early sessions focussed on education, normalisation, symptom management – to help clients to understand and manage their trauma responses. Resource-building helped them to identify what resources were available to them both internally and externally and which coping strategies were helping and could be enhanced; also which people were able to provide good support and how to use this effectively. Those employees in most distress were offered ongoing counselling. Most people found that symptoms eased within the first months so that they were able to resume work and normal functioning. A few have been provided with longer-term counselling.

Early assessments suggested that providing group sessions could be an effective helping strategy. Working together would enhance the impact of normalisation, enable discussion of effective coping strategies and help people to support each other. These groups were well attended by staff and managers and appeared to be extremely effective.

A key part of the response over the first year involved ongoing liaison with managers. In addition to regular telephone conversations and visits, they were given written guidance on how to support their staff. Personal support was often provided informally with managers reluctant to see themselves as needing help.

Counsellors provided a presence as the stations affected by the bombings were reopened, and on the first anniversary. As the anniversary approached, managers were visited so that their needs could be discussed. Written communications offering advice to managers and staff were circulated and the team provided on-site support for all the relevant areas.

Providing this response did have an impact – both on individual counsellors and the team as a whole. Additional support has been needed, both at the time and since in order to help with managing this impact. Group support, individual support and, further down the line, team-building has helped with this process.

This summary may suggest that the process was relatively clear and straightforward to provide, but it was far from that. Judgements and choices were made as the process unfolded. This chapter is intended to share some crucial learning points.

## THE CHALLENGES IN PROVIDING PSYCHOLOGICAL SUPPORT FOR CRITICAL INCIDENTS

There are many challenges for those who have a role in providing psychological support to organisations following critical/traumatic incidents. The summary below is written from the perspective of providing support in house within a large public sector organisation – however, it is hoped that it will highlight important areas to be considered and debates/questions relevant to all settings.

### Pre-incident Preparation in the Organisation from a Counselling/Psychological Perspective

Influence can be applied in several ways:

• Contribution to organisational training programmes
• Contribution to resilience-building and stress awareness in the organisation.

#### Organisational Training Programmes

Effective pre-incident training that prepares employees for incidents has an important role in minimising the impact of trauma. Employees and managers can learn about the potential psychological impact of incidents, how to cope with the symptoms, and to be familiar with the support that would be available to them. Crucially, first line managers can learn how to support employees in the immediate aftermath of an incident, and how to monitor the well-being of their employees in the ensuing weeks and months. Influencing the organisation may involve persistence in the context of competing priorities and limited training time.

#### Resilience-Building and Stress Awareness in the Organisation

This can provide another opportunity for the organisation to better prepare and equip staff for situations that place significant psychological demands on them. Organisations may recognise the impact of stress – if only in their sickness absence figures. This can provide an opportunity for working with managers and teams on building personal resilience. Undertaking this learning when not in crisis will help them maintain their resources when faced with more critical situations.

## Writing a Plan for Supporting the Organisation in the Aftermath of an Incident

A comprehensive written plan provides reassurance and clarity in a situation that is suddenly not clear, and is possibly overwhelming. Having such a plan frees up energy for responding to the many and varied demands that follow an incident without having to plan every detail of the response as it unfolds. Following the bombings on 7 July 2005, it became clear that although the counselling team's critical incident plan had provided a good structure for responding to previous incidents; it did not provide sufficient structure for an incident of this magnitude. The plan has been extensively rewritten to take account of all the learning points.

The important elements of a good plan are:

1. Clear roles and responsibilities.
2. Flexibility to take account of who may or may not be available.
3. At least one person who does not get involved in hands-on work and is able to maintain the overview.
4. A valuable role for everyone whether 'hands-on' or providing back-up.
5. A good process to follow for decision-making.
6. Practical information about exactly what to do to offer different kinds of support.
7. Information on how to obtain the necessary additional resources to do the work.
8. Timescales – broad planning for the immediate response, ongoing and long-term support.
9. Consideration of the needs at all levels of the organisation.

All team members need to be familiar with the plan and regular update training will also be helpful to ensure that people have the skills and confidence to carry out their roles when necessary. The plan should be regularly reviewed to keep up with various changes and developments.

Other key people in the organisation may also need to be aware of the plans. Wherever possible, plans for offering psychological support should be integrated with and link with other organisational emergency plans. Involvement in exercises to rehearse emergency plans is ideal. An organisational intranet may be a useful place to include information on individual and organisational response to incidents and the plans that are in place.

**Box 1. Example of a Critical Incident Plan for a counselling service in an organisation**

## INTRODUCTION

- A clear statement about the purposes of the plan, and how these objectives will be achieved.
- Information on the different types of incidents that may occur and how to assess differing needs for support.

## IMMEDIATELY AFTER AN INCIDENT HAS OCCURRED

- An outline of roles and responsibilities – what will be expected of everyone involved in providing the psychological response.
- What needs to be done immediately after an incident has been notified.
- Communications – what will be needed – both to the organisation as a whole and to the team(s) involved.
- Providing immediate support to local managers.
- Making on-site visits – how this will help, what to do and when.
- A list of practical resources that have been prepared in advance to take out on site.
- What additional resources – especially people – will be needed to do the work and how to access this.
- What additional administrative tasks that will need to be carried out.
- Dealing with previously arranged commitments.
- What additional support will be available for everyone.

## THE ONGOING RESPONSE

- Ongoing communications with the organisation, senior managers and significant individuals.
- Providing ongoing support to local managers and teams.
- Providing ongoing counselling and support for individuals.
- What resources are needed to support the ongoing response.
- Ongoing support for everyone involved.

## THE LONG-TERM RESPONSE

- Offering support with the rehabilitation process for those returning to work after an absence.
- Ending each part of the work – helping people to move on.

- Support through the first anniversary – for individuals, teams and the organisation as a whole.
- What do those who have been providing the support need in order to move on?
- Supporting information.
- Contact details for everyone.
- The format for offering different types of support – immediate, practical face-to-face support, telephone support, group support, support for counsellors.
- Templates for communications to the organisation as a whole at various stages.
- Guidance leaflets for managers and employees.
- Guidelines on relevant internal processes.
- Information and contact details for accessing the additional resources needed – both people and practical resources.

## Planning to Support the Counsellors/the Team

Berger (2001) provides a good in-depth discussion of the impact of working with trauma on the therapist. Providing good quality support to the counsellors and/or the team needs to be planned in advance. Counsellors will need additional good quality supervision when working with a traumatised organisation to ensure that the risk of vicarious trauma is minimised. In the same way that individuals may be helped by providing group support, group supervision is likely to benefit the counsellors. Regular communication with and within the team must be a priority so that everyone is aware of what is happening within the organisation, and with the counselling response. The necessary practical resources should be available, for example food, drinks, a bag of resources to support clients ready to take out on site. Monitoring should ensure that counsellors do not overwork.

## What Support Can/Should Counsellors Offer in the Immediate Aftermath of an Incident?

Managing people's distress in the aftermath of an incident can be stressful for those whose role and training is in other areas. Managers often feel the need to have expert help in these situations and there can be a demand for counsellors to be sent to the scene – *now*. This can be difficult – not only in terms of available resources but also the dilemma of knowing that professional counselling is not what people need during or immediately after an incident. Rational explanations about what support is and is not useful at this stage and help with obtaining appropriate support doesn't prevent the feeling that they have asked for help from the service that is supposed to be there to help support them, and have been told 'no'. It appears that *something* is needed immediately from the professionals, even if it is not counselling.

The anxiety and helplessness that forms part of a normal response needs to be contained and, once the manager feels less anxious, they are often able to support their staff very effectively themselves. Of course managers who have received good pre-incident training are likely to understand their responses and feel more confident about their ability to support people.

Our understanding of what people need in terms of practical support has developed significantly over the years. We know that when people are in shock they are most effectively helped by a person who is familiar to them rather than a stranger and that most people have the capacity to take on this role. Good immediate practical support should include education, advice and reassurance – giving information about how to access good support, advice about what to expect and how to cope, help with getting home (and ensuring that someone will be there) and giving people written advice to take away with them. Counsellors can also fulfil this role – as it is better provided by a stranger than not provided at all. Sometimes no amount of support will be contain the strong emotions and responses at this immediate stage, but providing it can help to break through the sense of isolation that trauma can engender.

In a context where incidents occur regularly, a peer support scheme may be useful. Volunteers can provide early practical and emotional support. Setting up such a scheme requires some commitment as volunteers need to be recruited and trained initially, and supported and offered refresher training in the longer term. The advantages of an enthusiastic and dedicated team of volunteers who give freely of their own time to support others are that awareness of trauma may be raised with a positive impact on organisational culture. It is important however that managers, counsellors and the volunteers themselves are aware of the boundaries – what support a volunteer can provide and where the limits are.

The challenge for each organisation is to work out what the immediate needs for support might be after an incident and how best this might be provided. The important point is that those who will provide it must be prepared at all times. One way of preparing is to have a 'grab bag' ready – with things that will help to provide on site support – e.g. tissues, rescue remedy, lavender spray, leaflets, lists of useful contact details, relaxation CDs, and forms to enable record-keeping.

Reddy (2005) talks of the need for skills of critical incident management. He calls the work during this immediate phase 'stabilisation' – helping a business to recover its functionality through helping to underpin management and other support services, which may be of more assistance to individuals at this stage than individually focussed work. Clinicians may need to leave clinical expertise on one side and instead be responsive at an intuitive, spontaneous, human and pragmatic level. Thus flexibility is a key skill in those who provide immediate responses to critical incidents.

Tehrani (2004) also discusses the importance of considering differing needs – for example obtaining medical treatment, practical support, and dealing with psychological symptoms. A crucial requirement is to consider how best to help people to re-establish feelings of personal safety and security in a way that does not add to feelings of being overwhelmed or out of control.

## The Dilemma of What Psychological Support to Offer to Individuals in the Early Weeks After a Traumatic Incident

Much has been written about whether or not psychological debriefing is an appropriate intervention in the early days following an incident and this chapter will not contribute further to that debate here. What is important is that organisations are offered a response package that is appropriate to the needs of both the individual organisation but also the particular situation at the right time. Reddy (2005) and Tehrani (2004) both describe the models of working with incidents that they use when working in organisations. Orner and Schnyder (2003) state that it is important that early interventions validate and complement individual coping strategies.

Brewin, Rose & Andrews (2003) suggest that practitioners refrain from focussed symptom-orientated early intervention in favour of monitoring survivors for psychological disorder and closer intervention if this develops. This advice mirrors that outlined in the NICE (National Institute for Health and Clinical Excellence) guidelines which suggest 'watchful waiting' in the early weeks following a traumatic incident. 'Watchful waiting' is open to interpretation – however, in negotiation with clients, practitioners can do more than simply watch and wait. Clients benefit enormously from reassurance and normalisation, education about post-trauma symptoms that may be experienced, advice about what to expect and how best to cope in the short term. Many people can and do recover from traumatic experiences without the need for professional counselling, but good support encourages the self-healing process. Empowering clients to take control of their own recovery assists the recovery process.

## How to Work Effectively to Provide Support to Teams

Other than psychological debriefing, little has been written about models for providing support to teams. However, working with teams who have been involved in traumatic incidents together can help to develop their ability to support each other, and to move forward together.

The four-stage model described in the case study is based on principles similar to those already described for working with individuals. It is focussed not on the incident, but on normalising, educating and promoting good coping strategies and a culture of peer support. It was important that managers attended the group sessions and were seen as being part of the process – both part of the process and supporting their staff. The groups needed an extremely experienced facilitator as the process was not always straightforward – as is common to trauma response there were times when people in the group were extremely angry which needed sensitive handling, and there were also times when individuals attempted to distract from the purpose of the group and had this not been carefully managed the group work could have been sabotaged.

Feedback suggests that this did provide a very effective method of working and probably reduced the need for one-to-one support. Employees were reassured by listening to others and their ability to support each other was enhanced. Managers were reassured about their ability to support their staff. In addition it seemed that the relationship between management and operational staff benefited from the process. One area in particular had had a history of difficult relationships which seemed very different after this incident and the team support that was provided. Many managers did not want to ask for one-to-one support so this provided a means for them to be supported. As a group, managers were focussed on supporting their staff and doing what needed to be done to move forward and seemed reluctant to acknowledge their own need for support. Often this could be provided informally however, through regular phone calls or over a coffee while ostensibly planning team support!

## Communicating at All Levels within the Organisation

Good communication at all levels is important to underpin the rest of the work that is being done to offer support after incidents. It is also important to think about what channel of communication – email, phone, face-to-face visits – is the most effective one to use in each situation. Also, what messages need to be communicated to different levels within the organisation. It may also be important to keep repeating some messages in order for them to be heard.

In the case study, senior managers needed an overview of what support was being offered, an assessment of the impact of the incidents on employee well-being, and some ideas on how this might move forward. Local managers needed much more practical advice on what to do.

## Ending the Work – Enabling People to Move On

The timing of the ending and moving-on process is paramount. The return to normality marks the final stage of the recovery process. Working in an organisation, an important part of this process is helping employees who have been away from work with rehabilitation back into work, by formulating plans and advising clients and managers and supporting the process.

For organisational trauma it is just as crucial to monitor and be aware when to scale down the interventions and negotiate this carefully in order to support the moving-on process. The first anniversary may be a significant factor in moving on. As in counselling the signs will be there when it is time to end, and this is the final part of the work – ensuring that everyone knows how to obtain further support in future if needed.

## Evaluation

An important part of the ending process is looking at the lessons that have been learned and making the changes that are necessary to enable future responses to be even more effective.

As Reddy (2005) points out, the field of critical incident management is an area of evolving expertise. There is little in the way of evidence of effectiveness of the different elements of trauma response, or overall response programmes. It is important therefore that professionals working in organisations give consideration to how they monitor and evaluate the interventions they use. However, giving attention to organising and providing the resources to systematically evaluate what you are doing while providing a critical incident response is not easy. It is possible to monitor how individuals are progressing and what their current needs for support are and to talk to them about what helps them and truly listen. It is absolutely essential to maintain up-to-date awareness of developments, research and current thinking. Counsellors should be clear about their objectives and continuously question whether what is being done is having the right impact, being open to whether another intervention might be useful. The learning continues while the work is being done.

## SUMMARY

In conclusion these are some of the most important points to consider when providing a response to a critical incident within the organisation.

1. The counsellor within the organisation has a crucial role in the aftermath of a critical incident. Having a comprehensive understanding of trauma, the counsellor must model not getting caught up in the helplessness and overwhelm, instead holding the hope of things moving forward and changing.
2. Good solid structures for support must be speedily and visibly activated, enabling people to regain a sense of safety.
3. Counsellors must be extremely proactive in visiting and making contact with managers, teams and individuals to offer support, remembering that overwhelm can result in people not seeking help appropriately.
4. Counsellors need to use their skills to communicate constantly in different ways at all levels, building strong relationships with key people and never underestimating the value of informal discussions as a means of providing advice and support.
5. The counsellor's role includes acknowledging and validating the experiences of individuals and the organisation, offering encouragement for doing a good job, and working towards empowerment.
6. The response must be critically evaluated, learning lessons for the future while simultaneously acknowledging achievements and a job well done.

# REFERENCES

Berger, H. (2001). Trauma and the therapist. In T. Spiers (Ed.), *Trauma: A Practitioner's Guide to Counselling*. Hove: Brunner-Routledge.

Brewin, C., Rose, S. & Andrews, B. (2003). Screening to identify individuals at risk after exposure to trauma. In R. Orner & U. Schnyder (Eds.), *Reconstructing Early Interventions after Trauma; Innovations in the Care of Survivors*. Oxford: Oxford University Press.

Orner, R. & Schnyder, U. (2003). Progress made towards reconstructing early intervention after trauma: Emergent themes. In R. Orner & U. Schnyder (Eds.), *Reconstructing Early Interventions after Trauma; Innovations in the Care of Survivors*. Oxford: Oxford University Press.

Reddy, M. (2005). Critical incident services post-Nice. *Counselling at Work*, Summer.

Tehrani, N. (2004). *Workplace Trauma: Concepts, Assessments and Interventions*. Hove: Brunner-Routledge.

# CHAPTER 13

# Managing Suicide and Sudden Death within Organisations

**Andrew Kinder and Emily Duval**
*Atos Healthcare*

Death and bereavement happens to all of us: 'Despite all the advances of modern science 100 per cent of people still die' (Parkes, Laungani & Young, 1997).

Death occurs in organisations as anywhere else, and the effect of this resonates across many people. Such incidents give the organisation an important opportunity to demonstrate its support and respect for its people, which will be noted by employees as well as by the bereaved families. Expert handling is required after a death by suicide or when a suicidal employee informs work colleagues of his/her intentions. This chapter aims to raise some of the issues surrounding suicide and sudden death at work and suggests a number of ways that an organisation can respond to such challenges.

## STRESS AT WORK

Much has been published on the subject of stress (Cooper, 2005). Stress at work has been calculated as costing industry anywhere between 5% and 10% of GNP in the USA and UK (Clarke & Cooper, 2004; Quick & Cooper, 2003). Stress has been shown to be a risk factor to many ill-health conditions including heart disease, depression, stomach ulcers (Cooper, 2005). Although stress as a concept has been criticised by some as being inadequately defined, it is an issue that attracts a lot of attention particularly within an organisational context. In recent years the UK's Health and Safety Executive (HSE) has argued that stress at work needs to be tackled through equipping managers with effective tools and has developed management standards to support this work.

*Employee Well-being Support: A Workplace Resource.* Edited by A. Kinder, R. Hughes and C.L. Cooper.

Traditionally human resources (HR) has had a central role in supporting managers who deal with stress at work including difficult situations such as managing a death at work or dealing with suicidal employees. Alongside its continuing strategic role HR has been moving away from a local HR manager and into a 'shared services' role where support is more distant and provided through a 'transactional' approach such as via a call centre with operators who provide guidance using prescribed scripts. These can be very helpful for processing transactions such as pay or recruitment but may feel quite remote for the difficult people issues which managers deal with such as bereavement.

The personal experience of losing a co-worker is emotionally draining, and often only appreciated by those who have shared a similar experience. Many organisations still have not set up a supportive counselling or welfare service which can result in the manager feeling overwhelmed, especially without the traditional front-line support from HR.

## NATURE OF SUICIDE

The Hazards trade union-run magazine claims that suicides due to excessive work, stress and harassment exceed 100 deaths per year (www.hazards.org). In 2000, the World Health Organisation reported a global mortality rate of 1 million deaths to suicide, approximately one death every 40 seconds; 16 per 100,000. Additionally, there are more acts of self-injury and non-fatal injuries occurring which do not result in death. Clark & Goldney (2000) point out that 6 million people are bereaved through suicide annually. Suicide is estimated to be 50–60% higher than the official rate due to the stigma issues of recording it as such. Death by suicide exceeds the death toll due to road traffic accidents, yet receives less attention.

The following are groups that are specially vulnerable to suicide:

- The elderly, particularly White men over 80 years (www.ioaging.org).
- People with mental health problems (e.g. schizophrenia, borderline personality disorder).
- University students, age 18–24.
- People with a history of depression.
- Alcoholics have 50–70% greater risk than the general population (www.ioaging.org).
- Survivors of suicide (those who have lost a loved one to suicide).

It has also been noted (Wallace, 2004) that:

- Women are 10 times as likely as men to attempt suicide.
- US research indicates that 57% of all sexually abused women attempt suicide at least once.
- 56% of all completed suicides are first-time attempts (especially males and older people).

- At least 24% of all suicide cases have had contact with mental health services within 12 months of completed suicide.
- Suicide is the second most common cause of maternal death in the year following childbirth.

Men are more likely than women to adopt violent methods of death such as hanging, shooting or jumping where the methods are fatal, whereas women tend to overdose, having more likelihood of recovery.

## SUICIDE IN THE WORKPLACE

Suicide is rare, and occurrences of suicide in the workplace even rarer. However, it does happen.

---

Lord Justice Sedley found that a workplace accident contributed to the suicide of Thomas Corr who was working at Luton IBC car factory at the time. He said that the 'suicide was proved to have been a function of the depression and so formed part of the damage for which IBC was liable'.

The UK Independent Police Complaints Commission (IPCC) found that PC Tomlinson had concerns about her work in the run-up to her suicide. They found that she had 'a perception of bullying, a loss of status following her removal from the firearms unit and an unwillingness to accept a transfer within Merseyside Police'. The IPCC point out that there was no direct link between these issues and her death but did carry out various disciplinary actions over the bullying (taken from www.ipcc.gov.uk).

---

Publicity over a suicide at work can be very damaging for any organisation, especially when there is a possible link between the death and work-related stress. A suicide may affect an organisation's reputation which could require damage control, undoubtedly impacting the bottom line.

Looking more specifically at suicide within the workplace, it is clear that such events will create unique and demanding situations for many different roles. It will affect the manager who needs to decide quickly how best to respond given their front-line role. It will involve the HR professional in terms of them giving advice or getting help to deal with the situation. Healthcare practitioners working in the organisation (e.g. workplace counsellors, occupational health advisers or practitioners working for an Employee Assistance Programme [EAP]) will be particularly involved in supporting people who could be at high risk of suicide either in treatment or in referring on to more specialist help. The following scenarios have been drawn from real experiences of working within organisations to illustrate the challenges faced by each of these roles.

## Issue for the Manager

> You are Bill, the manager, who has just received a telephone message on your telephone that Jane, a member of your team has said that she is going to commit suicide. You phone Jane back immediately and hear a very distressed individual who is talking incoherently. You are not sure whether she has been drinking or taking some sort of drug. She asks that you don't phone the emergency services and stay on the phone talking to her; she doesn't want you to leave her. You are alone in the office. What can you do?

Although highly stressful for Bill, it is pretty clear that he has an obligation to maintain Jane's health and well-being that overrides Jane's wish for him not to act. It would be a brave, perhaps foolhardy, manager who risked not calling the emergency services. Nevertheless, there are practical issues that this scenario raises such as whether Bill can find out where Jane is and how he can call the emergency services whilst keeping Jane talking. These situations can also take sudden unexpected turns, for instance if Jane suddenly hangs up without disclosing where she is, or if someone else comes on the phone saying that Jane is fine and that he will now take care of her. No matter what the eventual outcome, Bill will need support himself, perhaps by talking through how limited his options were and that the intervention he made was in good faith. It is important that this support is provided as soon as possible. The scenario highlights how an organisation needs to be able to get help quickly from a suitable healthcare practitioner to provide reassurance for Bill and to link into specialist help for Jane. Effective case management is especially important in repeat situations, such as where Jane regularly phones Bill when she feels suicidal.

## Issue for the HR Professional

> You are the HR Business Partner and receive a distressed call from one of the managers, Azi. He confides to you that he has been feeling bullied by his manager for over three months. Azi says he has no confidence left, is anxious about losing his job and is at his 'wit's end'. In the conversation Azi drops in that he has been feeling suicidal in the last week but wants you to keep this in confidence. He doesn't want you to take this any further or to take any formal action as he is worried that the bullying will get worse and that the bullying has not been witnessed by anyone.

The issues here are whether you should respect his wish to keep his call confidential and the degree to which he is a suicidal threat. Azi trusted you with this information and you could undermine your position by breaking this trust, especially if Azi was not really suicidal but used the word to highlight the depth of his feelings. What could you do if you disclosed what Azi said, and a subsequent investigation cleared his manager of any wrongdoing leaving Azi to accuse you of destroying his career? On the other hand, how would you be viewed by the organisation if you kept it confidential and he followed through with his suicidal threat? These 'no win' scenarios can be very difficult to navigate through. However, getting the advice of a healthcare practitioner is an important first step to help the

HR professional think through the options such as whether to try and get Azi to see a professional counsellor/psychologist or to think how to work with Azi in terms of getting him to gather evidence of the bullying and to make sure he understands how the organisation's harassment policy would actually work.

## RISK ASSESSMENTS USED BY HEALTHCARE PRACTITIONERS

Organisations are increasingly aware of the need to have clear risk assessment policies and assessing the suicidal risk of an individual is an important part of such a policy especially for a healthcare practitioner. Joiner *et al.* (1999) has identified a number of factors which would highlight an individual who is at greatest risk of suicide. For instance:

- Past suicidal attempts/behaviours
- Current symptoms of suicide
- Life stresses that may precipitate vulnerability relative to the norm
- Degree of psychological disturbance such as depression, anxiety, substance abuse, hopelessness and helplessness
- Degree of self-control in overcoming desire to take suicide actions
- Social support and alternative coping strategies.

Healthcare practitioners need to be trained in the use of such risk assessment including having clear guidance on what they can do to respond effectively to a client who is high risk. Unfortunately if someone is determined to commit suicide it may be very difficult to prevent. Even the powers of sectioning under the Mental Health Act (1983) can be insufficient. For instance, even a client under 'observation' in a psychiatric hospital can still find ways of taking their own life. In addition, resources in the community mental health team/GP practice are constantly under pressure and it is unrealistic to think that every case referred will receive prioritised and appropriate help/treatment. When the individual goes back into the community following a period of being sectioned it is possible they will not receive adequate support/monitoring.

## TRAINING OF WORKPLACE HEALTHCARE PRACTITIONERS

Practitioners working in organisations need to increase their confidence in carrying out risk assessments. It is important to help the practitioner think not just of referring on to the GP but also about what intervention would be appropriate in the case. It is amazing to think of the number of cases where the practitioner is told by the client that they are the first person trusted with the client's suicidal thoughts. Such disclosures demonstrate trust in the relationship and that practitioners can probably do more to help that individual within the workplace than has been previously believed. The practitioner therefore needs to think not just about referring to the GP but also about maintaining some contact with the individual/organisation, bearing in mind professional issues of confidentiality.

Suicide within our society is considered taboo. For a healthcare practitioner whose client has committed suicide it can have a detrimental and lasting effect (Kapoor, 2002). Reactions of other professional staff can also raise further issues about attitudes to suicide as the following reflections of a practitioner show:

> I felt really shocked when I heard this news as I hadn't really considered her an actual suicide risk and I felt concerned that I had not done my job in some way or had opened up the organisation to some kind of litigation. I also remember having a heated debate with a professional colleague who questioned why I was concerned and simply said that it was the client's right to choose. I couldn't agree with this and put forward the argument that we should intervene and try to prevent suicide since we were working within an organisation and had a 'duty of care' to the individual. I also argued that it was morally wrong as it impacted other people in a highly destructive way.

Training can help the healthcare practitioner explore their attitudes to suicide. The following is an account of a counsellor who went through a suicide training module:

> I felt challenged in my beliefs that suicide was always negative, hostile and morally wrong. For instance, I could see that it was less 'wrong' in having a 'living will' for no resuscitation in a terminal illness even if this was tantamount to suicide. I also became aware that I judged suicide in relation to its effect on others, so I was less sympathetic to a mother with a baby committing suicide compared to a young man who was adopted, a heroin user and HIV-positive. I discussed this with my supervisor afterwards and I realised that it was easier for me to sit on the outside in judgement, rather than to get on the inside of the person and listen to their distress.

Healthcare practitioners, especially counsellors, need to be able to stay within the client's suicidal thoughts/hopelessness rather than rushing into reframing the 'cognitive ambivalence'. They need to 'acknowledge and stay with both aspects of the client's hopelessness/helplessness and their apparent immutability' (Wallace, 2004) and to be able to reflect on the impact of their attitude to suicide because saying it is morally wrong puts a distance between them and the individual's feelings of pain and confusion.

## SUDDEN DEATH WITHIN THE WORKPLACE

Suicide is not the only issue that takes up a great deal of time within the workplace. A sudden death of an employee can also have a dramatic effect.

> A team member, Fred, dies in a tragic accident at work. You are Fiona, the manager, who has to break the news to Fred's family. You have to answer the difficult questions about what happened and are confronted with strong emotions such as anger, and distress such as crying hysterically. You knew Fred well and feel torn between the requirements of the organisation to 'manage' the incident (i.e. not to say anything until a formal

investigation has been completed) versus providing support and comfort to the family. You feel at breaking point when you realise that you need to sort out Fred's personal effects in his locker.

The organisation has a duty of care to its staff. Given Fiona's personal knowledge of Fred she may not be the best individual to liaise with the family. How can the organisation lesson the burden on Fiona by having other managers come in to deal with the situation? Fred's family may be keen to find out what happened to cause the accident; they may be eligible to receive from Fred's pension a death-in-service payment; they may wish to express strong feelings to the organisation for causing Fred's death and they may get involved in litigation against the company.

Sorting out Fred's personal effects and responding quickly and sensitively to the requests of the family are clearly important tasks straight after the accident and in the weeks following it. Fiona and the other managers involved need to be able to get personal support so that they don't become ill from the stress and they need to know what to do in terms of the organisation's policies and procedures. Crisis planning meetings which also involve healthcare practitioners would certainly help each person know their responsibilities and co-ordinate the activities effectively. Some employers use a counsellor to support bereaved family members, which can then give the managers space to deal with the more administrative matters.

## FIRST-AIDERS

In the event of injury or sudden illness, failure to provide first aid could result in that person's death. The employer should therefore ensure that an employee who is injured or taken ill at work receives immediate attention.

> You are phoned by a first aider, Helen, who has been working on someone who had a heart attack but unfortunately died. Helen has been hearing gossip that she did not perform the right sort of treatment and feels blamed for the death. You are responsible for the in-house first-aiders and realise that they are now talking to each other about how little support is available to them and that their training is inadequate to equip them for such situations. You are concerned that Helen is not coping, that she is feeling very guilty about what happened and seems to be having flashbacks about what happened.

First-aiders are not frequently called upon to deal with extreme situations such as a colleague who has had a heart attack or been seriously injured, but if they are it is vital that the organisation provides its full support to all involved to ensure that any emotional trauma is minimised. A first-aider who has the unfortunate experience of having someone die whilst they work on them can be a very distressing experience. Training first-aiders in the importance of understanding the nature of trauma on them, especially when dealing with death in the workplace, should give them a measure of emotional self-protection. A healthcare practitioner trained in trauma support should be a good starting point here so that information can be given to the first-aider about the nature of trauma, the symptoms of trauma and how to access trauma counselling. The healthcare practitioner, in conjunction with the person responsible for first-aiders, needs to monitor any first-aider involved in a traumatic event to ensure that any trauma symptoms reduce over the following weeks. If the symptoms continue it is essential that appropriate interventions which include specialist trauma counselling are established.

All these scenarios require sensitive handling on an individual basis and it is almost impossible to develop generic guidance which is sufficient to meet the needs of each and every situation. It is clear that a lot of management time will be expended in dealing with each situation although an organisation who has begun to think through such scenarios, especially where they have brought in expert advice to help, will be more equipped and can save management time as a result.

## THE AFTERMATH

For every suicide, there are at least six 'survivors'. These are people who had close relationships with the deceased, and who will likely experience profound grief. Suicide in families inevitably affects survivors as employees in their work settings. Carla Fine's *No Time to Say Goodbye: Surviving the Suicide of a Loved One* includes the story of one office employee who lost his wife:

> 'Everyone in my office seemed to avoid me after my wife's suicide,' says Jerry, a forty-seven year old computer software executive, whose wife shot herself fifteen months ago. 'People in my business are very involved in their jobs ... But when I came back to work after the funeral, no one even mentioned that my wife had died. Colleagues whom I had known for years would avert their eyes when they saw me; if we did talk, our conversation would be about the latest sales figures or basketball scores. I wanted to stand on my desk and scream, 'My wife is dead. Please, someone, acknowledge it' (Fine, 1997:137)

In Jerry's case although his wife was not an employee at his firm, her suicide resonated through his office. In these circumstances, perhaps a manager has the duty to recognise the disquieting effect the death has had on his employee, and the subsequent impact it has had in the office. It would be noticeable that Jerry was perhaps not functioning as well at work and this was partially due to the lack of acknowledgement about the suicide from his colleagues. Furthermore, being a survivor of suicide, Jerry is now in a higher-risk category, himself.

The second author of this chapter shares her personal experience with suicide:

> My boyfriend died by suicide in 1993. We were colleagues at the same company, and I happened to find out about his death two days later, whilst finishing my shift. A manager approached me in the corner of a crowded room and delivered the news. (He had died in his apartment the morning after the evening I had dropped him off. Apparently, the ambulance workers couldn't find his phonebook, but they did locate documents from his

place of work, which is how the company was informed.) I went into shock immediately. Feeling the walls closing in on me, I escaped and lumbered to my car in a stupor. In hindsight, I wished the manager had taken me aside into a private office and given me the chance to sit down before blurting out the news. I recognised that it must have been hard for the manager, too, as she was not used to delivering that type of news, but as the surviving girlfriend, I would have appreciated more delicate handling.

This is an example of how a manager poorly handled communicating the news of a suicide. Managers who have no previous experience in this area may be unwittingly insensitive in their delivery.

When suicide occurs in the workplace, it is essential to consider the impact on both witnesses and those who were close to the deceased.

For witnesses who may only be tangentially acquainted with the deceased, they will probably not grieve. However, they may experience symptoms of post-traumatic stress. The trauma associated with witnessing the event or discovering the body may prevent staff from returning to work or the death scene, as it would be a reminder.

It is imperative for managers to recognise this type of stress and how it may potentially affect an employee.

Societal attitudes about suicide may be reflected in the verbiage chosen following a death. To say someone 'committed suicide' suggests criminality, which may have an impact on survivors in mourning. Some practitioners are now using the phrase 'died by suicide'.

## WAYS TO RESPOND TO A SUICIDE:

Clark and Goldney have analysed how the impact of suicide on others can be very great and can last for long periods after the event, possibly several years, especially where there are feelings of guilt. However, they have identified how this impact can be minimised and provide some helpful practical measures that should be implemented following a suicide:

- The true cause of death should be told from the outset, including to children.
- Opportunity for relatives to view the body without being rushed and in private should be granted. A vigil over the covered body should be considered as an alternative if it the body is mutilated.
- A public funeral can help those affected as it gives the opportunity for all to offer an adequate tribute.
- Counselling can be helpful to enable the bereaved to rationalise feelings such as guilt or rejection and the practitioner should be alert to clinical symptoms of trauma or depression which require more in-depth medical or psychological intervention.
- Support groups exclusive to Survivors of Suicide are particularly beneficial.
- The bereaved may find it more beneficial to explore issues other than why the suicide occurred (i.e. the 'why' may never be solved).

The emotional impact after a suicide is profound. It is essential for colleagues and peers to understand that grief after suicide is complex.

While survivors of suicide also experience the 'traditional' stages of grief (shock, denial, anger, bargaining and depression), they are also faced with a multitude of other emotions and reactions, some of which include:

- Guilt, 'if only I . . .'
- Shame
- Confusion
- Relief
- Rejection
- Blame
- Rage
- Some post-traumatic stress disorder symptoms, such as reliving the event, avoiding reminders, feeling numb, self-destructive behaviours, mental blocks, hyper-vigilance.

## SUMMARY

Sudden death in the workplace is rare – and suicide even rarer – yet both happen. Preparedness of management can make all the difference for employees and the organisation's reputation.

This article explores the nature of suicide and raises important questions about working with suicidal clients. It identifies typical scenarios that managers, practitioners and HR working within an organisational context can face including where sudden death occurs, highlighting some of the ways that organisations can prepare for this. It underscores the importance for practitioners to examine their attitudes about suicide and the importance of carrying out risk assessments.

Organisations have a duty of care to their people, as enshrined in health and safety legislation, and therefore need to put in place preventative policies to minimise the chance of suicide (e.g. effective bullying and harassment procedures). Clear crisis management systems are imperative in order to deal with a sudden death, a suicidal employee or an employee who dies by suicide. This article has attempted to expand the understanding and emphasise the degree of sensitivity required for survivors of suicide in the workplace and beyond.

## ADDITIONAL FEATURES OF GRIEF AFTER SUICIDE

---

- Feeling alone and ostracised.
- Romanticising suicide as a 'hero's tragic end'.
- Loss of faith in mental health professionals.
- *In the workplace:* Resentment towards the company or management for exacerbating the person's stress, or for not intervening.

- Repeating the story over and over.
- Temptation to lie about cause of death.
- Time and energy spent reconstructing the final days.
- Desperately searching for 'why'.
- Losing track of time, 'fuzzy' memory.
- Feeling detached.
- Apathy, purposelessness.
- Beginning to feel hopeless, suicidal.

## RISK ASSESSMENT FOR THE WORKPLACE

High risk factors to consider:

- Employee talking about suicide
- Previous suicide attempts
- Previous history of depression or mental health condition
- Frequent use of alcohol or drugs
- Access to weapons or toxic substances
- Work-related stress, burn-out or fatigue
- Frequent absences or tardiness
- Significant life events, loss, changes
- Financial burden
- Limited social or family support
- Legal problems.

## IF YOU BELIEVE AN EMPLOYEE IS SUICIDAL OR EXPRESSING SUICIDAL IDEATION

- Foster a relationship, express concern and listen empathically.
- Encourage the person to talk about their feelings.
- Reassure confidentiality and gently explain when and if it may be breached.
- Be direct when talking about suicide – don't tip-toe around the subject.
- Don't hold back in asking someone if they feel suicidal, in fear that you may embarrass them.
- Ask if there is any person they would like to have called.
- Identify support networks available to ensure the person is not left alone while feeling suicidal.
- Refer the person to the EAP or Occupational Health.
- Create a supportive work environment.
- Reduce job stress and minimise work-related demands.

## IF A SUICIDE OCCURS IN THE WORKPLACE

- Inform emergency personnel and authorities immediately.
- Do not tamper with any part of the death scene.
- Follow company policy for informing next of kin and documenting the incident.
- 'Debrief' staff using open and honest communication.
- Identify other high risk staff who may be vulnerable and refer to OH.
- Stay vigilant about the 'cluster suicide' phenomenon.
- Arrange for counselling on site.

## WHEN RETURNING TO WORK AFTER A SUICIDE OR SUDDEN DEATH HAS OCCURRED:

- De-stigmatise mental health issues.
- Remind workers of support available through EAPs or Occupational Health.
- Coordinate an appropriate tribute for the deceased.
- Reassure, support, and respect those who were close to the deceased.
- Understand that survivors of suicide are placed into a high risk category, themselves and thus more vulnerable.
- Don't try to 'cheer up' workers or make sudden morale boosts – allow people to process their grief.
- Be prepared for the possibility that some staff may blame themselves, management or the organisation for contributing to the death.
- Foster a supportive working environment.
- Focus on worker stress reduction.
- Promote worker empowerment and mental health.

## REFERENCES

Clark, S. E. & Goldney, R. D. (2000). Impact of suicide on relatives and friends. In K. Hawton & K. van Heeringen (Eds.), *The International Handbook of Suicide and Attempted Suicide*. Chichester: John Wiley & Sons, Ltd.

Clarke, S. & Cooper, C. (2004). *Managing the Risk of Workplace Stress*. London: Taylor & Francis.

Cooper, C. (2005). *Handbook of Stress Medicine and Health*. Boca Raton, FL: CRC Press.

Fine, C. (1997). *No Time to Say Goodbye: Surviving the Suicide of a Loved One*. New York: Doubleday.

Heckler, R. (1995). *Waking Up Alive*. London: Piatkus.

Joiner, T., Walker, R., Rudd, M. & Jobes, D. (1999). Scientising and routinising the assessment of suicidality in outpatient practice. *Professional Psychology: Research and Practice*, **30**:447–453.

Kapoor, A. (2002). Suicide: The effect on the counselling psychologist. *Counselling Psychologist Review*, **17**:28-36.

Parkes, C. M., Laungani, P. & Young, B. (1997). *Death and Bereavement across Cultures*. London: Routledge.

Quick, J. & Cooper, C. (2003). *Stress and Strain*, 2nd edn. Oxford: Health Press.

United Nations (1996). *Prevention of Suicide: Guidelines for the Formulation and Implementation of National Strategies*. New York: United Nations.

Wallace, P. (2004). Personal correspondence – information compiled from a number of sources including the websites cited below. Roehampton University.

## Useful Website Addresses (correct as of January 2008)

www.befrienders.org
Befrienders listen to people who are lonely, despairing or considering suicide. They don't judge them, don't tell them what to do. They listen. That may not sound much – but it can make the difference between life and death.

www.mind.org.uk
Mind is a leading mental health charity in England and Wales which works to create a better life for those who experience mental distress in their lives.

www.uk-sobs.org.uk
Survivors of Bereavement by Suicide (SOBS) exists to meet the needs and break the isolation of those bereaved by the suicide of a close relative or friend. It is a self-help organisation with volunteers who have themselves been bereaved by suicide.

www.samaritans.org.uk
Samaritans is available 24 hours a day to provide confidential emotional support for people who are experiencing feelings of distress or despair, including those which may lead to suicide.

www.who.int/en
The World Health Organisation provides multiple fact sheets on the topic of suicide, including 'Preventing Suicide: A Resource at Work'.

www.ioaging.org
Institute on Aging provides information about suicide among the elderly.

www.suicidology.org
The American Association of Suicidology is an education and resource organisation, dedicated to understanding and preventing suicide.

www.apa.org
The American Psychological Association online help centre has articles on 'Coping with the Death of a Co-worker'.

## Helpful Books for Those Bereaved through Suicide

Bolton, I. (1991). *My Son . . . My Son: A Guide to Healing after Death, Loss, or Suicide*. Atlanta: Bolton Press.

Fine, C. (1997). *No Time to Say Goodbye: Surviving the Suicide of a Loved One*. New York: Doubleday.

Guinan, J. & Smolin, A. (1993). *Healing after the Suicide of Loved One*. New York: Fireside.

Jamison, K. R. (1999). *Night Falls Fast: Understanding Suicide*. New York: Random House.

Wertheimer, A. (1991). *A Special Scar: Experiences of People Bereaved by Suicide*. London: Routledge.

## CHAPTER 14

# Bullying and Mistreatment at Work: How Managers May Prevent and Manage Such Problems

### Ståle Einarsen and Helge Hoel
*University of Bergen, Norway, and Manchester Business School, University of Manchester*

## BULLYING AND MISTREATMENT AT WORK: PREVAILING AND DEVASTATING PROBLEMS

Exposure to bullying and mistreatment at work are serious problems for many workers in contemporary working life. Studies have indicated that as many as 30% of the working population are exposed to some kind of mistreatment at work (Rayner, Hoel & Cooper, 2002), with more than 10% labelling themselves as victims of bullying (Hoel, Cooper & Faragher, 2001). Bullying is prevalent in both private and public organisations and finds its targets among men and women alike. It occurs on all organisational levels, with female managers as a particular risk group (Hoel *et al.*, 2001). Furthermore, bullying may have overwhelming negative effects on the health and well-being of targets as well as bystanders, causing organisational problems such as absenteeism, turnover and loss of job satisfaction. For targets, exposure to bullying can cause severe emotional reactions such as fear, anxiety, helplessness, depression and trauma, altering their perceptions of the work-environment to one of threat and insecurity.

A survey of 'Fortune 500' manufacturing and service companies in the USA reported an average loss per company of US$ 6.7 million annually due to increased absenteeism and turnover as well as reduced productivity resulting from incidents of sexual harassment alone. On a national level, the costs of bullying have been estimated to be close to £2 billion annually for the UK

*Employee Well-being Support: A Workplace Resource.* Edited by A. Kinder, R. Hughes and C.L. Cooper.
© 2008 John Wiley & Sons, Ltd.

(Hoel, Sparks & Cooper, 2001), and in the region of US$ 0.6 to $3.6 million per 1,000 employees in Australia (see Hoel, Einarsen & Cooper, 2003 for an overview). Hence, bullying represents a considerable cost both to employees, employers and the society.

In this chapter we will describe the essence of workplace bullying, including its causes, and provide employers and managers with some guidelines on how to prevent and manage this very real problem.

## WORKPLACE BULLYING: WHAT IS IT?

The concept of workplace bullying, labelled by some as 'workplace harassment' (Björkqvist, Österman & Hjelt-Bäck, 1994) or 'emotional abuse' (Keashly, 1998), refers to situations where employees are exposed to persistent psychological mistreatment at work, with the effect of persistently humiliating, intimidating, frightening or punishing the target. Typically, the target is teased, harassed and insulted with little recourse to retaliate in kind. Sometimes bullying consists of highly aggressive, violent or clearly unacceptable behaviours. However, even seemingly harmless behaviours may become acts of bullying with rather extreme negative effects on the target if repeated over a long period of time. Being ignored by a manager in a meeting or in a social gathering may happen to anyone. However, if one is ignored time and time again for weeks, months and even years, it is, of course, another matter. While being closely monitored or facing an excessive workload are experiences most of us share, one may argue that such acts turn into bullying when applied excessively (Brodsky, 1976). Hence, when frequently and persistently directed towards the same individual(s), even less obvious aggressive behaviours may turn into an extreme source of social stress (Zapf, 1999) causing severe harm and damage, particularly if these acts create conditions where an employee becomes ostracised and isolated. Although the negative and unwanted nature of the behaviour involved is essential to the concept of bullying, the core characteristic is not the nature of the behaviours per se, but rather the *persistency* of the experience. Thus, bullying may be as much about the frequency and duration of what is done as it is about what and how it is done (Leymann, 1996). Yet, this is not to justify or say that single acts of aggression and violence at work are acceptable, far from it.

Bullying may take the form of direct actions, such as accusations, verbal abuse and public humiliation, or be of a more indirect nature, such as spreading rumours, gossiping and social exclusion. Another distinction may be made between work-related behaviours and person-related behaviours (Einarsen, 1999) as evidenced in an early Finnish study by Vartia (1991), who identified six typical forms of bullying behaviours where slander, social isolation, and insinuation about someone's mental health may be seen as examples of person-related bullying, while giving an individual too few or overtly simple tasks and constantly criticising the person or his/her work may constitute work-related bullying. Similarly, Rayner and Hoel (1997) suggested the following categories of bullying: threats to professional standing, threats to personal standing, isolation, overwork and destabilisation, in which the last refers to such acts as failure to give credit when due, giving someone meaningless tasks and unjustified removal of responsibility. In addition, bullying can, of course, also include physically intimidating acts, acts of sexual harassment, physical violence or threats of violence, although such acts seem to occur more infrequently.

A central aspect of the bullying experience is an imbalance of power between the parties involved, whether this reflects existing power inequalities or gradually evolves as a result of the bullying process. Such an imbalance may rule out the opportunity for retaliation and effective defence on the part of the target (Vartia, 1996). This imbalance of power may mirror a formal power-structure as would be the case when the perpetrator is in a higher position in the organisational hierarchy relative to the target. Alternatively, the source of power may be informal, based on knowledge and experience, or personal and social standing. Furthermore, bullying typically preys on perceived personal inadequacies of the target or their social standing, which in itself may undermine the position of the target (Brodsky, 1976).

# HOW AND WHY DO BULLYING AND MISTREATMENT HAPPEN?

## An Evolving Process

There are probably as many reasons for why bullying happens as there are individual cases. As far as the focus of managers is concerned, one may argue that to identify what may cause the problem is less important than stopping the negative behaviour, bringing the destructive process to an end and restoring a safe and productive working environment for all. In addition, bullying sometimes takes the form of a gradually evolving process where, in an early phase, the target is exposed to more discrete and subtle forms of aggressive behaviour that may be difficult to pin down (Einarsen, 2000). Progressively more direct aggressive acts may then evolve and the target becomes ever more isolated, or is made a laughing-stock in front of colleagues. In such a process, a range of causes may be involved, including reactions and actions of the target that may worsen the situation or that may be used to justify the actions of the perpetrators (Zapf & Einarsen, 2003). In a state of distress and confusion, the target may annoy others, perform less competently, and withdraw from social and professional activities, reactions that may elicit aggressive behaviours in others or even act to distort the target's perception of the environment.

## Psychopaths and Neurotics?

A rather popular view is that these kinds of behaviour are deeply rooted within the personality structure of the bully. In an interview study among 30 Irish victims of bullying, all targets interviewed blamed the difficult personality of the bully for their ordeal (O'Moore, Seigne, McGuire & Smith, 1998). Interestingly, self-reported bullies have been found to describe themselves as being high on aggressiveness and low on social competence (Matthiesen & Einarsen, 2007). Ashforth (1994) describes 'petty tyrants' as leaders who wield their power over others through arbitrariness and self-aggrandisement, belittling of subordinates, lack of consideration for others and through the use of an authoritarian or dictatorial style of conflict management. In behavioural terms these leaders often shout and scream at subordinates, criticising, complaining and demeaning them, and even lying and manipulating others in order to have their way. However, not much is actually known about the characteristics of bullies as most studies have relied on information provided by targets. What we know is that more men than women are considered to be bullies and that in many countries, bullying is predominantly top-down, with a majority of bullies being managers or supervisors (Zapf, Einarsen, Hoel, & Vartia, 2003).

An equally controversial issue is the role of victim personality. In this respect, studies have shown that although the personality of victims may play a role in some cases, this cannot be considered the main cause of bullying. In a study of the personality of 60 Irish targets of bullying, Coyne, Seigne and Randall (2000) found targets to be more rule-bound, honest, punctual and accurate in comparison with a control group. Furthermore, in a Norwegian survey among 2,200 participants, targets of bullying described themselves as being low on self-esteem, high on social anxiety and low on social competence (Einarsen, Raknes & Matthiesen, 1994). Nevertheless, a range of studies have, however, shown that targets are far from a homogeneous group in terms of personality. A study of personality and personality disorders among 85 Norwegian victims of bullying (Matthiesen & Einarsen, 2001) revealed one subgroup of victims displaying a range of psychological problems and personality disturbances. A second group portrayed a tendency towards becoming depressed and being suspicious of the outside world. However, the third group portrayed a quite normal personality. The last group has been found to be by far the largest group, as one study showed that two thirds of all targets do not differ from the general population in terms of personality (Glasø, Matthiesen, Nielsen & Einarsen, 2007). Employees with psychological problems, low self-confidence and a high degree of anxiety in social situations may of course be more likely than others to feel bullied and harassed, they may find it more difficult to defend themselves when exposed to aggression, and may be seen by others as easy or 'safe' targets for outlets of frustration. Yet, a Norwegian study showed that a large portion of the workforce may have such kinds of problems without having any problems with bullying (Einarsen et al., 2007).

## A Culture of Aggression?

Several studies (e.g. Archer, 1999; Einarsen *et al.*, 1994; UNISON, 1997) have revealed that bullying seems to exist in organisational cultures that permit or reward such kinds of behaviour (see also Einarsen, Hoel, Zapf & Cooper, 2003, 2005). Following such a rationale, bullying will particularly be frequent if the offenders feel they have the blessing, support, or at least the implicit permission of their superiors to behave in this manner. In an assessment of potential causes of bullying, nine out of ten respondents in a large-scale trade union survey in the UK agreed with the statement that bullying exists because 'the bully can get away with it' and because targets are 'too afraid to report it' (UNISON, 1997). In some organisations, bullying may even be institutionalised as a part of the leadership and managerial practice. Authoritarian leadership styles are still highly valued in many companies (Hoel & Salin, 2003). However, what some may consider 'tough' or 'firm but fair' management, may easily turn into 'harsh and unfair' management, be it as a prevailing cultural norm, or as a consequence of a mangers acting under stress, or being involved in interpersonal conflicts. Blaming it all on 'psychopaths at work' or even on a 'neurotic' victim is, therefore, in most cases a far too simplistic explanation for the question of why bullying takes place. Even if may be true in particular cases, it is still the responsibility of managers to develop an organisational culture where bullying is considered unacceptable and to intervene in individual cases to ensure that further mistreatment and victimisation are prevented.

## The Role of Leadership Style and the Psychosocial Work Environment

In addition to the prevailing values and norms of the organisation as reflected in its organisational culture, the quality of the leadership practices and the psychosocial work environment in a department seem to be important causes of bullying. A work situation characterised by role conflict and a lack of interesting and challenging work tasks, combined with a negative interpersonal climate in the work group, seems to be a high risk situation for bullying (Einarsen *et al.*, 1994). A high level of ambiguity or incompatible demands and expectations around roles, tasks and responsibilities may create frustration and conflicts within the work group, especially in connection with rights, obligations, privileges and positions. This situation may then act as a precursor of conflict, poor inter-worker relationships and a need for a suitable scapegoat, especially if the social climate is characterised by low trust and interpersonal tension. Another characteristic of workplaces where bullying occurs is widespread dissatisfaction with the leadership style of managers and supervisors, e.g. leaders considered to be authoritarian, aggressive or uninvolved. In fact, as many as 50% of targets claim to be bullied by a superior, again linking bullying closely to leadership (Zapf *et al.*, 2003). These findings can be summarised by Leymann's (1993) theoretical claim that four factors are prominent in eliciting bullying at work:

1. Deficiencies in work design laying the ground for stress, frustration, irritation, conflict and uncertainty among the staff, or laying the ground for inefficiencies in productivity and work performance.
2. Deficiencies in leadership behaviour or managerial practices, either by showing a tyrannical type of leadership, or by lack of leadership. The latter typically involves leaders who do not intervene in interpersonal conflict or in situations where employees engage in aggressive behaviours or other kinds of counterproductive work behaviour.
3. When stress and frustration prevail in the working environment, some employees may be more likely to be the target of aggression than others due to their socially exposed position. This may be related to the work organisation, the particular job in question, the composition of the workforce, or to some kind of permanent or transient personal vulnerability. For example, being the only black employee or only woman in a white, male-dominated organisation would be an example of this category.
4. Low moral in the workplace, e.g. with prevailing hostility, a lack of mutual respect, with elevated levels of interpersonal conflicts and friction. It may also be related to workforce or a work unit with a low work ethic. In this case, any employee who is particularly conscientious, honest or hard-working may be at risk of retaliation from the others, particularly if he or she blows the whistle on illegal or unethical conduct at work.

## THE PREVENTION AND MANAGEMENT OF BULLYING AT WORK

### Prevention of Bullying

Following the above discussion of the nature and causes of bullying in the workplace, we consider that successful prevention of bullying must contain the following elements:

- Create a social climate with an open and respectful atmosphere, with tolerance for diversity and where the existence of interpersonal frustration and friction is accepted but also properly managed.
- Ensure that leadership styles and managerial practices applied within the organisation lead to all employees being treated fairly and with respect, and that sensitivity to personal needs and vulnerability is taken into account.
- Ensure that managers have received necessary training in conflict management.

- Build a well-run organisation with clear goals, roles and responsibilities, and with high a work ethic.
- Create an organisational culture where bullying and mistreatment of employees are not tolerated.

## Intervening in Bullying Cases

When addressing a case, be it in the role of e.g. a manager, a supervisor, a personnel officer, or a consultant, we would argue that it is important to initially take a non-punitive approach towards the alleged offender or offenders. At the start, the primary objective should be to stop any unwanted behaviour and to restore a fair working climate. This simple rule should be communicated clearly throughout the organisation, and in particular to the parties involved in specific cases. 'Victim-blaming' or 'perpetrator-bashing' are both pitfalls that third parties must avoid in the management of individual cases. Furthermore, when investigating a case, all interviews and discussions with alleged offenders and witnesses must be impartial and fair and should aim to establish:

1. Whether bullying has occurred and how to stop it from recurring.
2. If it is not bullying, it may be something else, e.g. stress, interpersonal conflicts, misunderstandings. If so, to work to restore good working conditions for all.
3. Which organisational conditions or practices need to be altered in order to prevent future mistreatment or bullying scenarios.

It is important to bear in mind that most people, even most of those accused of bullying, will generally be opposed to bullying. It is, therefore, important to reach out to or connect with such views, as most employees are likely to want to co-operate to change the situation. However, if necessary, one needs to teach the bully basic social norms by means of coaching or personal guidance and, in cases where a manager is the culprit, provide specialised management training. In particularly severe cases of bullying, disciplinary actions – including dismissal – must be considered.

Victims of bullying are by definition in a weak position. Therefore, one must be prepared to protect the victim from further stigmatisation and retaliation. One must always be prepared for the possibility that the target shows disturbed behaviour patterns. People who are distressed often annoy others. Hence, targets may be demanding, in need of full attention and support, and highly sensitive to any sign of mistrust or disbelief. Many victims will also be in need of professional support and help, psychological and sometimes medical treatment for the after-effects of the exposure to bullying. There may even be a need for a rehabilitation programme to ensure reintegration of the target into the work group and into productive work altogether.

Although it might be tempting, one should avoid using individual cases as they emerge to raise general awareness about bullying within the organisation. This may be harmful to those directly involved, may reduce the possibility of reaching a quick and fair conclusion to the case, and will not necessarily create an anti-bullying atmosphere in the organisation as different groups of employees may side with the different parties involved. Thus, general prevention programmes must be implemented independently of any specific case of bullying. Such programmes must include efforts to improve leadership, organisational climate and working conditions, the development and communication of an organisational policy against bullying, as well as training programmes for supervisors and managers. Given that bullying is so closely associated with leadership, training managers in conflict management seems to be vital, as is a critical look at what kinds of leadership styles are nurtured within the particular organisational culture. At the end of the day the existence, prevention and constructive management of bullying at work resides with managers and supervisors of the organisation and the organisational culture they create or permit.

## THE NEED FOR A POLICY AGAINST BULLYING

It is the employer's task to ensure that any case of bullying or mistreatment emerging within the organisation is treated in a flexible, fair, ethical and legally responsible way, ensuring the rights of targets as well as alleged perpetrators. To be able to respond quickly to a bullying case, when emotions and discussion run high and when every party tries to rally support to their cause, is by no means an easy task, either for managers, or for involved parties or colleagues who may be bystanders or observers of the behaviour in question. Hence, a well-developed anti-bullying policy is a necessary and important tool (see also Richards & Daley, 2003), including both informal systems for support and guidance of targets, as well as a fair system for the management of formal complaints. Below we will put forward some ideas for the key features we consider such policies should contain. However, the actual content must be developed locally in co-operation with employee representatives or, where appropriate, with the local trade unions. The process of developing a policy through active participation and involvement of a broad cross-section of organisational members at different levels and functions may in itself also have a preventive effect.

The ideas and advice put forward in the following sections are largely the result of an ongoing debate among human resources (HR) practitioners and trade union activists, particularly in the UK, and are crystallised around certain key principles which are discussed below.

## A Statement of Intent and Commitment

The policy needs to start off with a statement which communicates the organisation's commitment and intent with respect to bullying and should consider the following:

- The right to work in an environment free of harassment, bullying and intimidation.
- A statement on the seriousness of the problem, e.g. that disciplinary action may be taken, and that bullying and harassment may be unlawful or even a criminal offence.
- That the policy applies to all employees, including managers, workers and any individuals subcontracted or seconded to work for the organisation.
- The responsibility of all employees to comply with the policy.
- Managers' responsibility for implementation of policies.
- That no recriminations against or further victimisation of anyone using the policy to complain will be tolerated.

It may also provide reference to other relevant policies or mission statements of the organisation. Moreover, it should refer to any legal provisions relevant to the policy.

## Definitions and Examples of Behaviour and Conduct in Breach of Policy

This section of the policy would describe the behaviours, acts and situations that are covered by the policy, how they will be judged and perceived:

- Where bullying is not defined in law, a definition of bullying and harassment as defined by the organisation should be provided. This could include definitions provided in legal documents, by official agencies, trade unions or employer associations, or by researchers.
- Examples of behaviours which are considered to be in breach of the policy.

It is important to emphasise that the focus of the policy is on behaviour and actions rather than the intent behind the acts, thus acknowledging that harassment and bullying can sometimes be unintentional. It may also be wise to state that, in case of an investigation following a complaint about bullying, the behaviours in question will be judged according to reasonableness, and that such a judgment must be in accordance with prevailing norms in contemporary society. Organisations may also wish to emphasise that the policy, in addition to focusing on exposure to repeated negative behaviour, which in isolation may not be so serious, also applies to serious isolated or one-off negative acts.

## Principles of a Safe Complaint Procedure: Reassurance of Fairness, Non-recrimination and Confidentiality

An essential part of any bullying policy is reference to a complaint procedure which will come into play when a complaint is filed (for a discussion see Merchant & Hoel, 2003). This would normally happen after the organisation has tried to address the issue informally. For a complaint procedure to work as intended it needs to comply with the following principles:

- Ensure that all complaints will be taken seriously.
- No attempted recrimination against targets (those who file the complaints) will be tolerated.
- Confidentiality should be offered to the complainant, alleged perpetrator or any witnesses, as far is possible for the progression of the case. Unconditional confidentiality cannot be offered as it may compromise the employer's general 'duty of care' for the organisation and all its members.
- Observe the rules of natural justice, e.g. that anybody accused of an offence should have the right to know the nature of the complaint.
- Principles of fairness and non-recrimination also extends to alleged perpetrators.

It is important to send a clear and unambiguous message that complaints will be taken seriously, that the procedure will be a safe route to address bullying, and that fairness is assured by means of management training and consistency in application of rules and regulations. The last-mentioned is important as it reduces the impact of subjectivity and increases organisational members' trust in the procedure. However, it must also be stated that malicious complaints will be considered a disciplinary offence. Moreover, to ensure that the investigation following a complaint is fair, and seen as fair, it is important to seek that, as far as possible, the investigators are, and are seen to be, independent of the complaint.

## How to Submit a Complaint as a Target of Bullying

We would recommend that the policy contains a section which explains what options are open to those who perceive themselves to be targets of bullying, allowing for both informal and formal possibilities. Informal approaches may include seeking advice from colleagues or dedicated 'advisors', talking directly to the perpetrator, seeking support or advice from counsellors or occupational health officers or by means of confidential informal mediation. An informal complaint (that is, a procedure involving as few people as possible and with interviews and discussions as far as possible held in an informal atmosphere), can also be made to the line-manager. However, it must be clear that using an informal route of complaint does not prevent later use of the formal complaint procedure. In addition the following issues need to be addressed:

- Although line-managers normally would be the first line of contact, targets should consider the possibility of talking directly to the alleged bully.
- For formal complaints the following must be clear:
  o How and where (to whom) complaint should be made;
  o Time-scale for response, stating the given time period within which a response will be made, e.g. a week;
  o Emphasise that the target should feel free to be accompanied by a person of their choice in interviews or when filing a complaint, e.g. a colleague or a shop steward.
- Making it clear where to complain if the perpetrator happens to be the line-manager, e.g. a dedicated HR person/representative.
- Outline the status and role of different advisors and how they may be contacted:
  o To provide advice on the rights of targets and the alternatives available to targets;
  o To provide practical help, e.g. assisting in drafting letters, assisting targets at meetings, etc.
- Provide information about the availability of professional support/counselling that can be offered to the target (complainant) as well as to alleged perpetrators throughout the process.

In this part there should also be a statement about the potential sanctions that may be applied to perpetrators if the complaint is upheld and how the employer will address the 'duty of care' towards the alleged perpetrator in the complaints procedures.

Finally, the policy needs explicitly to address how it will be monitored and evaluated. In this respect the following methods may be included:

- Register of complaints/incidents (and their outcomes) to be retained by HR.
- Regular review of policy and monitoring system.
- Collect information on negative behaviour as part of exit-interviews.
- Include questions on the effectiveness of policy as part of staff surveys.

## CONCLUSION

Bullying is a serious organisational problem which often is rooted in destructive leadership and organisational practices, often triggered by stress and interpersonal conflicts. To prevent bullying in the first place and to ensure that those affected are given an opportunity to have their complaint addressed, organisations need to develop and implement a bullying policy and a safe complaint procedure. However, although a first and important step, policies and procedures are, of course, no guarantee against bullying and abusive behaviours per se. At the end of the day the existence, prevention and constructive management of bullying at work resides with the managers and supervisors within the organisation and the organisational culture they create or tolerate. Instead of relying on a strategy for restricting the employment of potential bullies and targets, the focus must be on the acceptance and management of diversity in the workforce, combined with clear norms for acceptable behaviours, as well as sanctions against behaviours deemed unacceptable by the organisation.

## REFERENCES

Archer, D. (1999). Exploring 'bullying' culture in the para-military organisation. *International Journal of Manpower*, **20**:94–105.

Ashforth, B. (1994). Petty tyranny in organizations. *Human Relations*, **47**:755–778.

Björkqvist, K., Österman, K. & Hjelt-Bäck, M. (1994). Aggression among university employees. *Aggressive Behavior*, **20**:173–184.

Brodsky, C. M. (1976). *The Harassed Worker*. MA. Toronto: Lexington Books, D.C.

Coyne, I., Seigne, E. & Randall, P. P. (2000). Predicting workplace victim status from personality. *European Journal of Work and Organizational Psychology*, **9**:335–349.

Einarsen, S. (1999). The nature and causes of bullying at work. *International Journal of Manpower*, **20**:16–27.

Einarsen, S. (2000). Harassment and bullying at work: A review of the Scandinavian approach. *Aggression and Violent Behavior*, **5**:379–401.

Einarsen, S., Hoel, H., Zapf, D. & Cooper, C. L. (2005). Workplace bullying; individual pathology or organisational culture. In V. Bowie, B. S. Fisher & C. L. Cooper (Eds.), *Workplace Violence* (pp. 229–247). Cullompton, Devon; Willan Publishing.

Einarsen, S., Hoel, H., Zapf, D. & Cooper, C. L. (2003). The concept of bullying at work: The European tradition. In S. Einarsen, H. Hoel, D. Zapf & C. L. Cooper (Eds.), *Bullying and Emotional Abuse in the Workplace: International Perspectives in Research and Practice* (pp. 3–30). London: Taylor & Francis.

Einarsen, S., Raknes, B. I. & Matthiesen, S. B. (1994). Bullying and harassment at work and their relationship to work environment quality: An exploratory study. *European Work and Organizational Psychologist*, **4**:381–401.

Einarsen, S., Tangedal, M., Skogstad, A. *et al.* (2007). *Det brutale arbeidsmiljø*. Bergen: University of Bergen.

Glasø, L., Matthiesen, S. B., Nielsen, M. B. & Einarsen, S. (2007). Do targets of workplace bullying portray a general victim personality profile? *Scandinavian Journal of Psychology*, **48**:313–319.

Hoel, H. & Salin, D. (2003). Organisational antecedents of workplace bullying. In S. Einarsen, H. Hoel, D. Zapf & C. L. Cooper (Eds.), *Bullying and Emotional Abuse in the Workplace: International Perspectives in Research and Practice* (pp. 203–218). London: Taylor & Francis.

Hoel, H., Cooper, C. L. & Faragher, B. (2001). The experience of bullying in Great Britain: The impact of organizational status. *European Journal of Work and Organizational Psychology*, **10**:443–465.

Hoel, H., Einarsen, S. & Cooper, C. L. (2003). Organisational effects of bullying. In S. Einarsen, H. Hoel, D. Zapf & C. L. Cooper (Eds.), *Bullying and Emotional Abuse in the Workplace. International Perspectives in Research and Practice* (pp. 145–162). London: Taylor & Francis.

Hoel, H., Sparks, K. & Cooper, C.L. (2001). *The Cost of Violence/Stress at Work and the Benefits of Violence/Stress-free Working Environment*. Geneva: International Labour Organisation.

Keashly, L. (1998). Emotional abuse in the workplace: Conceptual and empirical issues. *Journal of Emotional abuse*, **1**:85–117.

Leymann, H. (1993). *Mobbing: Psychoterror am Arbeitsplatz und wie man sich dagegen wehren kann (Mobbing: Psychoterror in the Workplace and How One Can Defend Oneself)*. Reinbeck bei Hamburg: Rowohlt Verlag.

Leymann, H. (1996). The content and development of mobbing at work. *European Journal of Work and Organizational Psychology*, **5**:165–184.

Matthiesen, S. B. & Einarsen, E. (2001). MMPI-2 configurations among victims of bullying at work. *European Journal of Work and Organizational Psychology*, **10**:467–484.

Matthiesen, S. B. & Einarsen, S. (2007). Perpetrators and targets of bullying at work: Role stress and individual differences. *Violence and Victims*, **22**:735–753.

Merchant, V. & Hoel, H. (2003). Investigating complaints of bullying. In S. Einarsen, H. Hoel, D. Zapf & C. L. Cooper (Eds.), *Bullying and Emotional Abuse in the Workplace. International Perspectives in Research and Practice* (pp. 259–269). London: Taylor & Francis.

O'Moore, M., Seigne, E., McGuire, L. & Smith, M. (1998). Victims of workplace bullying in Ireland. *Irish Journal of Psychology*, **19**:345–357.

Rayner, C. & Hoel, H. (1997). A summary review of literature relating to workplace bullying. *Journal of Community and Applied Social Psychology*, **7**:181–191.

Rayner, C., Hoel, H. & Cooper, C. L. (2002). *Workplace Bullying. What We Know, Who Is to Blame, and What Can We Do?* London: Taylor & Francis.

Richards, J. & Daley, H. (2003). Bullying policy: Development, implementation and monitoring. In S. Einarsen, H. Hoel, D. Zapf & C. L. Cooper (Eds.), *Bullying and Emotional Abuse in the Workplace. International Perspectives in Research and Practice* (pp. 247–258). London: Taylor & Francis.

UNISON (1997). *UNISON's Members' Experience of Bullying at Work*. London: UNISON.

Vartia, M. (1991). *Bullying at Workplaces*. Paper presented at the Towards the 21st Century. Work in the 1990s. International Symposium on Future trends in the Changing Working Life, Helsinki.

Vartia, M. (1996). The sources of bullying: Psychological work environment and organizational climate. *European Journal of Work and Organizational Psychology*, **5**:203–214.

Zapf, D. (1999). Organizational work group related and personal causes of mobbing/ bullying at work. *International Journal of Manpower*, **20**:70–85.

Zapf, D. & Einarsen, S. (2003). Individual antecedents of bullying. In S. Einarsen, H. Hoel, D. Zapf & C. L. Cooper (Eds.), *Bullying and Emotional Abuse in the Workplace. International Perspectives in Research and Practice*. London: Taylor & Francis.

Zapf, D., Einarsen, S., Hoel, H. & Vartia, M. (2003). Empirical findings on bullying in the workplace. In S. Einarsen, H. Hoel, D. Zapf & C. L. Cooper (Eds.), *Bullying and Emotional Abuse in the Workplace. International Perspectives in Research and Practice* (pp. 103–126). London: Taylor & Francis.

# CHAPTER 15

# Counselling and Coaching in Organisations: An Integrative Multi-Level Approach

Vanja Orlans
*Metanoia Institute, London*

This chapter aims to highlight a number of factors that people in workplaces can reflect on in order to address the quality of those settings in terms of people issues, as well as thinking about what might need attention in order both to build on existing strengths and improve areas that might be functioning less than well. The issues highlighted emerge from the author's training and experience in both the therapeutic and organisational realms of practice with the aim of demonstrating the potential in bringing ideas and experiences from both of these domains together.

The 'organisation' is posited here as a relational field, created for a specific purpose and made up of a series of co-created intrapersonal, interpersonal and intergroup dynamics, generally across a range of hierarchical levels. While the purpose of the organisation has visionary, functional and economic aspects, which themselves interrelate with the people dimensions, it is argued that the human relational field is what gives the organisation its unique 'feel' or cultural identity. It is to the relational field that we generally need to attend in managing a whole range of challenges and potential difficulties.

The following sections deal respectively with the domains of counselling and coaching in the organisational setting; the notion of counselling and coaching as related realms of thinking and practice and the ways in which relational aspects of functioning are relevant to practitioners who identify either as counsellor or coach; and the importance of being able to work within an integrative frame of reference to incorporate the intrapsychic, interpersonal and group levels of functioning so as to provide the organisation and its members with a positive reflective space in which to tackle the complex challenges that can emerge.

*Employee Well-being Support: A Workplace Resource.* Edited by A. Kinder, R. Hughes and C.L. Cooper.
© 2008 John Wiley & Sons, Ltd.

## COUNSELLING WITHIN THE ORGANISATIONAL SETTING

Counselling now has a long history of involvement with the organisational setting. The British Association for Counselling and Psychotherapy (BACP) has a specialised division, the Association for Counselling at Work (ACW), which focuses exclusively on counselling issues in the work setting. This area of practice features also as a key activity in an expanding set of services to organisations, whether formally as Employee Assistance Programmes (EAPs) or as a human resources-related function within the organisational setting (Orlans, 2003).

Early approaches which aimed to bring counselling into the work setting revolved around the alcohol programmes developed in the USA in the 1940s. These were originally developed as a way of tackling the rising organisational costs of dealing with alcohol-dependent employees and the recognition that getting employees 'cured' and back to work as quickly as possible would be an effective outcome for the individual, their family and the employing organisation. This trend led, in time to the development of the 'broad brush' programmes which dealt with a range of emotional and practical difficulties experienced by employees and their families. In 1988 Whitbread established what was believed to be the first EAP in a British company. Less than a decade later it was estimated that over one million employees and their families in the UK had access to EAP support (Reddy, 1994). Under such a scheme, employees typically have access to financial and legal help and advice, as well as to counselling for emotional problems.

The extent to which an organisation involves itself directly with the EAP and its running in any executive sense will vary, depending on the values and strategic thinking of the organisation concerned. Confidentiality is a key issue in the operation of counselling at work programmes, and organisations will vary as to how they negotiate this issue. Bull (1997) charts the development of workplace counselling through a number of different phases. He suggests that the early initiatives evolved in the context of a disease model along the lines of Alcoholics Anonymous (AA). This progressed through a more client-centred phase, exemplified by the development of a broad brush approach to EAPs, to a period where the environment is acknowledged as having a potentially significant impact on the employee. The current position identified is one where the company is a potential 'client' for the counselling professional, alongside the individual client. This latter view challenges individual counselling professionals who deal with workplace issues to view their role more broadly than might have been reflected in a particular clinical training context.

The evaluation of counselling within the work setting can be viewed from a number of perspectives. Firstly, we can look at the general evaluation literature published within the psychotherapeutic fields. Empirical studies in this regard point to the overall effectiveness of therapeutic interventions at the individual level, highlighting research results that are not only statistically significant but also clinically meaningful – that is, clients experience clear gains from the process which hold over time (Lambert, 2004). McLeod (2001, 2007) has focused specifically on evaluation studies in the work setting. His review considers two categories: those concerned with psychosocial outcomes, and those concerned with 'value for money'. He concludes that two-thirds of studies reviewed suggest that counselling interventions are generally effective in alleviating symptoms of anxiety, stress and depression, and that there is some evidence that counselling interventions have a positive impact on job commitment, work functioning, job satisfaction and the reduction of substance abuse. In terms of cost-effectiveness, research studies are fewer and more complex in terms of the analyses. However, it would appear that workplace counselling schemes at the very least cover their costs, even though there were wide variations across companies and schemes.

Firth and Shapiro (1986) have highlighted the effectiveness of brief psychotherapy for the alleviation of job-related distress. They also suggest that it is more productive to identify and offer help to those individuals who are recognised as currently distressed, rather than offering general programmes to all workers. Barkham and Shapiro (1990) review a number of different interventions for dealing with job-related distress, and present some of the findings from a pilot study implementing brief psychotherapeutic models. Their results demonstrate the effectiveness of short-term psychological counselling interventions for presenting problems, both in terms of improvement in client functioning, and in terms also of cost-effectiveness to the organisation. Cooper *et al.* (1990) have outlined a programme of short-term psychological counselling which has been implemented in the Post Office, and present evaluation data on the effectiveness of this scheme. Results highlighted significant improvements in mental well-being and a reduction of days lost at work.

Although the results of these research studies are important, there are a number of complexities which need to be addressed within the organisational setting. For example, individual therapeutic gains reported may highlight a form of accommodation to existing environments, thus drawing attention away from environmental conditions. A broader perspective is likely to be necessary in order to assess the context more carefully (Orlans & Edwards, 2001). Carroll (1996) has also advocated a contextual approach to the evaluation or workplace counselling, highlighting the adoption of a range of perspectives – from clients, counsellors and the organisation concerned – in the evaluation of a counselling service.

## THE DEVELOPING PROFESSION OF COACHING

The fields of coaching and coaching psychology have seen enormous growth within the last decade with the practice of coaching rapidly defining itself as a new profession. The British Psychological Society (BPS) now has a Special Group in Coaching Psychology (SGCP) which was founded in 2004. At the end of 2006 the SGCP had 2,069 members making it one of the fastest-growing subsystems within the BPS. It is widely anticipated that the SGCP will seek to establish itself as a Division of the BPS with separate chartered status and related accredited training. Training courses in the field of coaching are already on the increase, as is the awareness of coaching as a potential resource for organisational employees. The Chartered Institute of Personnel and Development (CIPD), for example, highlights the growing trend for this new profession to establish itself with appropriate standards, and a general debate in the field as a whole is currently in progress concerning the best ways of developing an appropriate professional identity, as well as stipulating factors that might be used as appropriate benchmarks for competence (CIPD, 2006). In the context of the USA, Berglas (2002) has suggested that the number of executive coaches could rise from a documented 10,000 in 2002 to over 50,000 by 2007.

While there is considerable information that points to the growing professional field in coaching, there is alongside this a plea for more research on coaching outcomes and the specifics of practice (e.g. Linley, 2006), with the literature on coaching increasingly demonstrating attempts to address this issue (e.g. Stober & Grant, 2006). The overriding emphasis in this respect is for the field of coaching to create, develop and draw on valid research and sound practice in the delivery of its services and related trainings. We are also seeing different forms of coaching emerging, with an interest in differentiating, for example, between executive coaching and life or career coaching (Stern, 2004), or between executive coaching and management coaching (Peltier, 2001), with the latter emphasising a focus on the potentially useful nature of a coaching perspective within the management function of an organisation, and the importance of all managers thinking of themselves as potential coaches to their reporting employees.

In such discussions we can see that the definition of a 'coach' can have different emphases, from a more directing and modelling style, to a process-based interactive form more akin to the nature of counselling. Furthermore, it would seem that this service can be provided either by managers themselves, or by individuals who are independent from the relevant organisation. In some of these discussions the boundary between the personal and the professional becomes somewhat blurred. In my own experience as a supervisor of professional coaches, the issue of how to differentiate between the personal and the professional and, perhaps more challengingly, how to work with each in an appropriate way, is an ongoing ethical issue for practitioners, both in terms of unravelling the complexities intellectually, and in deciding on appropriate courses of action in practice.

Notwithstanding these developments and the enormous increase in interest in coaching as a profession, there are those who remain concerned about the training needed to cope with the complexities of some of the issues which present in the context of the organisational setting. Berglas (2002) for example, stresses the importance of rigorous psychological training in order both to formulate and deal effectively with presenting issues of executives. He expresses concern about the training level of some coaches and states that 'when an executive's problems stem from undetected or ignored psychological difficulties, coaching can actually make a bad situation worse' (p. 3). His concern is that coaching appears to offer easy and quick answers to problems that may need more in-depth attention. Unless the professional coach is trained to identify the difference between a fixable challenge and a more deep-seated difficulty then the outcome is not likely to be effective, especially in the longer term.

## COUNSELLING, COACHING AND THE RELATIONAL FIELD

Although both counselling and coaching have evolved as separate professional fields there is much overlap between the two, and even if we do not take as serious a stance as Berglas (2002), *not* to consider what is offered by both domains would be to leave out aspects that have potential usefulness in the organisational setting. For example, the fields of psychotherapy and counselling have significant amounts of theoretical ideas and related research studies that have a relevance to organisational functioning. Nevertheless, there are ongoing debates about how much overlap actually exists, with some pressure at times to define the fields as very separate.

Some of the tensions that exist can be located in an interest on both sides to identify a clearly defined profession with a related protocol in terms of training and accreditation. It has been argued, for example, that counselling is reactive and deals with emotional 'problems', while coaching is proactive, dealing with building performance (e.g. Stone, 1999). This distinction generalises the issues involved and suggests a potentially skewed idea about the counselling process. When we look at the different forms of counselling, for example, we can see that in some cases, perhaps more so in the psychodynamic tradition, we might see a greater emphasis on a 'problem' presentation, whereas in other approaches, for example in Gestalt counselling, there is an emphasis on moving beyond difficulties into a freer flow of energy and creativity. I have highlighted elsewhere (Orlans & Edwards, 2001) the ways in which counselling training can serve at times to minimise here-and-now contextual issues, with a resulting overemphasis on matters 'clinical', and have suggested the importance for the counselling profession of attending to this issue and working against any pull towards fragmentation. However, recent trends in psychotherapeutic theory and practice point to a much more integrative and 'here-and-now' focus across most modalities. In terms of coaching practice, coaches need to be challenged not to overemphasise 'task' while, for example, ignoring or minimising powerful emotions.

Whether people define themselves as counsellor or coach, in any organisation the presence of task, process and emotion will be relevant. What is needed is some considerable skill in teasing out the relative emphasis that needs to be placed on each and to manage the boundaries in a professional and ethical way. I am making a case here for the two professions to be open to learning from each other and drawing creatively on issues raised in both professional domains. The reason for this suggestion is that coaches who want to maximise their potential usefulness to the functioning of individuals and organisations will need to be able to recognise and tackle a number of emotional realms of experience. Likewise, counsellors who work in organisational settings need to understand the task functions in that setting, the values that are important, and the need for bottom-line issues of finance to be recognised as an intrinsic part of that setting.

However, both of these professionals are dealing with a relational field, which includes the intrapsychic, the interpersonal and the group level of experience. A holistic approach is advocated here, which seeks to understand these different levels and have the capabilities to work with them. This is not to say that coaches need to be therapists. There are ethical and professional decisions to be made in terms of where the best setting might be to work on particular challenges of a very personal kind, as well as a recognition that a person might need more space and time in a therapeutic setting to really tackle some longstanding patterns in their lives. What I am advocating is a set of capabilities that inform a high level of awareness of the issues that are being presented, and a capacity either to understand how these might be addressed within the existing contract, or how certain issues might be dealt with in some other setting. The relational field of the organisational setting presents just as complex a field as that considered by psychotherapists and counsellors. For both professions a clear conceptualisation and formulation of presenting issues is required.

There are a few examples in the literature which highlight this idea of integration. Leslie Greenberg (2002) uses the language of both therapy and coaching in the title of his book as well as in the contents. His idea of 'emotion coaching' is a basic educational one, designed to enable individuals to deal with complex information and communication patterns. In describing his approach, he uses the analogy of a teaching setting where the teacher offers the learner an opportunity to challenge themselves with a next step of learning within the learner's 'zone of proximal development' (Vygotsky, 1986). Mary Beth O'Neill (2000), writing in the context of executive coaching, talks about the importance of empathy, and highlights key counselling skills such as listening, respect, confrontation and concreteness. Whitworth *et al.* (1998), in their discussion of 'process coaching', a term which brings the counselling process to mind, highlight the importance of feelings as information rather than symptoms. They also address the complexity of the therapy versus coaching process in terms of formulation and accurate decision-making. While advocating caution and an open discussion with clients, they are making the point that 'both therapy and coaching, for example, might deal with the same difficult life circumstances such as betrayal in a relationship or failure of a business. Both therapist and coach might approach the situation similarly: looking for learning and looking for action that will lead the client to a more resourceful state' (p. 174). Clearly, the issues involved need careful analysis and also some in-depth discussion with the client.

However, the basic stance is one of integration and multi-level work, developed through open communication about issues that are not cut and dried in terms of the best professional involvement. Peltier (2001) highlights the many areas of overlap between the clinical and coaching contexts, bringing in the importance of ethical and professional frameworks for practice. I would suggest, however, that although professional and ethical codes are important, both for counselling and coaching, the complexity of many presenting multi-level issues will mean that there may be no 'correct' answer to a particular dilemma. I have discussed this elsewhere (Orlans, 2007) in the context of ethical issues in the therapeutic field and have proposed that open discussions, between professionals and involving also our clients, may be an important way in which the full complexity of presenting issues can be appreciated, and may also serve to keep professionals from imagining that they are too large or too powerful.

## THE IMPORTANCE OF A MULTI-LEVEL AND MULTI-DISCIPLINARY PERSPECTIVE

The issues that either coaches or counsellors are likely to be dealing with in the organisational context are likely to arise in the context of a relational field of experience. An integrative response to such issues needs to consider the presenting issue in context as well as from a multi-level perspective, which includes all realms of experience from the intrapsychic to the organisational. In order to work competently at these different levels, both coaches and counsellors need to ensure that they obtain a broad-based training which will include a reflexive focus on their own functioning as well as a sound understanding of a range of psychological, interpersonal and system issues. Ongoing consultation/supervision will also be required for these different professionals in order to keep support and perspective in the frame. Although I can see that different professional groups are probably going to feel most supported by their own professional settings, and are likely to want to keep a boundary around this and monitor who belongs and who does not, information and opportunity will be lost if there is not an adequate forum for ideas and cases to be shared with a view to mutual learning possibilities. The challenges faced by organisations in the post-modern era are substantial and deserve the very best response possible.

## REFERENCES

Barkham, M. & Shapiro, D. A. (1990). Brief psychotherapeutic interventions for job-related distress: A pilot study of prescriptive and exploratory therapy. *Counselling Psychology Quarterly*, 3:133–147.

Berglas, S. (2002). The very real dangers of executive coaching. *Harvard Business Review*, June, 3–8.

Bull, A. (1997). Models of counselling in organizations. In M. Carroll & M. Walton (Eds.), *Handbook of Counselling in Organizations*. London: Sage.

Carroll, M. (1996). *Workplace Counselling*. London: Sage.

CIPD, Chartered Institute of Personnel and Development (2006). *Coaching at Work*, Vol. 1, Issue 2, p. 12 (News Section).

Cooper, C. L., Sadri, G., Allison, T. & Reynolds, P. (1990). Stress counselling in the Post Office. *Counselling Psychology Quarterly*, 3:3–11.

Firth, J. & Shapiro, D. A. (1986). An evaluation of psychotherapy for job-related distress. *Journal of Occupational Psychology*, 59:111–119.

Greenberg, L. S. (2002). *Emotion-focused Therapy: Coaching Clients to Work through Their Feelings*. Washington, DC: American Psychological Association.

Lambert, M. J. (2004). *Bergin and Garfield's Handbook of Psychotherapy and Behavior Change*, 5th edn. New York: John Wiley & Sons, Inc.

Linley, P. A. (2006). Coaching research: Who? What? Where? When? Why? *International Journal of Evidence Based Coaching and Mentoring*, 4:1–7.

McLeod, J. (2001). *Counselling in the Workplace: The Facts: A Systematic Study of the Research Evidence*. Lutterworth, Leicestershire: British Association for Counselling and Psychotherapy.

McLeod, J. (2007). Counselling in the workplace: The facts: A Comprehensive Review of the Research Evidence. 2nd Edn. Rugby: BACP.

O'Neill, M. B. (2000). *Executive Coaching with Backbone and Heart: A Systems Approach to Engaging Leaders with Their Challenges*. San Francisco, CA: Jossey-Bass.

Orlans, V. (2003). Counselling psychology in the workplace. In R. Woolfe, W. Dryden & S. Strawbridge (Eds.), *Handbook of Counselling Psychology*, 2nd edn. London: Sage.

Orlans, V. (2007). From structure to process: Ethical demands of the postmodern era. *British Journal of Psychotherapy Integration*, 4:54–61.

Orlans, V. & Edwards, D. (2001). Counselling the organisation, *Counselling at Work*, 33:5–7.

Peltier, B. (2001). *The Psychology of Executive Coaching: Theory and Application*. Abingdon, Oxon: Routledge, Taylor & Francis Group.

Reddy, M. (1994). EAPs and their future in the UK: History repeating itself? *Personnel Review*, 23:60–78.

Stern, L. R. (2004). Executive coaching: A working definition. *Consulting Psychology Journal: Practice and Research*, 56:154–162.

Stober, D. R. & Grant, A. A. (Eds.) (2006). *Evidence-based Coaching Handbook: Putting Best Practices to Work for Your Clients*. Hoboken, NJ: John Wiley & Sons, Inc.

Stone, F. (1999). *Coaching, Counselling and Mentoring*. New York: American Management Association.

Vygotsky, L. (1986). *Thought and Language*. Cambridge, MA: MIT Press.

Whitworth, L., Kimsey-House, H. & Sandahl, P. (1998). *Co-active Coaching*. Mountain View, CA: Daview-Black Publishing.

# CHAPTER 16

# What Makes a Good Employee Assistance Programme?

**Mark A. Winwood and Stephanie Beer**

*AXA PPP Healthcare, and Employee Assistance Professionals Association*

## INTRODUCTION

An organisation's effectiveness is, to a large extent, dependent on the well-being of its staff. An employee assistance programme (EAP) is designed to help employers manage performance issues in the workplace and employees manage the balance between work and personal pressures which have become increasingly part of our everyday lives. An EAP is only as good as it is flexible to the ever-changing needs of employees, organisations and society and accessible to all of those employees and family members who may benefit from its service. It is imperative that the supports offered by an EAP reflect flexibility and accessibility.

In this chapter the authors will introduce the concept of EAP, the possible benefits an organisation might gain from purchasing an EAP and outline the essential core services and supports which constitute a good EAP service in the 21st century.

## BACKGROUND

In a modern society EAPs form part of the preventative measures employers can decide to implement in the workplace, encouraging investment in psychological support, in order to prevent sickness and absence and to improve productivity and job performance. According to the National Audit Office (2006): 'EAPs ... have been shown to reduce sickness levels and are cost effective'.

Employee assistance work has been traced back to the development of non-psychiatric counselling programmes following the classic Hawthorne Studies.

*Employee Well-being Support: A Workplace Resource.* Edited by A. Kinder, R. Hughes and C.L. Cooper.
© 2008 John Wiley & Sons, Ltd.

The focus then shifted from counselling normal employees to the treatment of troubled employees, especially those with alcohol problems; this was reflected in the emergence of occupational alcoholism programs. Employee assistance in the USA still has its focus on alcohol and substance abuse 'industries billion dollar hang-over' (Menninger & Levinson, 1954). In the USA, over 97% of companies with more than 5,000 employees have EAPs. The USA has the most saturated market for EAPs in the world (EAPA, 2007).

In the UK, EAPs first introduced in the 1980s, vary widely from the alcohol-based services in the USA. EAPs in the UK provide a much more broadbrush service. It is believed that the problems that people experience have a number of causes and therefore any number of effects; services which view problems through a single lens (e.g. alcohol) are in danger of not truly addressing an individual's concerns. In the UK, EAP penetration is much lower; the most up-to-date information from the Employee Assistance Programme Association's (EAPA) UK branch claims that 1,476 UK organisations have EAPs in place for their workforce covering 3.14 million employees, which is approximately 15% of the working population (PARN Research, 2003).

An employee assistance programme is a worksite-focused management tool to assist initially in the identification of employees' concerns and then develop interventions to assist in the resolution of these concerns. Such employee concerns typically include, but are not limited to:

- Personal matters – health, relationship, family, financial, emotional, legal, anxiety, alcohol, drugs and other related issues.
- Work matters – work demands, fairness at work, working relationships, harassment and bullying, personal and interpersonal skills, work/life balance, stress and other related issues. (EAPA, 2000).

These issues may directly or indirectly affect employee performance and well-being.

An employee assistance programme includes a mechanism for providing counselling and other forms of assistance, advice and information to employees on a systematic and uniform basis, and to recognised standards. The standards applied to any EAP are dependent, to a degree, upon the statutory regulations of the country/state the programme is operating from and the country/state the programme is delivering to. For example, if a UK EAP delivered a service to an organisation in Germany the service would need to be delivered taking into consideration the statutory regulations concerning assistance and psychological services in that country.

An EAP can focus on areas of interest to the purchasing organisation and the issues that may have influenced the purchase of the EAP such as: stress at work legislation (HSE, 2004), sickness absence, vocational rehabilitation, improving relationships in the workplace, reduction in grievance (by using early intervention strategies such as mediation), improving presence at work by relieving external pressures and distractions by providing a range of practical assistance services often labelled as 'worklife'.

An EAP addresses team and individual performance and well-being in the workplace. Employee assistance programmes should be defined by what they achieve in terms of outcome rather than what they consist of; this allows maximum opportunity for tailoring services to meet the needs of each client organisation. It is a strategic intervention and any organisation benefits should be quantifiable by outcome measurement.

EAPs are in a unique position. Unlike any other support mechanism in the mental health field they benefit both the individual and the organisation.

An EAP should never been seen in isolation from other supports that may be available within an organisation. Figure 16.1 illustrates how an EAP may interact with other services both internal and external to the organisation to affect the well-being of both employee and organisation.

There are three main models of programme delivery: external using an external provider, internal where the EAP professionals are employed by the organisation and deliver service to the employees of that organisation, and a hybrid model which is a mix of internal and external service. Some organisations

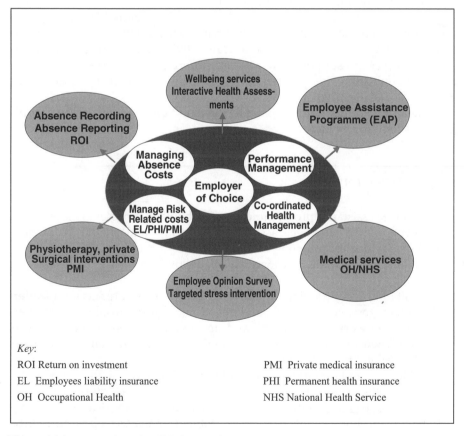

Key:

| | |
|---|---|
| ROI Return on investment | PMI Private medical insurance |
| EL Employees liability insurance | PHI Permanent health insurance |
| OH Occupational Health | NHS National Health Service |

**Figure 16.1** Interaction of well-being services

have established internal welfare systems whose services can be enhanced by an external EAP provider.

## WHY SHOULD AN ORGANISATION HAVE AN EAP?

In the last decade there has been an enormous increase in the pace of change in the commercial world. There is increasing pressure from government for corporate organisations to exercise their duty of care and provide support for employees who may have psychological difficulties. The Health and Safety at Work Act 1974.s.2(1) states it is the 'duty of every employer to ensure the health and safety of all his employees'. Recent legislation supported by the HSE requires organisations with more than five employees to do regular (yearly) risk assessments for stress with their workforce. In a 2002 Court of Appeal ruling, Justice Hale stated that 'any employer who offers confidential counselling and advice with access to treatment is unlikely to be found in breach of duty' (Sutherland vs Hatton, 2002). These issues are powerful reasons for employers to provide EAPs for their staff.

However, it must be noted that providing an EAP or counselling service does not automatically mean that an employer has discharged their duty of care. The case of Intel Corporation (UK) Ltd v Daw (2007): 'even if an employer has systems in place to support staff who are suffering from work-related stress, this is no substitute for putting an action plan into place to reduce their workload' (Delaney, 2007).

In short, EAPs represent a cost-effective solution to many of the 'people problems' employers face today.

## CORE TECHNOLOGY

The employee assistance programme Core Technology represents the essential components of the employee assistance profession and should be demonstrated by any quality provider.

The EAP Core Technology consists of the following:

1. Consultation with, training of, and assistance to work organisation leadership (managers, supervisors)) seeking to manage the troubled employee, enhance the work environment, and improve employee job performance, and outreach to and education of employees and their family members about availability of EAP services.
2. Confidential and timely problem identification/assessment services for employee clients with personal concerns that may affect job performance.
3. Use of constructive confrontation, motivation and short-term intervention with employee clients to address problems that affect job performance.

4. Referral of employee clients for assessment, treatment and assistance, plus case-monitoring and follow-up services.
5. Effective establishment and maintenance of service providers and management of provider contracts such as clinical affiliate management.
6. Consultation to work organisations and individuals on the availability and promoting access to other support services external to the EAP i.e. health service access.
7. Identification of the effects of employee assistance services on the organisation, the individual and individual job performance by outcome measurement.

Taking the core conditions into consideration, presence of the following components represent a comprehensive EAP programme.

## DIRECT SERVICES

### Short-term Psychological Intervention/Counselling

Research has shown that most counselling within employee assistance is short-term therapy, aimed at helping the client at a time of change, choice or crisis (Winwood and Karpas, 2002). The counselling service is also the most widely used aspect of an EAP, delivery of which depends on cultural expectations and statutory regulations. For example, in the UK initial psychological evaluation and, where appropriate, intervention occurs over the telephone by trained counsellors. In other parts of the world all intervention occurs on a face-to-face basis by psychologists or social workers. To a degree how it is delivered and by which type of professional is immaterial – what is important is that it is delivered well, by trained EAP professionals who are able to work to recognised standards.

Many EAP providers employ in-house mental-health professionals and also draw on a network of contracted psychologists/counsellors/social workers who work as clinical affiliates.

Recruitment criteria for affiliates for a major UK EAP provider can be seen in Box 16.1

**Box 16.1** The clinical affiliate network

---

**3. The Clinical Affiliate Network**

**3.1 Specific Qualities of a Clinical Affiliate**

There are two distinct types of Clinical Affiliate which make up the EAP network.

---

**3.1.1 Chartered Clinical/Counselling Psychologists (CCP)**

3.1.1.1   The CCP must be Chartered with the British Psychological Society, hold a current Practising Certificate and have EAP/Assessment experience.

3.1.1.2   The CCP will carry out an assessment of the customer's needs and will make a clinical recommendation for ongoing support which will include whether or not a short-term intervention is appropriate. In most cases, the customer will not be suffering from a recognisable clinical disorder. However, the CCP must be alert to any underlying disorders which may exist.

3.1.1.3   The CCP will be available for extended consultations if necessary to deliver short- term interventions. However, the CCP will not be required to provide ongoing psychological therapy/support to customers they have assessed unless by special arrangement.

**3.1.2 Accredited Counsellors/Registered Psychotherapists**

3.1.2.1   Essentially, four specific types of professional recognition are accepted:

3.1.2.1.1   An Accredited Counsellor/Psychotherapist with the British Association for Counselling and Psychotherapy.

3.1.2.1.2   An Accredited Counsellor/Psychotherapist with the British Association for Behavioural and Cognitive Psychotherapies.

3.1.2.1.3   A registered Psychotherapist with the United Kingdom Council for Psychotherapy.

3.1.2.1.4   An Accredited Counsellor with the Confederation of Scottish Counselling Agencies.

3.1.2.2   The Clinical Affiliate may be influenced by a variety of theoretical approaches/models of counselling. However, they will be experienced in short-term work with the emphasis being: focusing on solutions, dealing with specific customer issues and problem management. Appropriate short-term experience may have been gained, for example, in private practice, GP surgeries, student counselling services and workplace counselling/employee assistance settings.

*Source*: Employee Support, *Handbook for Clinical Affiliates* (AXA PPP Healthcare, 2007)

Both internal staff and clinical affiliates should all adhere to EAPA guidelines as well as their own professional standards. All clinical professionals should receive regular supervision (in line with their professional bodies' recommendations), be trained in working in an EAP context and be accountable to the EAP provider. All staff should be experienced in the delivery of short-term intervention and be able to work systemically with the dual or triangular relationships of client, corporate client and EAP provider. A key function for clinicians working in an EAP setting is one of assessment. Assessment should be continual, from formal assessment at the beginning of a contact or intervention to evaluation at the close of a case. Components of an assessment by clinical interview can be seen in Appendix 16.1.

All clinical work should be monitored by feedback from service users and also by the utilisation of formal outcome measures.

### Financial Support and Debt Management Services

Evidence suggests that employees often require practical input as a part of the holistic service provided by an EAP. Debt and financial difficulties rank as one of the most worrying aspects of life. A condition known as money sickness syndrome (MSS) (Henderson, 2006) has recently been described where the anxiety related to financial difficulties actually is a precursor to somatic illness and relationship problems. AXA Insurance has conducted national research to explore this and conclude that 43% of the population have experience symptoms of MSS; 3.8 million people admit that financial concerns have caused them to take time off work. They should be able to identify issues that might benefit from interventions from other services both within and external to the EAP as well as identifying those issues that pertain to a problem in the workplace.

### Legal Support and Information

Access to legal support is popular. EAPs should guide client organisations to decide to include employment law advice. Any legal professional again should adhere to all relevant codes of conduct.

### Child and Eldercare Services

An ever increasing number of working people are also carers to either children or elderly relatives. An EAP that is able to support employees with issues around sourcing childcare placements and care homes will help those individuals to spend more productive time at work whilst allowing experts to identify the most appropriate placements for the child or elderly relative. EAPs should employ appropriately qualified staff to deal with this service.

### Health Information

Increasingly EAPs are making health information available as an integrated part of holistic EA.

### Management Support and Referral

EAPs coach managers in management referral at the implementation stage. New managers' induction into the organisation should involve a session with an EAP 'expert' to inform, facilitate and encourage management referrals and demonstrate their usefulness.

It is important that the EAP recognises the role a manager has within the organisation. The EAP's role is to support that manager in their duty of care but also to offer guidance on how to assist their troubled employees and those members of staff who are not performing in the workplace as expected.

Management referrals should be well structured, explicit and clearly communicated to all parties. At the heart of any management referral is an expectation of measured change. What is the organisation hoping to achieve from the referral?

It is vital that employees who are formally referred into the EAP give informed consent for any information to be disclosed to the manager. Consent can be withdrawn at any time and must be explicit. Any disclosure is only given with the understanding that it is given on a need to know basis.

It is vital to decide who in an organisation are able to make formal referrals into the EAP. Referral forms may be helpful – see Appendix 16.2.

Management referrals need careful management from within the EAP to ensure treatment is 'on-track' and feedback to the referrer is carried out ethically and responsibly.

### The Pro-active EAP

The EAP should also work with an organisation's HR facility to help to identify those who have had recent life events i.e. birth, bereavement or becoming the carer of an elderly relative. The EAP should be an expert referral service, know its limitations and be able to facilitate the employee to obtain the correct support.

### Case Management

Case management is distinct from clinical/counselling supervision in that it focuses principally on the role that the EA service plays in supporting individuals. Case management aims to support the affiliate and to ensure that employees obtain the maximum benefit

Specifically, case management is to ensure:

a. that the EAP can confidently assume responsibilities for all direct assessment and counselling services provided to employees using the service. The case management team monitors and controls the progress of the customer's treatment at all times. The affiliate is accountable to the EAP during the period of assessment/intervention.

b. that affiliates are supplied with all the appropriate case documentation and any relevant information on both clinical and organisational issues.

c. that the assessment/counselling provided has been agreed at the outset and will comply with the relevant contract agreed with the employing organisation (e.g. how quickly customers are seen, number of sessions, location and specific issues of confidentiality).

d. that the assessment, counselling and referral are carried out according to required quality standards (e.g. the counsellor complies with the clinical recommendation of the assessor).

e. ongoing clinical support to affiliates to provide the correct identification of customers who may need help beyond the EAP service (e.g. customers requiring urgent psychiatric attention).

f. the ongoing training of affiliates in employee support assessment and/or counselling through the adherence to the core values and procedures of employee assistance work.

## INDIRECT SERVICES

### Management Information

The preparation of management information (MI) is the essential difference between workplace counselling and EAP. MI is the translation of an individual's use of an EAP into an organisational intervention. It is an opportunity to examine any clinical or organisation change that has been measured or reported.

### Account Management

The relationship between the organisation and the service should be managed by an account manager. This person acts as an intermediary between the clinical EAP service and the business world of the organisation, translating the multi-layered support offered by the EAP into clear organisational advantage.

There should be a process in place for EAP practitioners to alert account managers of any important organisational issues. 'Serious/at risk' cases should be logged and checked regularly and issues reported to account managers who have a relationship with the organisation and are best placed to intervene. Account managers are managers of an intricate feedback loop – they should also alert the EAP practitioners to issues in the organisation (i.e. redundancies etc.), allowing EAP professionals to be prepared, knowledgeable and to set-up/review protocols.

### Trauma Services

The EAP should be involved in the human aspect of any business continuity plan (BCP) developed by a client organisation. As well as having a protocol to intervene with any post-trauma support that is necessary, these plans should include as a minimum: triggers (i.e. who can activate the protocol), first-line support immediately post-incident, on-site capability and timings, process for supporting staff members and feedback to the organisation.

Any intervention should be evidence-based and take into account most up-to-date guidance from organisations such as NICE (National Institute for Clinical Excellence 2005).

The EAP should assist in 'organisational preparedness' for major world events including terrorism threats, flu pandemic.

### Access/referral to Mediation and Coaching Services

Traditional EAP interventions may not be appropriate for all situations. It is important that practitioners are aware of, and keep up to date with, other treatments which may assist an individual or an organisation

### Training

EAP professionals come from a wide variety of clinical and commercial backgrounds. Innovative EAPs should use their people to offer tailored training workshops to clients to assist organisations manage issues identified through EAP usage i.e. managing bullying at work, change management, mental health in the workplace, HR and the law updates, etc.

## PROTOCOLS

EAPs should be protocol-driven to allow consistency of service and individual organisational needs. Protocols can be shared with the organisation especially around services such as management referral and disclosure of confidential information allowing accurate promotion of the service. EAPs need to be accountable and auditable – clear readily accessible written protocols allow this to be assessed. They should be reviewed regularly by management in collaboration with purchasers.

## OUTCOME MEASUREMENT

It is important to be able to demonstrate to client organisations that the EAP is providing what it has promised to provide and also to demonstrate value for money and a return on investment. The measures and variables used should be agreed between the EAP and the organisation. Measures could include satisfaction survey data reported by service users, clinical outcomes routine evaluation (CORE), return to work data, and sickness absence data.

## ETHICS

The EAP is responsible for adhering to, promoting and clarifying the ethical stance of the programme. The EAPA provides clear ethical guidelines and it is the EAP's primary task to ensure that they are adhered to.

A key ethical issue is one of confidentiality. Confidentiality is at the centre of EAP delivery – it is no one's interest to deviate from the ethical codes around confidentiality. It is a contract between the EAP provider, the organisation and the service user. There must be clear guidelines around situations where confidentiality is breached. Such situations outlined in the Association of Counselling at Work's *Guidelines for Counselling in the Workplace* (Hughes & Kinder, 2007) can be seen in Table 16.1.

In any other situation it is vital that information about a client or service user is only disclosed with the relevant consent forms signed and understood. Any consent must be informed and time appropriate. An example can be seen in Appendix 16.3.

**Table 16.1** Circumstances when a disclosure may be made include:

- Where there is risk to self or others
- Where there is serious alleged crime
- Where there are legal requirements (e.g. protection of children or prevention of terrorism)
- Where there is significant threat to the health and safety of those within an organisation

## CONCLUSION

In this chapter the authors have attempted to demonstrate those characteristics essential for a good EAP provider. Programmes must be flexible, protocol-driven, with clear management information and with a strong ethical position.

It is no one's interest to breach ethics even if it means losing a contract – the EAP must adhere to the EAPA Guidelines at all times despite commercial pressures.

## APPENDIX 16.1

### Full Assessment Protocol

#### *Customer Details*

The relevant details of the customer would be age, sex, ethnic origin and marital status if they have not already been gathered.

#### *Presenting Problem(s)*

At the beginning it should be ascertained why the caller is ringing for help. What is the presenting problem and why is the customer asking for help now? A detailed analysis of the presenting problem(s) is required, which should first involve a quantitative assessment of the problem(s) in terms of frequency and severity. A question that needs to be considered is: Does the customer have any problems that would be classified as a clinical disorder by DSM-IVr or ICD-10 standards?

As well as the above, other relevant information that needs to be collected is for how long the problem has occurred and whether the problem is general or context-specific. The precipitating factors to the problem need to be assessed as well as factors that may be maintaining the difficulties.

#### *Impact of Problem(s) on Work Performance*

There needs to be an evaluation of how the customer's presenting difficulties might be impacting on work. It should be identified whether the presenting problem is having an impact on work performance, and if so how; relationships at work, and/or issues related to attendance. Aspects of work that are exacerbating the problem and those aspects that relieve or have no effect should also be identified. It should be asked whether the customer is at work or currently absent and, if so, for how long. If the customer is experiencing difficulties at work it is necessary to explore their support systems within the workplace. It is essential that there is an exploration and discussion around any changes that might be necessary in the workplace to support the individual to return to normal functioning.

#### *Current and Past Psychological/Psychiatric Support*

In this section of the assessment, it is first necessary to discover what support the customer is currently receiving for the presenting problem. This is vital to ensure that any interventions by the EAP do not conflict with or deflect any other sources of psychological support. A detailed history of previous psychological/psychiatric support needs to be recorded including the individual/agency providing the support e.g. general practitioner, psychiatrist, social services or voluntary agency. As well as psychological/psychiatric support for the presenting problem(s), any other forms of support for psychological or medical problems need to be ascertained. Knowledge of a customer's past or current physical illnesses, both acute and chronic, can be very important. In particular, any current medication, either prescribed or non-prescribed, the customer is taking needs to be discovered.

### Coping Mechanisms/Defences

This component of the assessment involves an analysis of the customer's functional and dysfunctional coping mechanisms and psychological defences. The customer's present level of functioning needs to be evaluated and any threats to their own safety or the safety of others needs to be assessed. Any dysfunctional coping mechanisms such as alcohol or drug abuse, gambling or excessive risk-taking activities need to be explored. Impulse control issues require exploration.

### Relevant Family History

A detailed history of the family of origin may often not be necessary. However, relevant experiences need to be explored e.g. alcoholism in family, the customer having suffered childhood abuse, history of psychiatric problems in family and any other members of their family experiencing similar problems. An examination of the customer's current marital/sexual relationship, if applicable, needs to be conducted. The age and sex of any children, whether from current or past relationships, is important.

### Intimate and Social Relationships

A brief understanding of a customer's ability to form and conduct interpersonal relationships of a sexual and non-sexual nature is a major component of any clinical assessment. The quality of current relationships is usually more important than quantity and the customer's perception of their level of social support is crucial.

### Education and Work History

The educational level of the customer is always useful to discover as is their experience of school and so on. For EAP work, the exact nature of the customer's work is important, with emphasis on safety-sensitive issues and specific concerns of the employing organisation, e.g. drugs and alcohol policy. The customer's relationship with their work colleagues and manager is important as is the customer's view of their work performance. Any formal procedures being followed by the customer or the employing organisation need to be discovered, e.g. disciplinary action or internal grievance procedures.

### Psychological-mindedness of the Customer

The customer's suitability for psychological interventions needs to be assessed. This can be achieved by understanding their psychological-mindedness and their ability to form an appropriate therapeutic relationship. The suitability of short-term counselling as opposed to other types of help needs to be evaluated, e.g. long-term therapy, self-help groups or medical interventions. We may ask you to collect specific assessment information for certain clients or to respond to changes in clinical protocol.

## APPENDIX 16. 2

### Formal Referral Form

Referring Manager's Name:
Telephone Number:
Fax Number:
E- mail address:

Employee Name:
Reason for Referral:

Expectation of referral, e.g. return to work, improved performance, reduction in sickness absence, etc.:

Consent: YES /NO

Contact Details:
Time Restrictions:

Feedback Required (*please tick info required or leave blank if not needed*)

- Current psychological state
- Cause – work-related, non-work-related, both
- Effect condition is having on work capability
- Expected absence timescales
- Any adjustments/support required at work
- Treatment recommendations and timescales
- Recovery timescales
- Risk assessment in relation to work only
- Other specific questions to the case

Initial Contact (EAP to contact manager once contact and consent obtained): YES/NO
*Please fax this form to the EAP on*: ************

## APPENDIX 16.3

### EAP Consent Form

CONSENT FORM FOR THE RELEASE OF INFORMATION TO YOUR OCCUPATIONAL HEALTH ADVISER/MANAGER REGARDING YOUR ASSESSMENT AND COUNSELLING

*Data Protection Act 1998*

**The general information we ask about you is known as your personal data.**

**Information about your health, medical history and any treatment you have received is known as sensitive personal data.**

**We require your informed consent in writing in order to accept and process your personal and sensitive data. By signing this consent form you are in agreement with this.**

I xxx xxxx, authorise the EAP to disclose to my Occupational Health Adviser/ Manager, information relating to the recommendations made, in the course of my referral, through the EAP service.

If you would like a copy of the report/notes please could you call us on 0800 12 34 56

**\*Circle as appropriate otherwise this form is not valid.**
*I agree / I do not agree for the information listed on this consent form to be released.

Signed . . . . . . . . . . . . . . . . . . . . . . . . . Date . . . . . . . . . . . . . . . . . . . . . . . . .
Full Name (in block capitals) . . . . . . . . . . . . . . . . . . . . . . . . . . . . . . . . . . . . . . .
Contact Details (tel. and address) . . . . . . . . . . . . . . . . . . . . . . . . . . . . . . . . . . . .
Referrer's Name . . . . . . . . . . . . . . . . . . . Position . . . . . . . . . . . . . . . . . . . . .
Referrer's Contact Details. . . . . . . . . . . . . . . . . . . . . . . . . . . . . . . . . . . . . . . . . .
Date of Referral. . . . . . . . . . . . . . . . . . . . . . . . . . . . . . . . . . . . . . . . . . . . . . . . .

**The content of all your counselling sessions is confidential**
**Please sign and circle appropriately this Consent Form to enable us to release information in response to the issues listed below to your Occupational Health Adviser.**

**1. Current psychological state**
**2. Cause of difficulties: work-related or non-work-related**
**3. What effect is the condition having on work capability?**

4. Expected absence timescales
5. Any adjustments/support required at work
6. Treatment recommendations and timescales
7. Recovery timescales
8. Risk assessment in relation to work only
9. _____

## REFERENCES

AXA PPP Healthcare (2007). *Handbook for Clinical Affiliates*. Kent: AXA PPP Healthcare.

Deaney, D. (2007). Employers must act on workplace stress: Intel Corporation (UK) Limited v Daw – 7 February 2007. http://www.personneltoday.com/Articles/2007/02/20/39311/employers-must-act-on-workplace-stress-intel-corporation-uk-limited-v-daw-7-february.html.

EAPA (2000). *Standards of Practice and Professional Guidelines for Employee Assistance Programmes*. London: Employee Assistance Professionals Association UK Chapter.

EAPA (2007). Employee Assistance Professionals Association UK Website http://www.eapa.org.uk.

Health and Safety at Work Act (1974). http://www.hse.gove.uk/legislation/hswa.htm

Henderson, R. (2006). Money Sickness Syndrome could affect almost half the UK population. http://www.axa.co.uk/media/pressrelease/2006/pr20060120_0900.html.

HSE (2004). Health and Safety executive, Management standards for wok-related stress. http://www.hse.gove.uk/stress/standards.

Hughes, R., Kinder, A. (2007). *Guidelines for Counselling at Work, Association for Counselling at Work*. Lutterworth: British Association for Counselling & Psychotherapy.

Menninger, W.C. & Levinson, H. (1954). The Menninger Foundation Survey of Industrial Mental Health. *Menninger Quarterly*, **8**, 1–13.

National Audit Office: Current thinking on managing attendance. http://www.nao.org.uk/publications/nao_reports/04-05/040518_researchpaper.pdf.

National Institute for Clinical Excellence (2005). *Post-traumatic Stress Disorder (PTSD). The Management of PTSD in Adults and Children in Primary and Secondary Care*. London: NICE.

PARN Research (2003). http://www.eapa.org.uk/secure/articles/PARN0307.doc.

Sutherland (chairman of the Governors of St Thomas Becket RC High School) v Hutton (2002). CA, EWCA Civ 76. In the Court of Appeal (Civil Division) on appeal from Liverpool County Court., per Lady Justice Hale, Lord Justice Brooke, Lord Justice Kay see IRLA (2002) 263 at paragraph 33.

Winwood, M.A. & Karpas, T. (2002). From 'Boozed-up' to 'Stressed-out'. The continuing evolution of EAPs in the UK. Presented at the BPS Counselling Psychology Conference, Torquay, May 2002.

# CHAPTER 17

# Tackling the Macho Culture

**Mark Brayne and Neil Greenberg**
*Dart Centre for Journalism and Trauma, and King's College London*

The grizzled cameraman standing at the back of the newsroom shifted slightly as the trauma briefing approached its end, cleared his throat and signalled that he had something to say.

The discussion for the previous half hour among the 30 or so people present had been of grief at the death of two much-loved colleagues – a cameraman and producer killed on assignment four days earlier by a roadside bomb in Iraq – and the wounding of their reporter.

The team had been speaking warmly and sadly of the dead, and had been encouraged in the introductory briefing to talk and listen to each other, and to allow themselves – as normal, sentient human beings as well as journalists – to express their sorrow.

The introduction had included reassurances that with good social support, most people recover well from traumatic loss. But the team had also been reminded that recovery often takes at least a few weeks and sometimes a little longer. And they had been advised that if traumatic distress *does* get stuck in the system, then – as advised in the 2005 guidelines from Britain's National Institute for Clinical Excellence (NICE) – it's a good idea to get professional help.

The floor was now open for questions or comments.

The man at the back spoke. 'I'd like to make a couple of observations,' he said.

Everyone turned to listen. The two briefers – one a former journalist now turned psychotherapist, the other an EAP professional – feared the worst. Would he rubbish the whole idea of trauma awareness and support? Would he undo all the good work that had been done in the previous half hour? But no.

'Listen to what the man says,' the journalist continued. 'I know what this is like.'

The briefers' anxiety began to abate.

---

*Employee Well-being Support: A Workplace Resource.* Edited by A. Kinder, R. Hughes and C.L. Cooper.
© 2008 John Wiley & Sons, Ltd.

'As many of you know,' he went on, 'I had a rough time in the first Iraq war in 1991. When I came back, the company sent me to see a doctor.

'I told him of course that I was fine, physically and emotionally. The doctor said that was OK, but he just let me know that I might just feel different in a few months or even a few years. The emotions might catch up with me, or something like that, perhaps in response to something quite different and even trivial.'

It rapidly became clear that this war-hardened cameraman knew a great deal about trauma. One of the most experienced, respected and toughest of his generation, with approaching 30 years of news reporting behind him, he had been held for several months in an Iraqi jail and had been treated rather badly.

He continued. 'I thought at the time that what the good doctor said was rubbish. I put it all behind me. I was tough, after all. This is what we journalists do for a living. But a couple of years later, just as the doctor had warned, I fell apart. It wasn't a lot of fun. I got myself help. A bit late, but it made all the difference. So, as I said, listen to what the man is telling us.'

Our post-trauma journalism briefing could not have been choreographed more effectively. Several people then spoke up, expressing gratitude that their emotional needs as journalists were now at last being taken seriously. The only problem, added another equally experienced colleague, is that journalists didn't start talking about this years ago. They had needed this for so long.

It's a statement that's equally true for other professional first-responders who deal with trauma as a core part of their job. But in tackling the macho culture of such areas of work, there are babies that must not be thrown out with the bathwater.

First-responders need to be tough – albeit not so tough that they are unable to accept the possible consequences of being exposed themselves to extreme human distress.

When a bomb goes off in a city centre, or a train is derailed, with consequential death and injury, or an aircraft crashes on a motorway, or when drunken young men start brawling on a Saturday night, the healthy response of most ordinary people is to run the other way, and very sensibly to absent themselves from personal danger.

Professionals who rush in the other direction, on the other hand, and towards danger rather than away from it – a group which includes journalists as well as policemen, firefighters, ambulance and rescue workers – can find themselves dealing with extreme situations.

Exposure to critical incidents is likely to be for them too, at times, emotionally difficult. But they have a job to do which requires them to be resilient, and in the heat of the moment to put their own emotions to one side – skills and qualities which can show themselves in sometimes unsettling ways.

As anyone who works closely with groups such as soldiers, doctors and mortuary workers – and again, journalists – knows, people who work with death and disaster have a black sense of humour which can seem very callous to outsiders. However, the ability to see the funny side of even the most extreme situations is an important part of staying sane.

It is of course politically very incorrect, but policemen, among themselves, will talk about suspects and the public in sometimes crassly insensitive terms. Journalists dealing with overwhelming stories of trauma and distress will talk excitedly in editorial meetings of earthquakes with thousands of dead as a 'great story'.

That too may seem insensitive to outsiders. But to those that deal with such incidents on a regular basis, a great story is exactly what it is.

None of this should be too sharply condemned. First-responders need at some level to be hardened to the emotional effects of horror. But they also need to be allowed to be vulnerable human beings, able to recognise, acknowledge and process the impact on themselves of the traumatic soup in which they so often swim. Even the hardest may find themselves 'wounded' from time to time. Hard does not mean impenetrable.

Organisations which employ such professionals need also to know that it is not just those on the front line of blood and tragedy who may need support and training. Those at the rear, who deal 'merely' with the aftermath, the traffic, the relatives, the reports or the pictures are also at risk. Trauma does not respect artificially drawn lines between professional groups.

So in tackling the macho culture of professions such as journalism, what are the lessons we have learned, and what still needs to be done?

Since 2002, the Dart Centre for Journalism and Trauma (www.dartcentre. org) has cooperated with a number of major news organisations such as Reuters, *Newsweek* magazine and the *Washington Post* in the United States, German television, the Arabic television news channel Al Jazeera and especially the BBC in Britain, in developing training programmes in trauma awareness and support.

We have drawn generously on the experience of Britain's Royal Marines and their programme of trauma risk management (TRiM), with a particular focus on internal culture change and open recognition of trauma and its impact.

Our underlying understanding of trauma was usefully reflected in the 2005 NICE guidelines, with their recommendation for 'watchful waiting' for the first few weeks after a traumatic experience, and with the reassurance that, on the whole, most people, with the right kind of support, will recover naturally.

We have therefore supported the BBC and other organisations in moving away from the idea that confidential counselling and a free, outside helpline number are the only answers – an approach which rather obviously can be seen by staff as management washing their hands of their own duty-of-care responsibilities.

We needed to de-mystify and above all de-pathologise the concept of trauma-related distress, taking our cue from the Marines in emphasising peer-led monitoring and assessment of trauma symptoms within teams, by colleagues or managers given basic training.

What we have added to the Marines' TRiM model, however, has been a very clear accent on generic and pre-assignment briefings, introducing the concept of trauma and post-traumatic stress disorder (PTSD) *before* individuals are exposed to potential stressors – so that on their return, no one need feel surprised or stigmatised by being asked how they are doing.

The approach has seven levels – summarised here in a short list, and then with explanations.

1. There has to be top-level political buy-in from the senior managers.
2. There needs to be a rolling programme of explicit trauma-focused training which is best integrated into existing management and entry-level training courses.
3. Generic and pre-assignment briefings about trauma should be normal practice. Where an assignment or project is likely to be tough, people need to be told.
4. Teams and individuals dealing with trauma need, in the moment and while it is happening, appropriate support and care.
5. On return from potentially traumatic assignment or at end of (or during) emotionally challenging projects, individuals should have an opportunity, within a few days, for what we call a 'structured conversation' with a trained colleague – to assess how they are doing.
6. A month or so later, there must be a follow-up contact, again to check on how the individual is faring, and to identify any continued or emergent distress.
7. If necessary (and in general infrequently), professional mental health support can be suggested and individuals referred on, ideally with the knowledge of an organisation's occupational health provider or department.

So, let us explain in more detail why we have found that this approach works.

First, culture change will not work without explicit and enthusiastic support from respected group and organisational leaders. Top management needs to be seen to be personally and publicly committed, regularly reinforcing the message. That can be very hard to achieve.

The benefits for those managers may be far more than they initially realise. In helping their organisation discharge its duty of care, senior managers may eventually be viewed in a more positive light as individuals not just sanctioning good journalism, but also demonstrating real interest in their staff.

Second, an established and accepted programme for training – and not just briefing – of managers and editors, existing and newly appointed, will ensure that those deploying staff into emotional harm's way recognise and normalise for their teams some of these points:

- Why and how trauma knowledge matters in their business.
- How real human beings – which includes journalists, however tough they might be – can be affected by psychological trauma.

- What are the current scientific understandings of trauma.
- How to discuss the issue with colleagues, and recognise if someone is getting into emotional difficulties. This requires nothing more than (often already existing) active listening skills coupled with a basic awareness of trauma and its impact.
- What, as manager or editor or colleague, one can do about such distress, and where a referral to a specialist might be advised.

The training package we have put together usually lasts one day, allowing plenty of discussion and sharing of experiences, and an afternoon of role plays. The course is designed to leave participants with very practical skills as well as knowledge.

It is worth noting, as with the newsroom briefing described at the beginning of this chapter, how participants in this training frequently bring powerful personal stories of often unrecognised trauma from their own or colleagues' past, and how grateful many are that the issue is now being openly tackled.

At the third level, there then needs to be an expectation of regular pre-assignment and generic trauma briefings, to emphasise the normality of dealing with trauma responses as part of day-to-day management. That trauma is part of the job needs to be seen as normal and routine in the same way as many other already identified risks for particular forms of work or areas of assignment, such as malaria, lifting heavy equipment, and of course, sometimes avoiding bullets.

Trainees often find this pre-deployment discussion one of the hardest parts. When colleagues are just donning their emotional Super(wo)man suits before dashing off to cover a war, a fire or a murder, how does one broach the issue of possible emotional distress?

The answer, of course, is that this should have already been done several times in the normal course of team and individual briefings, so that what is needed now is just a reminder. The possibility of exposure to trauma should be part of the formal pre-assignment risk assessment.

The messages we encourage managers and team leaders to convey in this pre-assignment briefing include:

- Thank, acknowledge and appreciate what is being undertaken, and in general the colleagues' continued good work for the organisation. The thinking here is to reinforce psychologically healthy attachments within the work group, which is what good management should do as a matter of routine.
- Explicitly name what might be involved – emotionally as well as physically. In tackling the negatives of the macho culture, half the battle is in encouraging individuals and teams actually to talk about the issue in an informed way. Managers and example-setting leaders who are uncomfortable talking about trauma will send the implicit signal that they would rather everyone else bottle up their feelings as well.

- Make reliable arrangements to keep in touch. Again, this is about reinforcing health-supporting attachment and contact. As anyone working in this field knows, colleagues away from base, even the most organisationally aware and responsible among them, very quickly adopt an Us-and-Them attitude towards 'London' or 'Head Office' – and supervisors can lessen any associated distress simply by encouraging regular contact.
- Encourage self-care. Looking after physical needs for sleep, water, food and exercise makes all the difference. People under emotional pressure, and especially, it seems, journalists, can very easily forget that their mind and body are their most important pieces of kit, and like their equipment need fuel, water, cooling off and maintenance.
- Reassure that some distress is not unusual when dealing with trauma. What matters is how it is dealt with – and that it is good to talk, although not, of course, compulsory.

This can be a very simple discussion. As we have found at the BBC and elsewhere, when done well it can make a great difference to how a journalist reporting the worst things human beings can do to each other is able to handle the emotional stress that comes with that.

Pre-assignment briefing is, however, only part of a three-dimensional package. At the fourth level in our seven-point list, we make clear that good management *during* an assignment or project is just as important as preparation or reaction afterwards.

- Arrangements beforehand to keep in regular touch need to be honoured and initiated. Managers need to be inquisitive, alert and supportive, and not simply reactive.
- Colleagues should be allowed and encouraged – and financed, although with internet email and now telephoning this is no longer quite so expensive as it was – to keep in close contact with home and friends.
- Leaders should set an example – for instance in getting enough sleep. Of course, that is not always easy, and eight hours every night may not be possible. But a team's attitudes are set in large measure by the behaviour of the individual in charge. As military forces now emphasise constantly in their training, sleep-deprived soldiers are simply unable to fight well. The same is true of all professions dealing with stress and trauma. Being tired is just not good for business.
- Be careful with the timing and pitch of any criticism. The emotional defences of teams in the field will be down, and their sensitivities high.
- Similarly, make sure the rest of the home team (including Finance . . .) is on side, and aware of the pressure teams are under.

These last two points often elicit wry smiles of understanding, and horror stories of the Accounts Department ringing a journalist who is in the middle of a firefight to query a month-old taxi receipt, or of insensitive output editors bellowing nasty feedback down an open telephone line just when someone has been travelling all day through mine- and guerrilla-infested battlefields to file their story.

As one journalist put it after the war in Afghanistan in 2001: 'I could cope with the dead bodies. What I couldn't cope with was that b\*\*tard on the five o'clock news who could only criticise what I was doing.'

- Before individuals return to base from a stressful assignment, encourage where possible a spell of 'decompression' with their colleagues – e.g. a day or two in a nice hotel or coming into the office for some easy days when they have arrived back safely.

This latter suggestion does not always go down well. Staff are needed for the next assignment; their partners want them home; there aren't the resources to pay for this kind of downtime.

In reality, though, giving people space and time to wind down, to talk and to relax a little with their trusted team mates – at company expense, and especially if they have just been through similar experiences – has a strikingly soothing and health-reinforcing effect.

It sends a *felt* signal that their work is appreciated. It allows arousal and alarm levels to abate naturally, before the colleague is pitched into dealing with the very different stresses of home life. And it protects journalists just a little from the jolting transition from war zone to home which many say is the single most damaging aspect of their work, and one which has destroyed many a marriage and relationship.

Moving to point five – what happens *after* an assignment – the opportunity to talk about what was experienced should again be part of a broader approach, one which recognises the importance of social and practical support in the first instance, and the value of small gestures – appreciation, what we in journalism call herograms (notes of special individual appreciation for work well done), emails, being met at the airport, parties, public acknowledgment and the like.

We make the point that factual information about what happened when 'you were out there', and about the array of normal emotional reactions to traumatic events, often reassures and soothes the nervous system. So it should be shared generously.

We do not make it compulsory that people talk with managers or colleagues about the emotional side of the assignment. But we do expect managers to make sure that the opportunity of a structured conversation is offered, and indeed encouraged.

And the conversation should not just be what journalists usually do with each other – 'Hi, good to see you back. Great work! Hairy stuff! You OK?' To which the answer, almost invariably, will be, 'Oh thanks, I'm fine' – a word which can mask a multitude of experiences good and bad, and which, we joke, can actually mean 'F\*\*\*ed up, Insecure, Neurotic and Emotional . . .'

One should not forget that stigma is a real and important issue which prevents many people, especially the more hardy ones, from asking for help even if they need it. Unless distressed individuals appreciate that the organisation really *does* care and wants to ensure that they really are fine, they are unlikely to be open and honest with their bosses or colleagues. The training emphasises the point that if you are going to take an interest in your staff – and of course all managers should – then that has to be a sincere interest.

So, drawing from but slightly adapting the TRiM approach developed by the Royal Marines, we encouraging teammates or managers to use the word FINE as a mnemonic for the structure of how they talk.

- F is for FACTS – What happened? When, where, how, who, etc. rather than focusing on emotions or feelings. We encourage here that the event or experience is talked through chronologically in the sequence of Before, During and After.
- I for IMPACT – How did the person personally experience what happened? Their thoughts (and feelings) *then?*
- N for NOW – How are you doing? Which can explore how well they're functioning in the present, and whether any distress is getting stuck in their 'system'.
- E for EDUCATION – Reassurance and reminders that human beings have natural responses to trauma, that on the whole and with time they recover pretty well, but that if things remain difficult, then a spot of professional support can be helpful.

The process is not one of forced catharsis. Not everyone needs to express huge amounts of emotion. Often the simple telling of one's story from start to finish is enough. What is important is that people get an opportunity to chat with someone who is interested in what they are going to say, and who may be in a position to offer or point to appropriate help and support if they need it.

Note that that counselling support is not necessarily brought into play just yet, unless of course the colleague is in obvious and serious distress, and finding it difficult to function. Rather, the expectation is (Level Six in the seven-point list above) that there will be a follow-up conversation or contact in a month or so, again to check on how the person is doing.

Usually, of course, there is not a great deal to worry about – and the mere fact of having expressed an interest, *within* the culture and given reassurances about normal reactions to trauma, allows people to come to terms with their experiences in a more productive and healthy way.

So what do we tell peers and colleagues to look out for? Again drawing on the Marines' experience, we use two very simple checklists, boiled-down versions of more comprehensive lists that have been proven very reliable in identifying PTSD-style symptoms.

Readers will be familiar with the Acute Stress checklist developed by Chris Brewin of University College London – watching out for:

- upsetting thoughts or memories
- upsetting dreams
- acting or feeling that bad things are happening again

- feeling upset by reminders
- physical reactions – e.g. fast heartbeat, stomach churning, sweatiness, dizziness
- sleep difficulties
- irritability or outbursts of anger
- difficulty concentrating
- heightened awareness of danger
- being jumpy or startled at something unexpected.

What we do, however, add is a useful further nine-ingredient cocktail of risk factors which help to identify distress that does not necessarily fit into straightforward patterns of PTSD – which after all is a less likely outcome from exposure to trauma than depression, anxiety or relationship difficulties.

- Did the person feel out of control when experiencing the trauma?
- Did they feel their life was threatened?
- Do or did they blame others, beyond the reasonable?
- Or did/do they indeed blame themselves, in the form of shame?
- Are they still exposed to substantial stressors?
- Have they been having problems coping with day-to-day life?
- Has their experience reminded them, in a distressing way, of previous traumas in their life, personal or professional?
- Do they have good or poor social support – perhaps the key risk factor?
- And finally, are they using alcohol or drugs to try to make themselves feel better? Not a habit normally associated with journalists, of course . . .

So, is this new focus on an awareness of trauma in journalism making a difference? We believe so. More and more journalists – in Britain, in the United States, in Germany, in Spain, in Scandinavia – are beginning to talk more openly about their emotional experiences of covering tragedy and violence.

'In the old days', says David Loyn, the BBC's experienced Developing World Correspondent, 'none of us would ever talk about this stuff. Now, sitting around in bars in the Middle East or Africa, there's little else we talk about.'

Loyn is a committed supporter of the trauma-and-journalism agenda, and member of the Dart Centre Europe Advisory Board. His perspective is personally coloured, and for every David Loyn in the business, there are still probably 10 who have never yet given a thought to the connections.

But the climate *is* changing.

In the Royal Marines, the difference to the macho culture made by nearly a decade of TRiM training was neatly illustrated in a conversation between one rank-and-file serviceman and the co-author of this paper, Dr Neil Greenberg.

Greenberg asked the fellow – a big and tough regimental sergeant-major type – what was done in his unit about trauma. The soldier responded: 'We have this thing called TRiM, Sir. The lads think it's a bit poncey – but they like to know it's there.'

Journalism in the UK is, as yet, nowhere near the level of acceptance which the Marines appear to have achieved towards talking practically about trauma.

But well-known journalists are beginning to write and broadcast about trauma and their own experiences. They are beginning to talk with counsellors. News managers are calling the Dart Centre for advice and starting to commission training.

Almost all broadcasters, although not yet most print media, have employee assistance programmes in the background with a confidential helpline – not the whole answer, but an important element.

And when two other Western newsmen were badly injured in a bomb attack in Iraq in 2006, the response when we spoke to the bereaved teams was not to button up and hope that giving them a few days off would sort it. The organisation involved openly acknowledged the emotional dimension of what had happened, and told colleagues that anyone who did want to see a specialist would be funded to do so. Grizzled veterans are beginning to ensure that the message gets credible backing from the newsroom floor.

Working with journalists who are dealing with trauma – sometimes accumulated over a career of many decades – the stories that the other co-author of this paper Mark Brayne now hears from people coming through his consulting-room door are sometimes heart-breaking but also typical.

The stories are not just about Iraq, a conflict of especial psychological toxicity for journalists covering the story from Baghdad. They speak also of trauma bottled up in many cases for a long time – from Africa, the Balkans, the Middle East and all the disasters and wars of the past two decades, and at the cost of marriages, health, even careers.

By respectfully tackling, and seeking gently to change, the macho culture, we can help first-responders to recognise that trauma responses come with the territory. We can give them a language to talk about that, and encourage them to give themselves and each other the space and the time to do so.

The change will take years, probably generations, to bring about. But the process has begun.

# PART 3

# Mental Health, Emotions and Work

CHAPTER 18

# Rehabilitation of Mental Health Disabilities

**David Wright**
*Atos Origin*

## INTRODUCTION

There is wide acceptance that those with physical disabilities should be in employment wherever possible and those who develop such disabilities while in employment should remain in employment. Often such disabilities follow a period of sickness absence or are associated with periods of sickness absence and there is a concomitant need to rehabilitate employees back into the workplace.

There is greater difficulty in accepting that the same considerations should apply to mental health disabilities and there are a variety of reasons for this unwillingness. The lack of understanding of mental illness coupled with a fear of the consequences is at the root of this misappreciation. The difficulty is associated with the more intangible nature of mental ill health and the varied and varying course of such illnesses.

Mental ill health is given as a cause of absence from work in an increasing number of cases. In the United Kingdom approximately 80 million working days are lost as a result of mental illness (Palmer *et al.*, 2007). Thirty-five per cent of incapacity benefit claimants in the UK are suffering from a mental disorder (TSO, 2002:12). The definition of mental ill health in these cases may be very wide-ranging from acute psychosis at one end of the scale to anhedonia at the other. Job dissatisfaction may become transmogrified into mental ill health. The experience of occupational health physicians is that this is increasingly the case.

## DEFINITION

One of the major difficulties in the consideration of mental health disabilities is the definition of what constitutes such a disability. Mental health problems

*Employee Well-being Support: A Workplace Resource.* Edited by A. Kinder, R. Hughes and C.L. Cooper.
© 2008 John Wiley & Sons, Ltd.

range from the major psychoses through minor/moderate mental health difficulties to stress and burnout to more general unhappiness. They may be considered to include personality traits, behavioural issues and learning difficulties.

Some jurisdictions have sought to limit the definition to the more serious conditions. In the United Kingdom the Disability Discrimination Act 1995 said that mental health impairments had to be clinically well recognised illnesses. In practice this meant that such conditions had to meet the definitions within: DSM IV (AMA, 1994) or ICD 10 (WHO, 1990).

This effectively removed personality traits, behavioural issues and stress from the scope of the Act. However, the newer United Kingdom Disability Discrimination Act 2005 removed this restriction and all such conditions could now be covered by the Act. Other jurisdictions will have other definitions and even within one jurisdiction there will be different definitions for different purposes. Examples of such legislation and directives can be found at:

- Americans with Disabilities Act 1990 (USA)
- Council Directive 2000/78/EC (European Union)
- Disability Discrimination Act 1995 (UK)
- Disability Discrimination Act 2005 (UK)
- Disability Discrimination Act 1992 (Australia).

The International Labour Office (ILO) in *Mental Health in the Workplace* (ILO, 2000) sought to make a distinction between mental health problems and mental illness, suggesting that illness occurs when mental health problems become such that clinical intervention following a diagnosis occurs. The argument becomes to a degree somewhat circular in that in order to make a diagnosis it is necessary to revert to the criteria of DSM IV and ICD.

The other associated issue is that different cultures have different approaches to mental ill health and may well use different definitions. This is particularly so when social and financial benefits become involved.

In many ways cases of the major psychoses are easier to deal with, as there is a clear diagnosis, the likelihood of treatment is high and all concerned understand that there is an illness present. That is not to say there is not the potential for major difficulties but it is easier to put them in context.

Whatever the diagnosis or category of mental health disability, it must be appreciated that it is an individual that needs to be managed rather than the disease itself. Healthcare practitioners can be guilty of managing the disease rather than the individual and in a clinical context that can be the appropriate approach. In an employment context it is the individual's needs and expectations that require management rather than the disease process itself. Due account does have to be taken of business needs and the needs of colleagues and customers together with the wider public.

## THE BUSINESS CONTEXT

The basis of employment is that there is a contract between the employee and the employer, in that the employee is paid by the employer for work done. If the employee fails to attend for work then that contract is broken. It may also be considered to be broken if work is below standard or there are behavioural issues in the workplace.

Any business is in business to do business and if they are frustrated in that then their business position may be in jeopardy. This applies to all employers whether they are in manufacturing, a service industry or in the public sector providing for example healthcare.

That having been said, in most developed societies there is a recognition that to dismiss someone from employment as the result of short-term illness would be unreasonable. This view may be enshrined in statute (Employment Rights Act, 1996), may be developed in case law, may be within the terms of the contract of employment or may be just considered a reasonable way to behave. More usually it is a combination of one or more of these.

The business position becomes more difficult should that absence be prolonged or if there are frequent absences. This is particularly so if there are associated performance and behavioural issues.

Large employers may be more able to accommodate absence or less than full performance from employees than small businesses. An employer with many thousand employees will suffer less impact from one ill employee than will a small employer with only a few employees. This will inevitably affect the ability to accommodate absence and affect the attitude of an employer towards those with mental health problems. Legislation may also reflect the needs of differing employers in relation to their size or field of work (HMSO, 1996).

There can be no doubt that management approaches to mental ill health can significantly influence the behaviours of employees towards their own perceptions of mental illness. If management is felt or seen to be unsympathetic to mental health problems then it becomes increasingly difficult for employees to admit that they have a problem, to discuss that problem, to seek help in rehabilitation and to return to work. Unsympathetic management may precipitate absence from work, as the individual may perceive that by absenting themselves they have at least removed one stressor. At that stage they may not appreciate that by doing so they have merely replaced one stressor with another that is more difficult to overcome.

Conversely an over-sympathetic management style can bring its own problems. It may be that the manager advises a few days off to get over a difficulty. The problem may then arise that this is not enough; days become weeks, weeks become months and the downward spiral to prolonged absence outlined below begins.

## IMPACT ON THE INDIVIDUAL

Absence from work for whatever reason will have a significant impact on the employee. The most immediate effect may well be financial. There are, however, much wider issues relating to self-esteem, social interactions and general well-being. The longer an absence goes on the greater these problems become. Should that absence lead to dismissal then these issues may well gain significance by several orders of magnitude.

The longer an individual is absent from work the more difficult it is to return to work (TSO, 2002:11). The psychological, sociological and emotional barriers to a resumption of work become increasingly strong. This is regardless of the reason for the original absence and it can be argued that in all absences there is at least a psychological component even if that is not the primary reason for the absence.

If the absence originally occurs as a result of mental health problems then the psychological barriers to a return may be even stronger. Even where a physical illness has been the cause of the original absence it may be that in the end the reason for continuing absence relates to mental health issues which may have come about as a result of the absence itself.

As indicated above the individuals may absent themselves from work as a means of reducing the stressors on themselves. In this they may be assisted by healthcare professionals who encourage an absence from work as a means of reducing the perceived stress of work. If healthcare practitioners do this they encourage the medicalisation of problems and reinforce illness behaviour.

It is clear that at the start of an absence the majority of individuals express a desire to return to work. Some see themselves returning to work as part of the rehabilitation process from their illness. Others, sometimes reinforced by healthcare practitioners, develop the belief that they must be completely well before they can consider returning to work. The inevitable consequence becomes one of never being quite ready and thus they move into a state of perceived permanent ill health.

It has to be recognised that the social care and financial benefits system that is in place will in these circumstances begin to have an increasing influence on the ability to return to work. This is particularly so if the illness or mental health condition leads or is perceived to lead to a less that fully productive work style. The individual may move into the so-called benefits trap where it is both easier and financially worthwhile to remain on benefits. A downward cycle of stress, anxiety and depression takes place as a direct result of being absent from work leading to loss of employment and entering the benefits system.

Differing systems will have varying approaches to the management of this downward spiral. This may range from increasing restrictions on benefits at one end of the scale to active programmes of rehabilitation at the other.

Whereas many of those with mental health problems do not consider themselves disabled others do. This in turn may well affect the attitude on the part of the individual to rehabilitation, recovery and a return to work. The stance taken on disability as a concept will undoubtedly be influenced by both social attitudes and any legislation that is present.

## MAJOR MENTAL ILLNESS

The major mental illnesses are well defined within DSM IV and ICD 10. They include:

- schizophrenia
- bipolar affective disorder
- psychotic depression
- organic psychosis.

If the laid-down criteria are met then the diagnosis can be made and treatment plans put in place. It is highly likely that specialist help will be sought and ongoing support be provided. Hospital admission may be necessary at least at the start of a treatment regime and indeed a crisis may provoke such admission and the initiation of treatment.

Once formal specialist support and treatment is in place, this can encompass clear consideration of the need for rehabilitation back into the workplace. This may be facilitated by disability legislation, which can provide a framework within which the patient, healthcare practitioners and the employer can work to effect a return to work. The requirements of such legislation will vary and may well have differing end points. The legislation may point towards social and financial support or, as in the case of the UK Disability Discrimination Acts of 1995 and 2005, may focus on avoidance of discrimination with requirements placed on employers to make reasonable adjustments to allow a return to employment.

Such legislation may well extend beyond the major psychoses but to a degree is easier to implement when there is a diagnosis, treatment and support regime in place.

As part of this employers need to understand that the major mental illnesses are likely to be long-term and/or episodic in nature. Treatment is likely to be prolonged and may be life-long. The fact that treatment may not be fully effective or may need changing is not always appreciated by employers. The episodic nature of illness is not always understood and recurrences may be considered by employers to be the patient's fault and must be the result of non-compliance.

The existence of an occupational health service will provide advice and support to both patients and employers in such circumstances. The arrangements for occupational health support vary greatly between differing jurisdictions and within any one jurisdiction. In some there is comprehensive access, in others none. Even when it is available both patients and employers may find it difficult to accept such advice, as there may still be significant management issues to address.

## MILD TO MODERATE MENTAL HEALTH PROBLEMS

Mild to moderate mental health problems pose the area of biggest difficulty. Patients in this bracket will have a wide range of disorders some of which can be categorised by DSM IV and ICD. Others may have no formal diagnosis or may be encompassed in potentially vague terms such as 'stress'.

The majority of patients in this category are unlikely to be having specialist psychiatric treatment and may have no medical intervention at all apart from advice to absent themselves from work. The latter is particularly likely if the perceived cause of the stress or other illness is considered to be work-related.

Many of these minor mental health problems are multi-factorial. There may well be work-related factors but it is highly likely that there are other factors in the domestic or social environment that contribute to the problem. It may be that a work issue is the final factor precipitating absence. It is easier for the individual to concentrate on the workplace issues as these can then be blamed on someone else.

It becomes important in this context to separate out the issues and to clarify where the problems lie. If indeed there are workplace issues, be they real or perceived, then they need to be tackled. By addressing these matters in the workplace the focus can then be moved to addressing the other domestic and social issues. Common workplace issues include:

- harassment and bullying (real or perceived)
- poor interpersonal relationships
- grievances (real or perceived)
- job dissatisfaction.

If there are significant workplace problems it is likely that they will affect more than one individual. Indeed if a number of individuals are absent with minor mental health problems there needs to be a review of the workplace to ascertain whether there is a common issue. This could relate to working arrangements, to management style as a whole, to a particular manager, to other workers or to trades unions. An audit will need to be carried to determine if there is a common problem and to remedy it. If this is not done there may in some jurisdictions be an infringement of employment or health and safety legislation. In addition there could be a case for civil action.

## BEHAVIOURAL ISSUES

The major psychoses and moderate to mild mental health problems may all have associated behavioural problems. In addition aberrant personality traits may lead to significant behavioural problems.

Many of the minor ill health issues in the workplace relate to behavioural problems of the patient or of others. Disciplinary proceedings whether justified or not may lead to stress-related absence and a resistance to a return to work.

Allegations of bullying and harassment may also lead to stress-related absence both in those who feel that they are the victims as well as those accused of being perpetrators. The real difficulty in these cases is that although they may be fully investigated the sense of grievance remains and the perceived victim remains absent with stress, anxiety and depression. It may be extremely difficult in these cases to bring about a return to work as the absence is often prolonged and as discussed above the longer the absence, the less likely is a resumption of work.

Whatever the cause of the behavioural problem there needs to be a clear distinction between illness and behaviour. Whereas illness may well be a factor in difficult behaviour and to a degree may excuse it, nevertheless it needs to be dealt with by the organisation as a behavioural problem. To do otherwise may have significant effects on other employees and could in turn lead to other employees feeling that they need to absent themselves from work on the basis of stress. This could in turn lead to legal actions under employment or health and safety legislation.

In the major psychoses, for example schizophrenia, aberrant behaviour may become so extreme that it can no longer be managed in the workplace. Dismissal from work may be the only option provided the provisions of disability and employment legislation have been complied with. In these instances, ill-health retirement may be appropriate if the rules of the pension scheme so allow.

In the majority of cases, however, poor behaviour cannot be attributed to ill health and whatever the pressures such behaviours should not be medicalised. To do so increases the difficulties in bringing about resolution. There is often great pressure from both the individual and business points of view to categorise poor behaviour as mental illness and thus seek to manage it as an illness or sickness absence. This is unlikely to have a satisfactory outcome as either the sickness absence or the poor behaviour continues.

Those who are absent as the result of stress brought about by the threat of disciplinary proceedings should also not be permitted to medicalise the problem, nor should the employer. The stress will not resolve unless the disciplinary issues are dealt with. Employers and their advisers need to be clear about what mental illnesses prevent attendance at disciplinary proceedings. In reality such illnesses are very few but would include acute psychosis and acute mania, mute and demented.

It may be appropriate on some occasions to obtain a formal medical opinion from an occupational physician or psychiatrist that the individual is fit to attend a hearing.

Additionally employers may well be advised to have in their employment contracts provisions about the management of behavioural issues and the need for employees to attend hearings, even if they are absent from work supported by sick certification.

It may be felt on occasions that a pragmatic way forward in these sorts of cases and in those involving minor mental health problems would be for employment to end. It may be felt that this would be to the benefit of both employer and employee. Employment can only end, however, by dismissal or resignation. Dismissal in such circumstances may contravene employment legislation and/or disability legislation. Voluntary resignation may mean that the individual is denied unemployment or other benefits as they would be considered to have removed themselves from work.

The sometimes somewhat naïve suggestion by healthcare workers or other advisers that such a course should be the way forward may lead to an expectation of ill-health retirement. Such an outcome can only occur if the pension fund rules are met. For ill-health retirement the majority of pension schemes require an element of ill health at least and most require that ill health to be permanent and of such seriousness that further employment is not possible.

## CONCLUSION

Mental ill health in the workplace is an increasing cause of sickness absence in the developed world. The range of conditions covered by this term is very wide and includes:

1. acute psychoses
2. minor mental ill health
3. stress
4. behavioural issues
5. job dissatisfaction.

There needs to be a clear appreciation on the part of employers of the range of mental health problems and their role in the management of them in relation to the workplace. Policies need to be in place in relation to:

- reducing workplace stressors
- managing sickness absence
- managing poor behaviour
- clearly distinguishing between illness, unhappiness and poor behaviour.

Employers will have to take account of legislation which will include:

1. employment
2. health and safety
3. disability
4. discrimination on grounds of race, age, gender, religious belief, etc.

There will be variations between jurisdictions but the principles will be similar. Such legislation will impose responsibilities on employers both from the health and safety point of view and in respect of the management of disability. It will also, however, provide a framework within which such problems can be managed.

Such legislation may directly require or impose by inference the carrying out of risk assessments. Such risk assessments should include those related to:

- physical hazards
- chemical hazards
- mental health hazards.

The aim in all management of sickness absence due to mental ill health should be to facilitate a return to employment as that is undoubtedly in the best interests of the patient and the business.

## REFERENCES

AMA, American Psychiatric Association (1994). *Diagnostic and Statistical Manual of Mental Disorders – IV*. AMA.

HMSO (1996). *Disability Discrimination Act 1995, Code of Practice*. HMSO.

ILO, International Labour Office (2000). *Mental Health in the Workplace*. ILO.

Palmer, K. T., Cox, R. A. F. & Brown, I. (2007). *Fitness for Work: The Medical Aspects*, p. 149. Oxford: Oxford University Press.

TSO (2002). *Pathways to Work: Helping People into Employment*. TSO.

WHO, World Heath Organisation (1990). *International Classification of Diseases – 10*. WHO.

# CHAPTER 19

# An Organisational Approach to the Rehabilitation of Employees following Stress-Related Illness[1]

**Louise Thomson and Jo Rick**
*Independent Researcher, and University of Sheffield*

## INTRODUCTION

There is increasing research evidence that psychological distress, depression and anxiety can be a significant cause of absence from work (e.g. Dwyer & Ganster, 1991; Hardy, Woods & Wall, 2003; Spector, Dwyer & Jex, 1988). Government statistics also reflect the increasing role of mental health and emotional well-being in the causes of employee absence (see Box 19.1). The cost of this type of absence was estimated as £3.8 billion in 2001.

**Box 19.1** Impact of absence due to work-related stress in UK in 2005/6

---

- 10.5 million – number of working days lost to stress
- 420,000 – number of people affected by stress
- 30.1 – average number of working days lost per affected case

Health and Safety Executive, 2006

---

As well as the expense to industry, long-term absence also places a large cost on the individual and the wider economy. If employees with stress-related illness are unable to be rehabilitated back into the workplace, it can ultimately

---

[1] This chapter is based on research funded by Health and Safety Executive and undertaken by the Institute for Employment Studies and Industrial Relations Services Research. The full research report is published by the HSE in Research Report 138. We would like to thank our colleagues and all those who took part in the study for their contributions.

---

*Employee Well-being Support: A Workplace Resource.* Edited by A. Kinder, R. Hughes and C.L. Cooper.
© 2008 John Wiley & Sons, Ltd.

lead to them leaving the labour market and moving into the benefit system. Statistics suggest that over 150,000 workers leave employment each year as a result of ill health and transfer to Incapacity Benefit (Cunningham, James & Dibben, 2004). In addition, approximately 180,000 are forced to change jobs because of their work-related illness (Jones *et al.*, 1998). In February 2006, there were over 977,000 people claiming Incapacity Benefit due to 'mental or behavioural disorders' (DWP, 2006), representing nearly 40% of all claimants and an increase of nearly 200,000 from five years previous to that. However, this diagnostic category includes many different types and severities of mental health problems, so it is difficult to make an exact assessment of the number of Incapacity Benefit recipients suffering from stress. Nevertheless, long-term absence due to stress-related disorders is less likely to end in a successful return-to-work than long-term absence due to illness or physical injuries (Watson Wyatt, 2000). Research also shows that the longer employees are off work due to stress-related illness, the less likely they are to return. For example, a study of the rehabilitation of Australian teachers with stress-related illness found that teachers who had not attempted to return to work within 505 days of their first absence were less likely to return at all (Young & Russell, 1995). The impact of the length of absence on the likelihood of a successful return to work is also seen with other causes of absence too, not just stress-related absence. There is only a 50% likelihood of the employee returning to work after an absence of six months, and this falls to 25% after 12 months' absence (BSRM, 2001).

The UK Government has set targets to reduce the number of working days lost due to work-related injury and ill health by 30% and due to work-related stress by 20% by 2010 (HSC, 2000). Although preventative measures are widely accepted as the priority for reducing the prevalence of work-related stress, it is necessary to accompany this with thorough procedures for rehabilitation. Furthermore, the figures reported above suggest that small successes in rehabilitation could translate into significant gains for both organisations and society. To reduce the amount of absence due to work-related stress and to avoid the permanent loss of staff through incapacity to work, organisations need to have in place an integrated and effectively managed rehabilitation process which is initiated in the early stages of absence caused by work-related stress.

However, UK organisations have a poor record when it comes to rehabilitation services. A recent European study comparing return-to-work practices in five EU countries found that UK had the lowest return-to-work rate of long-term absentees (6%), with The Netherlands having the highest rate (54%) (Zijlstra *et al.*, 2006). These differences in rehabilitation outcomes suggest that UK employers could achieve much better results in reducing absence and retaining employees. In their review of rehabilitation practices in the UK, James *et al.* (2000) concluded that few employers provide comprehensive and integrated rehabilitative services; few are able to draw on the advice and expertise of occupational health professionals when considering actions to assist an employee to return to work; and most have little knowledge of appropriate actions that will help employees back to work. Managers don't feel confident about managing long-term absence (Cunningham *et al.*, 2004; James *et al.*, 2002), and this is probably more so for absence due to mental health problems than for absence due to physical illness and injuries (Bevan, 2003).

In this chapter we aim to describe the stages of rehabilitating employees who are absent due to work-related stress, from the first day of absence through to their full return to work, and the actions organisations should take at each stage. We will illustrate these with case study examples taken from a study funded by the HSE (Thomson, Neathey & Rick, 2003). We will also discuss factors affecting the successful management of these stages of rehabilitation. In reviewing the research literature on rehabilitation of absent employees, it soon becomes evident that the main focus has been on physical illnesses and injuries (e.g. back pain). There is relatively little literature that examines the specific process of rehabilitation following stress-related illness. Therefore, we will use the framework and basic principles of rehabilitation strategies for physical illness as a starting point from which we can consider issues that are specific to stress-related illnesses (Pimentel, 2001).

## THE STAGES OF OCCUPATIONAL REHABILITATION

There are six main stages involved in the process of rehabilitating employees back into work following a period of absence due to work-related stress (see Box 19.2). These stages tend to occur in the sequence illustrated, but there may be cases where it is necessary for the stages overlap or change order.

**Box 19.2** Six stages of occupational rehabilitation

1. A representative of the organisation (e.g. line manager, HR or OH professional) contacts the absent employee within the first week of absence.
2. The employee is referred for a health assessment as early as possible to determine appropriate treatment and prognosis.
3. A rehabilitation plan is developed with the employee describing the timescale and steps towards a gradual return to work.
4. The employee is referred to a therapeutic intervention (e.g. cognitive behavioural therapy or counselling) if necessary.
5. A gradual return to work schedule should be initiated as early as deemed appropriate, and monitored and adjusted as required.
6. The employee's job should be adjusted to remove or reduce any aspects of work that may impede recovery or lead to relapse, and the employee's health and work monitored during and after the return to work.

For each of the stages we now describe the key actions and processes that appear to increase the likelihood of successful rehabilitation and return to work.

## Early Contact by the Organisation

The timing of actions seems to be important throughout the entire process of rehabilitation, but this is particularly true within the first days of an employee going off sick with stress-related illness. Early and supportive contact by someone within the organisations is thought be a vital initial step. This would usually involve a telephone call from the employee's line manager or the occupational health department within the first week of their absence. The purpose of this initial communication is to:

- offer general support to the employee,
- demonstrate the organisation's concern for them as an individual, and
- maintain a link between the employee and the workplace.

Discussions of interventions, treatments and work adjustments should be avoided at this stage, and it is important not to rush employees. What appears to be key is for the employee to remain connected in some way to the workplace and not to completely withdraw and become isolated from it, but at the same time they need to feel under no immediate pressure from the organisation to return to work. Ongoing contact with the employee which demonstrates the organisation's sincere care for their well-being and which stimulates the employee's enthusiasm for returning to work is important (Zijlstra et al., 2006). The organisation also needs to consider who is the most appropriate and best placed to contact the employee, and what information and support is available to that individual. If line managers are responsible for making initial contact, they must be given guidance and advice on how best to do this. Employees can sometimes feel threatened by early contact by a line manager or personnel manager, and initial contact via the telephone may be unproductive because of this. If this is the case, contact with the absent employee should be reattempted quickly by another party such as a close colleague, friend, or occupational health (OH) specialist, or by a different method such as a letter.

**Box 19.3** Case study example of early contact

---

The employee was visited at home during the first week of absence by the line manager and personnel manager. They reassured the employee, and told him to focus on getting better. He found this very supportive, and once he had been put at ease he felt that he could talk to the managers about what the problems at work were.

Thomson, Neathey & Rick, 2003

---

Despite the wide consensus that early and ongoing contact is important to aid recovery, many employers and line managers may be reluctant to initiate this for fear that it is seen as harassment. This is unlikely to happen if contact is made in the correct manner. If conducted in a supportive way, without putting pressure on or adding further stress to the employee, then contact by the line manager or colleagues is most likely to be appreciated by the absent employee rather than lead to hostility. Nevertheless, there may be certain cases when regular contact is not appropriate initially, and input at an early stage from OH advisers can help identify such times and avoid inappropriate contact. In addition, during the early stages of absence it is useful to discuss with the employee the importance of ongoing contact with the aim of identifying how this can best be achieved for both parties (CIPD, 2004). Keeping records of such discussions and of other times the employee is contacted is another important practice for monitoring the appropriate amount of contact. Hogarth and Khan (2003) also suggest that perceptions of harassment would be reduced by improving all employees' awareness of the organisation's approach to maintaining contact during absence. Both line managers and employees should be fully informed about the nature of the organisation's absence and rehabilitation policies, and that good communication and regular reviews form a central part in the organisation's efforts to help the employee recover and return to work.

## Early Occupational Health Assessment

An early health assessment by occupational health specialists, or GPs where this is not possible, appears to be most effective. OH experts have suggested that employees should be referred for health assessment after four weeks (Thomson et al., 2003), yet many organisations aim to refer employees with stress-related illness to OH earlier than that. The outcomes of the health assessment and the manner in which it is conducted are also important. For example, the physician must be sympathetic and supportive, their diagnosis needs to be accurate, and any referral for treatment should be timely and appropriate. However, evidence suggests that inaccurate diagnosis and inappropriate treatment of mental health conditions is relatively common (Boland et al., 1996; Gjerris, 1997). The organisation needs to consider who takes responsibility for communicating with the GP or OH physician, collating the information from the health assessment, ensuring it is sufficiently detailed and then using it in the next stage of the rehabilitation process. Ideally, the organisation should assign a dedicated person (e.g. a case manager) to this role, who will continue to co-ordinate the rehabilitation process to its completion (see below for a full discussion of the management of the rehabilitation process).

**Box 19.4** Case study example of early OH assessment

In this organisation, a referral to OH usually occurs after eight weeks of absence, but if stress is indicated on an absence medical certificate then referral is immediate. In one case, the employee's GP had prescribed anti-depressants and she was signed off sick. The employee was seen by the OH department within 10 days and immediately referred to a counsellor.

Thomson, Neathey & Rick, 2003

## Developing a Rehabilitation Plan

A rehabilitation plan will describe a timescale for returning to work, a schedule of gradual increases of work tasks and hours, any work adjustments or adaptations necessary, and also a series of reviews built into the plan. Most employees returning to work from long-term absence report that a rehabilita-tion plan is useful (Zijlstra *et al.*, 2006). As well the contents of the plan being an important contributor to effective rehabilitation, the *way* that such a plan is developed also has a major role. All stakeholders should be involved in agreeing the plan, and it is essential to have commitment from the line manager and employee. Employee involvement in the planning and execution of their own rehabilitation process is crucial (Ekberg, 1995). Participation and self-management in rehabilitation can allow the employee to regain a sense of control over their situation whilst also encouraging their intrinsic motivation.

In addition, timing is once again important when it comes to developing the rehabilitation plan. Deciding the right time to start discussing a return-to-work requires consideration of the employee and the nature of his or her illness. If initiated too soon, the employee could feel under more pressure which could in turn delay their recovery. But if left too late, the employee may lose motivation and confidence in their ability to return. Breaking the return process into smaller stages may help with getting this part of the process initiated. Start off by finding out if the employee is ready to think about returning to work, then move on to actually planning the return with them (what tasks will be resumed, which will be changed, etc.), and when they are actually ready to return then set the timetable.

**Box 19.5** Case study example of developing a rehabilitation plan

One employee described how he felt anxious every time he thought of work, and he initially felt that he would never be able to return. Developing a rehabilitation plan with the employee at this stage would have been inap-propriate. However, over time and once he was receiving treatment for his symptoms, he gradually realised that he would be able to return. During their regular reviews, the OH nurse would ask the employee if he ever thought about work. She could tell from the change in his reactions to this question when he was ready to start discussing a gradual return to work.

Thomson, Neathey & Rick, 2003

Regular reviews should be built into the rehabilitation plan in order to check progress towards the target of a full return to work, and also as a way of maintaining contact between the employee and employer to prevent isolation and complete withdrawal from the workplace. Again, the organisation needs to consider who is to have responsibility for initiating the rehabilitation plan, discussing and agreeing it with the employee, reviewing its progress, and co-ordinating the other stakeholders involved. The role of a dedicated co-ordinator or case manager is thought to be most effective here as it provides continuity of support as well as detailed knowledge of the case.

## Therapeutic Interventions

As part of their rehabilitation plan, employees who are absent with stress-related illness are commonly referred to a form of therapeutic intervention, such as counselling, cognitive behavioural therapy (CBT), or psychotherapy. There is increasing evidence that demonstrates the effectiveness of these therapies for work-related difficulties (e.g. Reynolds & Briner, 1993; Allison et al., 1989; Shapiro & Firth-Cozens, 1990). Recent reviews suggest that CBT is the most successful intervention for stress-related illness (Van der Klink et al., 2001; Seymour & Grove, 2005). There is also some evidence that other forms of therapies such as interpersonal therapy and counselling may also have positive effects (Department of Health, 2001). However, organisations need to consider the implementation and management of these therapies for their effectiveness to be maximised. For example, the referral of an employee to an appropriate therapeutic intervention must be based on accurate health assessment and diagnosis as well as voluntary participation in the intervention by the employee. Ineffective treatment is expensive both in terms of costs of treatment and the overall time to recovery (Goodman, 2000).

Box 19.6 Case study example of a therapeutic intervention

An employee who had received counselling described how it helped him to understand his feelings, to recognise the causes of those feelings, and to use various strategies to deal with them. His experience of stress had stemmed from feelings of lack of control over change, and through his counselling he had learned to set small targets for himself to give him a sense of achievement and regain a sense of control. He continued to use these strategies after his return to full-time work.

Thomson, Neathey & Rick, 2003

## Flexible Return-to-work Options

Flexible return-to-work options refer to the alternative working schedules used to *gradually* reintroduce an employee into their work, rather than expecting them to return immediately to the full hours and tasks that they worked prior to their stress-related absence. It aims to get them back into the workplace as early as possible, with a long-term view of gradually increasing the employee's tasks and hours until an eventual return to full employment. The earlier there is a return to some duties, the greater the likelihood of a full return. After an absence of six months there is only a 50% likelihood of the employee returning to work (BSRM, 2001).

A phased return to work is most commonly used, which allows a gradual increase in hours and duties over a period of about four to six weeks. Evidence suggests that this approach leads employees to achieve their former functional level more quickly (e.g. Thurgood, 2000). It also important that this process is monitored during the employee's return to work to ensure that the schedule is adhered to and that sufficient support and resources are available for this. The return schedule should be adjusted in length and flexibility as necessary.

**Box 19.7** Case Study example of a gradual return to work

---

In this organisation, the flexible return often started before the employee came back to work. In order to create the structure and routine of work, employees could be encouraged to set targets at home, such as getting up by a certain time, carrying out specific chores, and planning activities. Once the employee is ready to begin a phased return to work, a typical plan might start with two hours per day on two days per week. This would be monitored and reviewed with the individual and gradually increased as they feel able to take on more.

Thomson, Neathey & Rick, 2003

---

## Work Adaptations and Adjustments

Work adaptations are a familiar aspect of rehabilitation plans following occupational illness and injuries. They involve changing aspects of a returning employee's job, such as the tasks or equipment used, in order to avoid aggravating the employee's illness or injury. Such adaptations have been shown to lead to improved health and attendance in rehabilitation following physical impairments and musculoskeletal disorders (Butler et al., 1995; Ekberg et al., 1994; Ekberg et al., 1996; Jonsson et al., 1988; Kenny, 1995). In relation to rehabilitation following work-related stress, it is also important for aspects of work that were implicated in the causes of stress-related illness, or that might foreseeably impede recovery or lead to relapse, to be assessed and removed or reduced. This is a legal requirement under both health and safety legislation and disability discrimination legislation. The types of work adaptations that organisations make for employees following stress-related absence include changes to tasks or duties, changes to the way work is managed, additional training, or redeployment (Thomson *et al.*, 2003). However, despite the best intentions of rehabilitation and sickness management policies, there may be significant difficulties in the provision of workplace adjustments. Cunningham *et al.* (2004) describe a series of organisational case studies concerning the return to work of ill or disabled employees, which showed that the relevant workplace adjustments were not always made, that they were often slow in being made, and that line managers often failed to support the process. Some of the reasons why organisations resist implementing the work adjustments necessary for an early return to work include fear of change, potential cost increase, fear of re-injury and subsequent outcomes, and lack of knowledge on how to implement a return-to-work plan effectively (Di Guida, 1995).

**Box 19.8** Case study example of work adjustments

---

Prior to his stress-related illness, the employee had been become responsible for providing technical support in *two* areas. When he returned to work, his workload was reduced back to *one* area of responsibility, as it had been when he first started the job.

Thomson, Neathey & Rick, 2003

---

Ongoing monitoring and regular reviews with the employee and line manager should continue following the return to work, to ensure that the return schedule and work adjustments are still working and being given the necessary support.

# THE MANAGEMENT OF OCCUPATIONAL REHABILITATION

The different stages of rehabilitation and various activities described above have to be managed effectively in order to be successful. Two main elements contributing to the management of rehabilitation are the written policies or guidelines concerning rehabilitation and the actual management practice.

## Organisational Policies

A written policy or guidelines setting out the organisation's rehabilitation procedures can provide information for employees, line managers, OH practitioners, and HR personnel on what to do, when to do it, and who can help in doing it. These rehabilitation policies should be integrated and consistent with all other OH-related and personnel/HR policies (CIPD, 2004).The potential importance of return to work policies has been illustrated by Cunningham and James (1997) who found that those organisations with written return-to-work policies were more likely to use proactive measures of work adaptations and have more favourable trends in absence levels than those organisations that had no written policies. However, there is often a gap between espoused organisational policy and the reality of management practice when it comes to return to work (Cunningham *et al.*, 2004).

## Rehabilitation Management in Practice

The practice of managing the rehabilitation of an employee with stress-related illness can be lengthy and complex. There are various stakeholders involved in the rehabilitation process (the employee, OH, line managers, HR/personnel, insurance companies, legal services, health and safety specialists, trade union representatives, GPs, etc.) with complicated interactions between them, as well as different, sometimes competing, agendas. It is widely acknowledged that effective return-to-work practices are dependent on integrated and co-ordinated activities of all of these parties (Bruyere & Shrey, 1991; Kenny, 1994). However, in practice, it appears that a lack of co-ordination of activities and increasing lack of support for line managers in handling cases is common (Cunningham *et al.*, 2004). A case management approach to rehabilitation following work-related stress has been suggested as a way of achieving the desired integration of activities (Nowland, 1997; Kendall *et al.*, 2000). This involves appointing a dedicated case manager to co-ordinate the rehabilitation process. This person could be an OH or HR professional or a suitable trained line manager. Their function in maintaining, effective communication between parties, and setting out clear roles and responsibilities, will help to ensure that the employee's needs are met as priority.

The presence of multiple stakeholders can lead to questions concerning who is best placed to oversee the stages of rehabilitation. In larger organisations, which tend to have occupational health departments, an OH specialist will generally lead the rehabilitation process. In many other organisations, primary responsibility falls to the employee's line manager. In others, the HR or personnel department oversees the employee's rehabilitation. Rehabilitation can be a lengthy process, taking months, even years, so it is important to try to maintain continuity in the management of rehabilitation. For example, if an OH representative knows they are leaving their job in a few months, it may be better for the HR representative to take overall responsibility for a rehabilitation case.

Whoever has overall management responsibility for the rehabilitation process, it is clear that the employee's line manager plays a vital role in its success or otherwise. As they have daily contact with employees, and in-depth knowledge of their work, their environment and their colleagues, they are in a natural position to serve as rehabilitation agents (Pransky, 2001). Current trends see the day-to-day HR management procedures increasingly moved to being a line management responsibility (Larsen & Brewster, 2003). Therefore, the line manager usually has responsibility for maintaining contact with the absent employee, helping identify the causes of the employee's work-related stress, designing work adjustments and adaptations and suggesting feasible, phased-return options. The support and involvement of the employee's line managers is a crucial factor in effective rehabilitation following work-related stress (Dollard *et al.*, 1999; Pimental, 2002). Research is now starting to identify which precise managerial behaviours may help to prevent or alleviate work-related stress (Donaldson-Feilder & Pryce, 2006).

Because of the importance of line managers, they need to have a good understanding and awareness of the causes, signs and symptoms of work-related stress. To this end, policy documents, guidance and training may be useful tools to ensure that line managers know how best to manage staff who have been absent due to work-related stress. Without such training or awareness, line managers are unsure how they should communicate with employees with work-related stress, are unaware how they can provide opportunities to return through work adjustments, and are unable to provide appropriate support during their return (Cunningham *et al.*, 2004). Furthermore, such awareness can help line managers identify and intervene in situations where an employee is experiencing work-related stress *before* they become absent. Zijlstra *et al.* (2006) found that people who have been absent for a long period of time tended to contemplate absence prior to becoming absent, and that this period of premeditation can last several months for those with stress-related illnesses. If managers can become aware of any work-related problems during this period then it might be possible for them to avoid stress-related absence.

One of the challenging aspects of managing an employee's rehabilitation is integrating the needs of both the organisation and the employee into the rehabilitation plan. The overall aim of rehabilitation is to help the employee return to work and avoid any unnecessary absence, ill-health retirements or dismissals on grounds of capability (Hogarth & Khan, 2004). Whilst the employer usually wants to return the employee to work as quickly as possible, and to their previous job role, rushing this process and giving the employee too many responsibilities on their return can have the opposite of the desired effect and lead to further absence. The employee's symptoms, and the advice of the GP or OH adviser on the basis of these, will be the major determinants of when and how a return to work is most appropriate. Therefore, a flexible, co-operative and consensual approach is recommended, with employee and employer working together with the best medical advice to meet both sets of needs. Using this approach, it is important for the employer to provide positive expectations of a successful return to work, maintain a co-operative and supportive relationship with the absent employee, communicate the benefits of remaining active and in contact with the organisation, identify realistic objectives, and encourage visits back to work and an early phased return to increase the likelihood of successful rehabilitation (CIPD, 2004; Kendall, Linton & Main, 1997).

## CONCLUSIONS

Although the available literature on rehabilitating employees who have been absent with work-related stress is sparse, we do know enough about the key

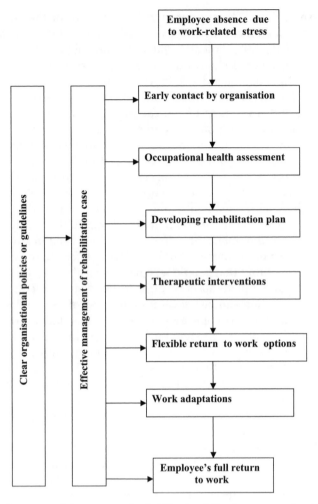

**Figure 19.1**   Summary of the process of rehabilitation following stress-related illness

factors which facilitate and inhibit return to work to enable organisations to try to improve the current rate of successful return to work. There are lots of activities that organisations can do to help rehabilitate employees following absence due to work-related stress. The success of these activities is dependent on which are most relevant for organisations and for each employee, and on how well they are managed. A summary of these factors is illustrated in Figure 1.

Organisations can use the following questions to help develop these activities (adapted from Thomson *et al.*, 2003):

### Early Contact by Organisation

• What is 'early' in terms of contacting the employee?
• Who should make contact?

- What guidance and support is available for the person making contact?
- What happens if the employee is not willing to talk to the organisation?

### Occupational Health Assessment

- What is the organisational practice regarding referrals for health assessment in cases of work-related stress (immediately or when a trigger point is reached?)
- How should line managers be advised on when to refer for a health assessment?
- Who is best placed to conduct the health assessment?
- Who is responsible for communicating with the GP or OH?
- Is the information available from the health assessment sufficiently detailed?
- How will sensitive information about the employee be handled?

### Developing a Rehabilitation Plan

- Who has overall responsibility for initiating rehabilitation plans?
- Who has responsibility for discussing and agreeing the plan with the employee?
- Aside from the line manager and employee, who else could be referred to?
- What preparation can be done in advance (e.g. establishing what different return-to-work options are available)?
- How are reviews managed, when, and by whom?

### Therapeutic Interventions

- Does the organisation offer any form of psychological therapy?
- When are these therapies used?
- How long for?
- Who should be the provider?
- How can access to appropriate types of therapy be assured?
- How will the organisation promote the long-term use of strategies learnt through counselling?

### Flexible Return-to-work Options

- How flexible are current return-to-work plans?
- How is the decision about initiating a return made?
- Who monitors the plan?
- When and how often is progress monitored?
- How are reviews and amendments decided?
- How does the organisation react to plans that are not working?

### Work Adaptations

- How, and at what stage, are work adaptations considered for an employee?
- What range of work adaptations is available?

## REFERENCES

Allison, T., Cooper, C. L. & Reynolds, P. (1989). Stress counselling in the workplace: The Post Office experience. *Psychologist,* **2**:384–388.

Bevan, S. (2003). *Attendance Management.* London: The Work Foundation.

Boland, R. J., Diaz, S., Lamdan, R. M., Ramchandani, D. & McCartney, J. R. (1996). Overdiagnosis of depression in the general hospital. *General Hospital Psychiatry,* **18**:28–35.

Bruyere, S. & Shrey, D. E. (1991). Disability management in industry: A joint labor management process. *Rehabilitation Counselling Bulletin,* **34**:227–242.

BSRM, British Society for Rehabilitation Medicine (2001). *Vocational Rehabilitation: The Way Forward.* BSRM: London: BSRM.

Butler, R., Johnson, W. & Baldwin, M. (1995). Managing work disability: Why first return to work is not a measure of success. *Industrial and Labor Review,* **48**:452–467.

CIPD (2004). *Recovery, Rehabilitation and Retention: Maintaining a Productive Workforce.* London: CIPD.

Cunningham, I., James, P. & Dibben, P. (2004). Bridging the gap between rhetoric and reality: Line managers and the protection of job security for ill workers in the modern workplace. *British Journal of Management,* **15**:273–290.

Di Guida, A. W. (1995). Negotiating a successful return to work program. *Journal of the American Association of Occupational Health Nurses,* **43**:101–106.

Dollard, M. F., Winefield, H. R. & Winefield, A. H. (1999). Predicting work stress compensation claims and return to work in welfare workers. *Journal of Occupational Health Psychology,* **3**:279–287.

Donaldson-Feilder, E. J. & Pryce, J. (2006). How can line managers help to minimise employees' workplace stress? *People Management,* 1 June, p. 48.

Department of Health (2001). *Treatment Choice in Psychological Therapies and Counselling: Evidence Based Clinical Practice Guidelines.* London: Department of Health.

DWP, Department of Work and Pensions (2006). DWP Tabulation Tool. WPLS data. Internet WWW page at http://www.dwp.gov.uk/asd/tabtool.asp (accessed 4 November 2006).

Dwyer, D. J. & Ganster, D. C. (1991). The effects of job demands and control on employee attendance and satisfaction. *Journal of Organizational Behaviour,* **12**:595–608.

Ekberg, K. (1995). Workplace changes in successful rehabilitation. *Journal of Occupational Rehabilitation,* **5**:253–269.

Ekberg, K. & Wildhagen, I. (1996). Long-term sickness absence due to musculo-skeletal disorders: The necessary invention of work conditions. *Scandinavian Journal of Rehabilitative Medicine,* **28**:39–47.

Ekberg, K., Bjorkqvist, B., Malm, P., Bjerre-Kiely, & Axelson, O. (1994). Controlled two year follow-up of rehabilitation for disorders in the neck and shoulders. *Occupational and Environmental Medicine,* **51**:833–838.

Gjerris, A. (1997). Are depressive disorders optimally treated in general practice? *Nordic Journal of Psychiatry,* **51**:49–51.

Goodman, D. (2000). Critical issues in the management of depression. *American Journal of Managed Care,* **6**, S26–S30 Supplement S.

Hardy, G. E., Woods, D. & Wall, T. (2003). The impact of psychological distress on absence from work. *Journal of Applied Psychology,* **88**:306–314.

Hogarth, J. & Khan, S. (2004). *Fit for Work: The Complete Guide to Managing Sickness Absence and Rehabilitation.* London: EEF.

HSC, Health and Safety Commission (2000). *Securing Health Together: A Long-term Occupational Health Strategy for England, Scotland and Wales.* Sudbury: HSE Books.

HSE, Health and safety Executive. Statistics: Stress-related and psychiatric disorders. Internet WWW page at http://www.hse.gov.uk/statistics/causdis/stress.htm (accessed 13 November 2006, revised 31 October 2006).

James, P., Cunningham, I. & Dibben, P. (2002) Absence management: The issues of job retention and return to work. *Human Resource Management Journal,* 12:82–94.

James, P., Dibben, P. & Cunningham, I. (2000). Employers and the management of long-term sickness. In J. Lewis (ed.), *Job Retention in the Context of Long-Term Sickness.* London: DFEE Publications.

Jones, J., Hodgson, J., Clegg, T. & Elliot, R. (1998). *Self-reported Work-related Illness.* Sudbury: HSE Books.

Jonsson, B. G., Persson, J. & Kilbom, A. (1988). Disorders of the cervicobrachial region among female workers in the electronics industry. *International Journal of Industrial Ergonomics,* 3:1–12.

Kendall, E., Murphy, P., O'Neill, V. & Bursnall, S. (2000). Occupational Stress: Factors that Contribute to its Occurrence and Effective Management – A Report to the Workers' Compensation and Rehabilitation Commission. Western Australia: Work-Cover WA.

Kendall, N. A. S., Linton, S. J. & Main, C. J. (1997). *Guide to Assessing Psychosocial Yellow Flags in Acute Low Back Pain: Risk Factors for Long Term Disability and Work Loss.* Wellington, New Zealand: Accident Rehabilitation and Compensation Insurance Corporation of New Zealand and National Health Committee.

Kenny, D. (1994). The determinants of time lost from workplace injuries: The impact of the injury, the injured, the industry, the intervention and the insurer. *International Journal of Rehabilitation Research,* 17:333–342.

Kenny, D. (1995). Barriers to occupational rehabilitation: An exploratory study of long-term injured workers. *Journal of Occupational Health and Safety,* 8:118–139.

Larsen, H. & Brewster, C. (2003). Line management responsibility for HRM: What is happening in Europe. *Employee Relations Journal,* 25:228–244.

Nowland, L. (1997). Applications of a systems approach to the rehabilitation assessment of clients with an occupational injury. *Australian Journal of Rehabilitation Counselling,* 3:9–20.

Pimentel, R. (2001). *Return to Work for People with Stress and Mental Illness: A Case Management Approach.*

Pransky, G., Shaw, W. & McLellan, R. (2001). Employer attitudes, training, and return to work outcomes: A pilot study. *Assistive Technology,* 13:131–138.

Reynolds, S. & Briner, R. B. (1993). Stress management at work: With whom, for whom and to what ends?' (prepared for special edition of *British Journal of Guidance and Counselling*).

Seymour, L. & Grove, B. (2005). *Workplace Interventions for People with Common Mental Health Problems: Evidence Review and Recommendations.* London: British Occupational Health Research Foundation.

Shapiro, D. A. & Firth-Cozens, J. A. (1990). Two-year follow-up of the Sheffield Psychotherapy Project. *British Journal of Psychiatry,* 157:389–391.

Spector, P. E., Dwyer, D. J. & Jex, S. M. (1988). Relation of job stressors to affective, health and performance outcomes: A comparison of multiple data sources. *Journal of Applied Psychology,* 73:11–19.

Thomson, Neathey & Rick (2003). *Best Practice in Rehabilitating Employees following Absence due to Work-Related Stress.* HSE Research Report 138. Sudbury: HSE Books.

Thurgood, J. (2000). Rehabilitation in practice: Providers and employers. In TUC, *Getting Britain Back to Work.* London: TUC.

Van der Klink, J., Blonk, R., Schene, A. & Dijk, F. van (2001). The benefits of interventions for work-related stress. *American Journal of Public Health*, **91**:270–276.

Watson Wyatt (2000). *Integrated Disability Management around the World 2000/2001*. Watson Wyatt Worldwide and Washington Business Group on Health.

Young, A. & Russell, J. (1995). Demographic, psychometric and case progression information as predictors of return-to-work in teachers undergoing occupational rehabilitation. *Journal of Occupational Rehabilitation*, **5**:219–234.

Zijlstra, F. *et al.* (2006). The impact of changing social structures on stress and quality of life: Individual and social perspectives. EU-funded project HPSE-CT-2002-00110.

# CHAPTER 20

# Stress Management for Employees: an Evidence-based Approach

**Stephen Palmer and Kristina Gyllensten**
*City University, London, and Gothenburg, Sweden*

## WORKPLACE STRESS

This chapter will focus on stress management and prevention for employees within the context of an organisational setting.

Research has consistently identified stress as an important factor causing both psychological and physiological ill health (see Cooper, Dewe & O'Driscoll, 2001; Hemingway & Marmot, 1999; Rosengren *et al.*, 2004; Vahtera *et al.*, 2004; Yusuf *et al.*, 2004). Indeed, a number of surveys have found that work-related stress has a negative impact upon organisational productivity as well as individuals' health (Cartwright & Cooper, 2005). For example, it has been found that exposure to high psychological job demands greatly increases the risk of major depressive disorder and generalized anxiety disorder (Melchior *et al.* 2007). The survey *Self-reported Work-related Illness in 2003/2004*, commissioned by the Health and Safety Executive (HSE) (2004) reported that stress, depression and anxiety was the second most prevalent type of work-related health problem in the UK. A survey conducted by an American insurance company, Northwestern National Life, found that 40% of the participating employers reported that their job was 'very or extremely stressful'. Similarly, a survey by Yale University reported that 29% of the participating employees reported that they felt 'quite a bit or extremely stressed at work' (NIOSH, 1999). Stress is not only a problem in the UK and USA; a survey of approximately 15,000 employees across Europe found that 28% reported that stress is a work-related health problem (Paoli, 1997). Furthermore, a survey of 147

---

*Employee Well-being Support: A Workplace Resource.* Edited by A. Kinder, R. Hughes and C.L. Cooper.
© 2008 John Wiley & Sons, Ltd.

million workers in Europe found that 28% complained of stress (Employment and Social Affairs, 1999).

## Definitions of Stress

Stress has been defined in many different ways in the literature. According to the HSE (2001:1) stress is defined as 'the adverse reaction people have to excessive pressures or other types of demand placed on them'. The American National Institute for Occupational Safety and Health (NIOSH) (1999:6) defines work stress as 'the harmful physical and emotional responses that occur when the requirements of the job do not match the capabilities, resources or needs of the worker'. A report by the European Commission (Employment and Social Affairs, 1999:3) states that stress is:

> the emotional, cognitive, behavioural and physiological reaction to aversive and noxious aspects of work, work environments and work organisations. It is a state characterised by high levels of arousal and distress and often by feelings of not coping.

Within cognitive definitions of stress there is more focus on the perceptions and beliefs of the individual. Palmer, Cooper and Thomas (2003:2) propose the following cognitive definition: 'Stress occurs when the perceived pressure exceeds your perceived ability to cope.' The cognitive behavioural approach has been found beneficial to manage and reduce symptoms of stress with clinical and non-clinical populations (e.g. Grbcic and Palmer, 2006a,b; White *et al.*, 1992) and is suitable for helping employees. Cooper *et al.* (2001) suggest that environmental factors that may function as sources of stress are called stressors and the individual's reaction to the stressors is called strain.

## The Transactional Stress Theory

Although there is much research focusing on work-related stress there is still controversy and debate regarding the processes in which hazards affect outcomes such as psychological well-being and physical health (HSE, 2002a). According to Cooper *et al.* (2001) contemporary definitions of stress suggest that stress is a transaction. This particular approach to stress proposes that stress is the result of the transaction between the individual and the environment (Lazarus & Folkman, 1984). Stress occurs when there is an imbalance between the demands made on the individual and the resources of the individual (Cartwright & Cooper, 2005). Within this approach it is recognised that the cause of stress does not exist exclusively in the individual or in the environment. Rather, it arises in the transaction between the two and the cause of stress can only be understood in the context of a process.

Therefore stress refers to the whole process involving stressors, strain and coping (Cooper *et al.*, 2001).

# RISK ASSESSMENTS AND THE MANAGEMENT STANDARDS

## Risk Assessments

Researchers have suggested that organisations should conduct stress audits or risk assessments in order to manage work-related stress (for example, Briner, 1997; Cooper & Cartwright, 1997; Cox, 1993). Likewise, the HSE recommends that organisations should conduct a stress risk assessment, and have developed guides for the risk assessment process (HSE, 2001; 2007). The aim of the risk assessment is to identify the potential hazards at the workplace and to guide consequent action. There are many ways suitable data could be obtained including focus groups, informal talks to staff, questionnaires, performance appraisals, sickness/absence data, productivity data and turnover data. Workplace stress is a multifaceted issue and it is important that employers do not rely on one measure of stress but consider data from several sources in order to capture an overall picture (HSE, 2001). The assessment should be able to capture local concerns and should involve employee participation (Mackay *et al.*, 2004).

Once the organisation has been prepared for the stress management prevention programme, a five-step risk assessment intervention is undertaken. The steps are (HSE, Health and Safety Executive, 2007):

1. Identify the stress factors - understand the management factors
2. Decide who might be harmed and how - gather data
3. Evaluate the risks - explore problems and develop solutions
4. Record your findings - develop and implement action plan(s)
5. Monitor and review action plan(s) and assess effectiveness.

## The Management Standards

The HSE, (2007) has identified a number of broad categories of risk factors that should be assessed when investigating whether stress is a problem within an organisation. These stressors areas were derived from extensive research of working conditions (Mackay *et al.*, 2004). On the basis of the stressor areas the HSE developed guidelines for standards to be achieved. These management standards for stress involve good practice in six key stressor areas: demands, control, support, role, relationships, and change. The exact nature of what is required in order to achieve a state will not be described here (see Cousins *et al.*, 2004). Nevertheless, it is useful to briefly outline the meaning of the six hazards:

- *Demands* – refers to workload, work patterns, and the working environment
- *Control* – refers to employee involvement with how they do their work, for example, control balanced against demands
- *Support* – refers to the encouragement, sponsorship and resources a person is receiving from the organisation and colleagues
- *Relationships* – refers to the promotion of positive practices at work and management of unacceptable behaviour such as harassment or bullying
- *Role* – refers to how much a person understands their role within the workplace and whether the individual has conflicting roles
- *Change* – refers to the way organisational change is managed and communicated.

As the standards are based on research on working conditions and are developed together with stakeholders, it is suggested that this approach of organisational stress could also be useful for continental European and US organisations. The six stressor or hazard areas can be a good basis for a systematic assessment of stress as suggested above or if this is not desirable they could be a basis for the beginning of a discussion of work stress. The 'Model of Work Stress' (adapted Palmer, Cooper & Thomas, 2001) is based on the six management standards or potential hazards and it highlights the relationship between these hazards, symptoms and causes of stress (Figure 20.1).

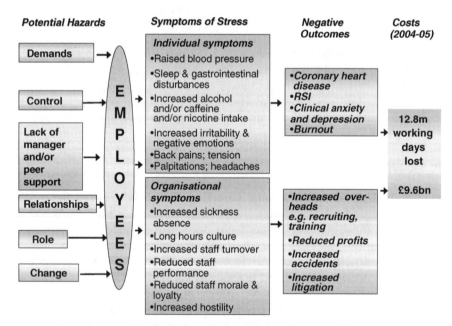

**Figure 20.1**   Model of work stress (*Source*: adapted from Palmer, Cooper and Thomas, 2001)

# STRESS INTERVENTIONS

## A Conceptual Framework for Stress Interventions

Following a risk assessment the organisation may need to design and undertake interventions that tackle the issues that the assessment has highlighted. Stress-preventative and -reducing interventions can take the form of primary, secondary and tertiary level interventions (Cartwright & Cooper, 2005). Primary interventions are concerned with modifying or eliminating sources of stress inherent in the workplace. Examples of primary interventions include job redesign, flexible work schedules and structural changes within the organisation (Cooper & Cartwright, 1997; HSE, 2002b). Many researchers suggest that this approach is likely to be the most effective as it is the most proactive and preventative of the three (Cartwright & Cooper, 2005) although this has been challenged (Reynolds, 1997). Secondary interventions are concerned with extending individuals' resources in dealing with stress (Cartwright & Cooper, 2005). Interventions include stress and pressure management programmes, relaxation techniques, educational activities and health promotion activities. Tertiary interventions are concerned with the treatment and rehabilitation of individuals suffering from serious health problems caused by stress although it can also include interventions to help employees deal with layoffs/redundancies. Outplacement and career coaching, counselling and employee assistance programmes (EAPs) are examples of tertiary interventions. Most activities appear to concentrate on secondary and tertiary level whereas primary interventions are less common (Cooper & Cartwright, 1997; Employment and Social Affairs, 1999). See Table 20.1 for a summary of the conceptual framework.

**Table 20.1**  A conceptual framework for stress management and prevention interventions

| Level of intervention | Examples of activities |
|---|---|
| Primary | Job redesign<br>Flexible work schedules<br>Structural changes<br>Improve resources |
| Secondary | Stress awareness or stress/pressure management<br>Training or coaching programmes<br>Relaxation and biofeedback training<br>Education<br>Health promotion |
| Tertiary | Counselling and psychotherapy<br>Outplacement or career counselling/coaching<br>Medical interventions<br>Rehabilitation |

## Secondary Level Interventions to Manage Work-related Stress: Taking an Evidence-based Approach

An evidence-based approach to organisational stress management and prevention programmes attempts to underpin practice based upon available published research. Although many papers have been published in the field of stress management, still more intervention research is needed in the field of occupational and organisational stress research (see Briner, 1997). This section will focus on research that can underpin secondary level interventions.

Stress or pressure management training is probably the most common secondary level intervention although there are a number of different interventions (Briner, 1997). The content and duration of stress management training programmes differ and they may be multimodal. Training programmes may focus on a combination of relaxation, biofeedback, meditation, life-style, exercise, nutrition, stress awareness education, modifying Type A behaviour, coping skills, time management, assertion training, cognitive restructuring and acquisition of cognitive skills and (Murphy, 1996; Cartwright & Cooper, 2005; Palmer, 2003; Cox, 1993). As part of the explanation of the nature of stress, a cognitive model of stress can be used to reinforce the impact of stress upon the individual and how the employee can use a range of psychological, physiological and behavioural skills, techniques and strategies to help him- or herself at the different stages of the model, 1 to 6 (see Figure 20.2, Palmer & Strickland, 1996). In addition, the organisational model of work stress can be used to explain the relationship between the

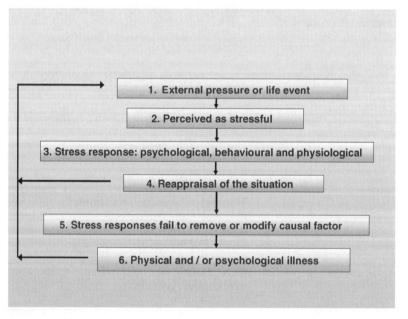

**Figure 20.2**   Cognitive model of stress Source: Palmer and Strickland, 1996

potential hazards, symptoms and outcomes (see Figure 20.1). The two models of stress complement each other.

In a review of the literature Cooper and Cartwright (1997) state that the evidence regarding the effectiveness of workplace stress management training is confusing and imprecise. Modest improvements in symptoms and strain were reported in the literature although levels of job satisfaction, blood pressure, or work stress changed little or not at all. Likewise, Briner (1997) proposed in a review of the literature that the limited evidence available regarding the effectiveness of stress management training indicates no long-term effects. Moreover, Briner (1997) suggests that a general 'feel-good' factor, following the training, may be more responsible for the short-term effects on psychological well-being than the content of the training. It should be noted that in clinical settings, individual or group cognitive behavioural training or therapy to reduce stress has been found to be effective (e.g. White *et al.*, 1992). A meta-analysis by Van der Klink and associates (2001) concluded that 'stress management interventions are effective and cognitive-behavioural interventions are more effective than the other intervention types'.

Stress management programmes can be effective in helping some employees deal with workplace stressors that the organisation is not prepared to change (Cooper, Liukkonen & Cartwright, 1996). Similarly, Cooper and associates (2001) suggest that skills training and increasing awareness of stress may develop employees' resilience and resistance to stressors. However, it is important to highlight that secondary interventions frequently deal with the outcomes rather than the external sources of stress. Training that aims to increase the employee's ability to cope with the working environment might sometimes be insufficient if the stressors are structural (Cooper *et al.*, 2001). The transactional model of stress highlights that it may be the interplay between the environment and the individual that creates stress and therefore an employee could learn techniques and strategies to ameliorate stress.

Many studies investigating stress interventions in organisations have methodological limitations (Cox, 1993). Indeed, it is quite difficult to conduct studies with rigorous designs in work settings. Common problems include lack of control groups, selection effects (most programmes are voluntary), non-specific effects, and diffusion, which is the tendency for the effects of an intervention, provided to one group of employees, to influence employees working closely with this group (Cox, 1993; HSE, 1998).

However, a randomised control trial which used a cognitive behavioural experimental condition, found that stress symptoms were significantly reduced in managers in comparison to the waitlist control group whilst the workplace stressors appeared to remain constant in both groups (see Grbcic and Palmer, 2006a,b). This provides further evidence of the effectiveness of the cognitive behavioural approach in non-clinical settings. The intervention used was a self-help manual based on cognitive behavioural techniques i.e. self-awareness training, recognising stressful thinking, goal-setting, prioritising, time management, motivation, overcoming procrastination, positive self-talk and lifestyle options. No trainers, counsellors or coaches were involved in the implementation and rolling out of this programme. This removed the apparent importance of the client relationship with the trainer or counsellor or coach which is normally believed to be a significant factor involved with client improvement in counselling and psychotherapy arenas (O'Broin & Palmer, in press).

Coaching at work has become a popular intervention to improve performance. However, quantitative research has not found significant decreases in stress (e.g. Gyllensten & Palmer, 2005) although qualitative research studies have found participants reporting reductions in stress (e.g. Wales, 2003; Gyllensten & Palmer, 2006). In contrast, quantitative research studies that have used cognitive behavioural and solution-focused approaches in the field of student and life coaching have found significant reductions in stress, anxiety and depression and improvements in mental health and well-being even when the coaching was not necessarily being used to address these issues (e.g. see Grant, 2001, 2003; Green et al., 2005, 2006). Further research is needed to confirm the efficacy of cognitive behavioural and solution-focused coaching used within the workplace but the Grbcic and Palmer (2006b) study would indicate that it could be effective in reducing and preventing stress. It may also address the needs of psychologically 'unfit' managers (see Jenkins & Palmer, 2004).

The main part of this chapter focuses on organisational aspects of stress. However, it is important to note that the experience of stress is unique and what acts as stressors differs between individuals. An event that one person views as stressful may be viewed as a positive challenge by another. Palmer, Cooper and Thomas (2003) suggest that the way an event is perceived by an individual will determine how they react and cope with the situation. Thus, the individual also carries a personal responsibility in the management of stress. In addition, employees can be held legally responsible for health and safety of themselves and others.

## SUMMARY

This chapter has focused on stress in the workplace. In particular, it discussed risk assessments and outlined a risk assessment process involving five steps. Moreover, the HSE's management standards were presented as these provide guidelines for good practice in six key potential stressor/hazard areas. A conceptual framework for stress interventions was outlined with a particular focus on secondary level interventions to enable the employee to deal with the stress triggered by the six hazards.

Finally it is important to highlight that comprehensive stress prevention and management programmes should be developed and adapted in order to meet the particular requirements of the organisation. Continuing assessment of the risks and requirements will help to ensure that this is the case (HSE, 2003). This is in line with the continuous improvement model recommended by the HSE. Although there is increasing evidence that workplace cognitive behavioural training, counselling and coaching programmes may be effective, organisations should not just rely on secondary and tertiary level interventions alone to manage and prevent stress.

# REFERENCES

Briner, R. B. (1997). Improving stress assessment: Toward an evidence-based approach to organizational stress interventions. *Journal of Psychosomatic Research*, **43**:61–71.

Cartwright, S. & Cooper, C. (2005). Individually targeted interventions. In J. Barling, E. K. Kelloway & M. R. Frone (Eds.), *Handbook of Work Stress* (pp. 607–622). London: Sage.

CompassPoint Nonprofit Services (2003). *Executive Coaching Project: Evaluation of Findings*. Retrieved 28 January 2005, from www.compasspoint.org

Cooper, C. L. & Cartwright, S. (1997). An intervention strategy for workplace stress. *Journal of Psychosomatic Research*, **43**:7–16.

Cooper, C. L., Dewe, P. J. & O'Driscoll, M. P. (2001). Organizational stress: A review and critique of theory, research and applications. USA: Sage.

Cooper, C. L., Liukkonen, P. & Cartwright, S. (1996). *Stress Prevention in the Workplace: Assessing the Costs and Benefits to Organisations*. Dublin: European Foundation for the Improvement of Living and Working Conditions.

Cousins, R., Makay, C. J., Clarke, S. D. *et al.* (2004). Management standards and work-related stress in the UK: Practical development. *Work and Stress*, **18**:113–136.

Cox, T. (1993). *Stress Research and Stress Management: Putting Theory to Work*. London and Sudbury: HSE Books.

Employment and Social Affairs (1999). *Health and Safety at Work: Guidance on Work Related Stress – Spice of Life – or Kiss of Death?* Luxembourg: European Commission.

Grant, A. M. (2001). Coaching for enhanced performance: Comparing cognitive and behavioural approaches to coaching. Paper presented at the 3rd International Spearman Seminar: Extending Intelligence: Enhancing and New Constructs, Sydney.

Grant, A. M. (2003). The impact of life coaching on goal attainment, metacognition and mental health. *Social Behavior and Personality*, **31**:253–264.

Grbcic, S. & Palmer, S. (2006a). A cognitive-behavioural self-help approach to stress management and prevention at work: A randomised controlled trial. Research paper presented at the Association for Rational Emotive Behaviour Therapy and Association for Multimodal Psychology Joint Conference, Greenwich, London, 24 November 2006.

Grbcic, S. & Palmer, S. (2006b). A cognitive-behavioural manualised self-coaching approach to stress management and prevention at work: A randomised controlled trial. Research paper presented at the First International Coaching Psychology Conference, City University, London, 18 December 2006.

Green, L. S., Oades, L. G. & Grant, A. M. (2005). An evaluation of a life-coaching group programme: Initial findings from a waitlist control study. In M. Cavanagh, A. M. Grant & T. Kemp (Eds.), *Evidenced-based Coaching: Theory, Research and Practice from the Behavioural Sciences* (Vol. 1, pp. 127–141). Brisbane: Australian Academic Press.

Green, L. S., Oades, L. G. & Grant, A. M. (2006). Cognitive-behavioural, solution-focused life coaching: Enhancing goal striving, well-being and hope. *Journal of Positive Psychology*, **1**:142–149.

Gyllensten, K. & Palmer, S. (2005). Can coaching reduce workplace stress? A quasi-experimental study. *International Journal of Evidence-Based Coaching and Mentoring*, **3**:75–87.

Gyllensten, K. & Palmer, S. (2006). Experiences of coaching and stress in the workplace: An interpretative phenomenological analysis. *International Coaching Psychology Review*, **1**:86–98.

Hemingway, H. & Marmot, M. (1999). Evidence based cardiology: Psychosocial factors in the aetiology and prognosis of coronary heart disease: systematic review of prospective cohort studies. *British Medical Journal*, **318**:1460–1467.

HSE, Health and Safety Executive (1998). *Organizational Interventions to Reduce Work Stress: Are They Effective? A Review of the Literature.* Sudbury: HSE Books.

HSE, Health and Safety Executive (2001). *Tackling Work-Related Stress: A Manager's Guide to Improving and Maintaining Employee Health and Well-being.* Sudbury: HSE Books.

HSE, Health and Safety Executive (2002a). Understanding the risks of stress: A cognitive approach. Retrieved 10 May 2004, from www.hse.gov.uk

HSE, Health and Safety Executive (2002b). Interventions to control stress at work in hospital staff. Retrieved 1 November 2005, from http:www.hse.gov.uk/stress

HSE, Health and Safety Executive (2003). *Beacons of Excellence in Stress Prevention.* Sudbury: HSE Books.

HSE, Health and Safety Executive (2004). *Self-reported Work-related Illness in 2003/2004: Results from the Labour Force Survey.* Sudbury: HSE Books.

HSE, Health and Safety Executive (2007). *Managing the Causes of work-related stress: A step-by-step approach using the Management Standards.* Sudbury: HSE Books.

Jenkins, D. & Palmer, S. (2004). Job stress in National Health Service managers: A qualitative exploration of the stressor–strain–health relationship. The 'fit' and 'unfit' manager. *International Journal of Health Promotion and Education*, **42**:48–63.

Lazarus, R. S. & Folkman, S. (1984). *Stress, Appraisal, and Coping.* New York: Springer.

Mackay, C. J., Cousins, R., Kelly, P. J., Lee, S. & McCaig, R. H. (2004). Management standards and work-related stress in the UK: Policy background and science. *Work and Stress*, **18**:91–112.

Melchior, M., Caspi, A., Milne, B. *et al.* (2007). Work stress precipitates depression and anxiety in young, working women and men. *Psychological Medicine*, 37:1119–1129.

Murphy, L. R. (1996). Stress management in work settings: A critical review of the health effects. *American Journal of Health Promotion*, **11**:112–135.

NIOHS, National Institute for Occupational Safety and Health (1999). *Stress.* Retrieved 11 April 2003, from http://www.cdc.gov/niosh

O'Broin, A. & Palmer, S. (2007). Re-appraising the coach-client relationship: The unassuming change agents in coaching. In S.Palmer & A. Whybrow (Eds.), *Handbook of Coaching Psychology: A Guide for Practitioners.* Hove: Brunner-Routledge.

Palmer, S. (2003). Whistle-stop tour of the theory and practice of stress management and prevention: Its possible role in postgraduate health promotion. *Health Education Journal*, **62**:133–142.

Palmer, S. and Strickland, L. (1996). *Stress Management: A Quick Guide.* Dunstable: Folens.

Palmer, S., Cooper, C. & Thomas, K. (2001). Model of organisational stress for use within an occupational health education/promotion or wellbeing programme: A short communication. *Health Education Journal*, **60**:378–380.

Palmer, S., Cooper, C. & Thomas, K. (2003). *Creating a Balance: Managing Stress.* London: British Library.

Paoli, P. (1997). *Second European Survey on Working Conditions.* Dublin: European Foundation for the Improvement of Living and Working Conditions.

Reynolds, S. (1997). Psychological well-being at work: Is prevention better than cure? *Journal of Psychosomatic Research*, **43**:93–102.

Rosengren, A., Hawken, S., Ôunpuu, S. *et al.*, on behalf of the INTERHEART Study Investigators (2004). Association of psychosocial risk factors with risk of acute myocardial infarction in 11,119 cases and 13,648 controls from 52 countries (the

INTERHEART study): Case-control study. *Lancet*, **364**:953–962. Retrieved 27 December 2006 from http://download.thelancet.com/pdfs/journals

Vahtera, J., Kivimäki, M., Pentti, J. *et al.* (2004). Organisational downsizing, sickness absence, and mortality: 10-town prospective cohort study. *British Medical Journal*, doi:10.1136/bmj.37972.496262.0D (published 23 February 2004). Retrieved 28 December 2006 from www.bmj.com

Van der Klink, J. J. L., Blonk, R. W. B., Schene A. H. & van Dijk, F. J. H. (2001). The benefits of interventions for work-related stress. *American Journal of Public Health*, **91**:270–276.

Wales, S. (2003). Why coaching? *Journal of Change Management*, **3**:275–282.

White, J., Keenan, M. & Brookes, N. (1992) Stress control: A controlled comparative investigation of large group therapy for generalised anxiety disorder. *Behavioural Psychotherapy*, **20**:97–114.

Yusuf, S., Hawken, S., Ôunpuu, S. *et al.*, on behalf of the INTERHEART Study Investigators. (2004). Effect of potentially modifiable risk factors associated with myocardial infarction in 52 countries (the INTERHEART study): Case-control study. *Lancet*, **364**:937–952. Retrieved 27 December 2006 from http://download.thelancet.com/pdfs/journals

# CHAPTER 21

# Perspectives on Managing Workplace Conflict

**Tony Buon**
*Robert Gordon University and ScotCoach*

## INTRODUCTION

This chapter explores workplace conflict from an experiential perspective and seeks to show how a reframing of our perception of conflict can help us to create a framework for responding to and managing workplace conflict that is empowering and transformative for individuals and organisations.

## PERCEPTIONS OF WORKPLACE CONFLICT

If asked to describe what constitutes workplace conflict, most of us would initially associate the word 'conflict' with experiences in our present or past working life that were negative, stressful or distressing. Those situations would most likely be characterised by a sense of frustration and powerlessness, and this would be true irrespective of whether we are in the role of a supervisor, manager or team member.

We would no doubt also be able to recall positive experiences of open communication where we felt heard and understood in the process of resolving our conflicts at work. These positive experiences of conflict would be characterised by a sense of shared power, trust and mutual respect, even though we may not always have achieved our preferred outcome.

In this sense, our experience of workplace conflict is not unlike our experience of conflict in our personal and family lives, in that whilst we do have significant and rewarding experiences of being able to work through our conflicts with each other; we still tend to have an over-riding perception of conflict as something undesirable, negative and difficult to deal with.

*Employee Well-being Support: A Workplace Resource.* Edited by A. Kinder, R. Hughes and C.L. Cooper.
© 2008 John Wiley & Sons, Ltd.

The following case study explores the question of whether a workplace that is relatively free of conflict can be regarded an indicator of a functional and healthy workplace and employee well-being.

## Case Study 1: The Power of Belief Systems

*Alan feels belittled by the way one of his colleagues. Bill always criticises his ideas and input in front of the rest of the department and his line manager at their monthly meetings. He believes that it will only make things worse to say something about it as this will just make him look 'thin-skinned' and weak, neither of which he feels are 'tolerated' in his organisation. He has therefore decided after a few months of hoping that it will just stop, to 'put up with' it even though he can feel his confidence to speak up at meetings is all but gone.*

### Discussion of Key Issues

Alan's decision to use avoidance as a way of dealing with this situation is underpinned by a number of powerful beliefs.

1. He believes that Bill's actions are belittling.
2. He believes that communicating openly about the situation will make him vulnerable and worsen the situation.
3. He believes that his managers and organisation will not understand or support his concerns.

Ultimately it is Alan's belief that dealing with the situation would result in a negative conflict and his desire to avoid that conflict that governs how he perceives his options for action. Perhaps even more importantly is the way in which this belief system is also a determinant for how the situation will evolve as it continues to impact on his sense of well-being at work and his ability to perform and make a contribution at work.

In answering the question above, it is clear that in this instance an absence or avoidance of conflict between Alan and Bill is not contributing to the organisation's function or the well-being of its employees. If we go wider than Alan's world view we can also see that there are other factors that are contributing to the evolution of this type of situation.

## CAUSES OF WORKPLACE CONFLICT

There are many individual and organisational precursors or contributing factors in the development of workplace conflict. A summary of the most frequently reported precursors or factors has been provided below. In reality a given conflict situation may have been caused by one or a combination of these factors and so the nature of that conflict situation may be straightforward or more complex.

## Individual Factors

- **P**oor interpersonal process skills
- Lack of negotiation and/or assertiveness skills
- Diversity and differences
- Competing needs and goals
- Misperceptions and misunderstandings
- Inappropriate use of personal or group power
- Underdeveloped emotional competencies
- Internal emotional states
- Personal problems outside of work
- Conflicting values and principles
- Lack of job satisfaction
- Low self-esteem
- Alcohol or other drug-related problems
- Relationship problems
- Physical or mental health problems
- Language difficulties
- Lack of autonomy or ability to make choices at work.

## Organisational Factors

- Flexible working practices
- Incomplete briefings and/or delegation
- Lack of team leadership
- Inappropriate management style
- Lack of training
- Office politics
- Ineffective conflict resolution processes or systems
- Lack of effective work performance management systems
- Over-reliance on e-mail communication
- Blame and shame workplace culture
- Overly competitive workplace culture
- Physical environment
- Poor information flow
- Unfair decision-making practices
- Lack of organisational due process
- Scarce resources
- Lack of clarity about roles
- Poor morale

- Promotion to people management roles on grounds of technical knowledge alone
- Lack of recognition
- Job design
- Lack of job security
- Unrealistic expectations
- Workload
- Power distribution.

## THE NATURE OF WORKPLACE CONFLICT

In reality an employee's experience of workplace conflict can be both negative and positive, and the factors that contribute to whether it is one or the other or a mixed experience are complex and multifaceted.

Before exploring these factors in more depth it is helpful to provide a brief overview of the levels of conflict or dissonance that tend to occur. These levels are indicative of the degree of internal feeling or emotion about the conflict that is being experienced by one or more of the parties.

Figure 21.1 (Weeks, 1994) summarises the levels of conflict that can be experienced starting with *discomfort* where nothing overt has occurred but the person affected has a feeling that something is not right. The next level can be described as an *incident* where an outward clash occurs but as yet the person affected does not feel any significant internal emotional response to the situation.

Once a conflict reaches the next level of *misunderstanding* one or more of the parties to a conflict has begun to hold negative images of the other but it is still relatively easy to resolve this level of conflict through information-sharing and open communication. However, when a conflict reaches the level of *tensions*

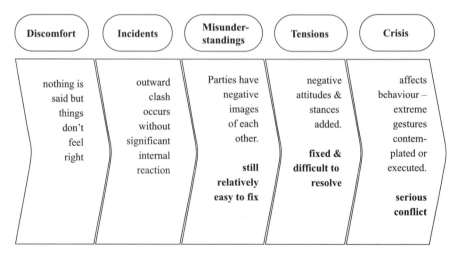

**Figure 21.1**   Level of conflict (*Source*: based on Weeks, 1994)

one or more of the parties has started to form fixed beliefs and positions about the other person and it becomes increasingly more difficult to resolve a conflict at this level.

At the final level of *crisis* the conflict may affect the behaviour of one or more of the parties and extreme gestures are contemplated or executed which further erodes trust and the opportunity to restore a healthy working relationship between the parties.

Clearly not all conflicts start at the lowest level of intensity and move their way up to a crisis as a conflict may stay at one level indefinitely and never escalate or it may de-escalate and improve. Alternatively, because of the nature of what has occurred, it may start at a very intense level and escalate very quickly into a crisis.

In general terms however, we can describe the way in which a conflict occurs over time as a continuum of conflict as can be seen in Figure 21.2

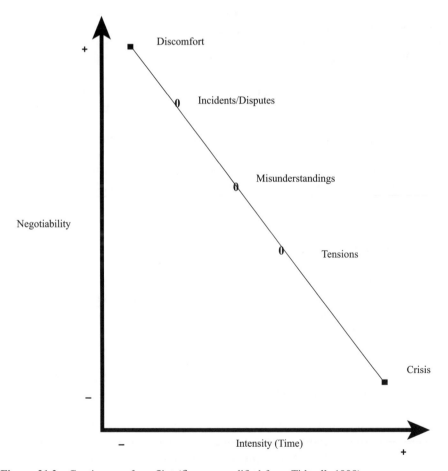

**Figure 21.2**   Continuum of conflict (*Source*: modified from Tidwell, 1998)

98). On the vertical axis is the degree of *negotiability* or oppor-
ɔtiate a resolution, and on the horizontal axis is the amount of
elapsed with the level of *intensity* increasing over time the
ɔnflict has continued to exist. What can be seen is that situations
ʌɪy become more intense over time and so have a lesser degree of
ɹegotiability.

It is also important to appreciate that the point at which a given
individual will feel a particular intensity of internal response to a conflict
will vary. A conflict situation or issue that appears as trivial or incon-
sequential to one person may evoke intense feelings of anger, betrayal,
injustice or hurt in another person. It is also very common for one party to
feel distressed by something that is happening and for the other person to
be unaware of this.

If we return to our case study of Alan and Bill it can be seen that this is what
has occurred whereby Alan has not spoken with Bill about the way his
behaviour is making him feel and it may well be the case that Bill is completely
unaware of the impact his behaviour is having on his colleague.

Whilst such individual responses to a given situation vary greatly, in general
terms it is known that situations involving inherent human needs such as
individual and group identity, recognition or developmental needs tend to
evoke powerful emotions and it is these unmet or unrecognised human needs
which underpin intensely felt conflict situations. At the core of such conflicts a
person may experience a sense of threat to their identity and begin to
experience significant symptoms of distress or stress.

In any conflict situation there will be elements of both unmet human needs
and the material or negotiable issues. As a conflict becomes more intensely felt
over time the challenge in creating a resolution is to assess these elements as
accurately as possible and then adopt the most appropriate approach that
addresses both of these aspects.

## Metamorphosis of Conflict

Building on the above idea of the evolution and escalation of conflict over time
is the concept of a 'continuum of behaviours'. In Figure 21.3 it can be seen that
there are a whole range of behaviours that may contribute to the evolution of
workplace conflict.

In any work group or team such behaviours will always arise and will vary
in intensity and duration depending upon: the nature of the conflict, the make-
up of the individuals, the collective history of the group or team and the skills
and experience of the managers and others intervening in the conflict situation
and the wider culture of the organisation.

Whilst a conflict may start at one end of this continuum involving behaviours
that are seemingly minor or can reasonably be regarded as just a normal part of
day-to-day working life, minor conflict situations have the potential to change
or 'metamorphose' (Fortado, 2001) into far more serious conflicts involving

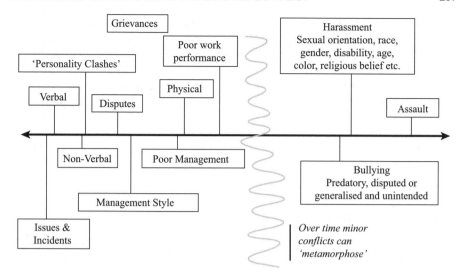

**Figure 21.3**  Continuum of behaviour (*Source*: Authors)

behaviours such as bullying or harassment and acts of retaliation, sabotage, physical assault or violence.

If a conflict is not handled through effective early intervention or is mishandled then the potential for this type of metamorphosis to occur increases especially where the conflict centres on unmet human needs and a high level of emotional intensity for one or more of the individuals is present.

In Figure 21.3 a wavy line is shown indicating that it is extremely difficult if not impossible to pinpoint or predict the exact point at which this change will occur. Case Study 2 further explores this phenomenon.

## Case Study 2: Metamorphosis of Conflict

*Claire was part of a team of specialist assessors working in a large insurance company. She had been in the job for a couple of years and was on her way to becoming a senior assessor. Until then she needed to collaborate still very closely with her colleagues in order to have certain reports signed off before they could be completed. Claire was very committed to her work but had a tendency to divert from company procedures and was not consistent in the way in which she recorded her work. The team of assessors were a very tight-knit group at work and socially but Claire was never really brought into the social group as she was seen to be a bit snobbish and often made remarks about politics or other topical issues around the lunch table that the rest of the group did not agree with and found off-putting.*

*Claire's supervisor, Stefan, was very close to the rest of his team and also had a problem warming to Claire and did not really like her. Claire felt increasingly excluded from the group and when Stefan or the other team members needed to speak with Claire about her work performance they were met by very emotional and defensive responses as Claire perceived this type of monitoring of her work as a form of persecution. Eventually Claire's work performance began to suffer further as she was feeling distressed more often at work.*

*When things became too distressing Claire went off on stress leave and brought a formal grievance of bullying and victimisation against her supervisor and other team members. After a formal investigation the grievance was not upheld and Claire took the matter to the appeal stage where once again it was not upheld. She did not return from sick leave and eventually made a claim of constructive dismissal which resulted in a compromise agreement before it went to a tribunal hearing.*

### Discussion of Key Issues

The factors that contributed to the way in which this relatively minor conflict changed or metamorphosed into a grievance of bullying can be summarised as follows:

1. Claire was not finding it easy to be accepted by the group.
2. Claire had some issues with her work performance that needed to be addressed by her supervisor.
3. Stefan and the team did not like Claire and did not feel comfortable letting her into their social group.
4. When the work performance issues were raised with Claire she over-reacted as she was feeling distressed about her sense of exclusion from the group.
5. Claire's over-reaction reinforced the group's belief that Claire was a 'difficult' person to work with.
6. Stefan was unable to maintain appropriate boundaries between his friend-ship with colleagues and his role as a line manager and so did not provide an equal level of support to Claire.

The dynamic in this team is clearly a very important factor underlying the way in which this conflict escalated into a formal grievance.

For Claire what started as a sense of not fitting in with and being accepted by the group eventually metamorphosed into a much more powerful sense of being victimised and excluded. In this sense her identity within the group was at stake and it is this powerful unmet human need which intensified and escalated the conflict for her. For the group, their belief that Claire was not a good fit within their team created a sense of threat to the established group identity and so they saw it as a failure on Claire's part to do what was needed to 'fit in' as opposed to anything they were saying or doing that prevented her from being a part of the group.

In addition, the way in which the situation was handled by the supervisor did nothing to change this dynamic or to prevent the escalation of the conflict within the team as Stefan was a part of that same group dynamic. In all likelihood, had he been able to maintain appropriate boundaries and provide support to all of his team members and manage Claire's work performance appropriately, this team would have learnt some valuable lessons about a diversity of approaches and personalities within a team and Claire would not have lost her job.

## NEGATIVE IMPACT OF 'DYSFUNCTIONAL' WORKPLACE CONFLICT

Where conflict is not responded to in a timely and effective way or where it has escalated over time or has become entrenched it becomes dysfunctional rather than functional. As a result a whole range of negative effects can be experienced at an individual and/or organisational level. The most frequently reported ways in which conflict can have a negative impact in the workplace are listed below.

### Individual

- Loss of commitment to job, workgroup and/or organisation
- Frustration, stress, anxiety or depression including physiological symptoms
- Strained or dysfunctional working relationships
- Increased use of prescribed medication or alcohol and other drugs
- Feelings of isolation
- Use or experience of harassment and/or bullying behaviour
- Loss of self-esteem
- Increased feelings of anger or a sense of injustice
- Feelings of betrayal
- Increased fixed positions, beliefs and behaviours with others
- Decrease in personal work performance.

### Organisational

- Employee turnover
- Reduced productivity and performance
- Absenteeism and presenteeism
- Increased formal grievances and investigations or claims
- Acts of sabotage or revenge
- Increased injuries and accidents
- Increased occupational health claims
- Loss of creativity and innovation
- Employee relations problems
- Loss of management time
- Customer/client dissatisfaction.

## RESPONSES TO CONFLICT

### A Neutral or Functional Perception of Conflict

If we return to the opening discussion about our predominantly negative perception of conflict it is suggested that in order to respond more effectively to conflict we need to reframe our definition of workplace conflict so that it is neither negative nor positive but neutral. Workplace conflict is instead viewed as an outgrowth of diversity and differences and is a natural process of communication (Weeks, 1994).

In accepting the inherently neutral nature of conflict we can then start to move the focus away from what is often experienced as a disempowering pathology at the core of most conflicts. We can also stop investing energy in avoiding the potential negative consequences of entering into conflict with others or in intervening in a conflict and instead focus on how we *can* respond effectively and positively to those conflicts at both an individual and organisational level.

In this sense it is not the conflict in and of itself that is negative but the negative or positive aspects of certain behaviours and the way in which we respond to those behaviours that determines whether that conflict is a constructive or negative experience.

The key question then is whether or not the conflict being experienced can be seen as functional or dysfunctional. In other words: What can this conflict situation tell me about myself, my working relationships, my team or my organisation?

Whilst the answer to this question is ultimately subjective and value-laden it is suggested that in asking it of ourselves and each other we begin to improve our level of self-awareness and therefore our capacity to respond more effectively.

### Positive Impact of 'Functional' Workplace Conflict

In contrast with the list above it is clear that where conflict is understood as a functional process and where individuals and organisations feel empowered to respond effectively and quickly then there are a whole range of positive outcomes that have been observed. When all of these outcomes are considered they translate into increased organisational and personal performance.

- Increased confidence and ability to problem-solve and negotiate with others
- Increased quality in decision-making outcomes
- Greater commitment to decisions
- Greater creativity and innovation
- Increased team or workgroup cohesiveness
- Greater self- and social awareness and ability to manage emotions and relationships at work
- Increased acceptance and learning about differences and diversity
- Increased use of shared power rather than I-versus-you power

- Increased level of self-responsibility whereby individuals take responsibility to have their job, team, function, organisation, the way they wish it to be
- Individual communication is more open, honest, transparent and vulnerable
- Individuals feel safe enough to try out new behaviours and take risks without fear of reprimand or put down by superiors or colleagues if they make mistakes
- Greater resilience of individuals, workgroups and the organisation as a whole
- Individuals are encouraged to work on the real behaviours/issues that need to change
- Individuals are encouraged to challenge themselves and support each other to both learn and grow
- Individuals feel valued and are inspired to give their very best effort on behalf of the organisation
- A more free and open and therefore less stressful working environment.

## Resources for Responding to Conflict

An individual's or organisation's capacity to respond effectively and positively to conflict is dependent upon the internal personal and organisational resources available to create and support that response.

The following list provides a brief overview of some of the key resources that are utilised in response to workplace conflict.

- Self-awareness
- Resilience
- Social and interpersonal skills
- Natural style of handling conflict
- Communication processes
- Third-party interventions
- Policies and procedures
- Management intervention
- Informal problem-solving processes
- Formal processes and organisational due process
- Training, development and coaching
- First contact or harassment contact schemes
- Employee assistance or welfare support
- Occupational health units or services.

## A FRAMEWORK FOR MANAGING WORKPLACE CONFLICT

Clearly there is no one correct way to respond to all workplace conflict as each conflict situation will present its own unique set of issues and challenges. There must then be an ability to be flexible and adaptable if our responses and interventions are going to be consistently effective. Whilst there are no guaranteed solutions it is not enough however just to get by on our intuition and pragmatism as this will undoubtedly lead us into great difficulties. We therefore need a framework within which we can discover what works.

In arriving at a framework for how to respond to and manage workplace conflict the following elements need to be considered.

## Power Imbalance and Organisational Due Process

Since October 2004 employers in the UK have had to put in place and follow minimum statutory grievance and disciplinary procedures. In our view irrespective of the legal requirement to comply with this legislation, it is essential to have in place a robust and meaningful set of complaint- or grievance-handling procedures as this forms the baseline for the way in which organisational due process is communicated and managed within an organisation.

Underpinning the need for this is the fact that the employment relationship has an inherent power imbalance and so all employees need to know that natural justice is enshrined in an organisation's policies and procedures. For these procedures to be effective they must be: institutionalised, perceived as equitable, easy to use, visible and well known, consistently applied to all and demonstrate in practice that employee rights will be upheld and acted upon (Ewing, 1977).

In addition, it is our recommendation that a separate and simplified complaints procedure be implemented for complaints dealing with allegations of bullying and harassment so that the employees involved are not compelled to discuss distressing aspects of the complaint at numerous stages of a grievance procedure before reaching a satisfactory conclusion.

## Informal Communication and Problem-solving Processes

Most grievance procedures will contain an informal stage, however in our experience a minority of organisations provide any indication as to how this informal stage should work and, whilst more employers are beginning to introduce some form of workplace mediation or informal processes for resolving conflict before it progresses to a formal grievance, this is not yet recognised as a mainstream approach.

In the face of an increasing number of protected categories of employment rights and in an effort to get it right and avoid potential risks, many managers may feel lacking in confidence or skills to even attempt to intervene in workplace conflict and so would rather have the matter dealt with on a formal basis. The danger is that this response to the legislative framework will lead to an over-reliance on a 'compliance approach' in managing workplace conflict.

This has been highlighted by the recent review of the Employment Act 2002 (Dispute Resolution) Regulations that came into force in 2004. Whilst these regulations were intended to encourage parties to resolve disputes as early as possible the headline finding of the recent review of these regulations by Michael Gibbons is that 'rather than facilitating early resolution of disputes the Regulations have exacerbated and accelerated disputes' (Gibbons, 2007). His key recommendations are that these regulations should be repealed and that all employer and employee organisations should be 'challenged to commit to implementing and promoting early dispute resolution, e.g. through greater use of mediation, early neutral evaluation and provisions in contracts of employment' (Gibbons, 2007).

A template for a *Workplace Informal Problem-solving Process* has been provided at Appendix 21.1.

The most effective way of preventing the incidence and escalation of conflict and in empowering employees to find their own solutions is to develop and utilise good informal and problem-solving processes and interpersonal process skills. We need to get past the fear of 'walking on eggshells' with respect to our differences with each other at work and past the fear of making a mistake as managers and accept that being good at responding to conflict means being open to learning about ourselves and our organisations.

It also means being given the opportunity to assess our own strengths, weaknesses and competencies and identify areas for change within our organisations. We have to have the opportunity to make judgement calls and learn what works and so become good self-managers and interveners in conflict.

## CONCLUSION

Even where an organisation has every resource available to it and good procedures for managing conflict and can say that they have ticked every box, if they do not have 'empowering cultural practices' (Gershon, 2006) within their organisation then they will still feel frustrated in their efforts to bring about the desired change in behaviour and find lasting solutions.

This means that an organization must work proactively at creating an environment within which people feel encouraged to take responsibility for creating solutions and feel safe enough to communicate openly about what the real issues are. It must also be a place where individuals are encouraged to learn and grow through conflict and so feel empowered to transform their problems into a way forward.

### Summary of the Framework

1. Assess the situation: what is the nature of the conflict? Are there are any unmet human needs involved? How much negotiability is there?
2. Understand the social, structural and statutory influences and implications.

3. Assess the response to the conflict:
   a. Is the conflict functional?
   b. What are the sources/causes?
   c. Do the conditions exist for resolution: opportunity, capacity, willingness?
   d. What are the best methods for handling the conflict? Informal or formal?
   e. Implement and then review the resolution or agreed approach.
4. Avoid counselling employees about personal problems that are impacting on work performance or contributing to the conflict; refer them on.
5. Make extensive use of informal communication, problem-solving processes and interpersonal process skills.
6. Utilise specific grievance or complaints procedures where appropriate but do not over-rely on a compliance approach.
7. Ensure that natural justice and due process are built into and observed in every process and intervention that is used.
8. Observe appropriate boundaries such as confidentiality and impartiality.
9. Underpin everything with empowering cultural practices.

## APPENDIX 21.1

### Template for Workplace Informal Problem Solving Process

1. Employees to speak with each other in the first instance about the issues and attempt to arrive at a workable solution.
   a. Clearly employees do not always feel that it is possible to speak directly with the person they are experiencing problems with for a whole range of reasons including that they may feel unsafe or may be concerned that in doing so they may make the situation worse.
   b. This step is therefore very much dependent upon the nature of the problem/issue/dispute with the other person, their past history with each other and their respective skills in communication and problem-solving.
   c. However if it is encouraged as a part of the wider culture within the organisation through the support, training and development provided by line managers the more comfortable and competent employees will become in resolving their problems with each other without intervention.
2. Where the employee feels unable to speak alone with the other colleague(/s) involved in the issue then they are to raise the issue with their line manager. Where the issue involves their line manager then the employee may raise the issue with their line manager's manager.
   a. Where employees have come directly to their line manager without attempting to resolve the issue with their colleague it is always important to explore this option with employees in the first instance so that their reasons for not doing so can be identified.

    b. Depending upon the circumstances it may be possible to provide some minimal coaching to the employee and assist them in feeling more confident about making an approach to speak with their colleague(/s).

3. Where the manager/s(s) assess that the issues raised invoke a duty of care or operational issue then they will need to intervene even though the employee may have asked that nothing be done by the manager.

    a. At this point in the process it may become apparent that the issues are such that the line manager needs to take advice from a more senior manager and/or Human Resources (HR) in which case they should advise the employee that this will need to take place.

    b. In doing so the line manager should also indicate that they will only disclose as much information as is absolutely necessary to seek guidance and that they will come back to the employee and let them know what if any action is to be taken by management prior to that action being taken.

4. Where there are no duty of care or operational issues and the manager does not need not to intervene the employee is to agree with the manager about what action they will take to resolve the issue with their co-worker/s(s).

    a. It is essential that, even where the manager is not to intervene in the situation, that the manager has a clear understanding with the employee about what action that employee is going to take.

    b. Managers should not leave a discussion with an employee about a problem they are having with a colleague without agreeing what the next step will be even if this next step is that having discussed the issue with their manager the employee is going to go away and think about what to do next.

    c. The goal here is to achieve clarity about what is to happen next and who is to act next and what that action is to be.

5. Options for action include one or a combination of the following depending upon the issues involved:

- Manager meeting informally together with all of the employees involved to facilitate discussion and resolution
- Manager informally meeting separately with the employees involved
- Employees meeting alone together without their manager to arrive at a resolution
- Issues dealt with by manager at a team meeting
- Employee/s(s) referred for counselling/other support
- Issues to be dealt with at mediation using trained internal or external mediators
- Issues dealt with by manager or colleague/s(s) using formal procedures.

Managers will need to make their own assessment in consultation with the employee/s(s) affected and possibly a more senior manager and HR about which of the above approaches will be most suited to the situation and of course an approach may be adopted whereby a number of these options for action are carried out over time.

6. Irrespective of what action is taken the option of taking no action is not recommended as to take no action will contribute to the development of misperceptions, misunderstandings and escalated conflicts.

   a. This reinforces the point discussed at 4 above and is meant to ensure that employees do not go away believing that by just telling their line manager about a problem that this makes it their manager's problem now even though nothing has been agreed on what will be done next and who is to do it.

   b. This is intended to reduce the opportunity for misperceptions and misunderstandings about what is expected by both the employee and the manager.

7. It may be possible that, after having an informal chat with the line manager, that the employee feels that they have satisfactorily clarified the issues of concern and that the matter has been resolved without the need for them or their manager to take any further action.

8. If this is the case then the employee will need to indicate within an agreed period of time after discussing the issues with their manager that they consider the matter to be resolved. Where there are no duty- of- care or significant operational issues to take into account no further action will need to be taken by the employee/s(s) or manager/s(s).

   a. As indicated above it is possible that an employee will feel that by speaking through the issues with their manager they have been able to clarify their position and now feel less troubled by the problem they are experiencing.

   b. What is to be avoided is a situation developing in using this process whereby employees feel that they can no longer just have a chat with their manager without wanting anything further to happen.

   c. This needs to be balanced against the importance of not allowing a situation to escalate and so in such situations it is still important for the manager to follow up with the employee and ascertain what progress has been made.

   d. If the employee reports that the problem has not been resolved but that they are still considering what to do and do not want the manager to intervene ([and there are no duty- of- care or operational issues)] then the manager will need to use their judgement to identify a way forward as it is important not to allow conflict situations to develop over a protracted period of time without any intervention or resolution.

9. All issues and agreed actions are to be followed up by the manager with the employees concerned to ascertain if progress has occurred.

10. Communication is to be on-going and open-ended until such time that the matter has been resolved.

   a. Managers should always ensure that, irrespective of what is agreed with the employee, that a follow- up discussion is held to gauge progress and ascertain when a resolution has been reached.

    b. A brief diary note of these informal discussions, their outcome and a note of the follow -up dates should also be kept by the manager.

    c. However minutes should not be made or kept of any informal meetings or discussions as this will undermine the importance of the informal nature of these discussions.

    d. It is essential that managers follow through on agreed actions and follow up discussions with employees so that the process gains credibility with staff and so that a consistent approach to problem- solving is developed.

11. It is not acceptable for employees to avoid normal day-to-day communication/interaction with any member of staff as a way of avoiding or preventing conflict.

    a. All employees need to accept that they must from to time work alongside people who they may not like and may wish to avoid and that this can be one of the challenges of working in a diverse workplace.

    b. Where it is apparent that certain employees are unable to maintain normal and civil communication with each other on a day-to-day basis then these situations will require that managers intervene so that those employees can be adequately supported, coached or counselled in the interpersonal skills necessary to maintain a civil working relationship with each other.

12. Employees are also able to seek advice/support from their union reps, welfare support, HR and harassment/first contacts.

    a. Even though employees may disclose problems of a personal and private nature to their managers during the course of an informal conversation about problems they are having at work, managers must not attempt to counsel employees about such matters.

    b. The focus here is for managers to offer appropriate support to the employee and make any necessary referrals.

    c. Where these private problems are adversely affecting their work performance then managers will also need to work with the employee on how they can improve their work performance.

    d. Employees may also present with problems that are work-related which could be more appropriately dealt with under another policy or procedure and in these instances managers can assist by obtaining relevant information or in making an appropriate referral to someone else within the organisation.

## ADDITIONAL GUIDANCE ON CONFIDENTIALITY AND DUTY-OF-CARE ISSUES

As all managers know, British occupational health and safety law requires that anyone who becomes aware of something that is a danger to the physical or psychological safety of a fellow employee has a 'duty of care' to report such information to someone who has the authority to deal with it.

Clearly line managers are not expected to have the answers or know how best to intervene in every situation that arises and so from time to time in order to ensure that best practice is being followed line managers may need to consult with or seek advice from a more senior manager and/or HR.

Where such issues arise and managers believe that the employee or other colleagues may cause harm to themselves, others or the organisation then such a duty of care may exist and the relevant details may need to be disclosed to others as determined by the line manager in consultation with their manager.

In other instances the employee may share information with their line manager that leads the manager to believe that managerial or operational procedures within the given division/department may be significantly compromised or impacted upon. An obligation may therefore exist to disclose the relevant details to others in consultation with their manager.

Even though employees have indicated that they do not wish anything to be disclosed or acted upon, managers will need to explain their duty-of-care obligations and assure the employee that any disclosures will be minimised so that only the information which is pertinent to the immediate situation is reported.

Where such disclosures are to be made to others the line manager will also consult with and inform the employee beforehand.

Where it has been determined by a senior manager and/or HR that further action will be required the employee will be advised of this before hand and informed as to what will be discussed, with whom and when this is to occur.

The underlying approach throughout the handling of such situations is to ensure at all times that situations involving potential bullying or harassment especially are not unnecessarily exacerbated and that conflicts are not escalated further.

## REFERENCES

Ewing, D. W. (1977). *Freedom inside the Organisation: Bringing Civil Liberties to the Workplace*. New York: Dutton.

Fortado, B. (2001). The metamorphosis of workplace conflict. *Human Relations*, **54**:9.

Gershon, D. (2006). The practice of empowerment. In T. Devane & P. Holman, *The Change Handbook*, 2nd edn. San Francisco, CA: Berrett Koehler.

Gibbons, M. (2007). *Better Dispute Resolution: A Review of Employment Dispute Resolution in Great Britain*. Department of Trade and Industry UK.

Tidwell, A. C. (1998). *Conflict Resolved?* London: Pinter.

Weeks, D. (1994.) *The Eight Essential Steps to Conflict Resolution*. New York, NY: Jeremy P. Tarcher/Putman.

# CHAPTER 22

# Whose Agenda Does Workplace Counselling Serve?

**Rick Hughes**
*British Association for Counselling and Psychotherapy*

In reviewing current agendas within workplace counselling a broad view is taken of 'counselling' interventions to include not only 'remedial' work with employees but also organisational and training initiatives which seek to enhance the employee's well-being in employment and consequently their contribution to the organisation. The variables which enhance or diminish the counselling influence are reviewed and particular attention is paid to what reflects best practice in employee support, particularly counselling provision.

## INTRODUCTION

It is often thought that counselling in organisations emerged in the United States in the 1950s in the form of employee counselling programmes to focus on specific workplace issues such as alcohol and addiction issues. However, if we regard 'counselling' as a form of organisational welfare support, then this may well have originated after the Second World War, in the United States, when the labour market changed significantly to include more women and immigrant workers, and specific programmes were developed to address this workforce transition (Kotschessa, 1994). In fact according to Midanik (1991), Employee Assistance Programmes (EAPs) can even be traced back to the Industrial Revolution of the late 19th century. In the United States, Brandes (1976) relates the evolution of staff welfare to the emerging political enthusiasm for 'Welfare Capitalism'. Indeed this development was a logical consequence to Roosevelt's 'New Deal' to bring about improvements in the circumstances and quality of life of ordinary people (Zevin, 1946; Hofstader, 1966) with attention paid to the emotional as well as physical needs of the vulnerable in American society (Trattner, 1974).

*Employee Well-being Support: A Workplace Resource.* Edited by A. Kinder, R. Hughes and C.L. Cooper.
© 2008 John Wiley & Sons, Ltd.

In Britain, as far back as 1800, Robert Owen (considered to be the father of the co-operative movement) can be credited with early comparable models of employee support by way of his revolutionary approach to labour reform at his Lanark cotton mills – his view being that people were the product of their environment. Kinder and Park (2004) trace back the welfare/counselling service of the UK Post Office to 1944 when the company took responsibility for the well-being for employees with advice on personal concerns such as accommodation, debt, childcare and bereavement issues.

Counselling provision has since evolved not only to become issue-specific, addressing such matters as alcohol and drug abuse, debt, careers, personal or relationship concerns but also to become a key player in influencing organisational change, development and personnel strategy (Reddy, 1993). Current developments and trends suggest a more differentiated range of provision rather than a move to integrate and merge employee support services.

The aim of this chapter is to review literature and previous studies of workplace counselling to assess whose agenda workplace counselling serves and to plot opportunities for future development. What follows is not intended to be a comprehensive review of the voluminous literature on counselling in the workplace, rather a succinct summary highlighting contemporary issues and exploring emerging trends. The reader is referred to the selected references for a more detailed insight into the issues discussed within this article.

The study of workplace counselling is influenced by a wide range of factors including contemporary debates, historical, economic and social developments, national and organisational cultures, theoretical orientations and changing work practices. The initial task of this research task was to scan several database resources (including Psychlit, ERIC, BIDS, Caredata, BEI, SSA and the Internet) to determine where research had been carried out previously. This exercise highlighted a complex web of research data from which emerging themes, trends and insights could be gleaned. Initial differentiation of the data was possible by considering the research orientations used. Research orientations are derived from humanistic psychology, organisational psychology, social psychology and behaviour psychology disciplines as well as psychotherapeutic orientations including person-centred theory, transactional analysis and psychodynamic theory. Each orientation tends to direct research from a specific base. This focuses attention on issues relevant to the discipline in question but makes comparisons difficult. For instance, an organisational psychology study will target the wider organisational dimension whereas a social psychology approach might look more at the social dimension within organisations.

Notwithstanding the different research orientations, there are a number of common core topics covering areas such as stress, motivation, employee assistance programmes, welfare, corporate culture, evaluation studies, organisational change, personal and professional effectiveness, productivity and training.

The objective of this review is to seek out the major agendas, sectioned under the following questions;

- What *is* counselling in the workplace – exploring the versatility and range of operations?
- What are the *aims* for counselling in the workplace – in particular what is the purpose, what needs are addressed?
- How does counselling *fit* within the context of management practices?
- How is counselling *implemented* in the workplace, what are the key ethical issues and how does counselling respond to the different variants of stress in organisations?
- How is counselling in the workplace *evaluated*?
- What can be used as a *benchmark* for future provision?

## WHAT IS COUNSELLING IN THE WORKPLACE?

The Association for Counselling at Work (ACW) in Britain states its mission:

> Engagement with employers and other stakeholders to enable every employee in the UK to work in a positive working environment that supports, nurtures and motivates, thereby achieving optimum efficiency and productivity. (ACW, 2007)

The breadth of this remit for counselling in the workplace brings its own concerns within the counselling community. There is some debate as to whether counselling in the workplace is actually 'counselling' in its formal sense. There can be confusion as to how directive the practice can/should be and whether advice and information-giving is part of this resource.

Even where attention is restricted to one-to-one work, the time-limited nature of the contract (Roman & Blum, 1988) has raised concerns, though similar short-term working is established in other fields such as primary care. To the private practitioner the remit for workplace counselling would appear to be hopelessly diffuse and even contradictory, yielding the possibility of numerous 'boundary' problems as the counsellor acts as change agent to the organisation as well as the employee. Schwenk (2006) highlights the multiple potential roles and responsibilities of the workplace counsellor.

This broader view of counselling in the workplace not only involves remedial one-to-one counselling, but also includes consultation on stress points and people management systems as well as counselling skills training for relevant personnel (Charles-Edwards, 1992; Hughes, 1998; Martin, 1997; Megrenahan, 1989; Newby,1983; Orlans, 1986). While some members of the counselling profession would be horrified at the danger which this breadth might hazard upon the sanctity of the therapeutic relationship, others would regard it as an inevitable and meaningful dimension of working within any organisation. Indeed, in student counselling, a full provision has long been regarded as one which attends not only to 'remedial' but also 'preventive' and developmental functions (Ratigan, 1989). In other words, a good student counselling service not only works therapeutically with individual students, but also identifies some general problems within the population and takes preventive or preparatory action as well as noting and acting upon identified stress points within the institution thus contributing to its development.

## WHAT ARE THE *AIMS* FOR COUNSELLING IN THE WORKPLACE?

### Counselling Provision – Legal Insurance, Functional Intervention or Social Responsibility?

A further debate, which receives increasing coverage, concerns the ultimate value, use and purpose of a counselling provision. Several well-publicised litigation cases have encouraged organisations to employ some form of staff support provision to provide an outlet for *stressed* or *traumatised* employees. A distinction needs to be made between what is defined as stress and trauma as both could elicit different types of litigation claims. Stress-related claims may be based on the employee being placed in a work context which repeatedly or continually causes excessive strain and on the employer's failure to take adequate measures to minimise or reduce the stress. Recent Court of Appeal rulings suggest that a counselling provision does not automatically immunise an organisation from its duty-of-care responsibilities (Jenkins, 2007), whereas trauma may relate to one-off incidents, such as the tragedies of 9/11 or the London bombings.

On the one hand it could be argued that an organisation without a counselling provision could be said to be failing in its legal obligation to provide a safe and healthy working environment, yet commissioning a counselling provision might equally be taken to imply an admission that the organisation contributes to stressful situations. Both scenarios could potentially be litigious (Loomis, 1986). Many organisations would argue that they are not the cause of stress but that stress is a consequence of how an individual perceives the work. A more realistic perception may be to recognise that organisations can cause stress and individuals can perpetuate or exacerbate it.

As is explored later under 'Evaluating Counselling', there are many studies that point to dramatic savings and cost benefits to those organisations that make use of a counselling provision. For those who utilise such a service this may represent sound business practice – a functional intervention which adds value to support and development programmes. Indeed, Cooper & Cartwright (1994b) found in their study of counselling programs in the UK Post Office that the significant improvement in the mental health and self-esteem of their participating employees led directly to major functional benefits for the organisation.

Some companies are known to widen counselling provision to accommodate families of employees (Berridge *et al.*, 1997). This may partially be motivated by a sense of social responsibility. Of course it also adds further weight to the increasingly familiar 'golden handcuffs' for employees, that is, the range of work and family benefits that make it difficult for employees to leave. But perhaps one can look at this as wider social responsibility. Employers who look after families of employees know that their staff have family lives and these will impact on their work-lives. It makes sense to invest in and cater for both. The needs of the family can parallel the needs of an organisation.

Friery (2006) highlights a range of reasons why purchasers choose a counselling provision, blending with it the cross-section of motives and aspirations, in order as:

- provide additional support
- duty of care
- support employees through major change
- help alleviate stress
- enhance welfare package
- support for HR
- protect organisation from litigation
- encourage retention/loyalty
- address sickness/absence.

This crosses over the reactive and proactive domains of employee support provision, suggesting that the optimum framework is achieved through some equitable balance.

### The Needs of the Employer and the Needs of the Employee

There may be an inherent conflict or tension between the needs of the organisation, which ultimately is functioning to provide a service or product, and those employees who, whilst supporting the endeavours of the organisation, will have separate financial and social needs (Briar & Vinet, 1985; Hopkins, 1998; Oberer & Lee, 1986).

Staff are rarely asked what they need or want at work, at least beyond the express purpose of getting a job done. Furthermore, Kotschessa (1994) found that many managers were inaccurate in their perceptions of employee needs. Yet, staff involvement facilitated through consultation exercises such as focus groups and quality circles helps to promote greater control over work which leads to increased staff satisfaction, decreased absenteeism and disputes and increased mental health (Isaksson, 1989). Indeed, even minimal involvement of staff can lead to improved effectiveness and productivity. This follows from the famous Hawthorne study by Elton Mayo who found that control groups improved performance simply by virtue of the *attention* given to them through their involvement and participation in the research (Mayo, 1945).

A *staff needs assessment* eliminates ambiguity and provides a focus for accurate staff planning and prioritising (Dooner, 1990). Jee and Reason (1992) claim that staff needs assessments can significantly contribute to job appraisal and redesign, team-working, autonomous worker groups, quality circles and joint planning and involvement in health-at-work schemes.

Whilst differentiating between organisational and individual needs it may be relevant here to highlight a difficulty expressed by some counsellors who work in organisations, namely, 'Who is the client?' (Schonberg & Lee, 1996). A counsellor works for several masters in this context: the provider who employs them, the employee they see and the organisation within which they practice (Googins & Davidson, 1993; Schwenk 2006). The counsellor has responsibilities to each master but conflicts often arise (Brady *et al.*, 1995). There has to be a structured and planned strategy for introducing counselling into the workplace (Hughes & Kinder, 2007) and this will help to highlight and assuage any conflict between organisational and individual needs. Attached to this tension is the concerned raised by Ivancevich *et al.* (1985) in citing workplace counsellors as 'interventionalists' who tend to be more comfortable with changing individuals than changing organisations. This further exacerbates the perception that counselling is a 'band-aid' approach unable or unwilling to deal with the organisation which chooses not to change, relying instead on the help of these 'interventionalists' to change individuals (Cooper & Cartwright, 1994a).

### Personal Development as a Catalyst for Professional Development

Human resource and people development departments are tasked with providing *professional development* initiatives. These support individuals through recruitment and selection, career development appraisals and skills training initiatives. Other broader management training programmes may be directed more towards leadership development via mentoring (Clutterbuck, 1985). However, noticeable by its absence in the literature is a coherent focus on *personal development*. Cognitive and behaviour profiling by way of psychometric instruments are regarded as expressly aligned within the professional development arena with limited overlap into the personal domain.

Goleman (1995, 1998) offers a more contemporary assessment of the importance of personal development through his advocacy of the principles of *emotional intelligence*. His initial book (1996) paid limited attention to this phenomenon in the workplace but became the major focus of his sequel, *Working with Emotional Intelligence* (1998). The gist of his work is to encourage the development of individual competencies, such as self-awareness, self-regulation, motivation and also social competencies including empathy and social skills. Much of this work parallels the 'core conditions' of person-centred therapy (Rogers, 1951) and the curricula of many courses on counselling skills (Hughes, 1998).

In Britain, the Association for Counselling at Work 1997 conference, particularly the input from Foster (1997), pointed to the importance of 'soft skill competencies', that is, listening and the use of empathy and being non-judgemental. While these can be stated in simple terms, the general appraisal is paraphrased by the idiom 'soft skills are in fact the hardest' (Foster, 1997; Natale, 1971; Spencer, 1983).

The focus for soft skills, which is the basis of Goleman's 'emotional intelligence' and is paralleled by the work of Cooper and Sawaf (1997), points to an emerging hypothesis that the development of emotional intelligence could contribute to a reduction in stress and conflict in the workplace. In addition this feeds into many other aspects of life at work, including motivation, personal effectiveness and communication. Simply considering communication, it is estimated that as much as 80% of the time of many managers can be spent in oral communication with others (Hughes, 1991). If managers lack effective communication skills a huge function of their role becomes disabled.

With or without a focus on emotional intelligence, counsellors have many key skills that can be utilised away from the therapeutic session. Coaching and mentoring are management processes which harness talent and provide facilitative nurturing to enhance empowerment of individuals in pursuit of greater personal and professional development (Clutterbuck, 1985; Flaherty, 1999; Thomas, 1995; Turner, 1998). The skill or process approach of the coach or mentor will be familiar to many counsellors and here lies further opportunity for training and staff development. However, some will argue that by diluting their role, counsellors overlook what they do best – counselling (Carroll, 1996:51).

## MANAGEMENT PRACTICES

Contextual variables within an organisation can have a dramatic effect on the aims and outcome of a counselling provision. Indeed, the context may determine whether a provision is accepted or not.

### The Role of Management

Recurring through this chapter (and the book) is the role that managers have, as key players in an organisation, in influencing not only how the business is run but also their weighted contribution to the corporate culture and subsequently how staff are valued and treated (Bunce & West, 1989; Cooper & Melhuish, 1980).

Essentially, the culture, aims and practices of the whole organisation are mediated through the relationship the manager establishes with the worker. The potential tyranny of this role is extended when we note that in most management systems the voice of the worker is communicated to the organisation through the manager. When we consider workplace counselling, two interesting points emerge regarding managers.

1. Managers (especially middle managers) appear to be the least users of counselling services (Gerstein *et al.*, 1993; Kotschessa, 1994; McSulskis, 1996; Shirley, 1985; Warr, 1992).

2. Managers are the most commonly identified cause of stress for others (Buck, 1972; Craft, 1993; Donaldson & Gowler, 1975; Poe & Courter, 1995; Woollcott, 1991). Argyris (1986) believes this is due to the perpetuation of 'skilled incompetence' where managers use practiced routine behaviour (skill) to produce what they do not intend (incompetence). Managers' relationships with others in the organisation determine the extent to which stress may be prevalent (French et al., 1982; Donaldson & Gowler, 1975).

## DELIVERY OF COUNSELLING IN THE WORKPLACE

### Internal versus External Provision

A further consideration is how counselling provision tends to be offered in the workplace. Much debate has existed over the merits of different formats of service provision, from an 'internal' service (Carroll, 1997) and the benefits of this against an 'external' provision (Woollcott, 1991).

In *Guidelines for Counselling in the Workplace* (Hughes & Kinder, 2007), the Association for Counselling at Work profiles a range of counselling service formats in a way to highlight the value of dexterity and variety. Seven different formats illustrate that service provision in Britain has now adapted to morph into an offering that not only meets employer and employee needs, but also responds to resource requirements and industry specific variables. Additional influencing factors will include labour and management relations, size of company, geographical location, corporate structures, employment policies and procedures, private or public sector (including profit or not-for-profit orientation) and perhaps most significantly, the corporate culture (Carroll, 1996).

### Issues around Confidentiality

Aligned to the debate on delivery format is the whole issue of confidentiality (Salt et al., 1992; Wright, 1985). There are ethical considerations with regard to confidentiality which will differ slightly between the formats of service provision. However, all will need to clarify the expectations and requirements of the service to the organisation in terms of feedback protocol. An organisation will want service usage feedback, as a function of outcome measurement and evaluation, the extent of which will determine the degree to which confidentiality may or could be threatened (Carroll, 1996).

It is important that some form of feedback is recorded as this becomes part of the ongoing monitoring mechanism and helps the service adapt and re-align itself as necessary. Accumulated feedback could be taken to change policies and procedures if such systems are found to be working against the interest of employees and the organisation as a whole.

While service providers can and do differ in their information feedback procedure most will report back to the employer, usually their named contact in the human resources or occupational health departments with summary client usage data, including presenting issue, frequency of usage, age range, gender, location and department, together with a view on whether progress was made. It is crucial to have a written-down procedure for information feedback agreed in advance and clearly communicated in to all staff. The Employee Assistance Professionals Association (EAPA, a professional body made up of EAP providers and established to uphold industry standards), advises on the appropriateness of feedback (EAPA, 1990). Other issues to consider are summarised in more counselling focused material (Hughes & Kinder, 2007). Formalised codes of ethics or 'ethical guidelines' also help to clarify boundary issues (Clarkson, 1994; Puder, 1983; Schonberg & Lee, 1996). However there is a constant tension on this matter within the British Association for Counselling and Psychotherapy (BACP) where ethical frameworks must span such radically different contexts as private practice and EAPs, not to mention the internal employee counsellor for whom confidentiality can be an even greater problem, at least in the view of clients.

The internal employee counsellor usually will be based on-site and needs to contend with the possibility of meeting former clients in communal areas. In practice, this visibility can be a useful means to promote the service, present a 'human face' and tame any possible adverse image associated with seeking counselling. However, confidentiality concerns will remain. A counsellor will have to juggle two main 'clients' – the organisation in which they work and the employee they counsel. This can cause tensions and merge boundary issues further (Lee & Rosen, 1984).

## Stress Intervention

This article does not and cannot review stress or the cause of stress per se. However, if counselling at work is about change management (facilitating change for a client), then nowhere is it more applicable than with dealing with stress and stress management.

Murphy (1988) draws attention to a model which is made up of three 'intervention' stages. He suggests that the *primary intervention stage* corresponds to tackling organisational stressors and requires policy or operational change. The *secondary intervention stage* represents the preventive use of stress management techniques, that is dealing with stress by working with the individual before stress becomes debilitating. The *tertiary intervention stage* equates to the counselling provision responding to the effects of stress upon the individual. These three intervention strategies broadly correspond to the 'preventive', 'developmental' and 'remedial' functions mentioned earlier as dimensions of an organisational counselling service (Ratigan, 1989). It could be argued that a full role for the EAP or the internal counsellor is to exert influence at all three intervention points. Indeed, Bunce (1997) argues that a combination of 'technical approaches' can be more effective than any approach used 'singularly'. Similarly, Glasser's (1985) development of control theory points to a more personal approach to stress management by encouraging the adoption of choice and control and by combining humanistic and cognitive behavioural counselling approaches, to seek out change within a situation *and* a change in the perception of the situation.

This three-stage intervention concept, affording consultation among all those concerned, may be regarded as the way forward for counselling if it is to play a full role within organisations. However, it needs to be recognised that this is a very different task from that of the private practice counsellor intent on maintaining very precise 'boundaries'. For counselling to progress towards its full potential within organisations it needs to be supported in its development by this wider view within the profession.

## EVALUATING COUNSELLING

Notwithstanding the legal or social benefits attributed to a counselling provision a further benefit may be the actual savings made by the organisation. Numerous evaluation studies have been carried out (McLeod, 2001) that point to significant savings for organisations that have a counselling service (MacDonald, 1986). These findings are generally based on factors such as reduced absenteeism, increased self-esteem and consequent increased productivity.

Evidence of counselling benefits might not be surprising (Keaton, 1990; Kim, 1988; Sexton & Whiston, 1991; Smith *et al.*, 1980;) but what is perplexing is that with this wealth of evidence many companies still choose not to act (Highley & Cooper, 1994). It is not known with certainty why this is the case. Possible reasons might include a general apathy from the human resource or occupational health departments, or in senior management, an unwillingness to believe in such benefits, a lack of understanding about counselling or a fear that funding a counselling service admits the organisation's culpability in regard to stress creation. In some cases it might be argued that failure to provide staff with appropriate support, when it is known that stress-related absenteeism exists, could amount to professional incompetence and neglect. Organisations have a responsibility to their staff and if they choose to ignore this then they must be accountable to the consequences (Jenkins, 2007; Goss & Mearns, 1997).

## CONCLUSION: BENCHMARK FOR COUNSELLING PROVISION

In assessing the different agendas for counselling service provision, Hughes and Kinder (2007) conclude with a checklist that encompasses all the variables discussed above and represents sound industry practice:

## Setting Up a Service

- Ensure there is a clear and unequivocal commitment and support from senior management
- Establish what the reasons are for setting up the service – purpose and outcomes sought
- Consider specific employee *and* organisational needs, particularly after any recent changes
- Assess how best to involve those connected with employee relations, especially unions
- Plan how best to communicate to staff the reasons for having a provision with senior-level endorsement
- Form a steering committee – those responsible for managing and implementing the service
- Establish boundaries of confidentiality and how this impacts on stakeholders and steering committee
- Assess how the provision will be promoted (PR and marketing strategy) whilst measuring service awareness and service usage.

## Integration between Service Provider and Purchasing Organisation

- Create formal guidelines, parameters and service protocols – what is offered how, when and by whom
- Clarify how these fit with key policies such as drug and alcohol, grievance and disciplinary, bullying and harassment, accident management policies (for trauma) etc.
- Consider the extent and limitations of confidentiality – who needs to be 'in the know' and why, including human resources, occupational health, welfare and/or management and in what circumstances information may be requested from the provider
- Prepare for and plan a crisis prevention plan for trauma, including clear lines of responsibility
- Consider the referrals process – self- or manager-referral with pros and cons of each format.

## Service Provider Issues to Address

- Consider appropriate data collection and record-keeping protocols, including compliance with current data protection legislation
- Choose appropriate delivery mechanisms for counselling – face-to-face, phone, online, intranet etc.
- Clarify an appropriate level of professional indemnity insurance required of counselling and related activities for practitioners
- Devise appropriate quality standards and consider what these seek to ensure

- Draw up a complaints procedure and ensure all who access the service are aware of this
- Clarify the facilities for the counselling sessions that will protect confidentiality – in-house requirements or external standards
- Specify an appointment system – how it works, including contact time (sessions) and frequency
- Establish referral-on procedures – roles and responsibilities of counsellor, service provider and employer
- Establish supervision arrangements that are appropriate to the workplace (see Copeland, 2004, for a wider discussion on this).

## Evaluation

- Ensure appropriate service monitoring and auditing procedures are in place
- Monitor usage figures and feed in to marketing/PR campaign
- Evaluate the service to determine whether it is ethical and meets disability, age, gender, ethnicity and religious needs.

## CONCLUSION

For several hundred years, the quest to maximise employee productivity has focused on providing a conducive and facilitative working environment for people to blossom in and perform optimally at their job tasks and roles. The motives for employee support and counselling provision merge into the vacuum of 'duty of care' and whilst this might appear to be employer-led, the consequence of this not being employee-focused is likely to render any initiative as half-baked. The most productively sound and cost-efficient outcome to counselling provision is only achieved with a clearly thought-out and planned recipe for employee support.

## REFERENCES

ACW, Association for Counselling at Work (2007). *Mission Statement. Strategic Review.* Lutterworth: British Association for Counselling and Psychotherapy.
Argyris, C. (1986). Skilled incompetence. *Harvard Business Review*, Sept/Oct.
Berridge, J., Cooper, C. L. & Highley-Marchington, C. (1997). *Employee Assistance Programmes and Workplace Counselling*. London: John Wiley & Sons, Ltd.
Brady, J. L., Healy, F. C., Norcross, J. C. & Guy, J. D. (1995). Stress in counsellors: An integrative research review. In W. Dryden (Ed.), *The Stresses of Counselling in Action*. London: Sage.
Brandes, S. D. (1976). *American Welfare Capitalism*. Chicago: University of Chicago Press.
Briar, K. & Vinet, M. (1985). Ethical questions concerning EAPs: Who is the client (company or individual)? In S. Klarreich, J. Francek & C. Moore (Eds.), *The Human Resources Management Handbook: Principles and Practice of Employee Assistance Programs* (pp. 342–359). New York: Praeger.

Buck, V. (1972). *Working Under Pressure*. London: Staples Press.

Bunce, D. (1997). What factors are associated with the outcome of individual-focused stress management interventions? *Journal of Occupational and Organisational Psychology*, **70**:1–17.

Bunce, D. & West, M. (1989). Innovation as a response to occupational stress. *Occupational Psychologist*, **8**:22–25.

Carroll, C. (1997). Balancing integration and independence. *Counselling at Work*, 18, Autumn, 5–6.

Carroll, M. (1996). *Workplace Counselling*. London: Sage.

Charles-Edwards, D. (1992). Death, bereavement and work. *Counselling Issues for Managers*. No. 1. London, CEPEC.

Clarkson, P. (1994). Code of ethics for the office. *Counselling*, **5**:282–283.

Clutterbuck, D. (1985). *Everyone Needs a Mentor: How to Foster Talent within Organisations*. London: Institute of Personnel Management.

Cooper, C. & Cartwright, S. (1994a). Healthy mind: healthy organisation: A proactive approach to occupational stress. *Human Relations*, **47**:455–471.

Cooper, C. & Cartwright, S. (1994b). Stress management and counselling, stress management interventions in the workplace: Stress counselling and stress audits. *British Journal of Guidance and Counselling*, **22**:65–73.

Cooper, C. & Melhuish, A. (1980). Occupational stress and managers. *Journal of Occupational Medicine*, **22**:588–592.

Cooper, R. & Sawaf, A. (1997) *Executive EQ*. London: Orion Books.

Craft, M. (1993). Defining the problem: what employees want. In R. Jenkins & D. Warman (Eds.), *Promoting Mental Health Policies in the Workplace* (pp. 50–61). London: HMSO.

Donaldson, J. & Gowler, D. (1975). Prerogatives, participation and managerial stress. In D. Gowler & K. Legge (Eds.), *Managerial Stress*. Epping: Gower Press.

Dooner, B. (1990). Achieving a healthier workplace: organisational action for individual health. *Health Promotion*, 2.

EAPA, Employee Assistance Professionals Association (1990). *Standards for Employee Assistance Programs*. Virginia: Employee Assistance Professionals Association.

Flaherty, J. (1999). *Coaching: Evoking Excellence in Others*. Woburn. MA: Butterworth-Heinemann.

Foster, J. (1997). Communication and counselling: touchstones for effective change. Keynote address. Association for Counselling at Work Conference. Oxford, May.

French, Caplan & Harrison (1982) (non-referenced). In C. L. Cooper, Finding the solution: primary prevention (identifying the causes and preventing mental ill-health in the workplace). In R. Jenkins & D. Warman (Eds.), *Promoting Mental Ill-health Policies in the Workplace* (pp. 62–76). London. HMSO.

Friery, K. (2006). Workplace counselling: Who is the consumer? *Counselling at Work*, Autumn, 24–27.

Gerstein, L., Gaber, T., Cheile, D. & Duffey, K. (1993). Organisational hierarchy, employee status and use of Employee Assistance Programs. *Journal of Employee Counselling*, **30**:74–77.

Glasser, W. (1985). *Control Theory*. New York: Harper & Row.

Goleman, D. (1995). *Emotional Intelligence: Why It Can Matter More Than IQ*. London: Bloomsbury.

Goleman, D. (1998). *Working with Emotional Intelligence*. London: Bloomsbury.

Googins, B. & Davidson, B. N. (1993) The organisation as client: Broadening the concept of Employee Assistance Programs. *Social Work*, **38**:477–484.

Goss, S. & Mearns, D. (1997). Applied pluralism in the evaluation of employee counselling. *British Journal of Guidance and Counselling*, **25**:327–344.

Highley, C. & Cooper, C. (1994). Evaluating EAPs. *Personnel Review*, **23**:46–59.

Hofstader, R. (1966). *Anti-intellectualism in American Life*. New York: Random House.

Hopkins, V. (1998) Is counselling for the organisation or employee? In L. MacWhinnie (Ed.), *An Anthology of Counselling at Work*, 2–4. Rugby. Association for Counselling at Work.

Hughes, J. M. (1991). *Counselling for Managers: An Introductory Guide*. London: Bacie.

Hughes, R. (1998). Emotional intelligence. *Counselling at Work*, 23:3–4.

Hughes, R. & Kinder, A. (2007). *Guidelines for Counselling in the Workplace*. Lutterworth: British Association for Counselling and Psychotherapy.

Isaksson, K. (1989). Unemployment, mental health and the psychological function of work. *Scandinavian Journal of Social Medicine*, 17.

Ivancevich, J. M., Matheson, M. T. & Richards, E. P. (1985) Who's liable for stress at work? *Harvard Business Review*, March–April.

Jee, M. & Reason, E. (1992). *Action on Stress at Work*. London: Health Education Authority.

Jenkins, P. (2007). Duty of care. *Counselling at Work*, Spring, 15–16.

Keaton, B. C. (1990). The effect of voluntarism on treatment attitude in relationship to previous counselling experiences in an Employee Assistance Program. *Employee Assistance Quarterly*, 6:57–66.

Kim, D. S. (1988). Assessing employee assistance programs: evaluating typology and models. *Clinical Supervisor*, 3:169–187.

Kinder, A. & Park, R. (2004). From welfare to workplace counselling. *Counselling at Work*, Spring, 14–17.

Kotschessa, B. (1994). EAP research: The state of the art. *Employee Assistance Quarterly*, 10:63–72.

Lee, S. S. & Rosen, E. A. (1984). Employee counselling services: Ethical dilemmas. *Personnel and Guidance Journal*, January, 276–280.

Loomis, L. (1986) Employee Assistance Programmes: Their impact on arbitration and litigation of termination cases. *Employee Relations Law Journal*, 12:75–88.

Martin, P. (1997). Counselling skills training for managers in the public sector. In M. Carroll & M. Walton (Eds), *Handbook of Counselling in Organisations* (pp. 240–259). London: Sage.

MacDonald, S. (1986). *Evaluating EAPs*. Toronto: Addiction Research Foundation.

Mayo, E. (1945). *The Social Problems of Industrial Civilisation*. Boston: Harvard University Graduate School of Business.

McLeod, J. (2001). *Counselling in the Workplace: The Facts*. Rugby: British Association for Counselling & Psychotherapy: Rugby.

McSulskis, E. (1996). Employee Assistance Programs: Effective, but underused? *HR Magazine, Society for Human Resource Management*, 41:19.

Megranaham, M. (1989). *Counselling*. London: Institute of Personnel Management.

Midanik, L. T. (1991). Employee Assistance Programs: Lessons from history. *Employee Assistance Quarterly*, 6:69–77.

Murphy, L. R. (1988). Workplace interventions for stress reduction and prevention. In C. L. Cooper & R. Payne (Eds.), *Causes, Coping and Consequences of Stress at Work*. Chichester: John Wiley & Sons, Ltd.

Natale, S. (1971). *An Experiment in Empathy*. Slough, Bucks: National Foundation for Educational Research in England and Wales.

Newby, T. (1983). Counselling at work – an overview. *Counselling*, 46:15–18.

Oberer, D. & Lee, S. (1986). The counselling psychologist in business and industry: Ethical concerns. *Journal of Business and Psychology*, 1:148-162.

Orlans, V. (1986). Counselling services in organisations. *Personnel Review*, 15:19–23.

Poe, R. & Courter, C. L. (1995). An executive stress hot-line. *Across the Board*, 32:7.

Puder, M. (1983). Credibility, confidentiality and ethical issues in employee counselling programming. In J. Manuso (Ed.), *Occupational Clinical Psychology* (pp. 36–57). London: Sage.

Ratigan, B. (1989). Counselling in higher education. In W. Dryden, D. Charles-Edwards & R. Wolke (Eds.), *Handbook of Counselling in Britain* (pp. 151–167). London: Routledge.

Reddy, M. (1993). *EAPs and Counselling Provision in UK Organisations: An ICAS Report and Policy Guide.* Milton-Keynes: ICAD.

Rogers, C. (1951). *Client-centred Therapy.* London: Constable.

Roman, P. M. & Blum, T. C. (1988). Formal intervention in employee health: Comparisons of the nature and structure of employee assistance programs and health promotion programs. *Social Science and Medicine,* **32**:503–514.

Salt, H., Callow, S. & Bor, R. (1992). Confidentiality about health problems at work. *Employee Counselling Today,* **4**:10–14.

Schonberg, S. E. & Lee, S. S. (1996). Identifying the real EAP client: Ensuing ethical dilemmas. *Ethics and Behavior,* **6**:203–212.

Schwenk, E. (2006). The workplace counsellor's toolbox. *Counselling at Work,* Winter, 20–24.

Sexton, T. L. & Whiston, S. L. (1991). A review of the empirical basis of counseling: Implications for practice and training. *Counselor Education and Supervision,* **30**:330–354.

Shirley, C. E. (1985). Hitting bottom in high places. In S. Klarreich, J. Francek & C. Moore (Eds.), *The Human Resources Management Handbook: Principles and Practice of Employee Assistance Programs* (pp. 360–369). New York: Praeger.

Smith, M., Glass, G. & Miller, T. (1980). *The Benefits of Psychotherapy.* Baltimore: Johns Hopkins University Press.

Spencer, L. M. (1983). *Soft Skill Competencies.* Edinburgh: The Scottish Council for Research in Education.

Thomas, A. M. (1995). *Coaching for Staff Development.* Leicester: British Psychological Society.

Trattner, W. I. (1974). *From Poor Law to Welfare State: A History of Social Welfare in America.* New York: Free Press.

Turner, M. (1998). Executive Mentoring. In L. MacWhinnie (Ed.), *An Anthology of Counselling at Work.* Rugby: Association for Counselling at Work.

Warr, A. G. (1992). *Counselling at Work.* Plymouth: Bedford Square.

Woollcott, D. (1991). Employee Assistance Programmes: Myths and realities. *Employee Counselling Today,* **3**:14–19.

Wright, D. A. (1985). Policies and procedures: The essentials in an EAP. In S. Klarreich, J. Francek & C. Moore (Eds.), *The Human Resources Management Handbook: Principles and Practice of Employee Assistance Programs* (pp. 13–23). New York: Praeger.

Zevin, B. C. (Ed.) (1946). *Nothing to Fear: The Selected Addresses of Franklin Delano Roosevelt 1932–1945.* Boston: Houghton Mifflin.

# CHAPTER 23

# The Emergence of Coaching as a New Profession and Its Global Influence

**Patrick Williams**
*Institute for Life Coach Training and Coaching the Global Village*

While coaching may be the latest and hottest trend to invade the marketplace, it is not really new. It is a derivative of the best thinking in self-improvement since the turn of the 20th century. Coaching found its place in history – and most recently in the business world – when it exploded into the corporate environment in the 1990s. Today, workplace coaching has dozens of specialty fields (just like medicine) for every kind of business concern, including personal career coaching, transitions and mergers coaching, start-up venture and entrepreneurial coaching, executive leader coaching (team coaching), and what many call life coaching. After all, behind every job is a real person.

Coaching and mentoring have been common in the corporate environment for decades. Executive coaching has long been accepted as a 'perk' for high-level management. In addition, people outside the corporate environment have found it beneficial to have a coach. People today hire a coach to help with career transitions, with the challenges of self-employment (such as isolation and increased distractibility), for entrepreneurial ventures, for parenting, relationships and even retirement. Life coaching has become available privately and through agencies, schools, churches and other community resources.

## The Roots of Coaching

Coaching evolved from three main streams that have flowed together:

1. The helping professions, such as psychotherapy and counseling
2. Business consulting and organisational development

---

*Employee Well-being Support: A Workplace Resource.* Edited by A. Kinder, R. Hughes and C.L. Cooper.
© 2008 John Wiley & Sons, Ltd.

3. Personal development training, such as EST, Landmark Forum, Tony Robbins, Covey seminars, and others who included one-on-one coaching as part of the delivery of these training intensives.

Many psychological theorists and practitioners from the early 1900s onward have influenced the development and evolution of the field of business coaching. The theories of William James, America's father of psychology, impact coaches as they help clients discover their brilliance, which is often masked or buried and can be experienced when they begin to design their life and work consciously and purposefully. Many of the theories of Carl Jung (1933, 1953, 1970, 1976) and Alfred Adler (1956, 1998) are antecedents to modern-day coaching. Adler saw individuals as the creators and artists of their lives and frequently involved his clients in goal-setting, life-planning and inventing their future – all tenets and approaches in today's coaching. In a similar fashion, Jung believed in a 'future orientation' or teleological belief that we can create our futures through visioning and purposeful living. Unfortunately, psychotherapy somewhere along the way adopted or was co-opted by the medical model, which sees clients as 'patients' having 'illnesses' and needing a diagnosis and treatment. Of course, serious mental illnesses clearly do exist, which can benefit from clinical psychology or psychotherapy; however, many people in the past were treated and labeled for what really were challenges in living. These situations or circumstances did not need a diagnosis or assumption of pathology.

### Influences of the Humanistic Psychology and Human Potential Movement

In 1951, during the human potential movement, Carl Rogers wrote his monumental book *Client-centered Therapy*, which shifted the dynamics of counseling and therapy to a relationship in which the client was assumed to have the ability to change and grow. This shift in perspective was a significant precursor to what today is called coaching.

Abraham Maslow (1954, 1993) researched, questioned and observed people who were living with a sense of vitality and purpose and who were constantly seeking to grow psychologically and achieve more of their human potential. He spoke of needs and motivations, as did earlier psychologists, but with the view that people are naturally health-seeking creatures who, if obstacles to personal growth are removed, will naturally pursue self-actualisation, playfulness, curiosity and creativity. Maslow referred to this as 'being motivation' (or abundance motivation), meaning that needs at this level are primarily for the nourishment and development of our 'being' or higher self. This is the foundational belief of coaching today. Maslow's treatise *Toward a Psychology of Being* (1962) set the framework that allowed coaching to fully emerge in the 1990s, as an application of the human potential movement of the 1960s and 1970s.

## Important Distinctions

It is important to recognise the major distinctions between therapy and coaching. Therapy deals more predominantly with a person's past and painful events (trauma) which brought them to seek therapy (healing). Coaching deals more with a person's present and seeks to guide him/her to a more desired future. With coaching, little time is spent in the past, except for brief 'visits', and the focus is on developing the client's future.

This philosophical shift has taken root in a generation that rejects the idea of sickness and seeks instead wellness, wholeness and purposeful living. Hence the emergence of life coaching! Coaching is a special form of consulting, that is a co-creative partnership wherein the main focus is the client's agenda and his/her desire to create a fulfilling life, personally and professionally. The coaching relationship allows the client to explore blocks to greater success and to unlock his/her biggest dreams and desires with the possibility of living life more on purpose and at a higher level of satisfaction and expression.

The shift from seeing clients as 'ill' or having pathology toward viewing them as 'well and whole' and seeking a richer life is paramount to understanding the evolution of life coaching. Life coaches help clients uncover their intentions and to live them, not just dream about them. I often say therapy is about *recovering* and *uncovering*, while coaching is about *discovering*.

Distinctions between coaching and other types of supportive professional relationships can further elucidate the specific role of coaching and the unique relationship dynamic between coach and client (Table 23.1).

## What the Future Holds

My view is that we are on the verge of a fundamental shift in how people seek helpers and why they seek them. People today need connection with a mentor/coach/guide more than ever before due to the rapid pace of change, difficulty in creating sustainable relationships, desire to live one's life purpose, and many other reasons.

I believe that the profession of coaching will be bigger than psychotherapy in a very few years. The general public will know the distinction between therapy and coaching and will be clear on when to seek a therapist and when to seek a coach. Additionally, coaching will permeate society in the coming years and be an available service to everyone, not just executives and high-powered professionals. There will be coaches in churches, schools and community agencies. Coaches will be seen in every organisation and group, from the family unit to the largest conglomerates on the planet.

A variety of specialisations will develop as the profession gains recognition. These will include:

1. relationship coaching, for singles and couples wanting to have the best possible relationship, and

**Table 23.1** The unique relationship dynamic between coach and client

| Therapy | Mentoring | Consulting | Coaching |
|---|---|---|---|
| Deals mostly with a person's past and trauma; seeks healing | Deals mostly with succession training; seeks to help someone do what you do | Deals mostly with problems; seeks to provide information (expertise, strategy, structures, methodologies) to solve them | Deals mostly with a person's present; seeks to guide him/her into a more desirable future |
| Doctor–patient relationship (*therapist has the answers*) | 'Older/wiser'-younger/less experienced relationship (*mentor has the answers*) | Expert–person with problem relationship (*consultant has the answers*) | Co-creative equal partnership (*coach helps client discover his/her own answers*) |
| Assumes emotions are a symptom of something wrong | Is limited to emotional response of the mentoring parameters (succession, etc.) | Does not normally address or deal with emotions (informational only) | Assumes emotions are natural and normalises them |
| The therapist diagnoses, then provides professional expertise and guidelines to give you a path to healing | The mentor allows you to observe his/her behavior, shares expertise, answers questions, and provides guidance and wisdom for the stated purpose of the mentoring | The consultant stands back, evaluates a situation, then tells you the problem and how to fix it | The coach stands with you, and helps you identify the challenges, then works with you to turn challenges into victories and holds you accountable to reach your desired goals |

2. protirement coaching (a term coined by Frederic Hudson, author of *The Adult Years (1999a)*, *The Joy of Old* and, most recently, *The Handbook of Coaching (1999b)*) for those entering the later years who want to redefine the last few decades of their life free of the traditional expectations of aging.

Other specialisations will include parenting and family coaching, health and wellness coaching, and spiritual development coaching.

The entire profession, as I see it, will foster the idea of life coaching as the umbrella under which all coaching rests, whether a client seeks specific coaching for business or job challenges, support during a life transition (such as career, relationship, loss or health), or for pure life-design coaching. A coach may also serve as a referral source for specialty coaching as needed or requested by a client.

Coaching is a profession experiencing dynamic growth and change. It will no doubt continue to interact developmentally with social, economic and political processes; draw on the knowledge base of diverse disciplines; enhance its intellectual and professional maturity; and proceed to establish itself internationally, as well as in mainstream America, as the most powerful and effective tool for success in every area of life. If these actions represent the future of coaching, the profession will change in ways that support viability and growth. Life coaching exists because it is helpful, and it will prosper because it can be transformational.

## The Coaching Advantage in the Workplace

Whether coaching is employed at a personal life level or in the workplace, the value of coaching in helping people reach desired goals cannot be overstated. Bob Nardelli, the former CEO of Home Depot, has said that 'without a coach, people will *never* reach their maximum capabilities'. This may or may not be true, but it is a powerful testimony to the advantage of coaching. Boardrooms across the globe are sitting up and taking notice, especially when the return on the investment of coaching is measurable, and even significant.

We are on the verge of a fundamental shift in how the workplace ensures employee retention, team cohesiveness, sales and production increases, and overall employee effectiveness and satisfaction. Coaching is on its way to becoming bigger and more successful than any other form of organisational investment in the future. Coaching exists for every type and size of business, from the self-employed sole proprietor to huge coaching programs within the top Fortune 500 companies. Boeing International even has a coaching department. Coaching has proven a worthy investment during its short yet remarkable history. In addition, other specialties have arisen, such as relationship coaching, health and wellness coaching, and retirement coaching.

Coaching in the workplace can take a variety of forms. External coaches can be contracted to provide individual leader or team/group coaching within an organisation. Alternately, some organisations either hire or train their own full-time internal coaches. Both have advantages, and which is used depends on the company and the situation. Many workplaces are also realising the value of training their leaders and managers to be coaches themselves so they can employ the successful tenets of coaching in their management and leadership. Leaders are learning to be less 'command and control' and more coach. The results have been remarkable.

> I never cease to be amazed at the power of the coaching process to draw out the skills or talent that was previously hidden within an individual, and which invariably finds a way to solve a problem previously thought unsolvable.
>
> John Russell, Managing Director,
> Harley-Davidson Europe Ltd.

Organisations are also adopting coaching as a way of turning problems into possibilities. This 'coaching culture' causes a paradigm shift in the workplace. Typical businesses will find employees complaining around the water cooler (or wherever else they gather today!). But where the culture of coaching is present, complaints are often replaced by comments such as 'I could sure use some coaching . . .' or 'It sounds like something that coaching might help you get clearer about.' While coaching is a burgeoning profession, it can also assist in creating an empowering culture when adopted in the workplace and fueled by internal sponsorship, training and encouragement.

### Coaching Tools

In the modern-day workplace, coaching is utilising theories and practices that have been around for quite awhile. These tools, an important part of coaching resources, include group dynamics, Johari Window, and 360 Feedback assessments, which allow clients to learn about blind spots – Achilles heels of behavior tendencies that block effectiveness – and hidden strengths that can be used more effectively. Style assessments or inventories (such as FIRO-B, Myers-Briggs, Peoplemap, and DISC) help people learn how they relate to one another most effectively.

Emotional intelligence (EI, Daniel Goleman) is very popular, especially since it has reinforced what everyone always knew but didn't want to admit: relationships within the workplace are important to the overall success of the company or organisation. Businesses improve (and show healthier bottom lines) if the employees are happier and communicate and function as a team that works well together and resolves conflict early.

The Peoplemap (E. Michael Lillibridge, PhD) is a user-friendly and powerful personality assessment that is quickly completed and easy to understand and apply. The client recognises and comprehends his/her general personality type and how it manifests in work, family and social environments. When people are aware of their strengths and their areas of potential challenge or conflict, they can be more sensitive to the ways in which other people view and respond to them.

As individual coaching clients obtain results from these assessment tools and make discoveries about themselves, they work with coaches who help them understand the information, determine what changes they want to make, and plan the strategy to reach desired goals. The coach elicits ways that the person can change behaviors. The coach does not *tell* the client how to change his/her behavior; instead, the coach supports the client in accessing his/her own wisdom to create an individualised strategy for change. Coaching involves motivational interviewing, powerful questions (discovery), intentional listening, collaborative brainstorming empowerment, creating consistency, and accountability.

---

Carol came to me for executive coaching to improve her role as vice president of a department with a major international bank. She was generally very happy with her work but was having difficulty with her team. Specifically, they often saw her as a tyrant and aloof. This was not her intention. Carol wanted her coaching to show her how to be a better manager. What she learned, however, was that a better manager is really a coach rather than a supervisor. A good manager brings out the best in team members, ensuring that the team works efficiently and smoothly. Carol had already completed the Myers-Briggs assessment as well as 360 Feedback with her staff. I introduced her to the Peoplemap (which contains only 14 questions!), and she was amazed at the report generated from her answers. Carol's profile showed her general tendencies to be Leader-Task, the most common combination for managers. I coached her around the strengths and blind spots of her personality type, which correlated perfectly with what was revealed on both the Myers-Briggs and 360 Feedback assessments. Carol learned how to more effectively communicate with the other 'types' on her team and to appreciate each of their unique contributions, as well as anticipate their potential conflicts. During our coaching, Carol also discovered that she needed to delegate more responsibility to her staff, coach her team rather than manage them, and find opportunities to have more fun while maintaining her vision for herself and the team.

Carol has realised that an effective team is like a family, and relationships can sometimes manifest personality conflicts. Her learning around the concepts of emotional intelligence helped her understand that each team member also has emotional needs in the workplace. Carol actually gave the Peoplemap to her entire team and had two conference calls to review the results. Everyone felt acknowledged and empowered to working more effectively as a team, and all appreciate Carol's openness and willingness to change. She became a model for her team members. Carol became a coach herself.

## Total Life Coaching as an Operating System

Although the most visible and lucrative areas for professional coaches are mainly in the areas of executive and leadership coaching for large companies, more and more small business owners and entrepreneurs are also hiring a personal coach. I believe that coaching is the single most powerful, most non-directive and most deceptively simple system ever devised for releasing individual human potential. Coaching is a client centered, whole-person, non-directive professional relationship that elicits wisdom from the client. The International Coach Federation (www.coachfederation.org) defines coaching as 'an ongoing partnership designed to help clients produce fulfilling results in their personal and professional lives. Coaches help people improve their performances and enhance the quality of their lives.' The definition goes on to say that

> Coaches are trained to listen, to observe and to customize their approach to individual client needs. They seek to elicit solutions and strategies from the client; they believe the client is naturally creative and resourceful. The coach's job is to provide support to enhance the skills, resources, and creativity that the client already has.

In *Total Life Coaching* (Williams and Thomas, 2005), it is stated that 'life coaching is more than a collection of techniques and skills. It is more than something you do. Life coaching reflects who you are – it is your authentic being in action.'

I believe that all coaching is life coaching. Total life coaching is the operating system that is always on, like Windows XP or Mac OS. It is always running in the background. In other words, no matter what the reason the client comes for coaching, quality coaching works with the whole person and all of his/her systems and relationships as necessary.

## Coach Training Opportunities

Many of you reading this book may want to research training and educational opportunities for becoming a professional coach. Others of you may want to learn coach-specific skills to add to your current profession or simply for your own personal development.

Since the use of the word *coaching* has become ubiquitous and is often used by those who are not specifically trained in coaching techniques, I believe it is imperative to get proper and respected training or education from a high-quality recognised school. The best source today is the International Coach Federation (www.coachfederation.org) which lists *only* the schools and training organisations that have chosen to become Accredited Coach Training Programs (ACTP). These schools must offer a minimum of 125 hours of coach-specific training and include practicum and testing, both written and oral, to verify their graduates' coaching proficiency according to accepted core competencies. Other schools are listed on the ICF site that offer Accredited Coach-specific Training Hours (ACSTH). These programs are not comprehensive coach training, but their courses are approved by the ICF as offering foundational coaching competency training and, in some cases, niche-specific skills such as executive coach training, relationship coaching, parent coaching and leadership coaching, among others.

In addition to these international and multicultural coach training organisations, there are now dozens of graduate schools offering certificate programs in coaching and, in many cases, a graduate degree of a master's or doctorate in coaching.

## THE EMERGENCE OF ACADEMIC DEGREES IN PERSONAL AND PROFESSIONAL COACHING: WHAT DOES THIS MEAN FOR THE FUTURE OF COACHING?

I predicted in my book *Therapist as Life Coach: Transforming your Practice* (Williams & Davis 2002, 2007) that with the evolution of the coaching profession and the proliferation of coach training organisations, the next logical step would be graduate degrees in coaching. There were just a handful of colleges in the last half of the 20th century and the beginning of the 21st offering such degrees. George Washington University became the first ICF Accredited Coach Training Program after starting as a certificate program within the Organisation Development department. The University of Sydney (Australia), spearheaded by Dr Anthony Grant, offered the first MA in coaching psychology in the late 1990s. Those were soon followed by other colleges offering at least classes in coaching, some leading to certificates in coaching as part of a degree in a related field, such as organisational development, management or leadership.

As of 2005, over two dozen colleges and universities offered either a certificate program in coaching or a full graduate degree in coaching. The valuable addition of academic institutions in the growth of the coaching profession is very welcome. This trend adds courses of study that underpin the actual coaching relationship, such as personality development, developmental psychology, theories of human change, research methodology, organisational development and cross-cultural issues.

This proliferation of academic programs in coaching also parallels the path of the field of clinical psychology. In 1949, the historical event called the Boulder Conference, in Colorado, was held to create the field of clinical psychology and PhD programs that would teach the science-practitioner model of academic studies. This model focused on both practical application of skills and the scientific rigor and knowledge of evidence-based research and research methodologies. A later conference in 1973 in Vail, Colorado (hence called the Vail Conference), offered an alternative for the learner who did not want to be a researcher and instead just wanted to learn the specific applied skills for being a masterful psychologist. This model, which became known as the scholar-professional model, created the momentum for the PsyD or Doctor of Psychology. Today, more students are enrolled in PsyD programs, even though there are more PhD programs by number.

Many of the graduate-level coaching certificates are offered by very recognisable institutions, including as Georgetown University, University of Texas, JFK University, Duke University, New York University, Villanova University, George Mason University, Fielding University – all accredited and long-established institutions of higher learning. Others, such as Walden University and International University of Professional Studies, are places allowing 'alternative education' and creative degree design with an emphasis on self-directed learning with a mentor and distance-learning modalities, coupled with classroom learning by the learners choice and committee approval. Colorado State University has initiated conversations with me to create a PhD program in interdisciplinary studies and health and wellness coaching.

Most of the graduate institutions are focused on executive or corporate coaching applications, but a few (such as IUPS.edu) are focused on a more general education in coaching and human development that can be applied across the client spectrum. And several in the UK are offering degrees or certificates in professional coaching (University of Wolverhampton, Middlesex University, Oxford Brookes University and others).

I interviewed representatives from four institutions with varied coach training programs, The University of Sydney, Fielding University, Georgetown University, and International University of Professional Studies—and asked them all the same questions:

1  Why a graduate degree/certificate in coaching?
2. Are you particularly interested in ICF guidelines for coaching certification?
3. What do you think the future of degrees in coaching is in relation to established coach training schools?
4. What is unique about your program?
5. How will your students impact research in coaching?

There is not space in this chapter to include all of their thoughtful and enlightening responses, but I can say that each of them saw their interest in being on the cutting edge of an evolving profession and assisting in creating or affirming an academic philosophy of coaching and evidence-based research on the skill sets of coaching and the predictable outcomes for coaches and clients—in other words, documenting what really works and why.

All of the four representatives I spoke with stated that graduate education in coaching adds to the credibility of the profession and may also assist in the future of self-regulation, as the various governments look highly on graduate degrees.

Anthony Grant, of the University of Sydney, states, 'This trend will encourage private coaching schools to raise the bar, and I'm sure we all agree that this is good for the students, good for the coaching industry, and good for the schools.'

Dr. Leni Wildflower, of Fielding University, says, 'There is room for, and a need for, both academic programs and coach training organisations. For those who want grounding in a long-term academic rigorous program, the degree programs are the answer. For those who just want the skill training and may use the coach approach as part of their job, or they want to be an entrepreneurial private coach, high-quality coach training may be the answer for them as well.'

Chris Wall, MA, MCC, of Georgetown University's coaching program, states:

> We have found over the past few years that the corporate consumers are more and more educated and savvy about coaching, and, in many cases, are requiring that coaches they hire be ICF certified. I am totally interested in raising the standards of coaching, including incorporating the newest thinking about coaching that is based on developmental theory, including cognitive capacity, and linking ways to align coaching moves with the evidence that is developmentally available. This will only serve to strengthen the power of coaching in the world.

And Dr Irv Katz, Chancellor of the innovative International University for Professional Studies, relates that,

> Research in coaching is essential if the field is to gain the credibility it deserves. Step by step, gains through coaching must be documented. The leadership in the field of coaching recognises this. And if coaches are going to do the research or be a part of the research being done, IUPS stands ready to assist those researchers in earning their doctorates.

So as you can see, the profession of coaching is growing in tandem with the academic theory, rigor, research and application that comes with graduate education. As the profession of coaching continues to spread globally, the impact of institutions of higher learning offering graduate certificates and degrees in coaching will be a trend to watch in the next decade.

Will this mean that in the near future you must have a graduate degree to be a coach? Probably not. But graduate education expands the knowledge base, challenges the status quo and raises the bar for training programs. And similarly, the standards of best practice as taught by the International Coach Federation and other coaching organisations will hopefully be endorsed and absorbed into the curriculums of the colleges. For our profession to be self-regulated and publicly recognised, it must have the partnership of academia and the coaching profession at large. This partnership and growth of our profession through research, applied theory and quality skill acquisition bodes well for all of us interested in seeing the profession of life coaching not just surviving, but thriving.

## REFERENCES

Adler, A. (1998). *Understanding Human Nature*. (C. Brett, Trans.). Center City, MN: Hazelden.

Adler, A. (1956). *The Individual Psychology of Alfred Adler: A Systematic Presentation in Selections from His Writings*. (H. L. Ansbacher & R. R. Ansbacher, Eds.). New York: Basic.

Hudson, F. (1999a). *The Adult Years*. San Francisco: Jossey-Bass.

Hudson, F. (1999b). *The Handbook of Coaching: A Comprehensive Resource Guide for Managers, Executives, Consultants, and HR.* San Francisco: Jossey-Bass.

Jung, C. G. (1933). *Modern Man in Search of a Soul*. London: Trubner.

Jung, C. G. (1953). *The Collected Works of C. G. Jung.* (H. Read, M. Fordham & G. Adler, Eds.). New York: Pantheon.

Jung, C. G. (1970). *Civilization in Transition.* (R. F. C. Hull, Trans.). Princeton, NJ: Princeton University Press.

Jung, C. G. (1976). *The Portable Jung.* (J. Campbell, Ed.; R. F. C. Hull, Trans.). New York: Penguin.

Maslow, A. (1954). *Motivation and Personality*. New York: Harper.

Maslow, A. (1962). *Toward a Psychology of Being*. Princeton, NJ: Van Nostrand.

Maslow, A. (1993). *Farther Reaches of Human Nature*. New York: Arkana.

Rogers, C. (1951). *Client-centered Therapy*. Boston: Houghton Mifflin.

## FURTHER READING

Williams, P. (1980). *Transpersonal Psychology: An Introductory Guidebook*. Greeley, CO: Lutey.

Williams, P. (1997). Telephone coaching for cash draws new client market. *Practice Strategies*, **2**:11.

Williams, P. (1999). The therapist as personal coach: Reclaiming your soul! *Independent Practitioner*, **19**:204–207.

Williams, P. (2000a). Practice building: The coaching phenomenon marches on. *Psychotherapy Finances*, **26**:1–2.

Williams, P. (2000b). Personal coaching's evolution from therapy. *Consulting Today*, 4.

Williams, P. & Davis, D. (2002). Therapist as life Coach: Tansforming your practice New York, W.W. Norton.

Williams, P. & Davis, D. (2007). *Therapist as Life Coach: An Introduction for Counselors and Other Helping Professionals*, revised and expanded edn. New York, W. W. Norton.

Williams, P. & Menendez, D. (2007). *Becoming a Professional Life Coach: Lessons from the Institute for Life Coach Training*. New York, W. W. Norton.

Williams, P. & Thomas, L. (2005). *Total Life Coaching: 50+ Life Lessons, Skills, and Techniques to Enhance Your Practice and Your Life*. New York, W. W. Norton.

# CHAPTER 24

# Mentoring and Employee Well-being

**David Clutterbuck**
*Clutterbuck Associates, and European Mentoring and Coaching Council*

*Formally structured or supported mentoring is strongly associated in both research and practitioner literature with employee well-being. This chapter explores several aspects of this association, with particular reference to the concepts of the psychological contract and work–life balance. It also examines the growing body of information about good practice in managing mentoring programmes.*

Recent industry surveys suggest that 72% of companies in the UK use mentoring in some manner (CIPD, 2006) and that they do so because they perceive that it delivers significant benefits to both the organisation and its employees. The literature on mentoring is awash with references to benefits for mentees and, to a lesser extent, mentors. Mentoring is reported both anecdotally and empirically to be associated with job satisfaction (Kram, 2004), job commitment (Joiner *et al.*, 2004) self-confidence/self-esteem and a variety of career outcomes (Turban & Dougherty, 1994).

From an organisational perspective, one of the most commonly reported benefits of supported mentoring programmes is their impact on employee retention. Allied Irish Banks, for example, reported a two-thirds reduction in first-year turnover amongst graduate recruits as a result of introducing a mentoring programme; GlaxoSmithKline found a 1,300% difference in turnover comparing its mentored and unmentored population; and various international surveys indicate that, overall, employees engaged in mentoring are only half as likely to have an intention to quit within the next 12 months compared with unmentored colleagues Anon (1999-2005).

Exactly *how* mentoring affects retention has not been investigated with any rigour. However, some of the likely explanations include the following:

*Employee Well-being Support: A Workplace Resource.* Edited by A. Kinder, R. Hughes and C.L. Cooper.
© 2008 John Wiley & Sons, Ltd.

- People like to feel they are valued by the organisation. Having someone who is interested in you as an individual and cares about your progress helps acclimatisation and organisational commitment (Kleinmann *et al.*, 2001).
- People often leave organisations because they cannot see a clear path of advancement. Where the mentor is at a more senior position, he or she can see a wider range of opportunities and is likely to be aware of how to work through potential career blockages.
- Having someone to discuss your work and job roles with outside immediate team/line relieves stress and increases job satisfaction (Kram, 1983, 1985). For example, the practicalities of managing relationships with boss and colleagues are amongst the most common themes for discussion within the learning dyad.
- People need from time to time to sit outside the confines of day-to-day detail, and consider the big picture, not just in pure work terms, but also how their work and non-work lives interface and how to manage each symbiotically rather than in conflict.
- Mature mentoring relationships, in particular, provide a safe environment for such discussions.

Similar effects have been recorded for mentor retention as well and similar explanations may apply:

- Mentors often feel valued by being able to help others (the so-called generativity effect described by Levinson [1978] and others).
- The intellectual challenge of working with someone, who does not report to you and asks stimulating questions, is often described by mentors as a significant attraction to the mentoring role and a source of their own learning.
- The opportunity to stop and reflect – taking a different pace for an hour or so has positive impacts upon mentor creativity and insight with regard to their own issues.
- Personal development is identified in current research as one of four key outcomes for mentors (Clutterbuck, 2005).

This chapter focuses on three issues relating to making effective use of mentoring in the workplace. One relates to the manner in which mentoring supports the psychological contract; one to how it supports work–life balance; and the third to the practicalities of designing, implementing and sustaining a mentoring programme. First, however, it is appropriate to determine what we mean by mentoring, as the term is often confused with other helping activities, such as coaching or counselling.

## THE ORIGINS OF MODERN MENTORING

As Figure 24.1 illustrates, there are two dominant models of mentoring and two of coaching. Sponsorship mentoring derives from a French depiction of the role

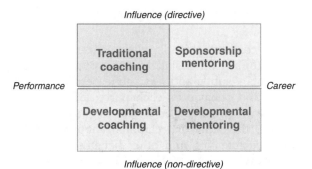

**Figure 24.1** Models of coaching and mentoring (*Source*: Reproduced by permission of Clutterbuck Associates © 2004)

a few hundred years ago. It came via the United States, where structured or supported mentoring programmes – aimed at reproducing in a relatively controlled manner the informal relationships that sometimes developed between older and younger employees – were first initiated in the late 1970s and early 1980s. The 'contracts' in these relationships were built upon an expectation that the mentor would use his (this was initially seen as an exclusively male phenomenon) power, influence and greater experience to guide and facilitate the younger person in their career, by opening doors and equipping them with contacts and political insight.

Introduced to Europe a few years later, this model generally failed dismally. Employers in Europe were encouraging self-development and self-management of careers; there was also a strong distrust of 'old boy networks'. Instead, a model of mentoring emerged based on a different interpretation of the original Greek story, one more firmly grounded in the Socratic tradition of stimulating insight through well-crafted questions. In this model, the mentor and the mentee learn from each other, through the quality of their dialogue; the power of the mentor is largely irrelevant and the mentor's experience is employed not to tell the mentee what to do, but to guide the creation of understanding and, ultimately, wisdom.

A similar evolution has taken place in coaching, where the traditional 'tell' style, which emphasises feedback *to* the coachee, is increasingly being replaced by a more developmental style very similar to developmental mentoring in terms of the processes used, and which emphasises intrinsic feedback (i.e. by the coachee through self-observation). The primary differences between developmental mentoring and developmental coaching are that the latter is almost always targeted at performance improvement, while the former takes a wider, more holistic perspective, often focused on career; and that mentoring includes a number of other roles, such as helping the learner develop their networks and negotiate organisational politics. A variety of spurious distinctions have been proposed from time to time – for example, that either coach or mentor has to be a subject expert. In practice, there are approaches to both roles that assume subject expertise and approaches that do not.

## MENTORING AND THE PSYCHOLOGICAL CONTRACT

The psychological contract, at its simplest, concerns the exchange of value between employees (or any other stakeholder group) and the organisation. It has many components – subtle and less subtle perceptions and expectations about the attitudes and behaviours each party should exhibit towards the other. In theory, at least, alignment on the terms of the psychological contract (both parties having the same expectations) should lead to increased job satisfaction, employee retention and other benefits on both sides (Guest & Conway, 2002; Conway & Briner, 2005).

One simple way of describing the psychological contract as a value exchange identifies three core elements of value:

- Worth (The creation of value-added. For the organisation, this is represented by shareholder value-added. For the individual employee, it may involve a mixture of reward/compensation, training and opportunities to gain experience, which improve their value in the job market. For the customer, worth is related primarily to value-for-money.)
- Respect (As in 'I value your contribution/custom' or in 'I feel proud to say I work for this company')
- Belief (What people believe to be important – the values that underlie decisions and behaviours. For example, at Body Shop, employees, managers and customers share common beliefs about the importance of environmental considerations. Individual shareholders may also share those beliefs, but institutional investors may not.)

Within each of these exchanges there is an interplay of expectation and perception of behaviour, on both sides. In some cases, each side can have a very different view of the other's intentions, which affects negatively the nature of the psychological contract. For example, in a large food manufacturer, senior managers complained in interviews that shopfloor employees showed no initiative and avoided responsibility; while the employees complained that the managers only gave lip service to empowerment and wouldn't listen to their suggestions or allow them to take actions to improve production. When there is a disparity of views – either about expectations, or actual behaviours, or both – this tends to translate into a sense of unfairness, a loss of trust and reduced organisational commitment.

Mentoring contributes to the worth element of the equation by helping the employee establish and pursue more coherent career plans, by helping them build wider and more effective networks and so on. The result is that the net value of the mentee on the job market (and to the organisation) is enhanced. Increased retention helps the organisation improve profits, not least because longer service is associated with increased service quality performance (Hesket *et al.*, 1997). Without a mentoring relationship or an alternative mechanism to make employees feel that they are both contributing and becoming a more valuable asset, long service may sometimes in contrast be associated with *reduced* customer service. As some airlines have discovered, vocal and cynical long-termers tend to be less obliging, less enthusiastic and less likely to take advantage of the learning opportunities that do come their way. Mentors often also gain a new lease of enthusiasm from a successful and challenging mentoring relationship.

Mentoring contributes to the respect element of the psychological contract by providing a forum where the mentee can be listened to and feel they are treated as an individual. Over time, the mentoring meetings help the mentee present ideas, grow in self-esteem and build confidence in their ability to manage both their current role and roles they aspire to. A Norwegian mentoring programme to develop women leaders found that over 80% reported greater role confidence – as did half of the mainly male mentors! In a safe environment of constructive challenge, mentees can work out how to build their reputation within the organisation, how to manage their boss (a critical skill for an employee with ambition) and how to understand and capitalise upon their emotional and intellectual drivers.

Mentoring assists the beliefs element of the psychological contract by exploring the culture in a positive but critical manner. Each dyad is a small forum to influence the organisation. For example, a large financial services firm had made a variety of pronouncements from the top about the importance of work–life balance; yet in the workplace, away from the ivory tower, employees were still expected to put work priorities over domestic needs and to give 12-hour days, or longer. When mentors had an opportunity to compare notes on what they found difficult – as part of a confidential process of continuing skills development – mentee frustration with the dichotomy between what was preached and what was practised became apparent. Recognising the depth of feeling about this, the organisation was forced to review its policies and practices.

At the same time, compatibility of beliefs and values is an important element in the quality of the mentoring relationship itself (Hale, 2000).

One of the events that frequently causes the psychological contract to break down is merger and acquisition. Mentoring helps repair the damage. In one case, a service company acquired a rival in a protracted settlement. Although the legal merger took nine months, the two groups of employees quickly knit together. The reason? Every employee in the newly acquired and smaller company was paired with a mentor in the larger company, with a specific brief of co-learning. The mentoring relationships resulted in a rapid build-up of trust and hence ease of working together.

Although many organisations do measure the psychological contract – usually through tangential means, such as employee satisfaction surveys, which provide only part of the picture – actively managing it is another matter entirely. Building trust at the level of organisation to individual is difficult in the extreme. But building trust at the individual level is a relatively easy way to establish the foundations of organisational trust. Our current, unpublished research into mentoring suggests that this powerful relationship between individuals is relatively independent of influence *by* the organisation (i.e. people form trusting, learning relationships whether they perceive the organisation to be friendly or hostile towards development), but that successful and effective mentoring relationships may have a positive influence on the prevailing climate of trust/distrust.

## MENTORING AND WORK–LIFE BALANCE

When we ask mentors and mentees what they talk about at the early stages of their relationship, they typically refer to careers and ambitions, politics and relationships. After about six months, however, another theme begins to insert itself firmly into the mix. Managing work–life balance is an issue of concern from young new recruits to well-established senior executives – and one which is often too difficult to tackle, except in the safe confines of the mentoring relationship.

For many coaches and mentors, one of the scariest scenarios is to be dragged out of the comfort zone of issues that are strictly work- or career-related and into those 'softer' issues that concern personal life outside of work. But these issues can provide some of the most rewarding insights and outcomes for both parties.

A starting point is to recognise and accept that work and non-work are not two discrete parts of a person's existence. They constantly intrude upon each other. The parent losing attention at work because he or she is worried about a dependent or the state of their marriage, or the employee not listening to a spouse over a meal because his or her attention is temporarily focused on a problem at work – these are the commonplaces of daily existence. The intrusion of work into family life is rampant. More than four out of five managers are regularly telephoned about work issues out of working hours, for example. Even amongst the top 100 employers, employees say that they frequently return home too tired to enjoy their home life.

The key to managing the conflict implied in work–life balance is to recognise the issue as one of complexity management (Clutterbuck, 2003). And the keys to managing this complexity lie in a handful of critical skills:

- Knowing what you want and value out of life
- Understanding and quantifying the conflicting demands on your time, mental energy and physical energy
- Setting boundaries on each aspect of your life
- Having the self-discipline to resist challenges to those boundaries.

Implicit in managing the complexity is taking the reflective time to consider these issues, to develop wider and more creative options, and to plan what you are going to do less of or stop doing. Here is where the mentor can have a significant impact, helping with the rigour of the learner's thinking and with opening up new options and alternatives.

The same principles apply equally well to the issue of *work–work* balance. Knowledge workers, in particular, are faced with a complex set of choices about how they spend their time at work. It's very easy to put a lot of effort into tasks that don't really matter. Considering the way someone uses their time and other resources across the board typically produces much better solutions than dealing with work and non-work issues separately. Some useful questions a coach or mentor can put include:

- What can you do to ensure you approach these work issues with a fresh and relaxed mind?
- How much and where do you feel you are in/out of control of your time and energy? Who is in control of them?
- What do you want to achieve in each key aspect of your work and non-work lives and why?
- How did the conflicts come about? What did you *not* do that encouraged them?

One of the most useful tools the mentor can use in helping the mentee consider work–life and work–work issues is the notion of lifestreams – core facets of working and non-working life, each of which needs to be managed, if people are to fulfil their ambitions. In our work, we recognise six lifestreams:

- Job – the current role and its demands
- Career – potential future roles and how to both make them achievable and prepare for them in a way that the learner will be effective in carrying them out
- Family/domestic – how we maintain the quality of the relationships with the key people in our lives
- Health and fitness – how we maintain the quality of our physical lives
- Intellectual growth – what we do to develop ourselves outside the narrow confines of work and career
- Spiritual – how we sustain a sense of belonging to a community and giving back.

The coach or mentor can help the learner recognise the need to address each of these lifestreams and develop plans for how they will progress in each.
The mentor can also help the learner:

- Work out his or her key priorities in both work and non-work
- Decide how much effort to put into each priority and what to *stop* doing
- Manage the guilt that so often accompanies tough decisions
- Negotiate changes of priority and behaviour with other people, who are stakeholders and/or influencers relating to the learner's circumstances
- Develop the skills to sustain control over their work–life balance, once it is established.

## Making Mentoring Work in Organisations

We have so far looked at two ways in which mentoring is associated with employee – and hence organisational – well-being. Rather than examine other associations, the rest of this chapter examines how to ensure that the promised benefits of mentoring are actually achieved. There are no reliable statistics on success rates of mentoring programmes, not least because success is difficult to define (for example – is it a matter of outcomes for the mentee, the mentor, the organisation or all three?). However, a credible guesstimate is that 50% of programmes fail to meet the minimum expectations of their sponsors and participants. Programmes that are inadequately resourced in terms of training, matching, ongoing support and measurement rarely succeed; well-prepared, well- supported programmes (e.g. those compliant with the International Standards for Mentoring Programmes in Employment) rarely fail at the scheme level and    have relatively few failures at the individual relationship level. Some of the fundamental differences between successful and unsuccessful programmes relate to:

### *Purpose*

Current research on goal-orientation within mentoring suggests that an alignment of goals between mentor and mentee and between both of them and the organisation is an important factor in the quality of mentoring relationships and the outcomes from them. Vagueness on the part of the organisation doesn't encourage participation or the additional effort to overcome set-backs in relationships that are slow to get off the ground.

Research also shows that altruistic mentors (people who perform the role from a vague sense of wanting to put something back) are less effective than those who have clear learning goals of their own from the relationship (Engstrom, 1997/8).

Investment up front is therefore needed to ensure that all participants and influencers understand the nature of the mentoring programme and the benefits – both to the business and to individuals – it is intended to bring. The most effective mentoring programmes almost all have a published statement of purpose and a process for ensuring that mentors and mentees align expectations.

### *Selection and Matching*

The practical reality is that very few companies have sufficient resource of developmentally oriented managers to provide a mentor for everyone simultaneously. So the resource has to be husbanded. Equally, clarity of purpose is more difficult to achieve with a very broad spectrum of people than with a well-selected target audience. Many companies have started programmes for a specific group – often built around diversity objectives – and then widened it as more people become competent and confident in the mentor role.

An essential element in introducing a scheme is to consult and involve the target audience. Many schemes have radically altered in structure and approach as a result of feedback from the intended beneficiaries.

Selection of mentees is relatively easy once a target group has been decided, but it is normally important that they take part willingly – commitment to the relationship is an important to success. Selection of mentors depends on a number of factors, including the appropriate gap in experience/hierarchy, geographical considerations and the specific competencies needed. Seniority in the organisation and ability as a mentor do not necessarily go together.

Matching needs, wherever possible, to involve an element of choice, to ensure commitment on both sides. Good practice seems to be to offer at least two options for the mentee to choose from, and to allow the mentor to say no. All relationships should be probationary for the first two meetings!

### Training

Without any training the best we have seen a scheme achieve is 30% of relationships in structured programmes delivering significant value for one or both parties. With training for mentors only, that typically doubles to between 60% and 65%. Training mentors and mentees, and educating other influencers, such as line managers, pushes up the ratio to above 90%. It is important to remember that mentees in developmental mentoring are expected to play a large part in driving the relationship and helping the mentor help them – so they need to acquire appropriate skills and contextual understanding.

### Leadership and Support

Another common characteristic of programmes that deliver the goods is that they have visible support from the top. In some cases, chief executives have spoken openly about how they are mentored, to legitimise mentoring as an important activity.

Mentors and mentees do not need micro-managing – the relationship thrives best on informality. They do, however, need support in the form of opportunities to meet again to share experiences and develop their mentoring skills further. This can form part of the review process. It is also important to have someone who they can refer queries to – a scheme coordinator or a pool of steering group members, who keep an eye on each pair.

It is the coordinator's role to:

1. Make the business case for mentoring.
2. Create a cadre of enthusiastic and active supporters, including a steering group of participants and sponsors.
3. Market the programme.
4. Install robust systems.

5. Remain in touch with the programme undercurrents.
6. Benchmark against other organisations.
7. Plan for their succession. (Running a successful mentoring programme is often a significant stepping-stone in their own career. It brings people to top management notice in positive ways that may not have been obvious before. As a result, there is a trend for them to move on to other, larger assignments, or be head-hunted by other organisations, or take a career shift to become full-time executive coaches and/or mentors.)

### Measurement

Measurement and review are essential to help mentors and mentees cement their relationships, to troubleshoot the scheme and to demonstrate that the scheme is delivering results. The critical times to measure are:

- At the beginning, to assess whether mentors' and mentees' expectations are aligned.
- After several meetings, to check that the relationship is evolving and that the participants are demonstrating appropriate behaviours.
- After 12 months or so, to establish what the benefits are to both parties and the organisation.

Effective measurement and review of both mentoring relationships and programmes are an important element of the International Standards for Mentoring Programmes in Employment. Many companies now employ a basket of measures that encompass both process and outcomes at both relationship and programme levels. A typical basket of measures will be between 10 and 12 issues, some 'soft' (such as whether mentor and mentee have achieved rapport) and some 'hard' (such as the impact on retention compared with a control group of non-participants). Our own clients also have access to an on-line measurement resource, which allows them to compare average scores on aspects of relationship quality against those from other organisations.

## Completing the Circle

Compared with some other aspects of the management of employee well-being, such as health and safety, job design and family-friendly policies, mentoring is not a first-tier intervention. Yet well-focused, well-designed mentoring can have a wide and subtle effect upon organisational culture and climate. The reason is that mentoring is essentially a process of learning conversations or, when performed well, of learning dialogue. The psychological contract works well when the organisation, its employees and the managerial intermediaries talk to each other openly, honestly and fearlessly. Work–life balance issues are resolved through the quality of dialogue between the organisation and its employees. Mentoring provides the practice arena, where these skills of open dialogue can flourish. An issue of current debate in mentoring circles is what constitutes a critical mass of experienced and practised mentors and coaches sufficient to bring about a dramatic and sustainable shift in the organisational culture. As yet, we have no data – but at least we are talking!

# REFERENCES

Anon. (1999–2005). *Emergent Workforce Studies*. Fort Lauderdale FL: Spherion.

CIPD (2006). *Annual Members Survey, Chartered Institute of Personnel and Development*, Wimbledon.

Clutterbuck, D. (2003). *Managing Work-Life Balance*. Wimbledon: CIPD.

Clutterbuck, D. (2005). *The Dynamics of Mentoring: A Longitudinal Study of Dyads in Developmental Mentoring Relationships*. Paper to European Mentoring and Coaching Council Annual Conference, Zurich.

Conway, N. & Briner, R. (2005). *Understanding Psychological Contacts at Work: A Critical Evaluation of Theory and Research*. Oxford: Oxford University Press.

Engstrom, T. (1997/8). *Personality factors' impact on success in the mentor-protege relationship*. MSc thesis to Norwegian School of Hotel Management.

Guest, D. & Conway, N. (2002). *Pressure at Work and the Psychological Contract*. London: CIPD.

Hale, R. (2000). To match or mismatch? The dynamics of mentoring as a route to personal and organisational learning. *Career Development International*, **5**:223–234.

Hesket, J. L., Sasser Jnr, W. E. & Schlesinger, L. A. (1997). *The Service Profit Chain*. USA: Simon & Schuster.

Joiner, T. A., Bartram, T. & Garreff, T. (2004). Effects of mentoring on perceived career success, commitment and turnover intentions. *Journal of American Academy of Business*, **5**:164–170.

Kleinmann, G., Siegel, P. H. & Eckstein, C. (2001). Mentoring and learning: The case of CPA firms. *Organizational Science*, **3**:383–397.

Kram, K. (1983). Phases of the mentoring relationship. *Academy of Management Journal*, 26.

Kram, K. (1985). *Mentoring at Work: Developmental Relationships in Organisational Life*. Glenview, IL: Scott, Foresman.

Kram, K. (2004). Mentoring and Developmental Networks in the New Career Context. *Proceedings of the 11th European Mentoring and Coaching Conference*, Brussels.

Levinson, D. J. (1978). *The Seasons of a Man's Life*. New York: Ballantine.

Turban, D. B. & Dougherty, T. W. (1994). Role of protégé personality in receipt of mentoring and career success. *Academy of Management Journal*, **37**:688–702.

## Other Useful Reading on Mentoring

Clutterbuck, D. (2004). *Everyone Needs a Mentor*, 4th edn. Wimbledon: CIPD.

Clutterbuck, D. & Lane, G. (2004). *The Situational Mentor*. Aldershot: Gower.

Cranwell-Ward, J. *et al.* (2004). *Mentoring: A Henley Review of Best Practice*. Palgrave, Basingstoke.

Hay, J. (1995). *Transformational Mentoring*. Maidenhead: McGraw-Hill.

Klaesen, N. & Clutterbuck, D. (2002) *Implementing Mentoring Schemes*. Oxford: Elsevier.

Megginson, D. & Clutterbuck, D. (2005). *Techniques in Coaching and Mentoring*. Oxford: Elsevier.

Whittaker, M. & Cartwright, A. (2000). *The Mentoring Manual*. Aldershot: Gower.

# CHAPTER 25

# Building Resilience – An Organisational Cultural Approach to Mental Health and Well-being at Work: A Primary Prevention Programme

**Derek Mowbray**
*Centre for OrganisationHealth®*

## INTRODUCTION

Despite the increasing provision of secondary prevention services to employees in the UK (EAPs, counselling, awareness training, occupational health services), the incidence of stress and mental distress in the workplace continues to be a significant factor affecting business and service performance, as measured by sickness, absence, staff turnover, the iceberg effect (a metaphor which denotes that the bulk of the issues to be addressed lie 'below the surface') and productivity. This chapter is about building organisational resilience to prevent the risk of stress and mental ill health arising.

Resilience is 'the ability of an organisation or an individual to expeditiously design and implement positive adaptive behaviours matched to the immediate situation, whilst enduring minimum stress' (Mallak, 1998).

In this chapter the focus on building resilience is the interplay between the organisation, the 'rules' relating to behaviour in the organisation, and the skills, knowledge and experience of leaders and managers in their interaction with employees within the organisation (Figure 25.1). This, in turn, influences degrees of trust, commitment and the psychological contract, which leads to psychological resilience to stress and mental ill health at work. The approach is

*Employee Well-being Support: A Workplace Resource.* Edited by A. Kinder, R. Hughes and C.L. Cooper.
© 2008 John Wiley & Sons, Ltd.

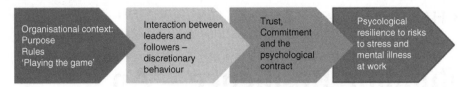

**Figure 25.1**   The interplay between organisation and resilience

predicated on the empirical evidence that people's interaction and behaviour with each other is influenced by the situation in which the interaction takes place (Mangham, 2005).

There is a substantial body of evidence to suggest that trust, commitment and a strong psychological contract between the employee and the organisation within which (s)he works (as represented by a leader or manager) leads to improved performance as defined by sickness, absence and staff turnover (Mowday et al., 1982, Mowday, 1998; Meyer & Allen, 1997; Geiger, 1998; Van der Post et al., 1998; Pool, 2000; Atkinson, 2007). The approach to building resilience presented in this chapter is to build trust, commitment and a strong psychological contract between employee and organisation, thereby creating an organisational cultural which enhances mental health and well-being in the workplace.

This chapter briefly describes the characteristics of a resilient organisation and some problems within organisations, provides an outline strategy to stop stress at work within which is a strategy to create resilience, offers a programme to build resilience, describes the appropriate behaviours in leaders to nurture resilience in individual employees, and offers a method of implementation.

## THE CHARACTERISTICS OF A RESILIENT ORGANISATION

The characteristics of a resilient organisation described below have been compiled from empirical research conducted in the public, private and education sectors including organisations from the UK Top 100 companies. Resilience is used as a proxy for low sickness, absence and staff turnover measures which indicate a low level of identified stress.

Organisations that show resilience have:

- A clear, unambiguous purpose, expressed as a simple 'big idea', an idea which all the staff relate to closely, and are proud to discuss with friends and colleagues (Purcell, 2004).
- An atmosphere of confidence, where all the staff are interested in each other, support each other, and project this confidence towards clients and customers (Johnston, 1996).

- Staff who behave respectfully towards each other, value each other's views and opinions, work in teams which are places of mutual support, where anything is debated without a hint of humiliation, where the critique of individual and team work is welcomed, discussed and where lessons are learnt and implemented (Ingram, 1996; Firth-Cozens, 2004).
- Staff who 'go the extra mile' by providing unsolicited ideas, thoughts, stimulus to each other, and where their interest in their customers offers something more than is expected, beyond courtesy, and beyond service, offering attentiveness and personal interest (Johnston, 1996).
- A culture that challenges the staff; provides opportunities for personal development through new experiences; that treats everyone with fairness and understanding (Hutchinson et al., 2003; Purcell, 2004).
- A culture where staff are personally driven towards organisation and personal success – intellectually, financially, socially, and emotionally (Mowbray, 2004).

These characteristics are derived from empirical research into the key factors that draw a distinction between high performing and other organisations. The features will be used to create trust, commitment (a strong belief and commitment to organisation goals; a willingness to exert effort on behalf of the organisation; a strong desire to retain membership of the organisation) (Porter et al., 1974) and a strong psychological contract - 'the idiosyncratic set of reciprocal expectations held by the employees concerning their obligations and their entitlements' (McLean Parks et al., 1998) between employees and their employers. Trust, commitment and a strong psychological contract are evidenced as having a significant impact on sickness, absence, staff turnover and the factors which lead up to these events (Purcell, 2004; Hutchinson et al., 2003; West et al., 2002; Firth-Cozens, 2004; Atkinson, 2007). It is the creation of a culture of trust and commitment which creates resilience and attenuates a risk of stress and mental distress in the workplace and offers primary prevention against stress at work.

## THE PROBLEMS WITHIN ORGANISATIONS

Probably the most significant problem within organisations arises from the lack of determination by leaders and managers to address the serious issues surrounding stress and mental distress at work. A possible reason is the complexity, ambiguity and idiosyncratic nature of stress, and the difficulty of dealing with the consequences of exposing the problems to analysis and resolution.

The fundamental problem facing organisations and their leaders is the behaviour between leaders and followers, sometimes referred to as 'discretionary behaviour' (Purcell, 2004). The interaction between two or more people is crucial to the success of an organisation (Mangham, 2005), and where this interaction breaks down, or fails to occur, stress and mental distress commences.

**Figure 25.2**  The iceberg effect

The problems within organisations are manifested in the levels of sickness, absence and staff turnover as well as under-performance. Other indicators include the numbers of staff suffering from harassment, bullying, various forms of discrimination and a host of other stressors such as lack of personal control, fatigue, 'burn out' and boredom (Spiers, 2003). These below-the-surface activities are a major contributor to low performance as they involve diverted attention, anxiety, depression, ambiguity, lack of safety and a growing desire 'to escape', creating an 'iceberg effect' (Figure 25.2). Services exist to support staff enduring misery, but they have little direct effect on the numbers eventually escaping to 'freedom'. The national average of staff turning over is 18% some of whom leave for 'positive' reasons, such as moving location, or changing career. The majority, however, are 'pushed' by organisational events (CIPD, 2006).

In the *Sunday Times* survey (March 2007) of the Best Companies to Work For, most of the companies voted for by staff had a staff turnover of over 10% per annum. The CIPD survey of costs of staff turnover (CIPD, 2006) showed that only 8% of all companies knew how much they were spending on filling vacancies and using temporary staff. The average cost per employee turning over was established in 2006 as £8,000. In the *Sunday Times* survey only nine companies with more than 500 staff were spending less than £500,000 on staff turnover. Eleven companies were spending between £2m and £6m per annum on staff turnover, most of which is effectively avoidable. The costs only include the visible costs. The iceberg effect is the period of time that staff think about leaving, when their concentration is elsewhere, and their productivity is low.

The average staff turnover percentage for the Top 100 Companies is 16%, close to the national average of 18%. Figure 25.3 shows the distribution and range.

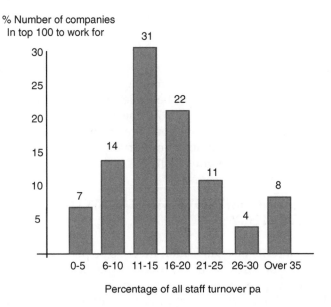

% Number of companies
In top 100 to work for

Percentage of all staff turnover pa

**Figure 25.3**   Turnover of staff 2006, top 100 companies to work for (*Source: Sunday Times*, March 2007 Grateful acknowledgement to Best Companies for providing the research data)

Unwarranted absence is another problem within organisations. In the CBI/ AXA healthcare annual survey (April 2007) it was revealed that 12% of all sickness and absence is unjustified and taken by employees as a routine, tacked onto the beginning and end of a weekend or bank holiday. The survey estimates that the absence costs per employee amount to £537. For a company of 250 employees this amounts to £134,250 per annum plus loss of productivity. All of this cost is avoidable.

## THE POSSIBLE CAUSES OF PROBLEMS WITHIN ORGANISATIONS

The possible causes of problems in the workplace can be identified as being associated with four dimensions of organisations:

- Organisation purpose
- Organisation architecture
- The 'rules' about organisation behaviour and processes, and
- The ways in which leaders and managers interact with their employees or 'play the game' (Mowbray, 1994).

The OrganisationHealth Questionnaire (Mowbray, 2007a) is an instrument based on the organisation development model (Mowbray, 1994), which helps leaders, managers and staff assess the degrees of commitment and trust that exist in the workplace. The approach is to assess the organisation as a context for nurturing commitment and trust.

The benchmarks against which the assessment is made come from empirical research. An unambiguous purpose aids commitment (Purcell, 2004); a flat architecture enhances decision-making and involvement (Hankinson, 1999); the size of the organisation being led has a significant influence on triggering stressors (Wall *et al.*, 1997); the team that encourages positive involvement, critical analysis without any form of humiliation, and the mutually supportive environment limits risks of stress and enhances resilience (Firth-Cozens & Mowbray, 2001).

## *STOP* STRESS AND IMPROVE MENTAL WELL-BEING AT WORK STRATEGY

The creation of a resilient organisation needs to be placed in the wider context of a strategy to stop stress and improve the mental well-being of people at work. A primary prevention strategy and intervention is being strongly advocated in the literature as an approach to sustainable reduction in stress at work (Cousins *et al.*, 2004).

The following strategic framework is adapted from Mowbray (1994, see Figure 25.4) and contains five strategic purposes:

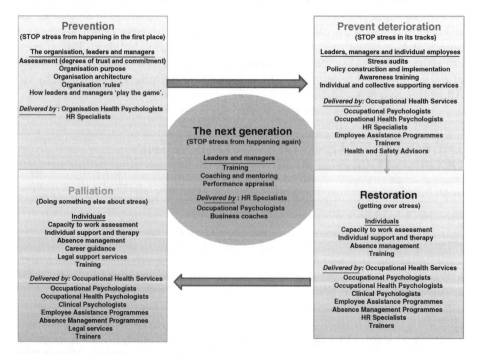

**Figure 25.4**  STOP stress and conflict at work–strategic framework (*Source:* Derek Mowbray, 1994 (adapted))

## Prevention (Primary Prevention) – Building Organisation Resilience

### *Purpose*

To build resilience to stress and mental distress in the workplace, and to prevent stress from happening in the first place.

## Prevent Deterioration (Secondary Prevention)

### *Purpose*

a. To raise awareness of mental health issues, and to provide tools to employees to cope with stress.
b. Once an individual is identified as suffering degrees of stress to stop stress in its tracks.

## Restoration (Tertiary Prevention)

### *Purpose*

To restore an individual to their normal working life having suffered an episode of stress for which they have been absent from work.

## Palliation

### *Purpose*

(For those employees who have been absent due to sickness for some time, and for whom there is little or no prospect of them returning to their original place of work, this strategy is) to ensure that this group of employees are encouraged into any form of work (paid or voluntary), including support in finding a job elsewhere.

## The Next Generation

### *Purpose*

To ensure that once the prevention strategy is implemented, future generations of leaders and managers continue to sustain the structures, rules and behaviours which ensure that the risks of stress is prevented from arising.

For a fuller description see Mowbray (2007c) and *New Ways of Working for Applied Psychologists*, Appendix 2 (DoH 2007).

## BUILDING RESILIENCE – AN ORGANISATIONAL CULTURAL APPROACH TO MENTAL HEALTH AND WELL-BEING AT WORK

Building resilience focuses on the primary prevention strategy. The emphasis is on creating, maintaining and sustaining trust, commitment and a strong psychological contract between employees and their leaders. The creation of trust and commitment requires a focus on the organisation as the context for personal interaction. It also requires the training and development of leaders and managers in the attributes which foster trust and commitment.

The *resilience model* has been constructed from empirical research into the influences which support trust and commitment, and the factors which create a strong psychological contract between the employee, leaders and managers. (Purcell, 2004; Hankinson, 1999; Wall *et al.*, 1997; Firth-Cozens, 2001; Hutchinson *et al.*, 2003; West *et al.*, 2002). The model relies heavily on the work to create the Bath Model of People and Performance (Purcell, 2004) with additional features relating to the organisation and is placed within the framework of Mowbray's model of organisation development (1994, see Figure 25.5).

### Purpose

#### The 'Big Idea'

A clear, simple, unambiguous genuine purpose for the organization which explains to others what it does will gain the commitment of the employee to the organization.

**Figure 25.5**  Resilience model

## Organisation Architecture

### *Structure*

The organisational architecture which is flat and allows the organisation to be divided into manageable sizes is more likely to attract the involvement of employees in the decision-making processes. This enhances commitment to and trust in the organisation.

## 'Rules'

### *The Job*

a. *Recruitment*

Matching personality, skills, knowledge and experience to the expectations of both the employer and prospective employee results in a 'fit' which enables the employee to gain confidence in his/her work. Confidence creates trust and a strong psychological contract.

b. *Pay*

Fairness, as perceived by the employee, is critical in issues of pay. Pay that reflects the value of work undertaken by the employee will be perceived as fair. Fair pay creates commitment.

c. *Challenge*

Individuals look for challenges in their work, which stretches their abilities and demonstrates attentiveness to their needs at work. This creates commitment.

d. *Security*

This refers to a guarantee that once a task is set it will be allowed to be completed without any suggestion of termination prior to the end of the agreed timetable. This helps create trust.

### *Training and Development*

Continuous personal and professional development offers opportunities for personal growth. This gains the commitment from the employee.

### *Teamwork*

Teams that work well have a culture of mutual benefit amongst members, based on trust and commitment to each other.

a. *Openness*

Teams that encourage openness in communication, observation and critical analysis of each other will become committed to each other and will grow to trust each other. This has a significant impact on the risk of stress amongst team members.

b. *Involvement*

Teams exist to achieve the idea of the whole being greater than the sum of the parts. This is achievable only if team members are involved together in issues.

c. *Communication*

Successful teams are made of members who look out for each other, and alert each other to any issues which will improve the overall effectiveness of the team.

### Work–Life Balance

Attentiveness by managers to the individual needs of employees will gain the trust and commitment of employees to the organisation and strengthen their psychological contract.

### Management Encouragement

Managers who encourage individual discretionary behaviour and some risk-taking will demonstrate their attentiveness to employees. This creates commitment.

### Career Opportunity

Managers who encourage employees to consider expanding their skills, knowledge and experience will gain the commitment of the employee.

## 'HOW TO PLAY THE GAME'

### Manager–Employee Relationship

This relationship must reflect attentiveness of the manager to the employee, manifested in discretionary behaviour, which, in return, will create attentiveness in the employee, and create commitment.

### Leadership Behaviours that Help Create Resilience

Implementing the resilience model requires leaders and managers to adapt their behaviour in a way which nurtures commitment, trust and a strong psychological contract. Good leadership needs to go beyond performance-monitoring and to look at the effects on staff well-being (Firth-Cozens & Mowbray, 2001).

The ability to adapt behaviour has been central to the psychological interest in organisations and leaders, and has been the focus of those interested in interaction within the context of organisations (Mangham & Overington, 1987). A more recent interest has been the comparison between leadership and parenthood (Durston, 2007), and the leadership competencies required to implement the Health and Safety Executive Management Standards (HSE, 2004; HSE/CIPD, 2007).

The focus on transformational leadership style (Bass & Steidlmeier 1998) and the development of emotional intelligence (Cooper & Sawaf, 1998) in leaders has partly influenced the construction of the Leadership Dimensions Questionnaire (Dulewicz & Higgs, 2005), which assesses leadership on four dimensions – leader performance, follower commitment, organisational context and leadership style. This approach fits well with developing trust, commitment and a strong psychological contract, and provides a benchmark for training leaders in the behaviours needed to enhance performance by reducing levels of stress.

The behaviours required by leaders and managers in their interaction with employees are identified in the literature relating to seduction (Calas & Smircich, 1991; Persaud, 2006), transformational leadership (Burns, 1978), emotion management (Landen, 2002), impression management (Rosenfeld et al.,1995) and charismatic leadership (House, 1977). From these the main competence to be developed is attentiveness – a focus on the individual in a manner which deliberately entices the person into an act. The more genuine the leader is in displaying attentiveness the stronger the seductive power. It is, therefore, important for leaders to be committed to and trust in their organisation, to the same depth as they expect others to be committed.

Other competencies that aid seduction are: being able to offer direction with committed ambition; being someone who attracts psychological status, who possesses levels of intelligence with humour, who can generate an impact by addressing the individual needs of the employee, who can create stress and then deflate it (developed from Persaud, 2006).

An overt leadership development programme based on the principles of seduction is being piloted (Mowbray, 2007b). An evaluation of the approach is included in the programme.

## Implementation

The preferred form of implementation follows the action research and learning methodologies (Johnson, 1998) with the addition of workshops on each of the topics outlined in the resilience model. The process, therefore, is to select leaders and managers to join action learning sets made up of about eight people and a facilitator. These sets meet each month over a span of 12 months minimum, and on each occasion a selected topic is examined with a view to members of the set bringing about change in their own behaviour as well as in others. In between the set meetings, each member is expected to bring about a change in the organisation, using one of the resilience topics as the focus. On each occasion the learning set meets, each member learns from the others about the successes and challenges they face in the change process, and use the resources of the other members of the set to help overcome the challenges and celebrate successes.

## REFERENCES

Atkinson, C. (2007). Trust and the psychological contract. *Employee Relations*, **29**:227–246.
Bass, B. M. & Steidlmeier, P. (1998). *Ethics, Character and Authentic Transformational Leadership*. Bingham, NY: Center for Leadership Studies.
Burns, J. M. (1978). *Leadership*. New York: Harper & Row.
Calas, M. B. & Smircich, L. (1991). Voicing seduction to silence leadership. *Organisation Studies*, **12**:567–602.
CBI/AXA (2007). Attending to absence: Absence and labour turnover. London: CBI.
CIPD (2006). Recruitment, retention and turnover. Survey Report. London: CIPD.
Cooper, R. K. & Sawaf, A. (1998). *EQ: Emotional Intelligence in Leadership and Organisations*. New York: Perigee.
Cousins, R., Mackay, C. J., Clarke, S. D. *et al.*. (2004). 'Management Standards' and work-related stress in the UK: Practical development. *Work and Stress*, **18**:113–136.
DoH, Department of Health (2007). *New Ways of Working for Applied Psychologists – The End of the Beginning*. Appendix 2.
Dulewicz, V. & Higgs, M. (2005). Assessing leadership styles and organisational context. *Journal of Managerial Psychology*, **20**:105–123.
Durston, I. (2007). *Everything I Need to Know about Being a Manager, I Learned from My Kids*. London: Piatkus.
Firth-Cozens, J. (2001). Teams, culture and managing risk. In C. Vincent (Ed.), *Clinical Risk Management*, 2nd edn. London: BMJ Books.
Firth-Cozens, J. (2004). Organisational trust – the keystone to patient safety. *Quality and Safety in Health Care*, **13**:56–61.
Firth-Cozens, J. & Mowbray, D. (2001). Leadership and the quality of care. *Quality in Health Care*, 10 Supp **11**:ii3–ii7.
Geiger, G. (1998). The impact of cultural values on escalation of commitment. *International Journal of Organisational Analysis*, 6:165–177.
Hankinson, P. (1999). An empirical study which compares the organisational structures of companies managing the World's Top 100 brands with those managing outsider brands. *Journal of Product and Brand Management*, 8.
House, R. J. (1977). A 1976 theory of charismatic leadership. In J. G. Hunt & S. L. L. Larson (Eds.), *Leadership: The Cutting Edge* (pp. 189–207). Carbondale, IL: Southern Illinois University Press.
HSE, Health and Safety Executive (2004). *Stress Management Standards*. London: HSE.
HSE/CIPD (2007). Managing stress at work – a competency framework for line managers. London: CIPD. London.
Hutchinson, S., Kinnie, N. & Purcell, J. (2003). HR Practice and Business Performance: What Makes a Difference? Work and Employment Research Centre. University of Bath School of Management. Working Paper Series 2003.10
Ingram, H. (1996). Linking teamwork with performance. *Team Performance Management*, **2**:5–10.
Johnson, C. (1998). The essential principles of action learning. *Journal of Workplace Learning*, 10.
Johnston R. (1996). *Advancing Service Quality: A Global Perspective*. New York: ISQA.
Landen, M. (2002). Emotion management: Dabbling in mystery – white witchcraft or black art? *Human Resource Development International*, **5**:507–521.

Mallak, L. A. (1998). Measuring resilience in health care provider organisations. *Health Manpower Management*, **24**:148–152.

Mangham, I. (2005). The drama of organisational life. *Organization Studies*, **26**:941–958.

Mangham, I. L. & Overington, M. A. (1987). *Organisations as Theatre: A Social Psychology of Dramatic Appearances*. Chichester: John Wiley & Sons, Ltd.

McLean Parks, J., Kidder, D. L. & Gallagher, D. G. (1998). Fitting square pegs into round holes: Mapping the domain of contingent work arrangements onto the psychological contract. *Journal of Organisational Behavior*, **19**:697–730.

Meyer, J. P. & Allen, N. J. (1997). *Commitment in the Workplace: Theory, Research, and Application*. Newbury Park, CA: Sage.

Mowbray, D. (1994). A Generalised Model of Organisational Design and Development. A pamphlet. Cheltenham: MAS.

Mowbray, D. (2004). The Aspirations for Organisations. A Pamphlet. Cheltenham: MAS.

Mowbray, D. (2007a). *OrganisationHealth Assessment Questionnaire*. Winchcombe, Gloucestershire: OrganisationHealth.

Mowbray, D. (2007b). *The Premier Programme*. Winchcombe, Gloucestershire: OrganisationHealth.

Mowbray, D. (2007c). *A Role for Clinical Psychologists in the Light of Health Work and Wellbeing – Caring for Our Future*. Cheltenham: MAS.

Mowday, R. T. (1998). Reflections of the study and relevance of organisation commitment. *Human Resource Management Review*, **18**:387–402.

Mowday, R. T., Porter, C. W. & Steer, R. M. (1982). *Employee-Organisation Linkages: The Psychology of Commitment, Absenteeism and Turnover*. New York: Academic Press.

Persaud, R. (2006). The Psychology of Seduction – Is Life a Seduction? Annual Gresham Lecture, Gresham College, London.

Pool, S. W. (2000). Organisational culture and its relationship between job tension in measuring outcomes amongst business executives. *Journal of Management Development*, **19**:32–49.

Porter, L. W., Steers, R. M., Mowday, R. T. & Boulian, P. V. (1974). Organisational commitment, job satisfaction and turnover amongst psychiatric technicians. *Journal of Applied Psychology*, **59**:603–609.

Purcell, J. (2004). The HRM-Performance Link: Why, How and When Does People Management Impact on Organisational Performance? John Lovett Memorial Lecture. University of Limerick.

Rosenfeld, P., Giacalone, R. A. & Riordan, C. A. (1995). *Impression Management in Organisations: Theory, Measurement, Practice*. London and New York: Routledge.

Spiers, C. (2003). *Tolley's Managing Stress in the Workplace*. Reed Elsevier.

*Sunday Times* (2007). 100 Best Companies to Work for. 11 March.

Van der Post, W. Z., de Coning, T. J. & Smit, E. V. (1998) The relationship between organisation culture and financial performance: Some South African evidence. *South African Journal of Business Management*, **29**:30–41.

Wall, T. D., Bolden, R. I. & Borril, C. S. (1997). Minor psychiatric disorder in the NHS trust staff: Occupational and gender differences. *British Journal of Psychiatry*, **171**:519–523.

West, M. A., Borrill, C., Dawson, J. *et al.*. (2002). The link between the management of employees and patient mortality in acute hospitals. *International Journal of Human Resource Management*, **13**:1299–1310.

# Index